CAMBRIDGE STUDIES IN
MODERN POLITICAL ECONOMIES

Editors
SUZANNE BERGER, ALBERT O. HIRSCHMAN, AND CHARLES MAIER

Work and politics: the division of labor in industry

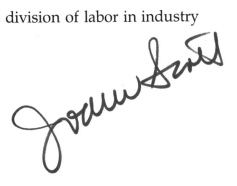

Work and politics

The division of labor in industry

CHARLES F. SABEL

Massachusetts Institute of Technology

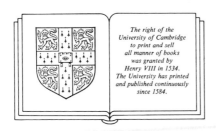

The right of the
University of Cambridge
to print and sell
all manner of books
was granted by
Henry VIII in 1534.
The University has printed
and published continuously
since 1584.

CAMBRIDGE UNIVERSITY PRESS

Cambridge
London   New York   New Rochelle
Melbourne   Sydney

Published by the Press Syndicate of the University of Cambridge
The Pitt Building, Trumpington Street, Cambridge CB2 1RP
32 East 57th Street, New York, NY 10022, USA
296 Beaconsfield Parade, Middle Park, Melbourne 3206, Australia

© Cambridge University Press 1982

First published 1982
First paperback edition 1984

Printed in the United States of America

Library of Congress Cataloging in Publication Data

Sabel, Charles F.

Work and politics

(Cambridge studies in modern political
economies)

Includes index.

1. Labor and laboring classes. 2. Division
of labor. 3. Industrial sociology. 4. Labor
supply. I. Title. II. Series.
HD4904.S23   306'.3   81-18085   AACR2
ISBN 0 521 23002 0 hard covers
ISBN 0 521 31909 9 paperback

TO M., R., AND S.

Exemplary friends, teachers by example

Contents

viii   *Contents*

Tables and figures

Tables

ix

Figures

Preface

I conceived this book about social transformation with one set of questions in mind and wrote it guided by another. When the ideas set down here first took shape in the mid-1970s, the strike waves of the 1960s in France, Italy, and West Germany were fresh in mind; but so too was the impression that, measured by many of their explicit ambitions, these movements had failed to revolutionize factory labor. Why had millions of normally cautious workers gone into the streets? Why were they back at their jobs? To understand what happened, I decided to find out as much as I could about the structure of industrial jobs and the demands industrial workers make on them. The naïveté of the questions seemed both a reminder of my ignorance of industry and a way to keep an eye turned to the passionate drama of hope, desperation, and power that is played out in any large conflict.

Visiting factories and reading about them, I convinced myself that workers were neither a homogeneous class united in opposition to management nor a mass of individuals eager for their own reasons to cooperate, even in limited ways, with the bosses. Rather, it seemed that in factory after factory in different countries and times the work force was regularly split along skill lines into distinct groups, perpetuating themselves in different ways. Each had a characteristic definition of its prerogatives and ambitions and little comprehension of those of the others. Given the right provocation, furthermore, each group was capable of fighting for its claims and allying with the others to pursue them. Political doctrines were often the language these groups used to express their demands; but what the work groups wanted often corresponded loosely at best to the ideas of the political leaders.

These general ideas, I imagined for a time, explained both the broad pattern of industrial conflict during the nineteenth century

xi

and the apparently contradictory recent events that had initially drawn my attention. The partial overlap between the distinct ends of the different work groups and those of management helped make sense of the alternation of conflict and cooperation on the shop floor. The possibility of alliances between groups sharing a common political vocabulary shed light on those extraordinary moments of mass defiance that occasionally shake our societies. The fragility of those alliances, a consequence of the allies' different aims as well as of the gap between the political symbols and the workers' real demands, seemed in important ways to account for the ease with which the authorities could restore order in the factories by making no more than limited concessions and playing on the workers' divided ambitions. The more I studied the complex web of understanding and misunderstanding that binds work groups to bosses and to each other, the easier it became to see why there could be so much conflict and so little fundamental change in the factories. Almost without knowing it, and certainly with no pleasure at the thought, I came to accept the failure of transformative hopes as a proof that the existing division of labor was a fact and limit of social life.

But as I put these ideas in order, applying them to different industries, countries, and times, I began to feel as though I were building a sand castle in the line of an advancing tide. I was explaining the obstacles to change. Yet as I learned more about the early history of industrial capitalism, it became clear that at certain turning points in the history of mechanized production the division of labor might have gone down a path different from the one it followed. More puzzling still, research on the reorganization of work now under way in many of the most modern factories suggested that in the future the division of labor in some of the rich capitalist countries might take a road intersecting some of these foregone possibilities. And it was clear that social struggles, including shop-floor conflicts, played an important part in determining how work is organized, though not in the way I had implicitly imagined. Change often seemed to come not from direct concessions to straightforward demands, but from management's attempts to regain control over an unruly work force by introducing new machines and forms of industrial organization. Under the right circumstances, I found, the clash of worker strategy and management counterstrategy could lead to transformations that neither foresaw. Whereas my initial question led me to underscore the restraint and partiality of workers' demands, the questions arising from this new perspective led me to underscore their potentially revolutionary character. The division of labor came to seem not a limit to the possibilities of transformation but, looked at over long periods, the result of a complex clash of visions of society backed by economic and political power.

This book, then, is an attempt to weave these concerns together: to show how unpretentious claims for decency defined in various and sometimes conflicting ways can contribute to profound transformations in the structure of society. The example is the factory and blue-collar workers, because some of the most dramatic and consequential conflicts in our society are fought between capitalists and workers and because the division of labor is so often regarded as the cause, not the result, of struggle. But the point is more general. The overarching aim is to explore the relation between our barely articulated ideas of honor and justice – politics in the broadest sense – and their quietly revolutionary effect on the social order.

According to one current fashion, these prefatory remarks should end with a kind of playbill in which are listed those who made any contribution to the production at hand. According to a second fashion, this acknowledgment is a more or less provisional substitute for the author's unwritten *Bildungsroman*. In my book, at least, an acknowledgment is neither. It is, rather, a page from that ledger in which each of us notes those persons who out of love, friendship, or duty have so marked either our lives or our work that it is impossible to think of either without thinking of them as well. Herewith, then, I would like to do publicly what I hope to have done, unmistakably, privately, and acknowledge my debt to these people: Suzanne Berger, Donald L. M. Blackmer, Janis Bolster, Sebastiano Brusco, Vittorio Cappecchi, Abby Collins, Joshua Cohen, Daniel Dexter, Sheila Emerson, Charles Ferguson, David Friedman, Robert A. Gates, Peter Gourevitch, Richard Herding, Gary Herrigel, Helen Hershkoff, Hilary Horton, Carl Kaysen, Susanna Kaysen, Helgard Kramer, Burkhart Lutz, Charles Maier, Donata Meneghelli, Marina Monteroni, Hartmut Neuendorff, Claus Offe, Adele Pesce, Michael Piore, Daniel Raff, George Rosen, Michele Salvati, Maria Pia Seirup, Werner Sengeberger, William Sewell, Jr., Harley Shaiken, David Stark, Frank Stille, Roberto Mangabeira Unger, Maurizio Vannicelli, Peter Weitz, and Jonathan Zeitlin. Different as they are to the world and to me, all are alike in this: Each is possessed of a kind of dignity that makes more plausible the dream of a better world.

Research for parts of Chapters 2, 4, and 5 was funded by a generous grant from the German Marshall Fund of the United States.

Cambridge, Mass.   Charles F. Sabel
March 1982

1

Workers and world views

This is an essay about the reasons industrialists create different kinds of factory jobs, about why workers put up with these jobs when they do, and about what they want when they do not. It shows how workers' ideas of self-interest, born of the principles of honor and dignity they bring to the factory, can be transformed by workplace struggles. And it shows how these struggles, colliding or combining with conflicts in the larger society and between nations, can reshape technologies, markets, and factory hierarchies.

The essay is a work of synthesis. It combines into a single framework research on industrial technology, factory workers, industrial organization, and labor movements from roughly 1850 to the present: the age of mass production, standardized goods, specialized machines, and unskilled workers. It concerns mainly France, Great Britain, Italy, the United States, and West Germany. Wherever possible I have tried to corroborate and supplement the available sources by my own interviews with workers, managers, and academics from these countries.

But the essay is also a work of reconstruction, for to unify the research findings, it is necessary to reinterpret them on the basis of methodological assumptions often radically different from the ones on which they were originally constructed. I try to show that most of the diverse and frequently contradictory studies of factory work and factory workers from different countries and periods form a whole if arranged according to new ideas of the relation between workers' consciousness and the division of labor.

Compare the available theories of working-class behavior and industrial conflict with even the most cursory review of the relevant facts, and the need for reassessment is immediately clear. For judged by the theories, blue-collar workers have become unpredictable. In different countries and at different times in the last twenty

1

years, peasant immigrants new to industrial work, traditional craftsmen, and technically sophisticated workers with recently defined
skills have openly challenged management's authority in the factory. In some countries one or another of these groups is still doing
so.[1] No single theory of blue-collar behavior accounts for this variety
of opposition; and no theory that predicts the militancy of any one
of these groups accounts for other crucial aspects of its behavior: its
acquiescence in authority as well as its revolts against that authority,
its inability to find allies as well as its willingness to join broad
political movements. From the point of view of the existing theories,
too much as well as too little is going on in the factories.

Instead of a comprehensive theory there are a series of case
studies, each proclaiming the workers of a particular plant at a particular time the heralds of a coming age. Every major change in
economic conditions, every important development in the division
of labor, has been an occasion to reopen the question of which
workers to count as typical of the future. Much investigative energy
has therefore produced a line of monographs that are convincing
taken one by one but implausible, at least at first glance, taken
collectively. Looking back upon the theoretical works of the 1950s
and 1960s, we see them standing today like the towers of a medieval
Italian city, each firm upon its own ground, imposing from close up,
and a little ridiculous in its claim to challenge the others.

Contemporary views of blue-collar workers

The post–World War II economic boom brought forth the theory of
the *embourgeoisement* of the working class. According to Ferdynand
Zweig's version of this theory,[2] the riches produced by capitalism
were so greatly and so fairly distributed that workers could begin to
emulate the consumption habits of the middle class. That they
would want to and that the result of this imitation would be their
absorption into that class were taken as foregone conclusions. In the
end, economic prosperity would make revolution seem as senseless
for the workers as it was presumed to be for the middle classes. The
everyday evidence for this thesis was so compelling that in his most
pessimistic moments even a champion of radical social transformation such as Herbert Marcuse came close to embracing it.[3]

A variant of the *embourgeoisement* thesis put forward by Robert
Blauner predicted the waning of revolutionary consciousness not
because of the rise in the standard of living but rather because of
changes in the division of labor. Automation, this argument ran,
was reversing the trend toward the decomposition of tasks. The

more workers supervised machines rather than executed the commands of supervisors, the more they would have the archetypical middle-class experience of exercising discretion. The more they had this experience, the more likely they were to discover the community of interests that bound them together with their superiors. Thus, as technology widened the circle of those responsible for maintaining production, the barriers between classes would dissolve. Automation would give workers the chance to satisfy their immaterial desires just as prosperity satisfied their material wants.[4]

Almost as soon as they were formulated, these two versions of the *embourgeoisement* thesis were challenged by opposing interpretations of the facts on which they were based. Against the claim that automation would lead workers to discover their moral affinities with the middle class it could be argued that as workers began to exercise more autonomy at the work place, they would increasingly resent the intervention of their superiors. Having learned the pleasures of exercising discretion, they would become less tolerant of the remaining restrictions on the scope of their responsibility. The solidarity born of this common resentment would be reinforced by the mutual dependence imposed on them by the apparatus of production itself, and the result would be the formation of a new class consciousness. Such, at least, was the theory of the rise of a new working class that Serge Mallet put forward before May 1968.[5]

Against the idea that a rise in the level of the workers' material standard of living would necessarily result in a dissipation of working-class militancy it was argued that workers can be as militant in pursuit of their consumer interests as they were in pursuit of political ends. As the worker comes to accept the putatively middle-class viewpoint that the purpose of life is to provide the highest possible standard of living for one's family, he can convert all the institutionalized and informal forms of workplace solidarity into so many instruments for getting his way with his employer. Unions, instead of forming and expressing class consciousness, become the weapons with which their members get what they want at the bargaining table. Because of the very zeal with which the worker participates in the race for material goods, he can become a threat to the stability of the state. Such, according to John H. Goldthorpe and David Lockwood, might be the unwitting revenge of workers with an instrumental view of their jobs upon the society that had ruined their communities and disrupted their relations with their kin.[6]

Before these debates had been carried to anything like a satisfactory conclusion, all the parties to them were discredited in roughly equal measure by the great strike waves in France, Italy, Great Britain, and Germany of the late sixties and early seventies. May 1968 in France, the *autunno caldo* of 1969 in Italy, the strike waves of 1969 and 1973 in West Germany, and the continuing crisis of industrial relations in Great Britain all proved that the working class has not become simply another group in industrial society. But these same events hardly proved any of the variants of the counterclaim that the progress of industrial society was creating a new revolutionary transformation of the state.[7]

Then, before the confusion created by these events had given rise to anything but the most fragmentary theories, the postwar boom came to an end. Accounts of working-class consciousness which presumed increasing prosperity were replaced by those which postulated economic stagnation, if not crisis. Neo-conservatives frightened themselves with images of irascible workers made greedy by a culture of prosperity, and ready to turn on the capitalists if their exorbitant demands were not met.[8] Leftists saw the working class shocked from its stupor, ready again to recognize that it is exploited and dependent. In these quarters the recession – at least in its early phases – brought a recrudescence of the classical Marxist view that the material situation of the working class leads to forms of discontent that are the precondition for the rise of revolutionary consciousness.[9] Yet a third reaction was to see the working class as condemned to live out cycles of militancy in which phases of belligerent assertiveness (corresponding to good times) are succeeded by phases of passivity (in bad times) – and nothing fundamental about the structure of society changes.[10]

Despite their differences, these theories all share three fundamental assumptions: technological determinism, essentialism, and reductionism. To understand their shortcomings and especially the incapacity of each to make sense of those aspects of experience captured by the others, it is necessary to examine their relation to these foundation stones of so much social science.

Three misleading ideas: technological determinism, essentialism, and reductionism

Technological determinism is the familiar idea that regardless of its political preferences, any society that wants to produce industrial goods must adopt certain structures of organization, patterns of authority, and ways of doing business. These modern institutional forms may correspond to a regime of free enterprise, or to the ideals of the socialist state; but in any case they and no others will prevail if industrial production is successfully organized.[11]

The objection to technological determinism is that performance standards can usually be met in several ways. The fit between what needs to be done and how it can be done is seldom as tight as the determinists imagine. We will see, for example, that plants using comparable technologies can divide the necessary work in different ways, and that the same goods can be produced using different technologies. By overstating the connections among products, technologies, and organization, each of the case studies under review drew general conclusions from historical particulars, only to be overthrown by succeeding research focusing on different situations.

Essentialism is a species of determinism. It is the claim that what is true for society as a whole is true of each of its parts. The more advanced an industrial society, the more clearly modern forms of organization predominate in each of its parts. As the differences between industrializing societies disappear, each society becomes internally more homogeneous.

The objection to essentialism is that radically different forms of organization, some apparently archaic, others modern, are often interdependent. We will see, for example, that advances in some industries create the preconditions for the survival of backward forms of industrial organization. The regnant theories either neglect this diversity or dismiss whatever seems backward as vestigial, destined to be swept aside by future developments.

Reductionism is the doctrine that experience unambiguously determines thought. Here it amounts to the claim that everyday experience of modern societies by itself determines what people in those societies want of life.[12] We will see in a moment that the reductionists differ in their views of what this experience ultimately teaches; but they are in agreement on its general significance. One lesson of life in industrial society, they argue, is that human wants are not fixed. Rather, they change over time, stimulated by, though always outstripping, society's capacity to satisfy them: The development of technology, for example, produces new goods that awaken new wants, spurring further technological advances, and so on. A companion lesson is that the purpose of social and economic institutions is to satisfy these changing desires. Institutions are no longer considered just or unjust in themselves, but only efficient or inefficient: efficient if they maximize social welfare given existing wants, technological capabilities, and resources; inefficient if they do not.

Combined with determinism, these ideas add up to the characteristic reductionist claim that industrialization means the end of ideology.[13] Call an ideology a moral conviction that society should produce certain goods (associated, say, with a particular vision of community), and/or produce them in a given, politically defined manner (according to plan, with public means of production, in small shops, etc.). Then, if industrialization produces a uniform experience of life and if the experience produces agreement that technology should be efficiently used to satisfy wants, these fixed ideas lose their meaning.

But if the reductionists agree that ideology is meaningless, they disagree about the significance of the pursuit of efficiency. At issue is the definition of efficiency itself. For the producer, efficiency means the least wasteful use of resources and technical capacities; for the consumer, it means the optimal satisfaction of wants. In economics, for example, Marxists take the producer's standpoint and argue that prices are ultimately set by the costs of production; neoclassical economists see the market, and behind it the preferences of the individual consumer, as the ultimate arbiter of value.[14] In sociology, too, there is an analogous division of opinion on how the inhabitants of industrial society understand the idea of efficiency.

Marxist and *marxisant* sociologists like Mallet and Blauner take the position that workers experience work as producers. The assumption is that humankind seeks self-expression in the graceful mastery of nature independent of the product. For this reason production cannot be efficient unless workers actively participate in organizing and controlling it; and it is this participation which colors the workers' view of society. For Blauner, workers supervising automated machinery have the prototypical entrepreneurial experience of exercising discretion and bearing responsibility, which cements their allegiance to an industrial order based on entrepreneurship.[15] Mallet has it that workers who supervise machines experience a new solidarity with one another *against* management, which they eventually see as dedicated to profits, not to the efficient use of machines. But in both cases ideology gives way before the producers' ethos of technical efficiency, even if the result is in one instance capitalism, in the other socialism.[16]

Sociologists like Goldthorpe and Zweig who have been influenced by neoclassical economics, on the other hand, argue that workers see themselves as consumers. The claim is that workers define themselves by what they have, not by what they do. The more they have of whatever convention defines as enviable, the more content they are, even if they must let themselves be treated as mute instruments of production at the workplace.

Zweig's argument is that a rise in living standards teaches workers that they have individual wants, and that satisfaction of these wants undermines classes in the sense of institutionally organized, culturally homogeneous, and politically self-conscious groups with a definite place in the division of labor.[17] With classes gone, the age of the efficiency-conscious individual begins. Goldthorpe's counterclaim is that traditional class-based institutions, if not self-conscious classes, will continue to exist because the actual, technologically imposed distribution of power in society makes such institutions indispensable to the satisfaction of workers' private wants.[18] The efficiency-minded consumer celebrates another victory, but this time as a collectivist.

The difference between these two variants of the reductionist view can be characterized in a more general way that focuses attention on their inverse limitations. Where the theory of the worker as consumer defines rationality as the choice of means given arbitrary ends, the theory of worker as producer sees reason in the choice of ends – to be a producer – without consideration of means. But because it is impossible in practice to define ends without respect to means and vice versa, the result is a fruitless and contradictory struggle to separate the rational from the irrational in the workers' behavior. Where one school sees the reasonable consumer who cannot say why he consumes what he consumes, the other sees the reasonable producer who has no idea of what to produce or how.

Theories that stress consumption habits, for example, assume that the workers' actual desires are conventionally defined. Thus W. G. Runciman treats groups of workers as collective subjects whose wants are determined in reference to their historical relation to other groups in society.[19] These wants are fixed for long periods. But social, economic, or political changes from time to time disrupt group identities, causing workers to develop new desires.[20]

One characteristic defect of these theories is their implication that changes in consciousness are arational, if not irrational. Translating to the analysis of group behavior the concept of efficiency they apply to the whole society, these theorists argue that rationality is the efficient use of resources given present wants. When a group's wants are in flux it has no foundation for the calculation of the means appropriate to its ends. Hence change of identity is seen as a hiatus of reason: a succession of unrelated wants that supersede each other capriciously.

Alessandro Pizzorno's theory of the cyclical character of worker militancy illustrates this dilemma well. Pizzorno argues that progress in the division of labor creates new groups of workers whose interests are not represented by the existing system of negotiations between capital and labor. For a group to be recognized as a bargaining partner, however, its leaders must overcome the opposition of the organized interests who benefit from its exclusion. To do this the group must coerce recognition by disrupting production. But effective coercion is possible only if the leaders overcome each member's tendency to shift the burden of struggle onto the others in the expectation that they will succeed without him while he benefits from their efforts. The solution to this free-rider problem is to convince workers to think of themselves as agents of a comprehensive social transformation that replaces the old world by an incomparably better one. What present sacrifice is too great compared with the plausible prospect of an incomparably better future? Moreover, by appealing to general interest in radical social change, the new group wins allies to its cause. Once admitted to the negotiations, however, it begins to redefine its interests. Ultimately, it drops its global demands and insists only on the satisfaction of the narrower economic interests shaped by its place in the division of labor and regarded by the bargaining partners as negotiable.

Pizzorno therefore sees workers as always behaving in one of two ways. In the periods of serious conflict associated with the creation of a new bargaining partner, they act selflessly for the common cause. But their solidarity with other workers and social groups is the result of collective enthusiasms, provoked by illusory promises. Only as these enthusiasms evaporate do the workers become reasonable again. After the struggles for recognition have subsided and their bargaining identity is established, they return to the selfish pursuit of sectional interest, the only behavior subject to rational calculation.[21]

A second defect of this kind of reductionist theory is a corollary of the first. Because they cannot see any fundamental, enduring features in the worker's personality, theories of the worker as consumer cannot say why he rejects one identity and arrives at another. Pizzorno, for example, cannot explain the *substance* of the collective identity that emerges from a period of struggle. On the one hand, he argues that the workers' bargaining-table demands reflect their place in the division of labor. But on the other, he argues that they had to forget their particular interests in order to get to the bargaining table in the first place. The result is an account of the origin of workers' demands full of ambiguities that cannot be resolved within the framework of a rigid distinction between periods of struggle and periods of negotiation.

On a superficial level, theories of the worker as producer seem to avoid these defects. The argument is that man the maker, *homo faber*, is dissatisfied with any system of production that does not treat him as such. This unnatural condition is called alienation. Lack of interest in work, resentment against bosses, and feelings of helplessness are its principal manifestations. Because they are presently alienated, workers in capitalist societies are in perpetual if often muted opposition to management. The balance of power in the labor market permitting, the opposition becomes overt when the weight of alienation becomes too great.[22] If the revolts are crushed by force or repressed more silently by economic blackmail in the labor market, dissatisfaction goes underground again. But at the next opportunity, with new allies and conscious of the errors of the past, the workers revolt against alienation again.

Thus the assumption that workers consider themselves producers implies a continuity in working-class personality of just the sort that theories of the worker as consumer deny. So by positing the worker as a producer it appears possible to see the rationality of his struggles and the coherence of his identity.

Closer examination of theories of alienation, however, reveals defects the inverse of those associated with theories of the worker as consumer, but equally crippling. The tables have simply been turned: Now the worker's militancy is declared rational, his workaday self said to be trapped in collective illusions. As in the case of the theory of the worker as consumer, we are told that the patient is really quite sane if we ignore his mad side.

Take the obvious problem of reconciling the view of the permanently resentful worker with the perspicuous fact that most workers assent to management's authority most of the time. One answer advanced by theorists of alienation stresses the role of force: Workers do not protest openly because they fear reprisals. Another invokes the idea of false consciousness: Misled in school and eventually by the press and television, workers learn to ignore or misunderstand the truth of their nature.[23] Both answers suggest that what the worker actually says and does is irrelevant to, not expressive of – even unintelligible in the light of – his essential nature. The alienated worker is comprehensible only in the rare moments when he struggles against alienation.

A related problem is the incapacity of reductionist theories of alienation to give substance to the worker's ambitions as a producer. Because *homo faber* is defined prior to and independently of what he makes, his choice of what to produce appears as arbitrary as the consumer's desire for particular goods. The theories address this difficulty in one of two ways, both of which disguise the problem rather than solving it.

One argument is that there is an immanent logic of technological development that determines what is produced and how. This theme plays a role in Mallet's work; and we will see that it is central to the analysis of Heinrich Popitz and Hans Paul Bahrdt. The objection, developed in Chapter 2, is that technological development is itself shaped by social choices imposed politically or through the market: Think of the way changes in oil prices and growing concern about the environment have forced changes in automobile design.

The second argument meets this objection, but at the price of diluting the theory's implicit claims to explain worker behavior. It is that the clash between the producer and the profit seeker catapults the former into politics. Once he sees that his interests are distinct from those of the capitalists, the worker is drawn to political activity to discover what his interests really are; and political debate, not the logic of technological development, decides what to produce. The difficulty is that the theory of alienation has as little to say about the progress of these debates as it does about the question why workers are sometimes militant, sometimes not. Where the first argument denies that the question of choice arises at all, this one denies that it is answerable with the help of the theory's categories.[24]

The essay that follows disagrees with these determinist, essentialist, and reductionist theories on almost all the points on which they are in agreement; it frequently agrees with at least one of them on points of analysis where they contradict one another. Where they try to explain away diversity in the division of labor, I attempt to account for its persistence; where they stress the unity between thought and the world, I emphasize the divergence; where they see the end of ideology, I see the constant struggle to impose moral order on the economy; where they see teleology, I see struggle and possibility. The full extent of our agreements and disagreements will become clear as the argument is developed in the body of the text. Here I want to introduce the logic of the analysis and the plan of the work by anticipating as much of the discussion as needed to contrast my major results with central features of the determinist, essentialist, and reductionist theories I have criticized.

Matching workers to jobs

The starting point of any more or less systematic exposition is somewhat arbitrary; I will begin somewhat arbitrarily with a discussion of the structures of the economy. The aim of Chapter 2 is thus to show how the manufacturing techniques pioneered in the nineteenth century and canonized by Henry Ford lead to the creation of radically different kinds of jobs. Building on theories of the dual labor market, I argue that employers facing stable demand for large quantities of standardized products pursue one kind of investment strategy, whereas those facing unstable or highly differentiated demand pursue another. These diverse investment strategies in turn lead to substantial segmentation in product and labor markets. The demands made on workers, their security of employment and possibilities of promotion, of acquiring new skills and exercising old ones – so runs the argument – vary substantially from one segment to another. Jobs in some of these segments of the labor market could be considered archaic in the sense that they require few skills (or many), and that they afford few (or many) opportunities for learning new ones. The claim is that the ensemble of these segments makes up the modern market economy. This argument does not deny that there will be advances in the division of labor. Technological innovation, international competition, and the growth of demand, I will argue later, in fact work together virtually to guarantee that there will be such advances. But progress in the division of labor will not cause one type of work to dominate the labor market. The coming changes will alter the mix of jobs in subtle ways, at one and the same time creating unskilled work, blurring the lines between craft and semiskilled jobs, and creating demand for various new skills. The distribution of skills that will result in the long run is difficult to determine, but in any case the existence of technologically advanced forms of work presupposes the continued existence of archaic forms and vice versa. I will have more to say about the assumptions underlying this typology in a moment.

Having outlined the various kinds of objective demands the economy makes upon workers, I turn to the demands workers make on jobs. Chapter 3 presents a typology relating groups of workers with shared expectations of work to the clusters of jobs roughly corresponding to the most important of their anticipations. The underlying assumption is anchored in the work of sociologists like Max Weber, anthropologists like Clifford Geertz and Pierre Bourdieu, and historians like Eugene Genovese and Edward P. Thompson. It is that during childhood and adolescence we acquire a set of fears and hopes, visions of success and failure: an intuition of possibilities that define at once our ambitions and our sense of social honor. The process by which these ambitions are acquired is called socialization. The set of hopes and fears, together with the map of the social world that it establishes, is called a world view.[25]

One defining feature of world views is that they legitimate, or at least obscure, disparities of power between social groups by making them appear to be facts of nature. In archaic societies, for example, women often occupy a subordinate position. Everything about the cosmology of these societies confirms women's subordination; alternatives are literally unthinkable. A woman who wants to exercise power in such societies can do so only by becoming as it were a keeper of the faith, an *éminence grise* whose strength derives paradoxically from strengthening the hold of the rules that mark the limits of her authority.[26]

In industrial societies the role of world views in shaping power relations is more subtle. Take as an example the case, analogous in many ways to one we will examine later, of two high-school graduates of equal academic ability faced with the decision to attend college or not. One we assume to be the son of wealthy, college-educated parents; the other is the child of working-class parents with only a high-school education. For the student from the wealthier home the costs of *not* going to college are high; the prospective rewards for getting a higher degree are great. If he does not attend college he counts, by the standards of his family at least, as a failure. If he completes his degree he enters a world that is both familiar and esteemed.

The situation for the working-class student is the reverse. Even if his education ends with his high-school graduation he is a success in the eyes of his family; if he attends college he enters a world whose rewards he may not understand well enough to value. Thus, leaving aside the question of the availability of tuition monies and the like, it is clear that the son of well-educated parents is more likely than his working-class schoolmate to continue his education, and that this disparity results not from some randomly distributed individual tolerance for or aversion to risk, but rather from the influence of the student's socially acquired world view.[27]

A second defining feature of a young person's world view is that it is not reducible to any series of experiences – either his own or his parents'. Nonetheless, it expresses in a general way the meaning of the social world in which they both move; conversely, single social and economic facets of that world will become significant only in the light of their connection to the world view.[28]

In this sense the relation between world view and social reality is analogous to the relation between theory and fact. World views and theories must both prove their use in practice. To be practical they must capture at least some of those features of the world they describe which would strike a hypothetical omniscient observer. They cannot be mere fantasies. Thus a world view, like any interesting theory, always contains something of the objective truth about the part of the division of labor and social structure to which it refers. But this is to say neither that a world view is the whole truth about the world nor, relatedly, that only one world view is appropriate to a given situation. An alternative conception may seize on objective features of the situation neglected by the first yet far from unimportant; it may also simply offer a different – but equally plausible – account of the same features by connecting them in a different way.[29]

Differences between world views of the "same" situation are not unimportant. They lead to differing predictions about the significance of events that will occur in the future. In the long, perhaps the very long, run, it may even be that one world view will prove incorrect enough to be hopelessly impractical. But in the short run, we can no more say that a world view is uniquely determined by, say, the technology of the part of society to which it refers than that a scientific theory is a mere extension of certain facts of nature.

Given the loose connection between world view and world and the diversity of economic activity that I take to be characteristic of modern society, it follows that there are a plurality of world views, some expressive and constitutive of the same and some of different realms of economic experience. Moreover, no world view need be comprehensive in the sense that it organizes all the convictions and beliefs of a single person into a single coherent whole. The set of propositions that make sense of working life can, especially if they are barely articulated, coexist with other, contradictory, propositions governing the experience of politics. This is particularly likely to be the case in liberal democracies like our own in which the dominant ideology distinguishes sharply between the roles of citizen and worker. In such societies, therefore, not only will there be diverse world views, but no single world view is likely to capture completely all of any one person's experience.[30] Where it is important to call attention to the distinction between a worker's view of his job and his political notions, I will refer to the former as his idea of a career at work. In general, however, I will speak of the worker's conceptions of the working world as his world view, it being understood that these conceptions have no unique implication for his politics, view of the family, and so on.

The catalog in Chapter 3 of the fundamental types of world views compatible with the different varieties of industrial work rests on a further assumption: that the operation of market forces tends to produce an equilibrium between the demands of employers for workers of a given kind and the expectations of workers for jobs with certain characteristics. Managers with only short-term work to offer, for example, recruit workers willing to take such jobs for reasons of their own. Workers with long-term ambitions refuse such employment and look for other jobs. By closely examining different segments of the labor market, then, we will be able to see how the overlap of certain crucial expectations permits at least a tenuous collaboration between capital and labor. Keep in mind the earlier discussion of world views and disparities of power: To say that relations between workers and management are, on this level at least, consensual is not to say that the power is equally distributed between them.

The relation between the mature worker's world view and the objective conditions of his job thus reproduces the relation between the world view of the school-age youngster and the milieu to which it refers. Because there must be some agreement between the worker's expectations and the requirements of the job he is actually offered, his world view is never just an illusion about work. But because agreement is limited to crucial expectations and the worker defines what is crucial, two workers doing the same job can have quite different ideas of what they are doing. Conversely, two workers with similar ideas of work may be doing jobs that seem quite different from, say, the employer's point of view. In those instances where more than one world view proves compatible with a single set of labor-market conditions, I will want to determine the similarities beneath their differences. Such, for example, will be the case when we discover peasants who expect to return to the land working side by side at unskilled jobs with industrial workers who expect to become craftsmen: Both can abide their work because they assume it will be temporary. When a single world view proves compatible with two different segments of the labor market, I search out the objective similarities of the two segments. Craftsmen, for example, can be employed on assembly lines or as feeders of automatic machines, provided that at least occasionally they can test their craft knowledge against unforeseen problems.

World views and workplace struggles

Chapter 4 takes the arguments considered in the preceding section two steps further by setting them in relation to workplace conflicts. It investigates how workers' world views shape their ideas of what is worth fighting for, and how industrial struggles, in turn, can change their original world views.

Again, the starting point of the discussion is an assumption common, in different forms, to the works of Geertz, Bourdieu, and Weber: the idea that world views are normative as well as explicative. They are not just models of the world, they are models *for* the world as well.[31] They are evaluative and simultaneously they create meaning: If we regard the world from the vantage point of a world view, the distinction between facts and values dissolves.[32]

Yet another way of making this point recalls the earlier criticism of theories of worker consciousness: In world views it is impossible to distinguish ends from means, the exercise of value rationality (choice of ends) from the exercise of instrumental rationality (choice of means). World views are like penal codes or codes of honor. They permit an exhaustive categorization of actions as licit or illicit, honorable or dishonorable – one member of each pair being defined negatively in terms of the other.[33]

This assumption suggests that many industrial conflicts arise from management's violation of the workers' expectations of propriety and justice, and that these violations are themselves expected. The conflicts come about when two conditions are fulfilled. First, prompted by the pressure of competition, for example, management attempts to rationalize or speed up work, substantially changing the terms of its relation to a given work group. Second, judging by its world view, the work group declares its integrity and place in the division of labor threatened, and rises to its own defense. Strikes by craftsmen in defense of wage differentials or freedom from shop-floor supervision would be one example of such conflicts.

Craftsmen learn as apprentices that management tries to profit from eliminating their prerogatives. When such challenges do come they are resisted as an affront to the craftsmen's ethos, an insult to their dignity, an attack on their well-being and the freedom they need to work. But they do not come as a surprise, for management was always suspected of neither respecting the dignity of skilled workers nor appreciating the moral basis of their work.

Elaborated in this way the argument also bears on three of the problems that vex theories of worker behavior. First, it becomes possible to take a preliminary step toward overcoming the theoretical division of the worker's personality into rational and irrational components. I show that for a wide range of conflicts it is the same person who rebels against management and accedes to its demands. The worker's militancy is not evidence that he has a second self, more or less rational as the case may be, than his accommodating everyday personality. Rather, his militancy is above all a sign of his determination to defend his everyday conception, which as a whole is comprised of illusions and truths inextricably mixed.

Second, it becomes possible to give an account of the diversity of the sources of opposition to management's authority: All groups are capable of some sort of resistance because all have a concept of intolerable injustice. No group acquiesces without reservation in management's authority; no group is in unreserved opposition to it. The capacity to raise and defend such moral claims is a fundamental feature of human nature.[34] Whether workers assert rights as consumers or as producers – the problem that preoccupies the available theories of worker consciousness – is a subsidiary matter at this level of analysis. Chapter 4 shows in fact how both sorts of claims can arise among workers doing the same jobs but holding different world views.

Third, this framework explains why diverse and recurrent outbursts of opposition seldom combine into anything like a concerted attack on management. Recall that the work groups have significantly different motives for accepting employment. The argument suggests that their motives for refusing to work will be different as well. Chapter 4 attempts to demonstrate both this and the corollary claim that workers perceive these differences. Comparing, then, the various, often contradictory, definitions of honorable and dishonorable situations, I argue that each group's defense of its own niche in the division of labor can isolate it from its most likely allies against management, the other groups in the plant. Thus workers may share a common enemy, but it would be wrong to conclude that they are therefore united. In fact, it seems that by helping to freeze the status quo in a divided factory, these single acts of opposition make it more difficult for the separate work groups to define and pursue common interests. Conflict situations, where work groups need each other the most, often prevent them from acting jointly to secure their ends.

The contrapuntal theme of Chapter 4 regards the opposite development: the way conflict can transform workers' ideas of their rights by amalgamating them with those of allies, extending them rapidly in the heat of battle, or elaborating them slowly to justify incremental claims. Returning to the earlier comparison of world views and theories, we can say that this aspect of the argument concerns collective attempts to replace inadequate theories of the world with better (though still imperfect) ones: collective learning through conflict.

There is, however, little systematically collected evidence that can be brought to bear on the complex of questions associated with transformations of consciousness. Most conflicts are disruptive enough to churn up established ideas, but few by themselves produce dramatic redefinitions of identity. Nonetheless, I have tried to consider the theme as fully as the available materials allow, integrating it wherever possible into the treatment of conflict in Chapter 4 and drawing examples from three of the most consequential and best-studied mass movements of workers in the West in this century: the New Deal in the United States, May 1968 in France, and the *autunno caldo* of 1969 in Italy.

A brief survey of Italian developments at this point will introduce the central conclusions of this aspect of the argument in a preliminary way.[35] Simplifying greatly, the politicized unskilled Italian workers were former peasants and artisans disappointed by their first, intensive experience with urban industrial work. In the 1950s and 1960s masses of Italians from rural areas, principally in the South, migrated to the industrial North in search of jobs. For some time they hoped to return to the South, using their savings to establish a secure existence. Then, peering as it were around the edges of their preconceptions, they began to catch glimpses of their actual situation in the North. They slowly realized that economic circumstance was trapping them in the industrial cities. As their confidence in a speedy return home diminished, they started to ask pointed questions about the industrial society they had entered and its relation to the more rural society they had abandoned. Unable to answer these questions themselves, they turned to ideologically sophisticated, left-wing Northern craftsmen for help.[36] In speech and thought they often took the ways of the Northern workers as their model. They did not, however, cast aside their old ideas and reject their previous self-conception as nothing but a false illusion: They held fast to central elements of their old identity, in particular to certain communitarian ideas of solidarity and fair exchange, reinterpreting these in the light of the theories of class solidarity among the skilled.

The demands by the unskilled for an egalitarian industrial society, demands that still command attention in Italian society, were the result of an act of collective theorizing. Realizing that their world view could not explain crucial aspects of their actual experience, they had to search for a new conception of themselves and the world. And in the process of articulating a new world view – a new theory of their relation to reality – that would be more faithful to their experiences, they transformed themselves and discovered new possibilities in the world as well.

The Italian example thus shows that workers are not fated to remain divided by the defense of unexamined and half-articulated world views. As workers are thrown together in conflict, the premises and implications of their separate world views can be both made explicit and transformed, uniting work groups instead of dividing them. It is, moreover, the process of politicization that connects and makes possible these developments.

Earlier I said that the worker's concepts of economic activity did not have to be coordinated with his political beliefs. They might contradict yet coexist with one another. The Italian example shows that a precondition for their separation is that neither set of concepts be fully articulated. Most of the time this condition is met. Acting according to the unexamined and only half-conscious premises of his workplace and political personality, the worker has no motive to examine their implications. A prisoner of his thought, he is freed of the obligation of testing its consistency.

But the moment a dramatic conflict or a long series of apparently humdrum ones puts his identity at risk, the moment he is forced to break free of his habitual self-conception, in that moment he finds himself obligated by the nature of his dilemma to determine the relation of his political beliefs to his economic world view. For political theories are the major source of the ideas he needs to interpret the experiences that his unelaborated workplace view of the world cannot explain.[37]

This process of political clarification has another implication as well: It forces each worker to rethink his relations to the workers in other groups. Whether they have contributed directly to his political education or not, they appear to him in a dramatically different light because of it. His identity is in flux, and he sees the mutability of theirs as well. And the – often fleeting – recognition that neither he nor they can arrive at any lasting solution to their problems without transforming the division of labor that separates them reinforces the solidarity first created by the sharing of still-vague political doctrines: Where defense of the status quo separates the blue-collar work force into its components, even an inchoate vision of the transformation of the division of labor can contribute to its unification.

As the alliance between unskilled Southern Italians and skilled Northerners shows, in such moments of recognition between work groups are established those bonds of trust which create the possibility of long-term cultural and political unity. If unity of this sort is what makes a group of persons into a social class, then a central conclusion of Chapter 4 is that classes are formed through the experience of common struggle. Groups do not share interests simply because they occupy the same or a similar place in the division of labor.

Another way to underline the significance of this aspect of the argument is to juxtapose it with determinist, reductionist, and essentialist ideas of social change. Four points of contrast are especially relevant.

First is the role of social diversity in the transformation of consciousness. The reductionist idea is that the transformation of consciousness amounts to its unification according to some master principle: As the economy is modernized, modern rationality spreads apace. By calling attention to what workers learn from one another, however, the Italian case suggests that the very diversity of economic experience, which in the determinist and essentialist view marks the immaturity of the world, may be a precondition for its transformation.[38]

A second contrast deals with the relation between the worker's old identity and his new one. In theories of the worker as consumer the relation is arbitrary because the worker has no continuous identity. The new personality does not bear any close relation to the old. But judging by the Italian example, the transformation of consciousness should be seen as a process of maturation. New ideas are actively appropriated, and unexpected layers of meaning in old concepts are revealed. Thus there is continuity as well as change in the identity of the subject; and it is no longer necessary to accept the idea that the workers' struggles and the process of change mark a hiatus of reason.

The third contrast, closely related to the preceding two, concerns the role of ideology. In the reductionist view ideologies ultimately give way to belief in the ostensibly apolitical idea of efficiency. My opposing claim is that political conceptions understood as visions of a just society always play a part in determining consciousness. The ideas workers exchange and reinterpret may be better descriptions both of their needs and of reality than their unexamined beliefs were, but they are in no sense the absolute objective truth about the world or human nature. Hence it is not necessary to accept the idea, identified with theories of the worker as producer, that the untransformed worker is like a madman, the transformed one like a man returned to his senses. In this regard, too, there is continuity as well as change.

Finally, there is the question of contingency in history and the limits of theories of worker behavior. Determinist, essentialist, and reductionist theories assume that the world is evolving. Change will come, necessarily calling forth a uniform response. The Italian example teaches that even similar changes in the division of labor need not produce similar results. Given different ideas as guides to the reconstruction of identity, and different powers of imagination, two groups facing similar situations can arrive at conclusions that are related (because both ultimately are expressive of comparable objective circumstances) but distinct.

The changes in the consciousness of masses of unskilled Italian workers might not have taken place in the 1960s but for the previous development in the trade-union movement and political parties. Had there been no socialist tradition in Italian politics, and had there been no splintering of some of the traditional leftist parties, it would have been more difficult than it was for the Italian workers to come by the starting materials for their ideas. By way of contrast, it is easy to imagine that one of the factors that prevented immigrants arriving in North America from coming to similar solutions was the absence of a politically established repertoire of collectivist ideas: Even the wrenching experience of the transition from agricultural to industrial work has no unambiguous meaning independent of the worker's theory about the world.[39] Of course it is possible to offer suggestions to explain why some ideas were available in the United States and others not. But these explanations would count as theories about the United States, colonies, or liberal societies, not about the transformation of immigrants' self-conception. Separating the latter from the former limits the range of theories about either. But the loss of scope is more than offset by an increase in explanatory power.

Finally, the Italian case makes clear that the study of industrial conflict is inextricably linked to the study of politics, and that both are tied to transformations in the division of labor. The outcome of the crisis of collective identity will depend on political considerations; the result of the long-term disruption of politics that often accompanies such a mass crisis of identity will depend in part on its resolution. The resolution of both will in turn influence in complex ways the subsequent strategies of labor and capital, provoking new experiments with the organization of production and the use of technologies. Chapter 4 broaches these themes. But fuller discussion of them is deferred to Chapter 5, where they can be set in relation to a broader analysis of changes in the division of labor and the breakdown of existing models of industrial organization. To make sense of these issues it is first necessary to explore the assumptions about the cultural and historical diversity of industrial society on which this whole study rests.

National culture and the division of labor

Debates about the transformability of whole societies offer analogies to the considerations about the transformability of workers' collective personalities presented in the last section. Setting out these analogies will focus attention on the general question of the uniformity and variability of industrial societies. At the same time it will allay the wary reader's suspicion that to offer an answer to the problem of the mutability of consciousness it has been necessary to undermine the foundations of the earlier discussion.

Previously I argued that the basic features of the division of labor and the segmentation of the work force have been fundamentally similar in industrial societies through most of their histories. This presumptive similarity was the warrant to draw empirical evidence from various countries and periods without attempting a rigorous comparison between nations, much less providing a comprehensive history of industrial society.

But the Italian example suggests that the experiences of originally similar work groups in two different countries may diverge radically, in ways that cause corresponding divergences in the nations' division of labor. But if societies may diverge in this way in the future, how do we know that they were similar in the past? What is left of the idea of a typical industrial society? It seems that, in leaving room for the variation in worker experience, my scheme, like a clock chiming thirteen times, has produced one answer too many. To show that the theoretical clockwork is in order it is necessary to put forward a view of industrial society and its transformation that allows for the possible emergence of distinct national species of production without vitiating the usefulness of the earlier generic discussion of the division of labor.

The collective personality of a nation is called its national culture. As used in the social sciences, the term "national culture" refers to the set of ideas about ideal social relationships and the just distribution of authority by which a society orders relations within families, within hierarchies, and between different social classes. A nation's culture in this sense might be styled its political world view; and it is not surprising that debates about the transformation of workers' world views have echoes in discussions of the fixity of national culture.

At one extreme is the position that each society has a kind of eternal and immutable soul. According to this view, authority relations must always be what they are because politics – in theory a laboratory in which to invent new relationships – in practice creates institutions that only perpetuate the original cultural motifs.[40] At the opposite extreme is the idea that national culture does not matter at all: Given comparable endowments of capital and labor, different nations will respond to like changes in the international economic order in the same way, and social arrangements will automatically adapt themselves to the requirements of efficiency.

The first view calls to mind the fixity of the worker's personality, as in theories that picture him as a producer who wants only to do things a certain way; the second, the unhindered mutability implied by the idea of the worker as a consumer who will do anything to increase his wealth. The first suggests that because authority relations at work reflect only national idiosyncrasies, no attempt to construct a generally applicable typology of workplace relations can possibly succeed. The second suggests that the sort of typology advanced here is needlessly complex, because the variations observed in national styles of organizing work can be traced not to variations in the histories and combinations of work groups, but to variations in their endowments of capital and labor or to lags in adjustment to market forces or technological possibilities. The first road leads to historicism in which each thing is unique and *individuum ineffabile est*; the second ends in reductionism in which all individuality gives way before the sweep of objective forces.

If either of these extreme positions is correct, my own cannot be; yet there must be something to each if the view that industrial societies share many common features without losing their individuality or being fated to share anything like a common destiny is to be borne out. First, therefore, I will present some evidence that casts substantial doubt on the extreme versions of the national culture idea; then I will offer a reconciliation of the two views that unifies the attempt to discover a general typology of work in industrial society with my speculations about the transformability of the industrial division of labor in different countries.

Imagine two countries whose contrary national political cultures prescribe relations between citizens that resemble authority relations between workers and managers in two different positions in my typology of the division of labor. If culture determines everything, relations between superiors and inferiors within each country will be the same regardless of position in the division of labor; if culture determines nothing, workers in the same position in the division of labor will have equivalent rights regardless of the differences between national political styles.

Take as the polar cases of political culture France and Germany. In France subordinates fear the discretion of their superiors; hence they insist that every exercise of power be authorized and limited by an impersonal rule. Orders are framed as interpretations of an objective bureaucratic regime, not as one person's command to another. Superiors, for their part, do not trust their subordinates to do anything that is not specified in a legitimate order. Those who plan tasks must therefore give exhaustive instructions to those who execute them, because the latter refuse to complement, augment, or revise the directions they have been given.[41] In Alan Fox's terms, French culture is "low trust" because it encourages separation of conception and execution.[42]

German superiors assume the opposite, namely, that their subordinates want and are able to acquire the kind of knowledge about their jobs that allows them to work autonomously. The task of the German supervisor is thus not to tell those charged with execution how to do their work, but rather to indicate to them what needs to be done. Conversely, in return for not being hedged in by a thicket of rules, German subordinates must count on their supervisors not to make abusive use of their discretionary powers.[43] German society is "high trust" because it discourages the separation of conception and execution.

The distinction between high- and low-trust social relations corresponds to a distinction, in my typology, between skilled and unskilled jobs. The skilled worker, I will argue, is characterized by his autonomy on the job. Having mastered the general principles of his craft, he applies these to solving particular problems; by solving particular problems, he deepens his grasp of general principles and readies himself for more advanced work. By contrast, the unskilled worker in theory never rises above the particular: His work consists of a series of discrete operations that remain unintelligible to him because their meaning is revealed only when they are placed in relation to a further set of operations about which he knows nothing.

If the national culture is indeed a rigid mold into which all social relations are poured, as one extreme version of the culture argument has it, then we would expect there to be very few or even no workers in France who fit the type of the craftsman, whereas Germany should be without unskilled workers.

Given their cultural ideals, the French should want to eliminate craftsmen on two grounds. First, the French try to minimize caprice by providing that whatever may and may not be done is foreseen by rules. But the essence of the craftsman is that he applies his general knowledge in unforeseeable situations; hence the danger in French eyes that, unrestrained by the law, he may use his ability to master uncertainty to a selfish end. The French would fear, too, that the very existence of craftsmen would subvert bureaucratic order by encouraging cronyism. When those in power know those beneath them, their interpretations of the rules, far from being objective, are just a subtle way of playing favorites. But the unfolding of the craftsman's talents makes it natural for him to approach his superior not as a judge, but as a teacher and advisor, and for the supervisor to see in a craftsman a pupil and successor.

An inverse logic would work to eliminate the unskilled worker from Germany. Supervisors would find it natural to give their subordinates only general instructions; the latter would have to discover for themselves how to apply these instructions to particular cases. Those who succeeded in this would find themselves in possession of the kind of wide-ranging expertise characteristic of the craftsman.

According to the opposite interpretation of the culture thesis, French and German ideas about authority are just another example of rules made to be broken. Under the pressure of world market competition, manufacturers in both countries will have to adopt the most efficient techniques of production and man them in the most efficient way, national traditions about authority notwithstanding. In international comparisons, of course, *ceteris* is never quite *paribus*. But this view of national culture suggests that in all factories producing the same products for the same markets by the same methods, workers will be organized in the same way: If efficiency requires certain German workers to be given a great deal (or very little) autonomy, those doing the same jobs in France will have neither more freedom nor less.

What a careful comparison of pairs of French and German factories using similar technology does in fact reveal gives comfort to neither extreme thesis, but does not fully discredit either. In France production *is* organized on the assumption that workers should exercise as little discretion as possible. In various industries workers are much more closely supervised than those in German plants using comparable technology.[44] The overall skill level is lower in the French industries; there are more layers of hierarchy because the general directives given by the people at the top of the hierarchy have to be rendered (by their subordinates) into exact instructions for those at the bottom; lines of promotion tend to be short because, unable to exercise discretion on the job, the workers cannot teach themselves new skills. Yet as the efficiency argument suggests, there *are* skilled workers in France; and as other studies show, their self-conception and the strategies of self-defense that grow out of it are comparable to those observed among skilled workers in the United States, Great Britain, and Germany. Conversely, despite traditions of mutual trust, there are unskilled German workers who can be compared in many ways to the unskilled of other countries. Nor do these generalizations hold only for the Occident: In Japan, whose national culture resembles Germany's in many ways, workers are encouraged to exercise discretion on the job. Even the least skilled are frequently trained to perform a number of tasks. Nonetheless, there are wide differences in the autonomy accorded different groups of workers; and the problems of the skilled and unskilled in Japan resemble those of their

Western counterparts, however much the solution to those problems may differ between East and West.[45]

A first conclusion to draw from these findings regards the unity of industrial societies. There is a good deal of free play in the organization of the industrial division of labor, but not an unlimited amount. Cultures will differ over where to draw the line between, say, skilled and unskilled workers; but all will have to acknowledge, more or less openly, the fundamental difference between the two. And this is just the kind of result that provides a foundation for the sort of general typology of work groups I propose: Finding the extreme groups identified in the typology even in the societies whose culture appears to provide the least room for them warrants my impressionistic use of comparative evidence.

A second conclusion regards the individuality of industrial societies. Despite their similarities, in the very act of organizing industrial work each society reasserts its identity. The authors of the study of French and German factories speak of an *effet sociétal* in summarizing the influence of each nation's ideas about authority and justice on the way it does all work. In a very general and inconclusive way this finding supports the claims made in Chapter 5 of this book about the potential diversity of industrial societies. But the claims made there go well beyond the reality reflected in present evidence, suggesting as they do the possibility of such wide-ranging transformations in the division of labor as might call into question the idea of a single type of industrial society based on Fordist principles of production. In assessing even in the most preliminary way the plausibility of such claims, something must be said about the limits of diversity and the sources of uniformity in modern society. Static comparison of the division of labor in various countries is insufficient. To form some idea of the potential diversity of future industrial societies it is necessary to pose the question of the origins of their common features in the past.

Imitation and autonomy: the historical sources of unity and diversity in industrial society

Most accounts of the diffusion of industrial organization into backward zones are written by economic historians or by other social scientists who think as economic historians do; hence it is no surprise that such accounts reflect notions of efficiency associated with reductionist arguments. From this perspective, industrial society arose autochthonously in England sometime between the middle of the seventeenth and the end of the eighteenth centuries, and in the

United States at the beginning of the nineteenth century. In all other countries – the late industrializers – the state has intervened in the economy to facilitate the break with traditionalism. But even where the state has promoted industrialization by imposing tariffs, or expediting the accumulation of capital or the introduction of new technology, the developments it has set in motion essentially resemble the ones that began spontaneously in England and the United States.

This conception points to two views about the unity of industrial society, the one only slightly less implausible than the other. The first is that economic development in time obliterates all traces of its institutional preconditions, so that all industrial societies come to be fundamentally the same. The more refined notion allows that industrial nations will bear the marks of their birth long into their maturity, suggesting as one conclusion that late industrializers will be systematically different from England and the United States.

Thus Ronald Dore tried to explain the difference in the organization of Japanese and British factories by the fact that Japan had to catch up in industrializing. In England, for example, the first generations of industrial craftsmen could simply top off the skills of their artisan forebears; in this way skilled workers came to think of themselves as craftsmen whose first allegiance was to their craft, not their employer of the moment. By the time Japan industrialized, however, the gap between artisanal and industrial skills had become so great that employers had to establish special schools to train the necessary craftsmen. The upshot was to institutionalize a system guaranteeing on-the-job training, long-term employment, and payment by length of service (*nenko*), which encouraged the skilled worker to give allegiance to his company, not his fellow craftsmen. Since World War II this system has extended to cover less-skilled workers in large firms as well.[46]

Even as an account of Japanese practices, this line of argument encounters substantial problems. In stressing efficiency considerations – on-the-job training as the rational response to the problem of forced-draft industrialization – it underplays the perpetual struggle that Japanese employers have had to wage against craftsmen's efforts to establish associations independent of single employers. The *nenko* was not the result of the straightforward application of old habits to new circumstances. It was deliberately created by skillful reinterpretation of traditional ideas of deference and solidarity, for example, the *oyabata–kotata* relation of master and apprentice.[47] But as Dore himself realized, the argument collapses of its own weight as soon as the comparison between early and late industrializers is extended to include countries such as Mexico, Sri Lanka, and Senegal. The organization of work in these countries shows no sign of reproducing Japanese circumstances.[48] Put the other way around, the conclusion is that the Japanese organization of work is a consequence not just of Japan's late development, but also of the fact that it was the Japanese doing the developing.

To come to grips with this surprising speciation of industrial society it is necessary to take a more comprehensive view of the diffusion of factory technology. To conceive of industrialization merely as a break, however accomplished, with an undifferentiated state known as traditional society is obviously to tie theory's hands with reductionist cords. It is more fruitful to think of the spread of factory production simply as another instance of the spread of techniques from one nation to another that has been going on as long as there has been military and economic competition between organized human groups. To take only relatively modern examples, the industrialization of the Third World does not involve fundamentally different processes from those underlying England's imitation of Dutch commercial techniques of the seventeenth century, French attempts to learn from English agricultural practices in the eighteenth, Latin American attempts to borrow the technique of liberal statecraft from the Old World in the nineteenth, or the Old World's imitation of American manufacturing practice at the beginning of the twentieth century.

For the purposes of my argument the crucial feature of this process of diffusion is that nations which adopt the new techniques from abroad always do so for a double and apparently self-contradictory motive: to become like their more advanced rivals, but to remain just as they are. They must at least meet the efficiency standards of their powerful competitors if they are to preserve their independence – hence the need to copy whoever has come up with the successful techniques of the day. But paradoxically, they imitate others the better to defend their individuality.[49]

Success at this process requires supreme self-confidence in the capacity to transvalue the enemy's means by putting them in the service of one's own ends. Tancredi, the young aristocrat in Giuseppe Tomasi di Lampedusa's novel of revolution in nineteenth-century Sicily, *The Leopard*, spoke for all the conservatives who have understood this necessity when he told his uncle, "If we want everything to remain as it is, then everything will have to change." And Trotsky spoke for the revolutionaries when, seeing the Red Army threatened by Mamontov's cavalry, he ordered, "Proletarians, to horse!"[50]

But even though the two impulses, imitation and individuation, may weigh equally on the minds of the leaders of the developing nation, it is likely that at first they will try to ape advanced techniques; only later do they consciously make of the technique yet another expression of their nation's personality. At first their very unfamiliarity with the new procedure makes them chary of experimenting with variations: Without knowing how a machine works it is impossible to know which parts, if any, cannot be tinkered with. Furthermore, even with an informed intuition about which parts can be improved, it takes time and money to hit on the best solution to local problems; and two things an underdog nation pressed by more efficient rivals lacks are time and money. To start with, then, it seems as though the recipient of new technology must purchase its future autonomy with the sacrifice of the loss of its old identity. The choice is between extinction and westernization.

But experience belies this first impression. Time passes and the developing nation realizes that despite its best efforts at imitation, the peculiarities of its history manifest themselves in a thousand ways in the application of supposedly universal techniques. More importantly, those whose religious sentiments, economic interests, or political advantages have been slighted by the general renovation, associated as it is with the prospect of a comprehensive revolution in social relations, begin to question the relations between the various elements of the modern ideas. They argue that some can be detached from the rest at no cost in efficiency, or even that the increased efficiency which the new techniques make possible is not worth the loss of the nation's cultural substance that their adoption seems to entail. A party of nativists grows up alongside the party of modernizers: Peter the Great calls forth the Slavophiles; the Argentine Liberals of Buenos Aires meet their nemesis in Rosas, the champion of the native provinces against the city of foreigners; Shah Resa Pahlevi meets his in the Ayatollah Khomeini.[51]

No matter who wins the struggle between modernizers and nativists, their clash ensures that the nation will begin to take full possession of the imported techniques. Deviations from allegedly ideal use of the new ideas, previously regarded as temporary shortfalls, unavoidable failures wed to the poverty of the country and the backwardness of its people, are reinterpreted as signs of national inventiveness; and once the unavoidable deviations are understood as virtues, the hunt for variations of the technology most suited to local circumstances begins in earnest.

Cursory though it is, this sketch of the diffusion of new techniques can focus speculation about the future balance between uniformity and diversity in industrial society. Since the middle of the nineteenth

century the late developers have very deliberately attempted to duplicate the achievements of the pioneers, first England and then the
United States. Everywhere there was debate about just what the inevitable progress of mankind inevitably held in store; nowhere was
there talk of the variety of possible futures that progress created.
Comtians in the Second Republic, their followers in Latin America,
German Marxists, American Social Darwinists, English Fabians, some
of them belligerently doctrinaire, most of them influential men of
affairs convinced that they were doing what needed to be done – all of
them were convinced that all nations were running the same race.
They asked only who would win and what the prize was to be. By the
time Henry Ford achieved a practical synthesis of nineteenth-century
advances in mass-production techniques, his solution seemed a triumph of the inevitable. None of the revolutionary factory-council
movements that emerged in many of the belligerent powers toward
the end of World War I had anything more than the most rudimentary conception of an alternative organization of work. Ford's ideas
would fascinate the Bolsheviks and German Social Democrats, Louis
Renault no less than Giovanni Agnelli. The first automobile factory in
Czechoslovakia to use assembly-line techniques, built by Skoda in
1925, was called America.[52]

However different the societies these men were shaping, their
belief in a common destiny – Fordism – tended to restrict the divergences between nations simply by making unlikely any systematic
development of the multitude of small innovations in technical design and work organization that local conditions made necessary. It
would be a mistake, moreover, to think that industrialists were any
less the prisoners of this rough-and-ready technological determinism
than workers or labor leaders. The Great Depression showed that
industrial magnates the world over were as convinced as the Left of
the necessity of technical innovation in the American manner, and
as uncertain how to organize a mass-production, mass-consumption
society. The difference was that the industrialists in Italy, Germany,
and Japan could count on state power to cancel their mistakes, and
capitalists in the other Western states pulled their chestnuts out of
the fire thanks to the war against the Fascists.

In retrospect it seems as though the Great Depression was also the
beginning of the end of the idea of a uniform industrial society.
Stalin proved that not all roads to industrialization run parallel; the
Swedes with their practical Keynesianism and Keynes with his macro-
economic theory opened debate on the extent to which an industrial, market economy could be subject to conscious political control.
German and Japanese armies did the same, more brutally, by creat-

ing a *Grossraumwirtschaft* in Europe and a co-prosperity sphere in Asia.

The success of American arms in World War II temporarily cut off this debate. The triumph of U.S. efficiency reinaugurated belief in the unitary character of industrial society; and American society became for a time the image of the future as much to the advanced states of Western Europe as to those in the Third World. U.S. failures, particularly in Vietnam; the successes of the United States' industrial competitors, not only West Germany and Japan, but also Brazil, South Korea, Taiwan, and the countries of Eastern Europe; the rise of the oil-producing countries of the Third World, but also the often wrenching domestic consequences of their pell-mell attempts to westernize – all of these have provoked renewed discussion in rich and poor countries alike about what is a necessary and what a contingent feature of industrial society, about which divisions of labor and distributions of wealth and power are compatible with the criteria of efficiency imposed by a world order certain to pit nation against nation in the future.

There can be no sure bets on the outcome of this debate. The recrudescence of reductionism during the postwar *Pax Americana* shows the paralyzing effect of overwhelming material success on speculation about alternative uses and extensions of modern technology. Nothing rules out the possibility that some nation, even the United States, may one day gain enough of the upper hand in the world to impose its practices as the embodiment of progressive reason. But this is unlikely. In Chapter 5 I argue that as the emergent industrial nations learn to use Fordist techniques of production, they will threaten the position of the established industrial powers in mass markets. To survive, countries such as the United States and West Germany will have to diversify production. Whether they can do this within the framework established by Fordist principles is uncertain. In any event, I will argue that experimentation with new forms of work organization may lead to the emergence of distinct national systems of industrial organization. The proof that this can happen is that it is happening already in Italy, where the industrialists' response to the conflicts of the 1960s and 1970s has opened the way to creation of extremely innovative high-technology cottage industries whose success in world markets flagrantly defies Fordist ideas.

But before we can begin to discuss the plurality of industrial futures that seem to be aborning, it is necessary to see what the epoch of the belief in convergence has left by way of common starting points for divergent developments. That is the burden of the analysis of industrial work, workers, and conflicts that follows.

2

The structure of the labor market

This chapter argues that the capitalist organization of production creates clusters of jobs offering workers systematically different opportunities for the use and acquisition of skills, and for regular employment. The capitalists create jobs of various types, and the worker tries to find one suited to his ambitions.

But the freedom of the capitalists as a group is not the freedom of the single entrepreneur. He is not at liberty to organize work as he will. The types of jobs he offers depend on the sort of investment strategy he pursues; and his choice of investment strategy depends on his firm's position in the market. We will see that since the last quarter of the nineteenth century, capitalist industrial societies have been dominated by firms of two kinds. The first count on sizable and stable demand for their products. They invest in technological innovations that reduce production costs and redistribute skills among workers: A few come to have jobs requiring ever-more-sophisticated and general knowledge; the rest are assigned increasingly routine and specialized tasks. Firms of the second kind are smaller. They face fluctuating demand and live in the shadow of the first group. They pursue short-term investment strategies requiring less-specialized use of labor and often employing technologies discarded by the larger firms.

From above, the perspective of the student of industrial structure, the economy thus appears to be divided into a technologically advanced sector made up of large, innovative firms, and a backward sector of smaller laggards. From within, the perspective of the entrepreneur, economic activity is a constant struggle to match machines to men according to rules of thumb and habits that differ from market to market. From below, the perspective of the worker, the economy appears to be a series of distinct labor markets whose various characteristics seem more or less advantageous, even more or less conspicuous, depending on his own interests. Chapter 3 surveys the economy from the third perspective, whereas this chapter reconnoiters the same terrain from the first two. Our starting point will be the emergence of a sector of larger, technologically advanced industrial firms in the nineteenth century.

The rise of Fordism

The giant factory employing thousands of mainly unskilled workers and specialized machines to turn out huge quantities of a single product is a relatively late creation of industrial society. Apart from the early textile mills of Manchester and New England, a few iron and steel plants, and giant workshops such as the Baldwin locomotive works in the United States, most industrial products were made in shops employing fewer than 100 workers. Production machinery was often a steam- or water-powered version of tools familiar to an eighteenth-century artisan. As late as 1883, when the Singer company was turning out some 600,000 sewing machines a year, final assembly often required skillful filing and manipulation of the separate pieces, none an exact copy of its model. In 1875 the largest plant of the Pullman sleeping car company, another symbol of the explosion of industrial energy, employed about 600 men, many of them craftsmen.[1] But in industry after industry changes were under way that transformed the nature of products and production. Studies of the nineteenth-century clock, shoe, sewing-machine, steel, chain, and bicycle industries in the United States and Great Britain, for example, all demonstrate a relation among the growth of mass markets, the standardization of products, and the introduction of specialized machinery.[2]

In each case, artisanal methods of production were first decomposed into simple tasks to meet the demands of expanding markets. As available supplies of labor were exhausted, specialized machines were devised to increase output at the bottlenecks, further reducing production costs and making the commodity available to still wider circles of customers. Subsequent growth in demand led to increased substitution of specialized machines for men, to decomposition of the remaining tasks, and to still broader market possibilities. The work of Alfred O. Chandler, Jr., on the emergence of modern management practices in the American railroad and telegraph industries reveals an analogous connection between the growth of stable demand and the rationalization and differentiation of administrative technique.[3]

Advances in the separate industries were cumulative, reinforcing each other in ways that moved the entire industrial economy closer to today's commonplace image of the large factory. Breakthroughs in machine technology, metallurgy, administration, and marketing in one industry were quickly applied in the others. As the general principles of mass production became clearer, experimental efforts focused more and more directly on their refinement. The culmination of this surge of discovery was the invention of the automobile assembly line at the Ford plant at Highland Park, Michigan, in 1913.[4] Ford's assembly line was the last consequence of the push toward the standardization of the product and the routinization of its production. It applied to the connection between manufacturing operations the logic of efficiency that other industries had brought to bear on the discrete operations themselves. It was therefore both the complement and the symbol of all that had gone before.

Ford's decision to produce only the Model T was a precondition for the routinization of production. The concentration of production allowed perfection of specialized machine tools designed for speed, precision, and simplicity of operation. An unskilled operator snapped engine blocks, for example, onto specially designed tables and watched a machine mill them automatically and accurately. Made this way, parts such as cylinder heads and engine blocks could be fitted together without the need for hand scraping of surfaces during assembly.

Once hand fitting had been eliminated and the specialized machines had been arranged in the sequence of manufacturing operations, the next and revolutionary steps were to reduce the transit time of workpieces from machine to machine and to systematize their assembly. Gravity slides and conveyors helped solve the first problem; the moving assembly line, an endless chain that carried subassemblies or chassis from work station to work station, solved the second. The assembly line may have been inspired by the disassembly lines in Chicago slaughter houses, which circulated carcasses from butcher to butcher, or by Ford's own gravity slides and conveyors. But however they hit on the idea of moving the work to the men rather than the reverse, Ford's engineers knew at once that they had discovered a new secret of mass production: The first crude moving line cut the time needed for final assembly from just under 12.5 to about 5.8 man-hours. It was as though the Ford engineers, putting in place the crucial pieces of a giant jigsaw puzzle, suddenly made intelligible the major themes of a century of industrialization. Because of the significance of this breakthrough in the history of mass production, I will use "Fordism" as a shorthand term for the organizational and technological principles characteristic of the modern large-scale factory.[5]

But the triumph of mass production was and remained incomplete. Around every large firm in the late nineteenth century there was a halo of small shops that supplied parts, built special machines, or manufactured similar products. In the United States in 1914, 53.8 percent of the workers were employed in plants of 250 workers or fewer, and fully a third in plants of 100 or fewer.[6] Today, despite an increase in industrial concentration, the situation is fundamentally similar: Wire cables for General Motors are likely to be twisted together in a parts plant near Detroit employing at most a few hundred workers, or in a much smaller firm in Mississippi; parts of some IBM computers might be assembled in a backyard factory just across the border in Mexico; some parts for FIAT cars are cast in factories no bigger than shacks. Japan's post–World War II successes in international competition are striking proof that the relentless search for industrial efficiency does not necessarily lead to the extinction of small firms: Of some 10 million workers employed in manufacturing between 1970 and 1977, a third were employed annually in firms of fewer than 100 and close to half in firms of fewer than 300, and there was no sign in the 1970s of increasing concentration of employment.[7]

Contemporary economies, as Marxists and neoclassical economists agree, therefore have a core and a periphery. At the core are the giant firms of each industry. They have substantial though not unlimited power to set the prices of their goods. At the periphery are the small firms, none large enough to influence markets and all therefore forced to sell their products at whatever price the competition establishes.[8]

The exact mechanisms by which prices and levels of investment are set in both sectors, and the remaining proceeds of economic activity distributed between wage earners and stakeholders in firms, are all puzzles to vex economists. Our concern here is with the division of labor and its relation to the use of technology and the organization labor markets. I therefore want to sidestep the narrow economic questions raised by this picture of industrial structure and turn to a model, proposed by Michael Piore, that captures its essential features from the relevant perspective.

Market structure and industrial structure

Piore's model rests on postulates that he draws from Adam Smith.[9] The first is that productivity depends on the division of labor: A top-of-the-widget maker and a bottom-of-the-widget maker together turn out more than two whole-widget makers working the same hours. Decomposition of tasks, furthermore, opens the way to the invention of specialized machinery that further increases productivity. An engineer observing a whole-widget maker at work sees a jumble of complex motions; observing a bottom-of-the-widget maker he sees a reduced set of regular gestures that he can reproduce by machine.

The second postulate is that the division of labor depends on the extent of the market. The subdivision of tasks not only increases output per unit of input, it also increases total output. If there is no market for the increased output, a firm will not expand production to take advantage of a more productive division of labor, even though by doing so it could reduce the selling price of its products.

The rest of the model addresses the relation between the actual demand for a product or group of products and the portion of that demand which affects progress in the division of labor. For strategic purposes, Piore argues, managers distinguish a stable and an unstable component of demand. The stable component is equal to demand at the bottom of the business cycle; the unstable component is equal to the difference between actual demand and the stable portion.

According to the model, not peak or average demand, but that demand for a product that persists at the lowest point in the industry's business cycle determines the degree of development of the division of labor.[10] Progress in the division of labor depends, as we saw a moment ago, on increased investment in product-specific equipment and forms of organization. Because they are more product-specific, the new techniques cannot be put to alternative use during downturns as easily as the old. To ensure that expensive machinery and workers with narrowly defined skills are always sufficiently employed, production capacity must therefore keep step with the changes in the stable component of demand. Figure 1 illustrates the relation between the total demand for a product and the portion of that demand which affects progress in the division of labor, the productivity of labor, and the unit cost of production.

The model thus suggests that each branch of industry or group of firms producing related goods can be divided into two sectors. The primary sector, which corresponds to the core of the economy in the previous description, will employ the technologically most advanced division of labor and will satisfy the stable component of demand. The secondary sector, composed of competitive, peripheral firms, will use less-refined and less-product-specific techniques of production; it will principally satisfy the fluctuating component of demand.

This distinction, Piore argues, is analytic: It is comprehensible to the managers in the industry because of its strategic relevance; but it

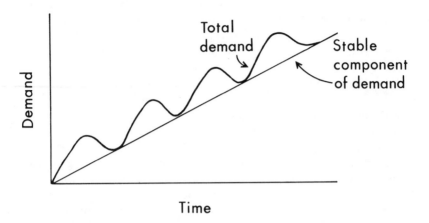

Figure 1. The stable component of demand. Adapted from Michael J. Piore, "The Technological Foundations of Dualism and Discontinuity," in Suzanne Berger and Michael J. Piore, *Dualism and Discontinuity in Industrial Societies* (Cambridge: Cambridge University Press, 1980), fig. 6, p. 66.

does not necessarily correspond to any clear-cut division between organizations. If demand for a single product in an industry is extraordinarily stable or growing at a reliably predictable rate, one or several large, advanced firms may cover it completely, leaving the smaller ones to compete in the volatile markets for other products. Or if demand for even the most stable product fluctuates, then the largest firms may leave space for smaller manufacturers of that good to supply customers at the peak of the business cycle. Finally, the same firm might produce for stable markets in a central plant and supply unstable ones through subsidiaries. The model predicts only that production units will be assigned to one or another sector of the market; it does not specify what the institutional arrangement of firms, products, and types of markets will be.

This model thus provides a convincing explanation for the coexistence of large and small firms. During a boom the latter might supply the former with parts or directly supply customers unwilling to stand in line for a particular good. Alternatively, small plants might specialize in the production of goods for which substantial, stable demand *never* exists. Thus the model explains why work clothes, white bread, and automobiles, for instance, are mass produced by assembly-line techniques in large factories, whereas fashionable ladies' garments, fancy grades of pumpernickel and high-quality pastries, and trucks, buses, and agricultural and construction machinery are manufactured in small lots by much more skilled workers and craftsmen using general-purpose tools and methods that often approximate artisanal techniques.

Simple as it is, the model thus clarifies a widespread and fundamental perception of the organization of the economy. It will help organize the discussion of labor in this chapter and the next. But before advancing a step and developing the relation of these ideas to the structure of labor markets, we must take a step back and discuss some of the suppositions on which they depend. In this way it will be possible to bring out the connection between the model and the analysis of the diffusion of technology offered in Chapter 1, as well as to take account of some important exceptions, contemporary and past, to the dominant pattern of dualism.

The political background of technological dualism: a historical perspective

The essential point, as true for this model of dualism as for any other model of the economy *senso strictu*, is that markets of all sorts are themselves the result of extraeconomic developments, and insofar as technological choices depend on the structure of markets, so are they as well.

The decision to invest in the elaboration of one technology rather than another, for example, is connected both with the existence of customers for the eventual products and with the right to control the proceeds from the products' sale. The first depends on the distribution of wealth and income, the second on property rights, understood in the broad sense of claims to returns on economic activity. Both in turn are the result of political choices: Governments can redistribute wealth and income directly and reshuffle property rights by protecting some claims and not others. Thus, deliberately or not, politics continually shapes economic activity. This understanding makes it possible to conceive the dominant forms of mass production not as the uniquely efficient form of industrial society but rather as the consequence of a series of complex, often unwitting, political choices whose history has only recently begun to be written. This same understanding also illuminates contemporary cases where economic dualism results from features of the organization of work and the use of labor rather than from the type of equipment in use in the factories.

Three strands of evidence point to the importance of extramarket developments in shaping contemporary technology and industrial structure. The first suggests that the factory system was not a simple result of technological advance, but a product of a particular distribution of property that encouraged a corresponding set of techno-logical developments. The second strand challenges the notion that the essentials of mechanization were a result of the factory system. The third calls attention to the ways in which differences in market structure, differences plainly rooted in divergent political histories, led to marked differences in the pattern of industrialization in coun-tries such as the United States, France, and Great Britain.

First, the existence of the modern mass-production factory system did not grow naturally out of collective experimentation with the efficient use of resources. Factories, it seems, did not initially pro-duce goods more cheaply than other methods of production. They were simply more profitable than other systems for their capitalist owners. And because they were created by a particular kind of soci-ety, their present organization may reflect the peculiarities of their social beginning.

There are two versions of this view of the origins of the factory, one stressing the political ambitions of the capitalists as a nascent class determined to keep control of the workers,[11] the other stressing the profit motives of individual capitalists. I will reproduce the sec-ond on the theory that it is easier to prove a felony than conspiracy to commit felony.

The argument, put forward by Jan de Vries, begins with the ad-vances in agricultural technique in seventeenth-century Britain.[12] These breakthroughs increased the surplus of food, lowering its cost relative to manufactured goods and causing demand for the latter to rise. Higher agricultural productivity also made some farm labor redundant. Industry, particularly the textile industry, migrated from the city to the countryside to take advantage of the cheap surplus labor by means of the putting-out system: Factors or middlemen bought wool, for example, and then paid peasants to spin it into yarn. As demand increased still further, merchants coerced their scattered workers into central factories, where they could be made to work longer hours and more days per year.

This was the crucial point. Even if productivity per working hour did not go up, the increase in total production per unit of calendar time that resulted from the increase in the number of working hours meant that the merchant's capital turned over more quickly, increas-ing his profits. Thus, sadly enough, simple coercion resulted in an increase in efficiency from the merchant's point of view. Once work had been reorganized in factories, entrepreneurs became attentive to the economies of scale made possible by further subdivision of an already regimented work force and by appropriate technological ad-vances; with such economies they lowered costs further, increased demand, and propelled forward the cycle of reorganization and innovation implicit in the model.

The second strand of evidence concerns the origins of the mechanical and organizational foundations of industrial society. The evidence is that the discovery of basic principles of machine design, their application to large- or small-scale industrial production, and the creation of efficient managerial techniques were all independent of the creation of the factory system by nineteenth-century capitalists. The most basic principles of machine design, for example, were discovered by Renaissance and Baroque instrument makers, military engineers, and scientists.[13] Their application to such industries as spinning and weaving in the seventeenth and eighteenth centuries often resulted in inventions suited to the circumstances of petty producers: The new machines required little capital and a family-sized labor force, and hence were well suited to the perpetuation of cottage industry.[14] For another example, precision machining techniques, which eventually made possible mass production of standardized goods, were envisioned by the French in the eighteenth century and perfected in the United States to meet military demand for guns with interchangeable parts easily replaced on the battlefield.[15] And long before the Americans had devised their system of divisional corporate management, the Germans, French, Japanese, Chinese, and Russians had all found their own ways of managing huge military and civilian bureaucracies often responsible for, among other things, large-scale industrial enterprises.

The third strand of evidence helps corroborate the preceding two. The organization of production by nineteenth-century industrial pioneers reflected differences in property holdings and cultural values: The basic principles of machine design were elaborated differently in different countries, depending on the constitution of their markets.

Roughly speaking, it is possible to distinguish two patterns of development. The first is the familiar one in which a mass market is associated with mass production. The clearest example is the United States, where the absence of guilds and feudal traditions of peasant deference left the population without preconceptions that might have slowed acceptance of mass-production goods: Because of the homogeneity and plasticity of taste in the United States, Nathan Rosenberg remarks, Americans were willing to buy the goods, from cutlery to clocks, that machines could make.[16]

Another example of mass-production, mass-consumption society in the nineteenth century was Great Britain. Here the creation of the mass market was rooted in the crown's failure, despite repeated attempts, to block eviction of the peasantry from its lands and the resulting growth in the swelling cities of a large, uprooted population open to and ultimately dependent upon the consumption of machine-made goods. Joan Thirsk has shown, moreover, how beginning in the late sixteenth century the English state itself contributed to the development of a mass market, first by tolerating cheap imports of such consumer goods as textiles, and then by encouraging, through chartered monopolies, the growth of domestic industry to satisfy the market.[17]

Compared to the Americans, however, British producers and consumers were only half-hearted supporters of mass-produced goods. Their insistence on variety in consumer goods and specialized producers' goods such as machine tools sustained at least until the end of the nineteenth century a sector of small firms whose operation, particularly evident in a city like Birmingham, pointed toward an alternative system of industrial development.

This pattern amounted to the mechanization of handicraft production. Instead of trying to satisfy a presumptively universal taste at the lowest possible price with a standard good, a manufacturer in this system aimed to customize his products, matching them to the diverse wants of a clientele willing to pay a premium for its preferences. Instead of using specialized machinery to make a single good, therefore, this second kind of producer used general-purpose machines. These were often a sophisticated version of the artisan's original tools, which could be quickly shifted from manufacture of one thing to another. Instead of unskilled labor he employed craftsmen, whose skill was required to make full use of the machines' potential. Where the emergent system of mass production housed more and more steps, rigidly defined, of a manufacturing process in a single giant factory, the unit of mechanized artisanal production was the small workshop specializing in one or a few operations and linked to the others by a complex web of subcontracting arrangements. As demand shifted, the workshops could be recombined in new ways to make new goods.

Thus, in nineteenth-century Sheffield, this kind of workshop economy born of traditional artisanal production was turning out a huge variety of razors, pocket knives, tableware, files, saws, and scissors. Small firms specialized in the forging, grinding, or hafting of a particular line of products, so that each item was passed from shop to shop on its way to the market. Using similar principles of organization, craftsmen in Birmingham turned out a huge assortment of buckles, buttons, toys, steel jewelry, and firearms.[18]

Where large expensive machinery could reduce the cost of production without limiting its flexibility, the new equipment was used in ways that were compatible with the decentralized character of the economy. In both cities, for instance, entrepreneurs rented steam power and work space to artisans. The torque produced by a steam engine was subdivided by means of looped belts and used to drive the small machines of independent producers grouped in the same building. Sheffield grinders in the mid-nineteenth century often worked in such "public wheels," as buildings full of workshops were called locally; and in Birmingham in the same period there were often signs reading "Power to Let."[19] In other cases the small producers themselves found means to solve common problems collectively. When production of brass and copper began to fall under monopoly control in the late eighteenth century, for example, artisans in Birmingham responded by forming producers' cooperatives to supply themselves with both.[20]

Although there were similar regions organized on workshop principles in all of the early industrializing countries, the center of this type of production was probably France. Here the peasants' successful defense of their interests before and during the Revolution, and the tradition of partible inheritance (later written into the Civil Code), kept the rural population on the land. This hindered the growth of mass markets because the poorer peasant households satisfied most of their own needs outside the market, whereas the wealthier ones, whose tastes were shaped by the consumption habits of local elites, demanded more differentiated goods than those produced in Great Britain. But even if there had been mass demand for standard goods, French manufacturers would have had difficulty organizing production to meet it. Guilds, the *métiers jurés* that were reinvigorated between the end of the sixteenth century and the French Revolution, helped enforce manufacture of a variety of quality goods in small shops, at least in the cities where the regulations were respected. And in any case the peasants' ties to the land blocked migration to towns, thereby limiting the supply of mobile labor.[21]

Industrialization in France, given these preconditions, did not therefore mean a simultaneous shift of labor from agriculture to industry and the creation of a system of factory production to satisfy the demands of the uprooted masses. French development, as one school of economic historians holds, was an alternative to, not a belated imitation of, the English pattern.[22] As small improvements in economic organization slowly raised the level of demand for manufactured goods, and as the constant subdivision of land from generation to generation reduced the size of the average peasant holding, the system of craft production spread out to the countryside. The artisans put work out to the peasants in order to profit from the lax guild regulation in the countryside, and take advantage of the available labor; the peasants aimed to supplement their farm income with part-time industrial work.

The productivity increases possible within this system were significant. Patrick O'Brien and Caglar Keyder go so far as to argue that average labor productivity in French and British industry was roughly comparable during much of the nineteenth century. Although their general conclusions rest on debatable assumptions about currency exchange rates and the boundaries of the industrial sector, their evidence does suggest that workshops in France were more efficient than those in Britain.[23]

How much of this increase in output is attributable to more efficient organization of traditional artisanal methods of production, and how much to the invention of new machinery and processes suited to the needs of decentralized, flexible production, it is difficult to say. But there is no doubt that the workshop economy in France and elsewhere was often technologically vital. A famous example of this vitality is the Jacquard loom, which was perfected for industrial use around 1815. This loom was the key to the booming silk industry in nineteenth-century Lyons. Designs were punched on cards, which then guided the weaving. For this reason the Jacquard loom is often regarded as the forerunner of modern numerically controlled machines. Mainly by reducing the time needed to set up the loom for each new product, it lowered labor costs and made possible a boom in flower-patterned façonné silks. The number of officially registered designs went from 30 in 1818 to 733 in 1824, and the number of looms in use rose from 1,200 to 4,202 in the same period.[24] But production remained extremely decentralized.[25]

Birmingham artisans, to continue the list of examples, were quick to use new materials such as copper, brass, tin, and steel, as well as new techniques such as pressing, stamping, die-sinking, and turning with metal lathes. Sheffield made breakthroughs in specialty steels and tin plating.[26] And even in the United States, perhaps the heartland of mass production, a workshop sector in southern New England devised a new technology for flexible production of textiles. Small and medium-size mill owners in this area were boxed in between manufacturers in Massachusetts who turned out mass-produced goods, British firms that made handwoven quality textiles, and local firms that supplied primitive but very cheap cloth. Their answer was to specialize in high-quality, fashionable products made on machines specially designed to facilitate rapid changes in the threads and weave: The invention of the differential gear was one result of their search for flexible technologies.[27]

To see why this alternative method of production, despite its successes, was overshadowed by Fordist principles, it is necessary to refer back to the earlier discussion of the dialectic of imitation. Had the system of mechanized artisanal production developed in isolation from or before the system of mass production, its principles might have been applied to a wide variety of industries, and the relation between core and periphery in the dualist model might have been reversed. The core of this alternative economy might have been a large number of small and medium-sized firms specializing in a wide range of finishing operations for differentiated markets. The periphery might have been a small number of large manufacturers of basic products, such as steel or dyestuffs, which enter into the production of a wide range of goods. As the example of the producers' cooperatives in Birmingham suggests, these large firms might furthermore have been owned collectively by their customers, who could thus benefit from economies of scale in the production of inputs without becoming dependent on a powerful manufacturer interested in standardizing the final good.

But coming as it did after and close to the system of mass markets, these workshop economies were drawn into the latter's wake. Once techniques of large-scale factory organization had proven their efficiency, delay in imitating them, even to adapt them fully to local circumstance, invited foreign domination. Wherever consumers were undecided between mass-produced goods and artisanal products, the existence of cheap, foreign goods was a threat to domestic manufacturers.[28] Similarly, if tastes were still unformed the availability of advanced mass-production machinery could play an important role in shaping the organization and final product of an industry. In this way the fascination of Continental mechanics and engineers with the demonstrably successful Anglo-American machine designs contributed to the speed of mass-production techniques even as it diverted attention from the perfection of more flexible technologies suited to the workshop sector.[29]

Developments in the British boot and shoe industry show these forces at work. Until late in the nineteenth century, British manufacturers were reluctant to adopt American-style technology. They produced, as R. A. Church has noted, a "considerable variety of styles and fashions"; and they feared that mass production would be "less economical for them than for the American makers, whose practice was to limit their range and thereby gain the benefits of long runs on fully mechanized production."[30] They also hesitated to introduce new machines in the face of opposition from the organized crafts-men whose jobs would be threatened by the new technology.

But beginning in the early 1890s, British manufacturers were threatened by a rapid rise in imports of mass-produced American goods. Although the total volume of the imports amounted at its peak to little more than a third of British exports of boots and shoes, even the limited success of the standard product raised the specter of a collapse of the established firms.

American shoe-machinery manufacturers encouraged these fears, and of course offered to sell the British the modern equipment needed to meet the foreign threat. At the same time British manufacturers were urged to experiment with new styles: Instead of attempting to reproduce old patterns by machine, the strategy was to introduce new products, suitable to machine production, which did not invite evaluation according to established standards of taste. The British listened. Tastes and techniques of production were gradually realigned; and after 1902 the number of pairs of imported shoes began to drop.

Besides fear of foreign competition, another reason for Fordism's success was its military potential. Careful observers in the mid-nineteenth century were aware that the capacity to mass produce munitions would one day be a precondition of military success. By World War I, as we will see in Chapter 4, the connection between Fordism and the war economy was an open secret. Thereafter, it was clear that a state that did not foster mass-production industry invited defeat on the battlefield as well as in the market.[31]

The further technological development proceeded down this path, the more difficult it became to conceive of any potential alternative as ever having been a serious competitor of the victor, and the more the shadow of Fordism obscured the continued vitality of other forms of industrial organization. Yet as historians are coming to see, parts of the workshop sector in the large industrial countries did survive in the penumbra of mass production by inventing new products and adapting technology to their needs.[32] The Lyonnais, for instance, still organized according to the principles of specialized production, developed new dyes, and pioneered the use of artificial fibers in the late nineteenth and early twentieth centuries.[33] And some small countries, such as Switzerland, recognizing that their domestic markets were not large enough to accommodate a system of mass production, made a virtue of necessity and specialized in the production of high-quality, customized goods.[34] The victory of Fordism was thus never as complete as it seemed. But the workshop sector was regarded as a vestige of an inefficient age, fated at best to play a secondary part in a superior order of production. The brilliance of Fordism's success as a model blinded observers to the limits to its hold over the factory.

Thus the spread of Fordism and the creation of the particular dual economic structure that it entailed was not, on the available historical evidence, a proof that a different pattern of mechanization based on different markets, rooted in correspondingly different patterns of property rights, could not have prospered. Nor does it seem, for that matter, that the Fordist system having once won out is here to stay: In Chapter 5 we will look at evidence that new market and technological possibilities are prompting the reorganization of parts of the industrial structure in the advanced capitalist countries according to the principle of the workshop sector. The present form of technological dualism, it seems, was and is not a technical necessity.

The political background of technological dualism: a contemporary perspective

Arguments like that of the foregoing section are necessarily speculative. History did not run the experiments needed to clinch the points. As we move closer to the present, however, the connections among the system of property rights, the structure of markets, and the organization of the economy stand out more clearly.

The dualist model, as we saw, presumes that capital costs are relatively fixed, labor costs relatively variable. But this is not necessarily so. If it is possible to buy a machine or a factory shed in the morning and sell it at the same price minus a day's depreciation at night, investment in capital equipment approximates a variable cost; if it is impossible to hire and fire workers or to vary the number of hours or the way they work, then labor is a fixed cost. What is a fixed and what a variable cost therefore depends on the structure of the capital and labor markets; and market structure, in turn, depends on political and institutional factors that cannot be deduced simply from examination of the technology of production.

Trade unions and their allied political parties, for instance, often freeze the organization of production by imposing contractual or statutory limitations on entrepreneurial freedom to set salaries, man machines, operate the plant, hire and fire, or introduce new equipment. The tighter the web of rules, the more decisions regarding manning levels or work schedules become long-term, hence risky, investments; and the greater is management's incentive to find some way of achieving its end without running the risk.

The employers' answer is likely to be subcontracting and the decentralization of production. Workers are easier to organize in large plants than in small. Contractual and statutory rules governing the use of labor are often much easier to enforce in large than in small factories. Hence, wherever employers fear that trade unions will freeze provisional changes in plant organization, they are tempted to establish subsidiaries or subcontract work to small, even one-man, plants.

When trade unions are particularly strong and pursue egalitarian policies, employers have an additional motive to decentralize production: to avoid homogenization of work conditions throughout the plant. Strong trade unions threaten to elevate every change favorable to the workers into a costly norm. A plant employing workers of diverse types is therefore particularly dangerous because it allows the union to establish the conditions of the best-off workers as the standard for the rest. As we will see from developments in Italy in the 1970s, volatile markets requiring abrupt and visible shifts in the organization of work can, when combined with aggressive trade unions, provoke extensive decentralization of production for both these reasons.

Alternatively, if the labor movement is even stronger, it can prohibit the emergence of a sector of small firms altogether, by setting wages for all workers so high that marginal producers are kept out of the markets. This is one consequence of prolonged Social Democratic control of labor markets in Sweden. There, in the absence of a secondary sector of the economy, the state coordinates responses to fluctuations in the level of demand by, for example, subsidizing firms during slack periods out of a fund accumulated during booms.[35]

A still more extreme case is that of the Soviet-type economies of Eastern Europe. Here the state aims through centralized input–output planning to treat the entire economy as a single, giant, primary-sector enterprise. In these economies petty production is tolerated as a means of responding to unforeseen contingencies and shortfalls in planned output; but its growth is sharply limited out of fear that a sector of small producers could pose first an economic and then a political threat to state control of national development.[36]

Thus, whether in historical or in contemporary perspective, not just the character but the very existence of economic dualism itself depends on the distribution of property and power: social conditions that theories of the economy posit rather than explain. Calling attention to the model's presuppositions exposes the limits of its applicability and will therefore facilitate the discussion of the breakdown of Fordism in Chapter 5. But discussion of these limits does not discredit the idea of dualism as a tool for understanding the dominant pattern of industrial development in Western Europe, the United States, and Japan in the twentieth century and its relation to the structure of the labor market, to which we now return.

The organization of the unstable sector

The analysis so far suggests both a typology of firms operating in the secondary sector and a surprising conclusion, given the initial notion of technologically determined dualism – that beyond their relation to the market, the distinguishing feature of these firms is their use of labor, not technology.

At one extreme, independent of any consideration of labor's organizational strength, secondary-sector entrepreneurs may prefer less expensive and less product-specific equipment than that used in the primary sector: Faced with uncertain demand, they refuse to burden themselves with high, long-term capital costs. Hence they employ older machines, discarded perhaps by more advanced firms, which they can purchase cheaply and sell to manufacturers in other branches when demand for their own product ebbs. The high production costs associated with the older equipment are tolerable for the simple reason that when demand is high, so too are prices, and high-cost producers can find a place in the market.

This kind of decentralization of production is likely when large companies are so content with the growth of stable markets and so at peace with the unions that they are neither pulled by the hope of extra profit nor pushed by the fear of losses to establish subsidiaries themselves. This is the image of American industry in the 1950s and 1960s that inspired the original model of dualism.

At the opposite extreme, segmentation can result from the strategic choices of large firms whose freedom to use specialized equipment according to the rhythms of the market is restricted by trade unions. Even if they are sure the boom will last long enough for them to recover their capital investment, they fear that the unions will freeze employment at a level above their expected long-term demand for labor. The solution is to set up a subsidiary employing the latest technology, but located in a region beyond the union's control. Here the industrial structure results from the need to segment labor, not capital.

In between are a variety of hybrid cases in which segmentation results from a complex mix of technical, economic, and political considerations. A firm with unrestricted power to hire and fire, for example, might try to meet peaks in demand by hiring extra workers and running extra shifts, creating an almost invisible intraplant segmentation of regular and temporary crews. In setting up a subsidiary, to take another example, a large company might use dated equipment as well as a docile labor force. Or fearing for whatever reasons the risks of buying new machines or establishing a subsidiary, a large, booming firm might subcontract to small manufacturers with modern equipment the few operations it cannot perform in sufficient volume even with extra shifts. The subcontractor of course considers the cost of amortization of his machine in the piece price he charges. But this cost is now distributed among all his clients, as is the cost of maintaining the machine: The large firm has the benefit of the new equipment without assuming long-term responsibility for the fixed costs. If demand persists, the firm will be tempted to purchase the machine itself. On the other hand, we will see in Chapter 5 how under the right circumstances subcontractors who begin as the dependents of large producers can break their dependence on large customers entirely and develop innovative products of their own.

This kind of decentralization is not necessarily a product of boom periods. It is a reaction to uncertainty, not growth per se. It therefore often results from severe business downturns. In the late 1940s and early 1950s in Italy, for example, crises of the textile and metalworking industries led to significant decentralization of production. As orders declined, workers were fired. Firms sold off older equipment, which was often bought by unemployed workers, sometimes with the help of their former employers. The new owners then began to produce on commission for the large firms, who thus transferred most of the risk of an unpredictable future to the subcontractors.

The ultimate extension of decentralization, born either of booms or of busts, is homework. Here, as Piore has argued, all costs are variable for the employer, because *all* tools and plant are owned by the worker.

Though they use technology in different ways, all secondary-sector firms have a common labor-market strategy: They employ workers who require no training. Firms that meet volatile demand can never be sure that they will continue to need the skills any particular training program produces; nor can they be certain that, once trained, the workers will not go into business for themselves rather than share the firm's shaky future.

Workers in secondary-sector firms therefore fall into two broad classes. The first, which includes the great majority, either have no skills or have informally acquired capacities that are taken so much for granted that employers do not have to regard them as skills at all – for example, a young woman's ability to sew. The second kind of workers are broadly skilled craftsmen who install, maintain, and supervise the operation of the capital equipment.

Skilled and unskilled workers in the same firm are likely to belong to different worlds. Should a secondary-sector firm need additional craftsmen, it recruits them on the local labor market rather than training an unskilled employee. The firm does not even have an incentive to promote or otherwise reward workers who train themselves on the job or discover better ways of organizing production. To take advantage of such suggestions would only make the production techniques more specialized and lengthen the time needed to break in the succeeding cohort of workers, thereby reducing the firm's capacity to respond to changes in the business cycle. Furthermore, when demand is slack, unskilled workers are laid off immediately. The skilled, who tend to be the most difficult to recruit in the first place, are the last fired. Advanced or backward, a secondary-sector firm is a dead end for the unskilled and no more than a way station for craftsmen.[37]

A Bavarian example

To illustrate the creation of markets for these kinds of labor, it is not enough to confirm that the investment and labor-market strategies of firms facing uncertain demand conform to predictions. The argument is that managers perceive their situation as the model describes it. So statistical analysis of the relation between the business cycle and the size and composition of the work force has to be supplemented by an examination of management's motives for its decisions. In lieu of a study of this sort, I will draw together several lines of research on the economic structure of some of the less prosperous regions of West Germany in order to illuminate the principal aspects of the problem.

In their work on the electronics and garment industries in the Bavarian Oberpfalz, Knut Gerlach and Peter Liepmann show that West German firms established subsidiaries in peripheral – usually rural – regions to reduce the effects of the business cycle on urban manufacturing centers. Compared with Bavarian and national averages, a disproportionate percentage of the new jobs in these industries in the Oberpfalz, they demonstrate, were in subsidiaries.[38] They found, too, that the atypical industrial structure of the Oberpfalz was particularly vulnerable to large fluctuations in employment. Gerlach and Liepmann conclude that because of the "direct dependence of firms in peripheral regions (in this case the Oberpfalz) on firms in the center of economic activity (in this case: Nuremberg, Munich, Oberfranken), necessary changes in the level of employment are carried out in the periphery so that their effects are not felt in the center."[39] But how exactly might production be organized in the peripheral plants so that the parent firms can take advantage

Table 1. *Percentage of unskilled and semiskilled workers in West German industry by type of plant*

Percentage of the total work force	New subsidiaries		Relocated subsidiaries		Relocated plants	
	Main plant	Subsidiary	Main plant	Subsidiary	Old site	New site
0–20	8.2	11.8	21.2	19.0	8.0	13.2
20–50	27.1	14.0	21.3	3.2	38.1	35.3
50–70	23.0	14.1	30.3	31.5	22.3	19.2
70–100	41.7	60.1	27.2	46.3	31.6	32.3

Source: Dietrich Fürst and Klaus Zimmermann, under the direction of Karl-Heinrich Hansmeyer, *Standortwahl industrieller Unternehmen: Ergebnisse einer Unternehmensbefragung,* Schriftenreihe der Gesellschaft für regionale Strukturentwicklung 1 (Bonn: Gesellschaft für regionale Strukturentwicklung, 1973), pt. 2, p. 37.

of the distinction between stable and unstable components of demand without disturbing the routines in the central works?

A study by Dietrich Fürst and Klaus Zimmermann of the location decisions of firms in Bavaria, Hessia, Schleswig-Holstein, and Rheinland-Pfalz examines the relation between the central factories and their subsidiaries.[40] In addition to completely new plants, too heterogeneous to be of interest here, they distinguished three categories of firms: relocated plants, new subsidiaries, and relocated subsidiaries. Main plants that had been relocated in new industrial regions, they found, resembled main plants with subsidiaries much more than new or relocated subsidiaries. Thus, as the segmentation model suggests, the organization of production was shaped more by a plant's relation to the market than by its geographic and social environment.

Tables 1 and 2 demonstrate that unskilled and semiskilled workers were a considerably larger percentage of the work force in new and relocated subsidiaries than in either main plants or old subsidiaries. More than 70 percent of the work force was unskilled or semiskilled in roughly half the new and relocated subsidiaries. In almost half the new subsidiaries and just over half the relocated ones, more than 70 percent of the workers were women. The corresponding figures for main works of all categories were much lower; and this pattern conformed closely to the one found by Friedrich Buttler, Gerlach, and Liepmann in one of their studies of the labor market in the Oberpfalz.[41]

Fürst and Zimmermann's interviews with managers show, more-

Table 2. *Percentage of women in West German industry by type of plant*

Percentage of the total work force	New subsidiaries		Relocated subsidiaries		Relocated plants	
	Main plant	Sub-sidiary	Main plant	Sub-sidiary	Old site	New site
0–20	33.1	24.6	29.4	24.2	35.0	38.4
20–50	17.3	17.2	29.4	17.2	28.1	27.0
50–70	14.8	12.3	20.6	6.8	21.1	11.5
70–100	34.8	45.9	20.6	51.8	15.8	23.1

Source: Fürst and Zimmermann, *Standortwahl*, pt. 2, p. 39.

Table 3. *Factors influencing choice of plant location in West German industry by type of plant*

	All plants	New subsidi-aries	Relo-cated subsidi-aries	Relo-cated plants
Access to interregional transportation	1	1	1	1
Availability of land	2	3	5	2
Inexpensive land	3	4/5	6/7/8	3
Supply of unskilled labor	4	2	2	11
Supply of skilled labor	5/6	7	9/10/11	5
Supply of female labor	12/13	8/9/10	4	16

Note: Numbers indicate degree of importance of factors, with 1 denoting the most important.
Source: Fürst and Zimmermann, *Standortwahl*, pt. 2, p. 104.

over, that the shift from a skilled work force was an important motive for the move: For new and relocated subsidiaries, the availability of unskilled labor was the second most important reason to locate at a particular site; probably because of peculiarities of the production techniques, the availability of unskilled women was important only in the case of the relocation of subsidiaries.

In contrast, as Table 3 shows, managers relocated main plants to take advantage of lower real-estate prices and the reservoirs of skilled workers typical of regions with declining industries. When main plants were relocated under such conditions, more than half of the old work force moved along with capital equipment. As a rule, it

Table 4. *Forms of plant-site tenure in West German industry by type of plant (%)*

	Subsidiaries		Relocated subsidiaries		Relocated plants	
	Main plants	Subsidiaries	Main plants	Subsidiaries	Old sites	New sites
Rented/ leased site	18.0	39.6	28.6	66.6	51.7	28.2
Purchased site	82.0	60.4	71.4	33.4	48.3	71.8

Source: Fürst and Zimmermann, *Standortwahl,* pt. 2, p. 56.

was the skilled workers who followed the plant to its new site: Managers in main plants were as careful to safeguard the skill level in relocated factories as the managers of subsidiaries were to lower it.

Table 4 shows that new and relocated subsidiaries tended to be built on rented or leased sites, whereas main plants, whether relocated or not, tended to stand on land that the firm owned or wanted to buy. Management's choice was obviously no more dictated by the availability of land than it was by the availability of various types of labor: Entrepreneurs with main plants to relocate had no trouble finding land to buy. Again, as the model suggests, managers of subsidiaries preferred leasing because they feared long-term investments.

The figures in Table 5 support this interpretation. The relatively high percentage of relocated main plants employing modern production techniques indicates that these plants were regarded as long-term investments. Conversely, the low percentage of subsidiaries using modern techniques supports the suggestion that, in management's judgment, instability of demand did not justify investment in sophisticated, product-specific technology with long payback periods.

Table 6 presents findings that suggest management's planning horizons. In subsidiaries with substantial sales (which used more sophisticated planning techniques than smaller firms), managers based investment decisions on short-term expectations: Almost 20 percent of the subsidiaries in the two largest size categories expected to make their investments pay off in three years or less.[42]

In short, the new and relocated subsidiaries served comparatively

Table 5. *Use of modern technology in West German industry by type of plant (%)*

	Subsidiaries	Relocated subsidiaries	Relocated plants
Modern technology in use	28.3	24.3	55.4
Modern technology not in use	71.7	75.7	44.6

Source: Fürst and Zimmermann, *Standortwahl,* pt. 2, p. 57.

Table 6. *Length of the planning horizon in West German industrial subsidiaries by turnover (%)*

	Turnover (DM)			
Length of planning horizon	0–less than 400,000	400,000 –less than 1 million	1 million –less than 5 million	5 million and above
0–3 years	—	—	18.8	18.2
3–10 years	28.6	21.4	31.2	54.5
10 years or more	71.4	78.6	50.0	27.3

Source: Fürst and Zimmermann, *Standortwahl,* pt. 2, p. 170.

unstable markets, the main plants of the parent firms comparatively stable ones. Operations requiring long-term commitment to expensive machines and skilled workers were concentrated in the main plants; and, as Georg Raum observes in his study of the distribution of skills in the Oberpfalz, "labor intensive steps in mass production processes are farmed out to the subsidiaries. Jobs in these plants are designed so that they do not need to be performed by skilled workers."[43]

Because the subsidiaries had familiar and reliable production equipment (which might have been previously written off), and because they stood on rented or quickly salable land, this division of labor meant that parent firms could expand production quickly by founding satellite plants in booms. When demand slackened, the parent firm chose between shutting down the subsidiary completely and merely laying off a substantial portion of the work force and, unburdened by high variable costs, awaiting better times. In the latter case, management could assume that "since subsidiaries tend to be monopsonists on the local labor market, laid-off workers will not have found employment elsewhere during times of little demand and can be hired back when the market revives."[44] This monopsonist's privilege probably accounted for the tendency to set up subsidiaries in small, even tiny, villages whenever transportation facilities permitted.[45]

In these examples there has been a match-up between main plants and stable product markets, on the one hand, and subsidiaries and unstable markets, on the other. But to recall an earlier point, there is no inviolable relation between formalities of organization and types of product markets; the division between the sectors of the product market can correspond to many different institutional forms. This is so even within a relatively small area: In the Oberpfalz there were subsidiaries producing for stable markets and main plants selling in unstable ones, as Raum's study shows.

Table 7 presents his results. Ranked by composition of the work forces, electronics subsidiaries employing more than 300 persons occupied a middle position between smaller subsidiaries and main plants of all sizes. Two related causes probably account for the disproportionately high number of craftsmen and the disproportionately low number of women workers in these plants. First, a plant of this size employs capital-intensive production techniques requiring more frequent, expert maintenance and supervision than do superannuated technologies. Second, the more advanced, expensive machinery is likely to be operated nights and holidays, and management tends to hire men rather than women to run it, either because of the prejudice that women are physically unable to stand the work load or because of laws prohibiting them from working at night.[46]

From this it follows that these large subsidiaries were integral to the production operations centered in the main plants: They no longer produced, at least not primarily, for unstable markets. Conceivably, these subsidiaries were the outgrowth of a cautious strategy reported in a related study:

Large firms not infrequently make use of the possibility of avoiding a necessary and costly expansion of capacity – in connection for example with goods whose product life is thought to be rather short – by the expedient of setting up subsidiaries in already existing factories in rural areas. As soon as future developments can be anticipated with some degree of certainty, these plants can be converted into "stable" subsidiaries, or capacity can be expanded in the main works.[47]

The group of small independent garment firms included in Raum's study illustrates the reverse case: main plants producing for unstable markets. As Table 8 indicates, the skill distribution of the workers in the smaller independent firms in the branch falls halfway between

Table 7. *Composition of the work force in the electronics industry of the Oberpfalz by plant size and type*

	Percentage of the total work force	
	Women	Skilled workers
Independent plants		
10–300 workers[a]	41.02	21.24
301–500 workers[b]	55.15	16.39
Subsidiaries		
10–300 workers	80.19	5.91
301–1,000 workers[b]	61.11	11.05
More than 1,000 workers[c]	60.87	13.12

[a]Survey includes 4 plants in this category.
[b]Survey includes 8 plants in this category.
[c]Survey includes 3 plants in this category.
Source: Georg Raum, "Die Arbeitsplatzqualifikationsanforderungen der Zweigbetriebe," mimeographed (Regensburg, 1975), p. 31.

the composition of the work force in the large independent firms and that in the smaller subsidiaries. The ratio of women to men is higher than in the large independent plants producing for stable markets, and the ratio of skilled to unskilled workers is lower. Comparison of these results with those shown in Table 7 calls further attention to this point. The smaller, independent electronics firms employ, relatively, far fewer women and unskilled workers than the small, independent garment producers. Within the electronics industry, in fact, this group of firms employs the largest percentage of skilled workers in the work force, whereas within the garment industry, firms of this size employ a smaller percentage of craftsmen than do large subsidiaries and independent plants.

A study of the Bavarian labor market prepared for the state government suggests the origins of these firms. According to the study, homework, once an important part of the Bavarian economy, was increasingly concentrated in small firms. Furthermore, sales and employment in the Bavarian garment industry taken as a whole were influenced more by changes in the business cycle than by employment and sales in the West German clothing industry in general; and finally, increases in the productivity of Bavarian firms were below the national average.[48] These last two results are just what one would expect if production for the secondary market had been collected into the small factories: Productivity levels in these plants

Table 8. *Composition of the work force in the clothing industry of the Oberpfalz by plant size and type*

	Percentage of the total work force	
	Women	Skilled workers
Independent plants		
10–300 workers	84.90	28.68
301–1,000 workers[a]	75.83	35.62
Subsidiaries		
10–300 workers	93.24	22.50
301–500 workers[b]	94.16	34.53

[a]Survey includes 7 plants in this category.
[b]Survey includes 3 plants in this category.
Source: Raum, "Die Arbeitsplatzqualifikationsanforderungen," p. 31.

would not match those in the capital-intensive sector, but fluctuations in sales volume and in the number of employees would be greater.

In short, there can be independent plants whose existence depends on the vagaries of the unstable market, just as there can be subsidiaries supplying stable markets. To repeat: Although the considerations underlying the segmentation strategy are simple, its institutional realization is complex. Only case-by-case analysis attentive to all the background political conditions that make markets can discover the structuring principle in the maze of organization.

The organization of production in the stable sector

The core features of production in the secondary sector follow directly from the original model: The prohibition of long-term planning rules out so many possibilities that it is easy to see the essentials of short-run strategy. The primary sector is more complicated. The original model offers only inconclusive hints about the connection between the progressive subdivision of labor and the organization of production. Additional postulates are needed to fill in the gap.

One plausible assumption is that progress in the division of labor produces a steady and equal erosion of the skills of all the workers in the plant. This would be the result if each task could simply be divided into two operations, each more efficiently performed by separate workers than by a single worker doing both together. The same result is reached by supposing the repeated invention of machines doing half the task of each skilled worker and serviced by completely unskilled operators.

There are, however, important reasons for rejecting these and related assumptions in favor of another proposition: that under Fordist conditions an increase in the division of labor creates demand for a mixture of new skills even as it destroys old ones. It seems likely, in fact, that as the continual division of tasks slowly reduces the average skill level, some craftsmen will be able to augment their skills, while new possibilities for semiskilled work will open up at the middle range of the blue-collar hierarchy. It is a commonplace of the sociology of organizations that specialization within bureaucratic organizations increases not only their efficiency, but also their susceptibility to disruption.[49] Analogously, as production becomes more mechanized, it becomes more prone to ever-more-costly disturbances. It is thus impossible to dispense with a core of skilled workers. Whether they are engaged in repairing the existing equipment or in installing the next generation of technology, they must be capable of understanding each task as part of a larger complex of tasks, as a case of the application of the overarching principles of construction. They must grasp the principles of a given technology abstractly enough to repair defects that occur for the first time.[50]

The upshot is that just as each generation of technology in a sense subsumes the principles embedded in the old, so technological progress leads to an upgrading of the skills of workers who service, repair, draw plans for, and even participate in the design of new machines. Though skills may pass from artisans to metalworking craftsmen, or from machinists to electricians, and although the percentage of skilled workers in the work force may decline, the specialization of labor affords at least a few workers the opportunities for advancement. I will refer to craftsmen privileged by technological progress in this way as workers with upgraded skills.

This line of reasoning also suggests several conclusions regarding the intermediate range of skills between those upgraded by advances in production techniques and those reduced to the point where they are not officially acknowledged as skills at all. Two developments whose interconnection will emerge later create demand for these intermediate skills. First, whenever machines must be routinely and frequently serviced in the course of production, certain of the craftsman's activities can be separated from the rest, formalized, and defined as a lower (and less-well-paid) skill grade. The machine setup man (*Einrichter*, *régleur*, *attrezzista*) who replaces dulled bits and other cutting tools or periodically readjusts the speed of automatic machine tools exemplifies this type.

The second type of workers with intermediate-level skills are machine tenders in automated process plants. They must master intricate procedures that, far from being formalizations of existing tasks, first become necessary with the implementation of new technologies. As we shall see, it is precisely because supervision of some machines cannot be reduced to rote operations that these jobs require an appreciable degree of skill.

The intermediate range of the skill hierarchy is thus a hybrid. It consists both of tasks no longer requiring the professional skills of craftsmen and those not yet demanding or generally applicable enough to be considered new crafts. It is also a hybrid in that it is the meeting ground for workers threatened with dequalification by technological change and workers to whom technological change offers opportunities for advancement. Jobs at this skill level tend to be held either by craftsmen no longer able to find employment for the full range of their skills or by formerly unskilled workers whose new positions of responsibility privilege them with respect to their old workmates.

Despite these differences, these two types of intermediate skills are similar in fundamental ways. Both rest on knowledge of particular machines as opposed to understanding of general construction principles. Both, for this reason, can be defined only with respect to the production techniques in a given plant. In contrast to upgraded skills, both are plant-specific. I will refer to them as downgraded skills when directing attention to their origin in changes in the division of labor, and as plant-specific skills when emphasizing their common roots in the mastery of particulars.

Last is the third and largest category of jobs: the one that groups tasks classed as unskilled. However demanding they may be, anyone familiar with the ways of an industrial society is presumed capable of performing them without further training. These jobs are a hybrid, too, but in yet another way: They combine elements typical of both the primary and the secondary sectors of the labor market.[51]

On the one hand, production in unskilled final assembly and packing divisions is often more labor intensive than the production process as a whole. The corresponding organization of work is reminiscent of production techniques employed in the unstable sector of the economy. Because these divisions have to respond quickly to small shifts in consumer demand, it is more efficient to organize production on the basis of a series of easily learned and variable techniques, such as welding, fastening nuts, or tightening screws, than to invest in expensive automatic equipment that might assemble only one variation of a product.[52]

On the other hand, these divisions are part of a production process that is in general capital intensive. The market planning that guarantees minimum levels of utilization for the capital equipment as a whole obviously works to stabilize unskilled jobs as well. Without final assembly there can be no production; and by definition, there is always demand for the products of firms in this sector of the economy. Although the labor force is likely to be reduced during recessions, nothing but a severe economic crisis will lead to even the temporary shutdown of a whole division. In other words, the most senior workers, or those most in favor with their superiors, need not fear for their jobs.

Two conclusions follow. First, because the definition of tasks is the same in both places, the same sort of workers who find employment in the unstable sector find work in this part of the stable sector as well. Second, at least some of the unskilled workers in the stable sector will hold their jobs far longer than the typical worker in the secondary market will be able to hold his.

At least one major objection can be raised against this scheme, and I will try to meet it before testing the explanatory power of the categories by applying them to a concrete case.

Intermediate skills: the skill cycle and the intellectualization of craft knowledge

No one seems to doubt the existence of upgraded and unskilled jobs. But questions have been raised about the type of intermediate-level jobs I am calling plant-specific: Do they in fact require substantial amounts of skill? Or are they rather a kind of placebo, empty of real responsibility and perpetuated only to give the workers a misleading sense of significance?

The view of the dualists, principally Peter Doeringer and Piore, is consistent with the ideas put forward in the preceding section. They argue that as work is rationalized, a series of middle-level jobs involving knowledge of the machines in particular plants is created. These skills are not transferable from firm to firm, as are traditional craft skills; but they are indispensable to production. Furthermore, because they require intimate familiarity with particular machines, they can only be taught on the job.

Organizing the transmission of these skills from one generation of workers to another is a problem of management. A single worker has little incentive to learn skills valuable to only his current employer. Furthermore, the small number of workers required for each particular job means that training must be essentially individual, and therefore expensive. Finally, older workers will not instruct younger ones without assurances that their pupils will not replace them. One solution to these problems, Doeringer and Piore argue, is the system of job ladders and seniority rights found in large American firms: As workers get older they advance up the job hierarchy, learning new skills on the job and acquiring, through their time in the plant, protection against younger competitors and rights to further promotion.[53]

The opposing, radical school denies that jobs in the middle of the official skill hierarchy require any skill. Most skilled jobs, according to this view, were abolished by the introduction of mass-production methods that took place in the United States, for example, around the turn of the century. Management, alarmed by the successes of the International Workers of the World, supposedly feared that the resulting work force, homogenized and with no hope of advancement, could easily be radicalized.

It therefore decided to control the workers' ambitions by creating a sham skill hierarchy: The desire for career and promotion would be satisfied by slow progress through a series of essentially identical, routine jobs, distinguished only by title and pay, with the higher wages of the top-ranked jobs being the small price for the moral subjugation of the labor force. The effect of these job ladders was to develop in the workers what David M. Gordon calls " 'hierarchy fetishism' – a continual craving for more and better job titles and status, the satisfaction of which leads eventually to intensified hunger for still more and better job titles and job status."[54]

Which of these arguments is preferable is an empirical question; and it seems to me that the evidence weighs heavily against the radical and for the dualist position. To argue the radical case at all, in fact, it is necessary to confuse employers' ambitions for the reality of the factory and partial truths about factory life for fundamental developments. Above all, it is necessary to overlook striking evidence of the workplace power of the putatively unskilled, powerless workers in intermediate-level jobs.

Much of the radical argument for the sham character of the skill hierarchy consists of citations of capitalists' assertions – endlessly repeated since Taylor began popularizing his notions of scientific management – that workers need no training to do their jobs. No doubt many managers would like this to be true, if only to confirm their uncomplimentary ideas about workers and their own indispensability. But managers say many things that radicals find patently wrong: for example, that capitalism is the only rational form of production. If the second idea is self-serving ideology, why not the first? At any rate, the simple fact that successive generations of managers keep announcing the final victory over their reliance on the workers' skills is hardly convincing proof of their success.

There is one piece of evidence for the radical thesis, however, that is surely not the result of anyone's wishful thinking: Intermediate-level posts do tend to go to people with connections, either to other workers in those sorts of jobs or to the managers who do the promoting. Examples will come up later. If promotion is a matter of cronyism and favoritism, why not conclude that the skill hierarchy exists solely to foster both? The difficulty with this argument is that it confuses one of the uses of an institution with the first causes of its existence. Assume for a moment that management deep down thinks the dualists are right: Training is necessary; most people can learn most jobs; most training is done on the job. It creates a skill hierarchy to train the necessary workers. But once the hierarchy is in place it will no doubt try quietly to discipline the workers by rewarding its favorites. Currying favor with management, after all, is not necessarily a proof that a worker is incapable of learning what everyone else can learn.

Thus the idea of a skill hierarchy and on-the-job training is compatible with both the idea that management encourages subservience through its promotions policy *and* the idea that workers, once they have learned their new jobs, do have substantial skills. Put another way, the fact that servility counts in promotion does not exclude the possibility that skill counts as well. No one seems to doubt, for example, that junior university faculty and young lawyers must be both servile and competent to get ahead.

Now to the overlooked evidence. Many ethnographies of work attest the discretionary powers of workers with intermediate-level skills (and often – a point for later discussion – those of unskilled workers as well). In his study of refinery workers, for example, Duncan Gallie concluded that there can be

little doubt that the operators do still have a crucial role and that the quality of their work performance is critical to the quality of the product, to the time it takes to produce, to its cost, and perhaps most important of all to the physical preservation of the plant and of the work force itself . . . But it was not only in avoiding error that the operator's work performance could save the Company the immense costs of lost production. Critical too was his ability to anticipate problems in a way that could not be formally defined as part of his duty. The really skilled and experienced operator was renowned as having a sixth sense, an ability to hear almost imperceptible changes in the sound of the units which would enable him to detect a coming problem. If a difficulty could be anticipated, one could often take action that would avoid altogether the need to close down the unit. It was the unexpected breakdown that could prove so costly.[55]

Giuseppe Bonazzi came to analogous conclusions after studying the skill hierarchy in an automobile motor factory.[56]

Factory studies also regularly report another piece of evidence which supports the idea that intermediate-level workers do a great deal of learning on the job: Their skill level and shop-floor influence increase with the plant's age. When a plant is new, management overstocks it with engineers and supervisors out of fear of problems with the equipment and the workers' inexperience. Workers are so closely controlled that they may resemble the radicals' picture of them as essentially powerless.

But management soon begins to trust that the equipment will not explode and the workers will not accidentally blow it up. High-paid technicians and supervisors begin to be withdrawn, and the workers are left more to themselves. Meanwhile the plant slowly begins to deteriorate, and machines develop quirks that only their operators can anticipate and control. At this point the workers do begin to have the skill to disrupt production in those subtle ways, even short of a strike, which alert management to the fact that they are a power to be reckoned with. Here is William Kornblum's description of the mill operators in an older rolling mill in Chicago:

Nominally all jobs on the mill are considered unskilled or semi-skilled when compared with craft occupations, but in the rolling mill it is generally recognized that the mill hands are on an equal footing with all but the most experienced millwrights and electricians. First, while the mill hand may have no generalizable skills, he is intimately familiar with the idiosyncrasies of a particular mill. This is a familiarity which may take years to acquire, depending on the range of sizes and shapes of steel rolled and on the age of the mill. Old installations such as No. 3 Mill are said to be held together with "bailing wire and spit." The machinery seems to have a personality of its own and the men who coax steel through it know they cannot easily be replaced with new men. This contributes to an egalitarian spirit among mill men of different seniority; all are pitted together against the whims of a cantankerous old steel mill.[57]

We will see in the discussion of the new working class that there are important limits to the power of such workers, and that they know it. But at the very least, their skills are not the phantoms of technical prowess destroyed at the beginning of the century.

This point raises a final question. Supposing that the skills of intermediate-level workers *were* shams, why should they take them seriously? The idea that workers inherently are, or (in other versions of this theme) can easily, through manipulative school programs or payment schemes, be made into, hierarchy fetishists is unconvincing.[58] Enlightened conservatives since Tocqueville have demonstrated again and again the ways in which all social classes challenge existing hierarchies, and how each challenge undermines the legitimacy of the hierarchies that remain. It would be hard to explain the tremendous amount of bargaining over workplace rules – which establish the limits and substance of hierarchy in the factory – if this general observation did not apply to workers as well. At the very least, the idea of hierarchy fetishism does not square with the fact that workers, as we shall see in Chapter 4, often make tremendous sacrifices fighting for the creation of job ladders as a means of establishing, in a limited and imperfect way, their *right* to promotion and to limits on the power of their supervisors. Schooling and work in a capitalist society may, among other things, shake workers' confidence in their capacity to produce without the capitalists; but it does not turn them into passive instruments of the latter. To understand what workers do and do not count as facts, and what hierarchies they accept, it is necessary to have a precise idea of their expectations. And the first step toward discovering these expectations is to realize that they are not simply the product of capital's manipulations.

A second strand of the radical argument concerns the other type of intermediate-level skills: those having to do not with continuous-process plants but with stand-alone machinery tools such as lathes, millers, and grinders. Once again the claim is that managers are bent on using technology to destroy craft skill, in order to increase their power on the shop floor. But this time the argument is that the bosses are about to carry through their plans, not that they already have done so.

Harry Braverman's example is the development of numerically controlled machine tools, which in his view were partly designed to separate conception and execution of tasks: A white-collar technician writes a program that guides the machine's movements, even to the point of instructing it to change tools or lubricate the workpiece; the craftsmen and the machine setter, dispossessed of their skill, are replaced by an untrained operative who fastens the workpiece in place and starts the program.[59] To this example David F. Noble adds the claim that, had it not been for the interests of managers in large firms in consolidating their shop-floor power and driving smaller competitors out of the market, numerical-control technology would have grown up in a different way. Instead of concentrating on systems requiring computers beyond the financial reach of small shops and encouraging the creation of a distinct corps of programmers, engineers would have pursued an idea developed in the late 1940s: record playback. As its name suggests, this type of machine recorded the motions of a machinist making a part. Playing back the tape put the machine through the same paces, allowing identical parts to be made automatically. Record playback would thus have automated many machining operations without eliminating the skilled machinist (or requiring expensive programming), and for these very reasons, Noble argues, the technology was abandoned.[60]

Again there is some truth to the argument. It is easy to find engineers and machine-tool manufacturers who thought the development of numerical control would make craft skill obsolete. Braverman, for example, cites predictions of the minimal skill requirements for use of numerically controlled machine tools that appeared in advertisements in the *American Machinist* and in writings by an executive of the Ex-Cell-O Manufacturing Company.[61] And there are indisputably shops, large and small, in which unskilled operators produce parts by pushing buttons. But once more the fondest ambitions of those who make and sell the machines are only part of the story of their development and use, and not the most important part. Examined closely, the radical history of the development of numerical-control technology is both self-contradictory and patently implausible. And the supporting evidence concerning the use of numerical control is offset by findings that the new technology is easily suited to the needs of small producers and that managers, instead of attempting to expropriate the workers' skill, often allow or encourage them to program operations themselves.

The contradiction in the historical argument is that numerical control was first developed to execute metal-contouring operations that could have been performed only by a machinist with superhuman skill. "Aircraft industry requirements for high-complexity, four- and five-axis machining jobs," Noble himself writes, "were simply beyond the capacity of record-playback (or manual) methods."[62] Obviously there was no point in perfecting a machine whose main purpose would be to record impossibly difficult manipulations.

But putting this difficulty aside, the argument is still unconvincing. Why assume that record-playback technology threatened skills any less than numerical control? If managers create a small cadre of skilled supervisors to record manipulations for the initial part, craftsmen on the shop floor are no better off than they would be under the subjugation of a programming office. Because many manufacturers by the late 1970s were in fact using record-memory or lead-through systems in just this way to program a variety of industrial robots and numerically controlled sewing machines, it is hard to see why they would have rejected the method twenty years earlier if it had suited their purposes.[63]

A further difficulty for the radical story is that research on the deployment of numerically controlled machines undercut its conclusions. Precise, comparable data on the size of shops using numerically controlled machinery are hard to come by. But the declining cost of data processing and the creation of straightforward, general programming languages, a kind of computer Latin easily translated into the dialects of different machines, have made numerically controlled equipment appropriate to the needs of small shops and available at an affordable price. The technology has also become more accessible to small users because of the rapid spread of computer numerical control: small computers, mounted on or near the machine tool, that allow the operator himself to type in instructions by means of a keyboard.

By the middle of the 1970s, in fact, it was already clear that many small firms had successfully come to grips with numerical control. In the United States and Great Britain in that period, for example, firms with between 10 and 49 employees held more than 20 percent of the stock of numerically controlled machine tools.[64] By 1979 *Iron Age* had noted "substantial growth" in the use of computer numerical control. "Not an insignificant part of this growth," the report continued, "represents first time users, the little guys who never could afford to get NC before. That's a big, new market."[65] Also in 1979, the French Agence National pour le Développement de la Production Automatisée (ADEPA), a government agency that sells computer systems and controls to small firms and assists them to finance and use the new equipment, trained about two thousand users. Demand for its services is growing rapidly.[66] In Italy the widespread use of numerically controlled machines in small shops is increasingly seen as a symbol of the success of the sector of high-technology cottage industry that I will discuss in Chapter 5.[67]

The explosive success of firms like Manufacturing Data Systems, Inc. (MDSI), in Ann Arbor, Michigan, and Encode, in Newburyport, Massachusetts, which both provide computer services and general-purpose programming languages primarily to small numerical-control users, corroborates these pieces of evidence. MDSI, for example, has been growing at 30 percent or more a year since it was founded in 1969.[68] Conversely, there is no evidence that increasing use of numerical-control machine tools by itself produces industrial concentration. If large capitalists had even half-formed conspiratorial thoughts of putting an end to their smaller competitors, they chose the wrong method.

Nor have they been very successful at separating the conception from the execution of machining tasks, assuming that was their intention. Observations of the operation of numerical-control machine tools in Great Britain, France, the United States, and Italy show that economically efficient use of the new equipment often requires that programmers have substantial knowledge of machining and that operators have substantial knowledge of programming.[69] Otherwise, programs tend to be roundabout, if they function at all; and machinists, who observe the metal cutting first hand, have no quick way of correcting them. On the one hand, therefore, large firms and small often train machinists as programmers or (much more rarely, at aerospace firms using the most sophisticated programming languages) instruct programmers in basic metalworking skills. On the other, they train operators in the rudiments of programming, if not more. At Caterpillar Tractor in Peoria, Illinois, for example, the *introductory* training film for numerical-control operators explains how to read the punched tape that controls the cutting tool's speed of rotation, and how to vary the velocity with which the workpiece is fed to it. Such knowledge allows workers to regulate the pace of the overall operation; and managers, according to the radical view, ought not to want them to have it.

Thus, if there are shops where unskilled workers load and unload numerically controlled equipment, there are others where workers with augmented craft skills are indispensable. Even in the largest plants, operators and programmers frequently cooperate to "prove" the first version of a tape; nor it is unusual for operators to use computer numerical control to edit the program after it has been proven. To take an extreme example, the Weybridge plant of the British Aerospace Corporation pays its numerical-control operators at a standard rate for supervising the execution of the programmer's tape and adds a bonus for corrections that reduce running time.

By the end of the 1970s, the idea that numerically controlled machine tools and skilled workers could be complementary had become simply another fact of business life for many observers, users, and manufacturers of numerical-control equipment. An office of the regional government in Piedmont that surveys the skill requirements of technologically advanced firms noted in 1978, for one example, that "it has been some time since anyone thought that machine tools could be entrusted to 'monkeys,' as the first advertisements for the new machines tried to make one believe."[70] The *Wall*

Street Journal, for another, complained on its editorial page in 1980 about the shortage of skilled workers capable of operating and programming numerical-control machine tools.[71] And in 1979 the Tree Machine Tool Company of Racine, Wisconsin, circulated a brochure advertising its $49,500 Journeyman milling machine as an instrument to augment the return to skill *or* as a substitute for it. According to the brochure, the Journeyman provided

Skilled Help Help
If you've got skilled help running manual machines, the Journeyman can double their output.
• Positioning is 20 times faster than manual machines.
• Machine can be programmed by running first part.
• Run your first part in 50% of the time of a manual machine.

Unskilled Help Help
If you can't find – or afford – skilled help, the Journeyman lets you run the first part, and your unskilled help run the second one!
• Machine can be programmed as you make the first part.
• With program in memory, anyone can run the second part.

• Easy to use, new operator can make parts the first day.
• Costs $5.00/hr. to own – no programming equipment required.
• Ideal for jobbing and medium-run manufacturing shops.[72]

To make sense of the aspects of the early history and deployment of numerically controlled machine tools that do not correspond to the radicals' expectations, it is necessary to see both not as a simple assault on manual prowess but as the result of a more general development in machine-tool design culminating in the intellectualization of skill. By the intellectualization of skill I mean the process of technological advance by which skill gradually comes to be defined as the capacity not to perform a certain operation by hand but to instruct a machine to perform the necessary manipulations: Adding lead to a column of type to fill the assigned space is a manual operation, as is controlling the motions of a lathe by a hand crank; programming a computer typesetter to lead a page or a numerically controlled lathe to cut at a certain speed is an intellectual one. Once the zigzag path that leads to the intellectualization of skill in machine tools is traced out, it will be clear why the development of numerically controlled machines has not meant and is unlikely to mean the destruction of all grades of skill between the very bottom and the very top of the blue-collar hierarchy.

The development of machine-tool technology since the nineteenth century at the latest, Rosenberg's studies suggest, has often followed a simple pattern. First, special machines using new principles are designed to solve the problems of a particular manufacturer. Next the innovative machine-tool maker or one of his competitors discovers that with slight modification or even none at all the original machine can be used to execute a whole range of related operations: Its origins notwithstanding, the special-purpose machine is transformed into a general-purpose machine tool. The Brown and Sharp Company in the United States, for example, set out to make a machine to produce better shafts, needlebars, and footbars for sewing machines, and eventually developed a universal grinding machine; a problem in the machining of twist drills used in the manufacture of Springfield muskets prompted the company to devise a universal milling machine that soon became indispensable in almost every branch of the metalworking industry.[73]

The close relation between the design principles of special-purpose and general-purpose equipment means that the machine can often be used in two radically different ways depending on the skill of the operator. A craftsman with extensive knowledge of tools, jigs, and fixtures can use the machine for a wide variety of tasks, many of which could not have been accomplished at all with previously existing techniques. An unskilled worker simply performs the same operation time after time, loading workpieces into a machine whose tools, fixtures, and jigs have all been regulated by a setup man.[74] In this sense even a conventional machine tool is like a computer, the skilled operator like a programmer, and an unskilled worker like the technician who runs a program simply by pressing the start button.

Which way a machine tool is actually used, as we know from the earlier discussion, depends on market conditions. The more stable the market for a good, the more managers will use unskilled labor to execute rigid routines. This means that if initially volatile markets settle down, firms may switch from skilled to unskilled labor, deskilling the work force without introducing more-specialized machines, as in the American metalworking industry between 1910 and 1930.[75] If the market for a standard good expands sufficiently, of course, the next step is to refine the design of the machine tool still further, trading universality for increased efficiency at a few tasks. Jigs and fixtures needed for routine operation might be built in and the original construction modified to increase the machine's speed and accuracy over the limited range of normal use. To continue the analogy, the machine tool has now become a hardwired device, a kind of single-purpose computer that rapidly executes a program (honed to suit the purpose) embedded in the physical circuits of the apparatus.

The development and deployment of numerically controlled

machine tools repeats this pattern, but at a more abstract level. The invention of a universal grinding or milling machine synthesizes the powers of a number of discrete machines; the use of numerical control augments the flexibility and precision of each of the universal machines. The latter are *like* programmable devices; numerically controlled machines *are* programmable devices. Skill becomes intellectualized: A program is a step-by-step description of how to do a particular operation. But this difference aside, the history of numerically controlled machines and of their effect on skill levels is in crucial ways a continuation of what has gone before.

Whatever the visionary pretensions of some of its designers and their admirers, the first numerically controlled machine tools were in fact built as special-purpose machines, suited to the exotic task of contouring complex aerodynamic surfaces such as turbine blades and wings. Had the U.S. Air Force not subsidized the development of the first machines through cost-plus contracts with the manufacturers, they would certainly not have been produced as quickly as they were. Because of this subsidization, the machines met the Air Force's needs and virtually no one else's: At the military's insistence, for example, the new machines were programmed in APT (Automatically Programmed Tools), a programming language with all the sophistication necessary for describing superhuman manipulation, but none of the generality and simplicity required to express economically and in an easily learned way the huge range of everyday machine operations.[76] It took almost twenty years and breakthroughs in programming methods (for example, the creation of MDSI's Compact II) and computer design (for example, the invention of microprocessors that opened the way to computer numerical control) before the original idea of numerical control was embodied in practical, general-purpose machines.

Finally, as soon as numerically controlled machine tools did come into general circulation, their use began to reflect the diversity of labor and product markets. Regardless of their size, firms producing a range of specialized products in small numbers tend to man numerically controlled machines with craftsmen who bring their skill to bear on programming the run; this is as true for a small manufacturer of specialty machine tools in Rhode Island as for a leading manufacturer of cigarette-packaging equipment, GD, in Bologna. Again regardless of size, firms turning out long runs of standard products are constantly tempted to man numerically controlled machines with unskilled labor; this is as true for a small shop selling pipe-hanging fixtures to utilities and replacement parts for widely used machine tools as for an aircraft engine manufacturer turning out long runs of an old-model turbine blade that have to be milled to close tolerances. And in case after case, the extent of deskilling or the form of collaboration between machine operators and programmers depends on the balance of power between labor and management, as well as on relations between different groups in the work force. Sometimes, for example, management cannot substitute unskilled for skilled labor because the unions prevent it; sometimes it cannot give the machine operators the right to collaborate in the editing of programs because the programmers (as at a British aerospace firm) claim this as an exclusive right.

Firms organized on Fordist lines in the future, therefore, are likely to deploy numerically controlled machines much as they currently use machine tools. The programmer, often a craftsman with upgraded skills, will team up with a master machinist to do the work presently done by tool and diemakers and the builders of prototypes. Unskilled operators will load and unload the machines once the program has been proved, just as though they were operating single-purpose machines. A corps of setup men will make small adjustments in machine settings and programs to account for minor variations in tools, materials, machine construction, and product design, much as machine setters do now.

The problem with the radicals' argument thus turns out to be that it is not radical enough. Because they do not consider the way markets, themselves the result of political conflicts, shape the use of technology and skill, they see the organization of work as a direct contest of will. On one side are the capitalists with their mad dream of total control, on the other the workers, who aim to express and develop their powers through work. But until firms expand the range of their products, experimenting with new things rather than perfecting the production of old ones, the idea of work as self-development will remain as chimerical as its opposite, the idea of work as subservience to another's design.

For as long as the same products are made day in, day out, managers and workers, each for their own reasons, will be tempted to reduce work to routines that minimize the costs and efforts of production. Even if the world is too unpredictably variable to permit them to succeed completely, incomplete success is enough to check creativity. What better symbol of the stalemate between the nightmarish fantasies of some managers and the transformative hopes of the radicals than the continued need, in the realm of stand-alone machines as in the realm of continuous-process production, for workers with intermediate-level skills to adjust idiosyncratic men and machines according to the exigencies of a rigid master plan?

The division of labor at Renault

Preliminary as they are, these considerations can be tested only by empirical studies more sophisticated than the available ones. Two complementary kinds of problems make the bulk of contemporary research on skill levels and the division of labor only marginally useful for present purposes. First, available studies of aggregate changes in skill levels over long time periods are not analytically precise enough to test the model: As a rule, such studies distinguish unskilled, semiskilled, and skilled workers, whereas my categories turn on a finer characterization of knowledge.

Second, the microeconomic studies of skill that do distinguish skill grades with the requisite precision tend to be too restricted in scope to permit conclusions about secular changes in skill distribution. These studies generally compare skill levels in a single shop before and after a major rationalization of production techniques. Many of these comparisons support the idea that under Fordist conditions, rationalization creates a demand for new craft and intermediate-level skills while the average skill level of the work force remains steady or slowly declines. But aspects of the redistribution of skills that involve relations between several plants or that are noticeable only during specific phases of the long-term development of the division of labor cannot be captured by this snapshot method.[77] Furthermore, both sorts of studies ignore the ways in which, for political reasons, management exploits and embellishes skill hierarchies rooted in technological considerations.

One major piece of research that largely avoids the first two of these defects is the study by Pierre Naville, Jean-Pierre Bardou, Philippe Brachet, and Catherine Levy of the relation between technological development and the organization of work in the Renault automobile factories.[78] They trace developments in all Renault plants from the end of World War II to the end of the 1960s: the age that will someday be called the heyday of Fordism in the West, if one line of speculation in Chapter 5 proves correct. Their categorization of skills is detailed enough to permit comparison of their results with predictions derived from the preceding discussion of the division of labor. The automobile industry was and continues to be a central element in the capitalist societies of Western Europe and North America. Renault is of decisive importance to the French automobile industry: In 1969 it employed 79,718 workers directly, about two-thirds this number in subsidiary plants, and an unknown, but certainly much higher, number indirectly in more than four thousand nominally independent plants that supply the concern with parts and services. A study of the redistribution of skills at Renault during a twenty-year period therefore illuminates major developments of one epoch in the organization of industrial work.[79]

The preceding section discussed subsidiaries that, despite their peripheral location, were integral parts of manufacturing systems geared to stable markets. The history of the organization of work at Renault is a variation in the large on this theme. For as technological progress and advances in the organization of work made it possible to employ less-skilled workers for certain tasks, management set up subsidiaries using the new techniques in more backward regions, and left the most skill-intensive operations in Billancourt, the original center of production.

The division of labor among the various Renault plants resulted from this strategy. The Billancourt works (36,363 employees, of whom 25,827 were blue-collar workers) contained a series of somewhat outmoded production divisions; as might be expected of a parent plant, it could produce almost all the parts necessary to construct a car. But the most important divisions at Billancourt were the machine-tool shops that built machines used in the peripheral works. The Cléon works (5,996 employees, of whom 4,832 were blue-collar workers) was an ultramodern copy of the aluminum foundries, motor division, and speedometer-assembly division at Billancourt. The last major works, at Le Mans (9,265 employees, of whom 8,045 were blue-collar workers), specialized in the manufacture of tractors and other agricultural machinery; but it also supplied the other plants with mechanical parts such as transmissions and suspension arms.[80]

The data presented in Table 9 help establish the connection between the geographic distribution of Renault's plants and changes in the workers' skill levels. Table 9 shows that, whereas the relative number of unskilled and semiskilled workers at Billancourt rose only slightly between 1953 and 1969, it jumped almost 10 percent in the peripheral works: By 1969, 85.5 percent of the workers in the outlying plants were unskilled or semiskilled. The obvious conclusion is that skills were being diluted on final-assembly lines and in divisions producing parts, because just these divisions were concentrated in the peripheral plants.

The data in Table 9, however, shed no light on developments at Billancourt. Machine shops there coexisted with outmoded production divisions that served as models for the more advanced provincial plants. Indeed, the composite figures in Table 9 could mask contrary changes in skill levels in the two areas of production.

Table 10 makes clear that this was the case. It shows changes in

Table 9. *Changes in the skill level of the Renault work force: unskilled and semiskilled workers as a percentage of all blue-collar workers*

Plants	Years		
	1953	1965	1969
Billancourt	67.4	64.7	70.0
Peripheral works	75.8	81.5	85.5
Firm as a whole	68.3	72.2	78.5

Source: Pierre Naville et al., *L'Etat entrepreneur: le cas de la Régie Renault* (Paris: Editions Anthropos, 1971), p. 165.

the percentage of skilled workers in the blue-collar work force in two sectors of production, defined as follows: Sector A, the sector of direct production, included those workers immediately concerned with production of automobile parts and assembly of the final product; Sector B, the sector of indirect production, included workers who built, maintained, inspected, or supervised the operation of many of the machines used by workers in Sector A.

Table 10 suggests that the dilution of skills in direct production corresponds to a rise in the skill level in indirect production. As the firm's history leads one to expect, the difference in skill levels was most marked between Sector A in the outlying works and Sector B at Billancourt. Ideally, these data could be refined to show that the absolute skill level of at least some of the workers in the indirect-production sector rose with time as well. But even though the data do not permit this refinement, the increasing use of skilled workers in this sector is consistent with the hypothesis that progress in the division of labor does not lead to a simple leveling of all skills: The dilution of skills in directly productive divisions requires an increase in the aggregate skill level in the indirectly productive divisions.

Table 10 also suggests conclusions about limits to the progressive subdivision of tasks in direct production. From Table 10 it is clear that, for comparable production units, the extent of skill dilution was greater in the peripheral plants than at Billancourt. One reason, already indicated, is simply that the production techniques in the peripheral plants were more modern: They permitted a more thoroughgoing division of labor. But a second cause of relative backwardness of the Billancourt divisions is likely to have been that the long tradition of de facto control by skilled workers of some parts of the production process gave rise to a corpus of written and unwritten law that made it difficult for management at Billancourt to ex-

Table 10. *Changes in the skill level of the Renault work force by production sector: skilled workers as a percentage of all blue-collar workers*

Plants	Sector A (direct production)			Sector B (indirect production)		
	1953	1960	1965	1953	1960	1965
Billancourt	14.3	13.2	13.0	19.2	19.4	23.3
Peripheral works	12.5	7.2	5.6	11.7	10.7	12.8
Firm as a whole	14.0	10.9	9.5	17.7	16.0	18.3

Source: Naville et al., *L'Etat entrepreneur*, p. 166.

ploit even those possibilities for rationalization which did exist. I will come back to this point in the discussion of craftsmen's strategies of self-defense.

Yet even where, as in the peripheral plants, management had a free hand in the organization of production, Table 10 indicates that there were limits to the dilution of skills. Even in the least skill-intensive production divisions there had to be an irreducible core of maintenance workers and machine setters; and their numbers grew in proportion to increases in productive capacity. Obviously, the subdivision of labor makes no economic sense when it causes greater increases in supervision, maintenance, and training costs than savings by way of increased productivity. Management will not invest in new machines to substitute cheap for expensive labor if the new machinery destroys the last vestiges of the worker's dedication to his job, while making it impossible to assign to anyone the responsibility for the damage that indifference or hostility breeds.[81]

The work of Naville and his colleagues also documents the relation between the general tendency during this period toward skill dilution, as indicated by a rise in the percentage of the work force without skills, and the concomitant process by which intermediate-level skills were created through the partial routinization or rationalization of traditional craft tasks. Table 11 shows the composition of the *skilled* work force in five production divisions in Renault plants.[82] The five are representative of the range of combinations of skilled and unskilled workers in the manufacturing divisions, with the repair shop being the most skill-intensive unit and the automatic-machines division being the least.

Roughly speaking, as the ratio of all skilled workers to the entire work force of a division decreased, the ratio of setup men to other kinds of skilled workers increased. Therefore, even where the divi-

Table 11. *Skilled workers and machine setters as a percentage of all blue-collar workers at Renault by production unit*

	Mainte-nance	Small metal presses (short runs)	Heavy-duty stamping	Assembly	Automatic machines
Skilled workers	87.2	11.7	10.6	8.0	0.7
Machine setters	—	12.6	5.5	4.9	7.2

Source: Naville et al., *L'Etat entrepreneur*, p. 195.

sion of labor between shops enabled management to go furthest toward eliminating traditional skilled work, management was forced to create a corps of workers with intermediate skills to organize and supervise production.

Table 11 reveals, more precisely, three general patterns of work organization, each made possible by and depending on the other two. The first is represented by the maintenance shop, where 87.2 percent of the workers were craftsmen, none of them setup men. Though no history is given of the changes in the repairmen's tasks, this shop seems to count as a center of workers with upgraded skills.

The polar opposite of the maintenance shop was the automatic-machines divisions, where 0.7 percent of the workers were craftsmen with a full complement of skills, and where for every such craftsman there were approximately ten workers with intermediate-range skills. This division illustrates the organization of production in shops doing long production runs: Unskilled workers fed the machines; workers with intermediate skills occasionally changed their settings.

The third organizational pattern is most obvious in the milling division. The general skill level was much lower there than in the maintenance shop but still appreciably higher than in the automatic-machines division. Here short production runs required frequent adjustment of the machines: Workers with intermediate-level skills, in other words, clustered where the model suggests that they should.

Finally, consider the unskilled workers. The Renault study confirms that unskilled work in the primary sector is stable. As Table 12 shows, it is possible to pass a working lifetime doing unskilled work in certain production divisions with no hope of advancement. The

Table 12. *Relation between years spent at present job and skill grade of the hourly workers in selected production units at Renault*

	Production units				
	Mainte nance	Milling (short runs)	Heavy-duty stamping	Assembly	Automatic machines
Percentage of hourly workers who have worked at present job:					
5 years or less	54	48	56	56	35
5–10 years	15	26	26	22	11
10–15 years	12	4	5	6	15
15 years or more	19	22	13	16	39
Percentage of hourly workers with skill level:[a]					
140 or less	14	77	82	80	67
140–50	1	4	10	17	26
150–60	47	7	3	2	2
160–209	38	12	5	1	5

[a]Classifications based on Parodi Skill-Grading System.
Source: Naville et al., *L'Etat entrepreneur*, pp. 201, 205.

upper part of the table shows the distribution by time spent at the then-current job of the *horaires*, the unskilled workers whose wages are reckoned by the hour. The lower part of the table shows the distribution by skill grade of these same *horaires*. Naville and his colleagues did not correlate the *horaires'* length of service with their skill grades, so it is impossible to say exactly how many workers had been how long at which jobs. Still, in the heavy-duty-stamping, assembly, and automatic-machines divisions, the three production units with the lowest average skill level, the total percentage of workers who had been working at their jobs for ten years or more was much greater than the total percentage of workers in the upper two skill grades who had been on the job this long. So even on the somewhat implausible assumption that those who had been promoted out of the lowest skill grades were those who had also served longest at their last jobs, there were many workers who had spent more than a decade at the least-skilled jobs in the plant. The automatic-machines division was the clearest example: 93 percent of the *horaires* were classed in the two lowest skill categories. Assuming that the remaining 7 percent, the most-skilled *horaires*, had been at their last jobs for more than fifteen years, a total of 32 percent of the *horaires* had spent an equally long time at the bottom two skill grades. An additional 15 percent had spent more than a decade there. Under the no less implausible but less conservative assumption that all promotions had occurred during the five years preceding collection of the data, the results would be even more dramatic.[83]

This is as far as an anaylsis of skill levels alone takes us. For, by itself, an account of the distribution of skill cannot make sense of an obvious, and as we shall see, significant fact: Wherever one looks, the same kinds of workers wind up with the same kinds of jobs. Just as the managers in the subsidiaries in the Oberpfalz prefer to hire unskilled women, we will see that the managers at Renault, as well as those in the West German and American automobile industries, go out of their way to recruit unskilled agricultural workers, native-born and foreign. West German automobile manufacturers do the same. In Great Britain the automotive-parts manufacturers historically hire unskilled women.[84] To understand why women, immigrants, and agricultural workers so often are found in unskilled jobs in both sectors of the economy, and why they tolerate them when other workers often do not, it is necessary to look at the broader question of the differences between their reasons for taking industrial jobs and the ambitions of other groups in the work force.

3
Careers at work

Suppose for the moment that capitalists compartmentalize labor markets as described in the previous chapter. Why do workers put up with the possibilities for work, often appallingly limited from a middle-class point of view, that capital offers?

To many the question will seem as ridiculous as asking why men put up with injustice and oppression. An obvious answer is that they have to: Rebels are crushed by those who want the world as it is; those who refuse bad jobs find none better. But even if it were proved that fear suffocates revolutionary thoughts, brute necessity is not an exhaustive explanation of why workers accept certain jobs.

There is much evidence, we will see, that workers choosing jobs often pick one that most of us would find unappealing. Immigrants, for example, frequently prefer relatively high-paying, unskilled, insecure, dead-end jobs to jobs that pay less but offer the chance to learn skills – jobs, in other words, with a future.[1] There are also cases of unskilled workers who more or less accidentally reveal an extraordinary aptitude for some line of work, and then refuse promotion.[2] Nor is it uncommon for very skilled craftsmen to refuse to compete for promotions for which they are and know themselves to be superbly qualified.[3] And there are, to take a final and more pointed example, many instances of workers bearing the economic and psychological hardships of unemployment rather than accepting just the kinds of jobs that immigrants seem most willing to take.[4]

Such evidence against the view that workers choose their jobs for want of real choice may seem to square with reductionist and essentialist ideas about those who fail to get ahead. If you think of society as a giant, all-purpose machine that works ever more efficiently, you are likely to think that those directing the operation and slow perfection of the machine contribute more to the satisfaction of wants than do those who execute orders. Assume also that for efficiency's sake

78

rewards must be proportionate to social contributions, and that it is human nature to want as much as one can get, and you will conclude that only persons who are inept, unambitious, shortsighted, or all three end up in inferior jobs.

Neoclassical economists, for example, see an immigrant worker's lack of skills and tolerance for unemployment as a combination of his incapacity to learn what the market accredits, his preference for leisure over work, and his unwillingness to sacrifice high pay in the present for training that pays off in the future.[5] A sociologist who shared these general views might explain the worker's situation as the result of his attachment to preindustrial traditions; a cognitive psychologist might suspect that a rudimentary capacity to reason abstractly qualifies him only to follow orders on an assembly line. By extension, each group's position in the division of labor might be accounted for by reference to its drive and productive skills, these latter depending on its ability to manipulate the categories that define the social and physical worlds.

If the idea of the worker as the victim of indomitable force makes of him a tragic hero, these reductionist and essentialist theories are oblique glorifications of the middle class. In a society that admires ambition, work, and mental agility, they amount to polite ways of saying that blue-collar workers are in varying degrees lazy, clumsy, and intellectually sluggish. But experience teaches that, as a rule, self-congratulatory theories embarrass only those who defend them.

As long as anthropologists from the "civilized" countries regarded "native" thought as a primitive precursor of science, they regarded the natives as incompetent logicians. Then the scientists realized that they had failed to understand the complexities of the natives' distinctive logic.[6] In the same way, middle-class sociologists and economists who think that workers get exactly what they deserve or want ignore what workers really want and can do.

To return for a moment to the example of immigrants in unskilled dead-end jobs: As a rule, *Gastarbeiter*, the immigrant "guest workers" in West Germany, work longer hours and save a greater percentage of their earnings than the average American worker; a Turk or Yugoslav working in West Germany can save 50 percent or more of his income, whereas an American worker saves less than 10 percent.[7] Surely these *Gastarbeiter* know what it means to toil and plan for the future. Why, then, do they settle for dead-end jobs? At home, many of them managed the accounts of small firms, repaired machinery, and kept up farm buildings. They possess a greater variety of skills than most of us. Is it cognitive sluggishness that makes them willing to follow orders on an assembly line? And what of the craftsmen who give up their sleep and jeopardize their family life in order to upgrade their skills at night school? Their fortitude and ambition seem indubitable. Why, then, do they step out of the way when a less-qualified, college-trained engineer demands to be promoted to a plum job?

From these examples it seems unlikely that workers are work-shy or incompetent, or that they have confused ideas about their possibilities. A more plausible view is that they work hard and skillfully, but in pursuit of ends that an omnibus notion of success as making it to the top of the middle-class heap does nothing to illuminate. Put another way, the evidence suggests that workers may accept gross disparities in the distribution of power and wealth; but they are nonetheless quite particular about what is an acceptable job.

This chapter discusses the various standards of blue-collar success and how these bear on various groups' choice of jobs. It presents an explanation of labor-market behavior opposed to both the apologetic idea that workers get their due and the despairing claim that they take whatever capital wants to give them.

The analysis turns on the idea of a "career at work," another name for a worker's world view. By a career at work I mean a series of remunerative tasks that successively challenge and require the development of whatever powers one takes as the measure of human worth. To claim that different work groups have different ideas of success or careers at work is to claim that they differ about which powers define dignity, which jobs count as disgraces and which as accomplishments, not that some groups are more accomplished than others or less devoted to the idea of accomplishment.

The exceptional case underscores the point: I will argue that the one work group which abandons the idea of testing and developing its powers in *any* job also comes close to embracing the idea that human relations are temporary, purposeless events, single lives little more than a series of accidents. For all the others, the idea of a continuous, developing personality corresponds with and rests upon diverse notions of a career at work. The idea of a career at work becomes a compressed cosmology that defines what virtue is and how to test it: in short, a world view.

The advantage of this method is to show how the meaning and consequences of each element of a worker's thought are shaped by its relation to the others. The economic and sociological views criticized a moment ago assume that the worker's ideas are an inferior approximation of some universal rationality. The idea of the world view suggests that the worker's world must be understood as an independent and integral whole in which ideas of ambition and dignity, early experiences at school and on the labor market, outbursts of rage at management, and even acceptance of certain hardships combine according to stylistic canons that the worker recognizes as his own. These canons shape his response to the unforeseen. A theory that does not take account of them cannot say what he is likely to do next.

The disadvantages of this method become clear when it is compared with, for example, neoclassical economics. A theory of this type promises to draw from the individual's reaction to objective circumstance an explanation of both the behavior of individuals and the social order which that behavior produces. The market disciplines persons to act self-interestedly, and self-interested persons perpetuate markets. By contrast, the method of world views leads to a kind of collective psychology of particular groups that says little about fundamental characteristics of all individuals or general patterns of social organization. An understanding of the connection between the craftsman's experience as an apprentice and his later behavior on the labor market, for example, sheds no direct light on the organization of socialization: the institutions that train individuals for the parts they have to play. Nor does it immediately illuminate the psychology of learning, the question how individuals learn what society has to teach.

The choice of method is therefore unappealing: On the one side is undisciplined holism that may not lead to science; on the other, scientistic universalism that obscures the integrity of particular kinds of social life. Yet given the task of making sense of industrial work, there can be no hesitation between them. If progress in the sort of investigation undertaken here had to depend on each discipline's resolution of the fundamental problems of individual and collective behavior, there would be no progress. Just as the understanding of particular languages is indispensable to the determination of the universal structures of language, the hope must be that an attempt to lay bare, in a particular and limited sphere, the relations between some of the questions asked in various social sciences will contribute to their ultimate resolution.

To this general defense of the method of world views I want to add a further consideration that authorizes its application to the problem of blue-collar work. Certainly one compelling argument for distinguishing the world views of different work groups is that throughout history, powerful persons, those who normally preside over social development, have found it in their advantage to do so. One of their sources of strength is the knowledge that certain groups are suited by experience and outlook to certain places in the division of labor. Hence they use socially established patterns of deference and subordination, intertwined as they are with the world views of various groups, as a template for hierarchical relations within large organizations. An especially clear example is Frederick the Great's decision to duplicate the hierarchy of the *Ständestaat* in his army, making soldiers of the serfs, noncommissioned officers of the free peasants, and officers of the nobles.[8] Contemporary small businessmen and personnel managers often have rules of thumb about which kinds of job applicants will fit various jobs.

What follows tries to make explicit some of this unspoken knowledge of the powerful. For the more widely the diverse world views of workers are known, and the more thoroughly understood they are, the less danger there is that each group's idea of dignity, often comprehensible only to itself, will be used to manipulative ends.

The craftsman's ethos and where it can lead him

From the point of view of the middle class, the craftsman is a contradictory figure, capable of tasks that presuppose self-esteem and assertiveness, yet in a more general way lacking both. Despite his apparent social proximity to middle-class managers and social scientists, he has remained as mysterious to them as the other parts of the working class. The craftsman's autonomy on the job is frequently attested: Not only does his independence often make supervision superfluous, but he frequently outwits managers in complex negotiations over work rules and piece rates.[9] Under the right conditions, we will see, the skilled worker can rise through the class structure to do work usually thought to be the prerogative of the engineer, the small industrialist, or the corporate executive.

Yet it has been repeatedly shown that the craftsman's attitudes toward education, child rearing, and the social hierarchy are those typical of what might be called a subaltern social class. Where the middle-class manager teaches his son to question rules and inquire into the justification of hierarchy, the skilled worker often teaches his son to accept both respectfully.[10] And although the craftsman may display formidable talents as a manager of his own or someone else's business, he often seems to lack drive and self-confidence, allegedly the stuff of which all good managers are made. Reliable studies show that skilled workers with advanced vocational training and confidence in their skills are still reluctant to compete with college-trained engineers or managers for jobs.[11] Furthermore, skilled workers are occasionally content to do work which is all but indistinguishable from that done by the unskilled: dirty, routine work that almost any reader of this book would find unbearable, and irreconcilable with the image of the deliberate, self-assured artisan mirrored on the perfectly regular surface of a masterpiece. The aim of this section is to show how all these traits of the craftsman's character are rooted in the idea of skill and technical prowess that he learns as an apprentice in his craft.

The formal organization of apprenticeship programs varies widely from industry to industry and country to country. Generally the "European" system of apprenticeship combines specialized technical training, beginning at the secondary level, with practical vocational experience. The "American" system also mixes classroom and on-the-job training (with emphasis on the latter), but begins typically after completion of a normal secondary education. Apprenticeship programs of both types are usually administered jointly by representatives of industry and labor. The state plays an increasingly important role in regulating who becomes an apprentice and what he learns; and apprenticeship programs are slowly being merged with or complemented by vocational training programs organized as part of the larger national system of secondary education.[12]

But to judge by the few studies of the experience of apprenticeship itself, however organized and by whomever administered, the programs teach two related lessons. The first concerns objects and techniques, the second the social preconditions and implications of the craft's knowledge.[13]

Most obviously, apprenticeship teaches the rudiments of a particular skill: how to make shoes or cut complicated curves in metal using certain materials and tools. The fundamentals, basic manual skills and the reading of blueprints or basic principles of electricity or hydraulics, for example, can be taught in school. The craftsman, however, must be able not only to make things, but to make them as quickly as possible with the available materials and tools and minimum waste. This he can learn only on the job. And as he gains practical experience on the job, he learns a second lesson about learning itself – that he will never know all there is to know about the materials and techniques of his work, and that what he does know can be learned only in collaboration with other craftsmen. There is always a leather cutter with a new trick to cutting an extra set of uppers from a peculiarly shaped hide, always a machinist who can teach him what to do when a particular lathe chatters and cuts chips of a strange color, or how to reduce the setup time for a particular piece.

One implication of this lesson for the young worker is that his new craft collectively possesses a huge store of concrete knowledge, increased in some ways by each generation and passed by example from master workmen to tyros. Another is that technical mastery is a standard by which to judge other craftsmen. Jointly they lead him to distinguish *within* the craft itself a hierarchy of prowess, without, however, forgetting the collective origins of technical knowledge.

Learning this principle in social valuation, the apprentice cancels his past and circumscribes his future. He cancels his past insofar as he now accepts his craft, and not the occupation of his parents or schoolmates, as the legitimate field in which to demonstrate his capacities. Thus, although post–World War II research confirms that, as in the past, young craftsmen are often relatives or neighbors of older ones,[14] it is also true that successful apprentices can be recruited from the families of white-collar workers, small industrialists, and merchants, and even, under conditions to be detailed later, directly from the peasantry. What these social groups have in common is their capacity to teach diligence, attention to detail, and the peculiar mixture of reverence for tradition in the large and the capacity to disregard it in the small that is characteristic of anyone who is successful doing things the old way. Apprenticeship encourages these traits, giving them at the same time a concrete form that often separates the young worker from the culture of his family and unites him all the more securely with his mates. The French say, *Le métier fait l'homme*, the craft makes the man.

Incorporation into a new social world also defines the craftsman's hopes for the future, and in ways that shed light on his apparently inconsistent behavior in the labor market. What counts for him now is technical prowess, not place in an officially defined hierarchy of jobs: Titles are not important, savoir faire is. Careful studies by Siegfried Braun and Jochen Fuhrmann show that this is precisely the opposite of the middle-class attitude. The middle class conceives of a career not as a series of successively more complex jobs, but as a progression through a socially recognized hierarchy of posts, each patently more prestigious than the preceding one. The craftsman wants to be able to do something; there is evidence that he is often indifferent to or ignorant of the career possibilities – understood in the middle-class sense – that apprenticeship opens to him.[15]

These characterizations apparently collide with stereotypical notions about the attitudes of craftsmen and the middle classes toward formal education. Research by Gavin Mackenzie, for example, reveals that craftsmen tend to view education narrowly, as a ticket of admission to a certain job; the middle class, on the other hand, tends to see in education an end in itself, an initiation into the higher experiences of life, which transcend and require critical reappraisal of social norms.[16] Extrapolating from these views, craftsmen would seem to be ready for officially defined careers, the middle classes for the intrinsic pleasures of work.

But these attitudes toward education are ambiguous with respect to the broader notion of a career at work. The craftsman's idea of education as an admission ticket is consistent with the idea that membership in a craft is like citizenship in a small republic: an honor in itself, but only the precondition to any particular activity. The idea of education as initiation is consistent with the view that the initiates ought to get the most prestigious jobs. It is in fact these latter interpretations which prevail, with profound consequences for the labor-market behavior of both groups.

First consider the craftsman's situation in isolation from his potential middle-class competitors. Take the case of a gifted apprentice in a rapidly expanding economy. Admission to the craft is itself an accomplishment that establishes his place in the community. But the apprenticeship has also given him a sense of professional pride, of being educable despite typically frustrating experiences in his early school years. This professional pride provides the germ of future ambition, but of a kind peculiar to the craftsman. In pursuit of ever more complicated technical problems to solve, of ways of expanding his technical capacities, he soon discovers that the most interesting tasks are reserved for craftsmen with upgraded skills. He discovers, in other words, that he must be more than a simple craftsman if he is to accomplish the truly interesting tasks of the craftsman's job. Thus come thoughts of promotion to more demanding jobs or of establishing himself independently in a small shop.

The social landscape of the advanced industrial societies is dotted with figures who have risen from the ranks in this way, though they are often disguised as artisans, white-collar technicians, and managers, so that their origins in the craft world are concealed. In West Germany workers with upgraded skills are often night-school engineers (*graduierte Ingenieure*), typically skilled workers who have supplemented their shop-floor experience with intensive courses in the theoretical underpinnings of their craft. They are highly prized as production engineers, as designers of parts, and, less frequently but still in significant numbers, as managers. In the machine-tool industry, where everything depends on the firm's ability to meet the clients' particular needs quickly, their practical experience in design and construction makes them excellent candidates for the very highest positions.[17] In Italy workers of this type are the backbone of a booming sector of small metalworking shops (to be investigated in detail later), which produce extremely sophisticated gearshifts, machine tools, and the like for world markets. But they can also be found programming or revising the programs for numerically controlled machine tools in large, technologically sophisticated plants. At GD, as I mentioned earlier, only workers with extensive knowledge of traditional machining techniques make efficient use of advanced numerically controlled machine tools. Hence the programmers, officially white-collar workers, are usually recruited among the skilled. Similar developments have been reported for the United States. In France such workers seem to flourish chiefly as independent artisans, perhaps because the elaborate system of educational certificates referred to earlier makes promotion within large industry difficult.[18]

What unites these successful workers despite all the variety of their apparent social places is a shared recognition that they continue to belong to and judge themselves by the standards of a community of craftsmen. Asked by Braun and Fuhrmann whether there were fundamental differences between white- and blue-collar workers, a night-school engineer, himself nominally part of the white-collar world, replied that, aside from the time clock and the wearing of different work clothes, he saw none:

> Blue-collar workers have to do a bit more manual labor, but I don't think there is any difference in the economic situation. And that's as it should be. And I can't think of any differences [in the styles of life]. For that matter, there are no differences in the way they think. At least not in respect to craftsmen. But a simple laborer, he hasn't developed himself intellectually, so naturally he thinks differently. He can't see how things are connected, and if someone tells him something, he parrots it. But an intellectually alive person thinks his own thoughts, independently of whether he is a blue- or white-collar worker.[19]

Braun and Fuhrmann found, moreover, that white-collar workers who had risen by upgrading their craft skills remained loyal trade unionists. These workers "feel that they belong in 'production,' or that they belong on the shop floor, not in the administration. Both sentiments explain their solidarity with the union."[20]

Similarly, in his studies of the *ami du trait*, Bernard Zarca describes a master carpenter who continues to be absorbed in the ethos and substance of his craft even after he has become something of an intellectual, as well as proprietor of an internationally known firm employing thirty men. One of his principal activities is preparation of an *Encyclopedia of Carpentry*: "Through his craft he discovered intellectual work, of which he can be unabashedly proud: he is no product of a school system which allows non-stop accumulation of cultural capital denied to others, but rather a man who has traveled what is, considered socially, an unlikely road – that which runs from the concrete to the formal."[21]

Next consider what happens when workers with upgraded skills, instead of being allowed free reign, must compete for attractive jobs with middle-class engineers and managers. Burkhart Lutz and Guido Kammerer investigated this competition in a study of the changing place of night-school engineers in the West German machine-tool industry. They found that, so long as productivity could be raised by refining existing methods, night-school engineers were easily equal to the task. But when techniques were revolutionized by fundamental breakthroughs, only engineers and scientists recently trained at leading research centers understood the new ideas well enough to apply them practically.[22] Hence, in order to keep up technically, management was forced to hire at least a core of academically trained specialists. This decision taken, management became the passive spectator of a struggle for power between the middle-class academics and the night-school engineers.

The university graduates in the plant insisted on careers in the middle-class sense. They demanded to be promoted to leading positions in the firm, positions traditionally occupied by night-school engineers. They understood promotions as signs that they had not failed.[23] And the night-school engineers ceded the places to them for two complementary reasons traceable to their opposed idea of a career at work. First, the night-school engineers saw nothing desirable per se about securing a typically middle-class position. The bourgeois world was foreign to them; they knew only that it is not a world that gives first honor to technical prowess. Second, the night-school engineers already were successful by the standards of the craft world: They had already demonstrated their capacity to solve the most various and complex technical problems. Given these values, the costs of competition were high relative to the expected gains from victory. It thus made good sense to retreat to jobs in which they could exercise their technical capacities, narrowly defined, abandoning the most prominent positions in the firm's hierarchy to their adversaries without a struggle.[24]

The more intense the competition between the groups, the more aware the upgraded craftsmen themselves became of the differences in culture and ambitions that shaped their respective behavior all along. Lutz and Kammerer found that conflict with middle-class university graduates forced the craftsmen to acknowledge, proudly but resignedly, their social identity. In those plants where university graduates either had not begun to achieve or were still far from achieving control over the higher reaches of the labor market, the night-school engineers had only indistinct ideas about the differences between themselves and their potential competitors. But in plants where the struggle between the two groups was well under way or already decided, the craftsmen easily saw the differences. They regarded their own strengths as practical experience, skill, and inventiveness in the execution of tasks and the ability to accommodate themselves to new situations and to cooperate with others. The advantages of the university graduates were good general education, careerism, polished manners, and the ability to lead.[25]

A series of interviews conducted by associates of the Institut für sozialwissenschaftliche Forschung (ISF) with craftsmen in a large Bavarian metalworking factory produced similar results.[26] The workers were asked whether everyone in West Germany has the same chance of success. Their answers show that perception of the inequality of opportunity for advancement increased with increases in skill grade, that is, with increasing contact with middle-class technicians and managers. A relatively unskilled twenty-four-year-old machine setter thought success in society depended "on character, a firm character. You have to have a trade. Higher up the heap people may be getting paid off – I don't know."[27] A senior foreman (*Obermeister*) in the test division maintained that professional success depended on financial means necessary for admission "into the right circles." He also believed that the firm's owners and upper-level managers took special pains to ensure that "no one rises too high."[28] Similarly, a night-school engineer was convinced that men like himself could advance only if "they work hard on themselves . . . Everything plays a role – your profession, financial situation, contacts – but the order of importance of these things is different in different cases – and naturally from your wealth, which really ought to stand at the beginning of the list. Wealth is the thing, I would give the priority to wealth."[29]

The experience of another night-school engineer revealed even more clearly the way in which progress through the firm's hierarchy recalls craftsmen to their working-class roots. As director of his company's piece-rate and social benefits systems, he spared no effort to identify himself with his superiors, only to discover that some inner resistance prevented him from succeeding. He distanced himself clearly enough from the "uneducated proles." But as a "factory man," he felt a greater sense of solidarity with blue-collar workers with upgraded skills – night-school engineers, for example – than with university-trained engineers: He could be "free and easy" with the former, but he had no chance of competing with the latter because of their "lip." He would gladly have learned to talk in a commanding way, and even considered attending courses on public speaking. He gave up the idea because of an aversion to "people who just talk because they have never done anything."[30] Thus he drew back from abandoning the last shred of his identity as a man of technical prowess even when a narrow sense of self-interest seemed to dictate just that abandonment.

The portrait of the craftsman that emerges from all these studies, then, is that of a man proud of his fellowship with companions whose skills he respects, a man hesitant to forgo that fellowship for a place in a world whose values he mistrusts insofar as he understands them. He can be successful from a middle-class point of view: Think of the master carpenter managing his business and writing the history of his craft. But he is successful only so long as he does not have to become consciously ambitious. His drive and resignation are rooted in the same values. Those values also shape his reaction to the situation that remains to be considered: the case in which the labor market, instead of favoring at least in a limited way the craftsman's ascent, offers him limited and decreasing possibilities to use the skills he learned as an apprentice.

Craftsmen in decline

Downgrading of the craftsman's skills can occur with violent abruptness or so gradually as to be all but imperceptible. The introduction of new products or production techniques – the change from mechanical to digital watches, for example – can suddenly extinguish whole crafts. Piecemeal routinization of production techniques, on the other hand, often means that workers who have not aggressively developed their skills in vocational courses find decreasing use for the skills they already have. Craftsmen's defense against both dangers is linked, because they realize that the acceptance of *any* erosion of their position on the labor market increases the possibility of a sudden collapse of strength later on. Discussion of their comprehensive, collective strategy of conflict with management is reserved to the next chapter. Here I simply want to indicate one of the ways in which the skilled worker's socialization into his craft allows him, acting as an individual, to find a compromise solution to the problem of a decline in his value on the labor market.

Friedrich Weltz, Gert Schmidt, and Jürgen Sass report on a series of developments that bear on this problem. In a study of middle-sized and large plants in the West German metal industry, they found that the skilled worker typically knows far more about his profession than is required for the tasks he actually performs. He possesses "surplus skills" in that "he occasionally solves problems far more complex than those anticipated by the official definition of his routine skill level – which he nonetheless acknowledges as correct." The firm makes use of these surplus skills to adapt the existing production process to short-run shifts in demand (avoiding the costs of reorganizations that might have to be reversed), and to shift from one process of production to another (thereby reducing dependence on the external labor market). But why, if the firm depends on him in this way, does the craftsman accept a job classification that neglects mention of his best efforts? And why, instead of refusing to perform demanding tasks that bring no material reward, because they are not part of his official work, does the craftsman claim that precisely these jobs are "a gratification which makes his work more attractive"?[31]

Considerations of economic self-interest suggest an answer to the first question. In a sense the craftsman is already a victim of dequalification, because he routinely performs tasks assigned to workers with at most intermediate-level skills. If he demands full recognition and remuneration of his capacities, the firm will reduce labor costs by introducing new technology requiring still lower skill levels, a move that will further jeopardize his position. He therefore acquiesces in de facto dequalification in return for an implicit guarantee of continued employment, especially in difficult times when shifting markets make his skills potentially valuable to the firm. But why should he find periodic stints of demanding work "a gratification"?

The answer to this question goes not to the craftsman's calculation of self-interest, but rather to his self-conception. The periodic exercise of his old capacities allows the craftsman to convince himself that, despite vicissitudes, he is still a member of the community of the skilled. The unanimous enthusiasm expressed by the workers who spoke with Weltz, Schmidt, and Sass for challenging jobs shows just how much this membership is valued. To a certain, but hardly quantifiable extent, the opportunity to do uncompensated but exacting work is in fact a partial compensation for dequalification, and hence a part of the compromise solution.

But looked at in another way, this reaction is the complement to the craftsman's response to competition with the middle class and a first hint at his capacity for self-interested exclusivity. For in continuing to define himself as a skilled worker, the downgraded craftsman is implicitly setting himself off from those with whom he actually works, the un- and semiskilled.

These latter, he reasons, have never had the steadfastness or drive necessary to learn a trade: Recall the slightly disparaging remarks of the upgraded craftsman who saw more of a difference between the unskilled and the skilled than between the skilled and white-collar workers. After all, he argues, the craftsman's skill consists not in the capacity to do particular things, but in general technical prowess that enables him to learn new tasks quickly and execute them with extraordinary precision. Employers often agree. A current West German study of shipyard workers in Bremen threatened by unemployment shows that some of the younger craftsmen accept jobs as semiskilled production workers in an automobile plant, justifiably confident that their self-evident virtues will soon win them promotion to craft jobs or low-level supervisory positions.[32] Quick promotion from the assembly line can only reinforce their sense of superiority over those who are left behind. Membership in the community of craftsmen can thus distance the skilled from other groups in the working class just as it isolates them from the middle-class world.

This discussion of the labor-market position and ethos of skilled workers suggests four general conclusions. All are familiar from studies of the most disparate kinds of social experience; but as they are easily, in fact frequently, forgotten, it is worthwhile to set them out by way of summary.

The example of the most successful of the craftsmen with upgraded skills shows, first, that the boundary between blue and white collar, between manual and intellectual work, or in yet another formulation, between the working and the middle class, is arbitrary. Under favorable conditions craftsmen seem able to learn almost any job in the firm. Which jobs are actually open to them and which are reserved to the holders of academic degrees is thus in the last analysis a matter of collective social choice, a political question in the largest sense.[33] Stalin, for one, understood this. He used the *praktiki*, men who had acquired various degrees of technical expertise through experience on the shop floor, as a weapon in his struggle against the old technical elites: Whenever he thought he could strengthen his hand by doing so, he simply encouraged the promotion of the former into jobs usually held by the latter.[34] A democratic society would presumably find other criteria for determining who ought to have access to which jobs; the point here is that none of the studies presented so far suggests that there is anything peculiarly rational about the distribution of job entitlements between those with and those without academic degrees.

Nor, second, does this account of skilled work lend the slightest support to the theory of *embourgeoisement*, the idea that the closer workers get to the middle class the more they want to become part of it. If anything, the evidence suggests the opposite: The closer workers with upgraded skills come to the middle class, the greater is their explicit pride in their own culture of skill, a culture they are anything but eager to betray.

Third, this account of skilled work undermines the related notion that upward social mobility makes workers more accepting of the class structure. The higher workers rise in the class structure the more clearly they perceive the barriers to further mobility, and the more acute is their sense of being unjustly limited in their possibilities. Studies of technical workers in France and Italy, moreover, reach a similar conclusion.[35]

Fourth and finally, downward social mobility – proletarianization, if the word is permitted as a description of the descent from skilled to unskilled work – does not automatically cause craftsmen to declare their solidarity with those who have known nothing but menial jobs. On the contrary, while they are slipping down the skill hierarchy they often try to cling, at least for a time, to their old identity, even at the price of remaining aloof from their workmates. In the next section we will see that fear of falling even lower in the skill hierarchy can have a paralyzing effect on workers with plant-specific skills as well.

Workers with plant-specific technical skills

The continuous subdivision of work has lowered the average skill level of the entire work force and has made it all but impossible for the unskilled to learn the fundamental principles of machine operation on the job. But as we have seen, progress in the division of labor does create two new opportunities for advancement for the unskilled. For one thing, unskilled workers can compete with downgraded craftsmen for jobs created by the rationalization of craft skill: An attentive drill-press operator, for example, can discover when and how to change bits or to adjust the speed of his machine, and how to judge the accuracy of his work, without learning how to fix a drill press or read blueprints. The French call workers who advance in this way *auto-régleurs*, a word that calls attention to their release from tutelage. In addition, the unskilled may be promoted to jobs having to do with the supervision and control of automated and semiautomated processes. These jobs are not related to traditional craft work by origin, and the skills they require are not denatured versions of craft skills: Hence unskilled workers moving up to fill them are not likely to collide with craftsmen on the way down.

Chapter 2 argued that, their differences notwithstanding, these two kinds of intermediate-level jobs gave workers similar responsibility for maintaining the flow of production. But there is an even more fundamental reason for grouping them together: Workers who hold them tend to see their relations to management and to other work groups in a similar way. This section develops the claim that the labor-market situation of these formerly unskilled workers determines their self-conception and their relation to work apart from their specific role in the production process. The early history of this group of workers, their experiences at home and school, will remain for the moment in the background; they are treated in the following sections on the unskilled.

In the 1950s and 1960s, sociological studies of workers with intermediate skill levels emphasized their special relation to technology rather than their position on the labor market. Mallet, Popitz and Bahrdt, Lutz, and Alfred Willener all argued that production processes based on new technologies were compatible with only certain ways of organizing workplace relations.[36] Rather than being individually subjected to management's authority, workers would collaborate with one another, guided by the technical rationale implicit in the machinery itself. The conflict that was to develop between workers (collectively attempting to organize production according to the logic of production itself) and managers (following the dictates of the market or asserting their own authority) would supposedly lead the real producers to claim control of the modern factories. A generic account of this transformation of consciousness will be unjust to the subtleties of the various theories; so I will limit discussion to the single work that makes the strongest case for the technological determination of consciousness: the study by Popitz and Bahrdt of the West German steel industry.

Popitz and Bahrdt argued that changes in workers' consciousness of the work force corresponded to the transition from team to articulated (*gefügeartige*) cooperation on the job. Team cooperation was practicable where progress in the division of labor did not require the worker to be continuously present at his post during the production runs. The rhythms of the machines, the arrangement of the shop, and the distribution of skills allowed one worker to relieve or assist another temporarily. Relations among blast-furnace workers served as an example: "A heavy chunk of slag – a bear, as it is called – which gets caught in the channel of the second smelter, is much easier to remove when the fourth smelter lends a hand with his pole." The reciprocal doubling of work roles "presumes that all the relevant workers are conscious of belonging to one group."[37] This sense of solidarity itself expressed the workers' realization that they were less dependent collectively than individually on the mechanical rhythms of production.

By contrast, Popitz and Bahrdt defined articulated cooperation as that system of work relations which resulted from the destruction of the workers' freedom of motion. A precondition of articulated cooperation was that each worker be so tightly bound to his post that he could no longer replace or assist the others. At most, he could compensate for their mistakes by varying his own work routine: "If, for example, the control man [in a rolling mill] sees that a relatively cold ingot will require additional passes through the mill, he adjusts the gap between the rollers accordingly. That means that the edge miller can only begin his work two or four passes later."[38]

The transition from team cooperation to articulated cooperation entailed two changes in the consciousness of the participating workers. Popitz and Bahrdt contended that these two changes in consciousness were complementary; together they induced the worker to elaborate a view of just social relations of production not unlike Saint-Simon's technocratic vision of socialism.

The first change had to do with the worker's new isolation. In a system of articulated cooperation, the worker theoretically knew that he was most helpful to the others in his group when he performed his task so well that they needed to take no notice of it when performing their own. Successful cooperation meant, paradoxically, *not* forcing the others to take special pains to cooperate. For the others, a successful worker was only an extension of the smoothly functioning production apparatus. According to Popitz and Bahrdt, the workers were therefore no longer conscious of one another as persons, let alone as members of a group: "Articulated cooperation makes . . . the individual's personal engagement unnecessary. The next worker is no longer one's 'mate' in the somewhat romantic sense in which industrial sociologists still often use the term, a sense which is still manifest vestigially in the usages of mines and smelters today. On the contrary, one's fellow worker is one's 'colleague,' someone who is the master of a clearly defined situation thanks to certain capabilities."[39]

The second change in the worker's consciousness was a growing independence from the control of his supervisors. The source of the worker's new autonomy was the special character of his knowledge of production. He did not have the grasp of the fundamentals of technology characteristic, in different ways, of the engineer or maintenance worker. But he knew far more than they about the quirks of his machine. A master of the art of making a certain group of machines produce the most it could produce (or, as Popitz and Bahrdt say, someone with "technical sensibility"), the process worker was of great value to the firm. If the company suddenly had to put production in the hands of someone who would either make mistakes or fail to catch breakdowns in time, the costs could be ruinous.

Once the firm had found a man who could do the job – and there is, given the nature of the art, no sure way of knowing whether he could before he did – it had no incentive to disturb his judgment by allowing supervisors to interfere with his work. Nor, according to this argument, could management threaten to replace him: The definition of articulated cooperation suggested that no one else on the same shift knew precisely what he did. The automation worker thus seemed to possess a unique kind of knowledge and a unique place among workers with similar kinds of knowledge. For both reasons he appeared indispensable to the firm.

The worker's consciousness was then defined by his independence. His relation to technology seemed to free him from the interference of supervisors. His position on the firm's labor market – another result of his relation to technology – made him secure enough to defend his freedom should his superiors or colleagues demand disobedience to the imperatives of technology.

Following this line of reasoning, Popitz and Bahrdt spoke of the immanent "loss of the function of the worker's immediate superior."[40] In their study of wage systems in the French steel industry, Claude Durand, Claude Prestat, and Willener went further and predicted a technologically imposed "de-hierarchicalization" of the organization of work.[41] Lutz shifted the focus from the decline of the supervisor's authority to the awakening of the worker's political consciousness. He suggested that there was a tendency for "spaces freed of domination" to develop in highly mechanized industries.[42] And once independent, the worker would discover his true nature and its political implications. Lutz expected that "in these spaces freed of domination, and on the basis of new knowledge into his own motives for working – knowledge which had lain buried beneath the ruling ideology of achievement – the worker would become conscious of himself as a producer; and this consciousness would give rise to demands to participate in the management of the firm, if not for a regime of worker self-management."[43]

But the more clearly the political implications of the analysis were spelled out, the more obvious it became that the whole argument turned on the assumption that workers conceive of themselves, at least latently, as producers.[44] Otherwise, it was difficult to see how a relatively small increase in workplace autonomy (if that was really what was going on at all) could produce such dramatic results. But a process worker in a chemical plant, for example, begins and ends his career without any generally applicable skill. Does the kind of knowledge he does have automatically make him think of himself as a producer? If so, does his position in the division of labor guarantee the security of employment required to defend his autonomy? The preconception of the worker as producer foreclosed discussion of these questions. It also drew attention away from the question of the worker's perception of industrial work and, more generally, away from that of his relation to the labor market.

Recent studies of work in automated plants suggest, however, that it is precisely the latter relations which decisively shape both the self-conception of workers with these new skills and their disposition to fight for reorganization of the workplace. These findings account for the relative docility of workers who could inflict enormous costs on their employers if they sabotaged production.

First, it has been shown that the very capacities which make these workers valuable to employers make them extremely dependent on their bosses as well. Unlike craftsmen, they do not have skills that can be transferred from plant to plant. Although they know the hidden difficulties of operating one set of machines with a given group of colleagues, they cannot apply general knowledge about technology to another plant. They are keenly aware that the chance to manifest the talents they have depends on a mixture of luck and influence. Most important of all, they know what limits the special character of their knowledge imposes on their freedom of action. A worker interviewed by Popitz and Bahrdt gave the following report of his promotion from unskilled to semiskilled worker:

When I heard that they were looking for people for the new furnace, I thought, that's the way to get a furnace job forever. But a lot of people were looking for that kind of work. There was a guy from the wire mill who wanted the job, but the plant people wouldn't let him go. And if somebody hadn't died, I wouldn't have gotten the job anyhow. My father-in-law did his bit too, because without a little favoritism nothing happens here in the plant. We can be frank: Here in the plant, one guy pulls the other after him.[45]

Moreover, recent studies of technological innovation and the reorganization of work in highly mechanized plants show that, even after the formerly unskilled have been promoted to become process workers, they are constantly reminded that the extent to which they exercise any skill depends on luck and their employer's good will.

The theorists of technological determination seemed to assume that, once defined, tasks in the technologically advanced sector would remain unchanged for long periods of time. They confused the permanence of the firm with the permanence of a given division of labor.[46] More careful investigations show that market pressures to cut costs lead to ever-more-perfected systems of automation and to frequent redefinitions of the responsibilities of process workers. Instead of conceiving of themselves as a functional unit, held together by each man's consciousness of the necessity of cooperation, the members of a work team may often see themselves as competitors for the jobs that will remain after the next phase of innovation.

Management often encourages this implicit competition by offering "polyvalence" premiums to workers who master a job other than their own,[47] and by periodically reorganizing work to eliminate "superfluous," costly automation workers.[48] Far from regarding their past as unskilled workers as a mere episode in their careers at work, outlived and overcome, the workers in automated plants often fear that before they have a skill with a generally acknowledged name, they will be victims of dequalification.

Process workers in a recently modernized West German Exxon plant, for example, asked to judge the security of their jobs, gave resigned answers. The optimist among those interviewed said:

This job is pretty secure because it takes a long time for a man to make sense of this equipment, and that means it costs the company a lot to train him . . . How things will look when I am older I can't say. Probably not so good.

The skeptic said:

In an oil refinery, a job is never secure, because of the technical side of things . . . If [Exxon] invests a few million in automation, maybe in equipment to do automatic analysis, I can imagine that they could do without two or three men. That would be hard for one of us, mainly for an older one.

And according to the pessimist:

Nothing is certain. You've got to turn up every day with the feeling, today I'm still here, but I can't say if I'll still be here tomorrow. It can happen that they say, "We're combining these two jobs, so you had better go off and start loading asphalt." And off you go.[49]

More generally, the studies of work in the automated plants found that worker satisfaction depended crucially on the economic bargain between capital and labor, rather than on some alleged intrinsically pleasurable harmony between man and machine. Horst Kern and Michael Schumann concluded:

The thesis of Serge Mallet and others that automation workers develop a new professional consciousness or new forms of identification with the content of their work is not confirmed by our results. The high degree of satisfaction which automation workers express with regard to their work is based on a favorable evaluation of the strains associated with the job and with the general conditions of work in the plant. This satisfaction is coupled with a marked degree of integration in the plant. The circumstance that all the privileges connected with these jobs are to a large extent tied to a particular plant call forth in the worker a sense of dependence on the firm. This sense of dependence is not reciprocal. The workers are well aware that replacements and substitutes can be found for them with relative ease. A professional consciousness cannot develop on this basis.[50]

Likewise, Michael Mann explained the willingness of process workers in an English instant-coffee factory to follow the company to a new location as the result not of their intrinsic satisfaction with their jobs but of their economic dependence: "The worker cannot afford to return to the unskilled labor pool outside the factory."[51]

These conclusions return the discussion to its starting point: the similarity in the way the two types of workers with intermediate-level skills view their place in the division of labor. What counts for process workers is their place on the labor market; and the same is true for semiskilled workers in other industries with jobs requiring fragments of traditional craft knowledge. After doing semiskilled work for four and half years in a West German metalworking plant, Konrad Thomas concluded that the "semi-skilled are, relatively, the least free workers. They don't possess patents as skilled workers, which is the minimum required if one is to be respected and given a chance to succeed . . . To a high degree the semi-skilled are bound to the jobs they have. No matter how unpleasant the jobs may in fact be, they regard them as invaluable. (They, the semi-skilled, never know if they would have it better in another plant)."[52]

The electronics industry is an even clearer historical example of a symbiosis between worker and plant that rests on the worker's limited but traditional skill, not his control of advanced technology. Because of the precision required for some operations, the necessity of responding to small shifts in consumer preferences, and certain engineering obstacles, it has long proved uneconomical, if not technically impossible, to mechanize some stages of production. Where machines failed or were inflexible, the industry used (and continues to use) women with accurate fingers. Firms in Germany and the United States, the world leaders in this industry, provided such workers with a whole range of social services with the hope of making job change unthinkable to them.

Before World War II, Siemens, for example, employed a large number of blind women in a single, unlit room: Only the blind had the dexterity to build certain parts.[53] The women received housing, privileges at the company store, and, of course, the right to lifetime employment. They could not have been more integrated into the company or more dependent on it, nor it more dependent on them.

When a delegation of Japanese experts inspected the plant, the German management convinced their potential rivals of the impossibility of duplicating Siemens's methods of production by showing them the blind women at work.

Henceforth I will use the terms "plant-specific" and "intermediate-level" interchangeably to identify the skills of those workers who know that management is as solicitous of them as it is attentive to the deterioration of any piece of company property, and as willing to replace them should circumstances require.[54]

Unskilled workers

No one is proud of doing unskilled work. It may require ingenuity, but it does not spur the worker to perfect his technical prowess. It may pay reasonably well and be reasonably secure, but it seldom gives even that fragile sense of indispensability which consoles and sometimes emboldens the man who has been lucky enough to get a semiskilled job. Most workers with unskilled jobs, in fact, seem able to bear them because they do not expect to – and often do not – hold them very long. As a rule they try to use unskilled work as a means of accumulating the capital they need to put their skills and talents to use as they want. In other words, it is precisely because they have good reason to doubt the economist's claim that they are lazy, inept, or shortsighted that they are willing to do unskilled work at all. I will argue that there are three groups of unskilled workers, distinguished from one another by their different ideas of what to do instead of unskilled work.

Consider a peasant with a plot just a bit smaller than the minimum required for subsistence. Think next of an artisan or small shopkeeper whose shop is just a bit too small to survive in the local market, or of a young person who quit school early and is trying to save enough to buy a car or pay for the additional education that would open the door to a white-collar job. Finally, imagine a housewife whose husband earns just a shade too little to pay off the mortgage; her younger sister, just out of school, supporting herself until she decides on a husband or a career; and their sixty-year-old father, stuck in a low-level job, with no hopes of promotion, thinking only of his family, his hobbies, and retirement.

All these workers are in a situation where a little extra income will allow them to carry on in pre- or, to stretch the meaning of the word a bit, postindustrial occupations. The peasant could return to his plot, the artisan and shopkeeper to their shops, the married woman to her home; the older worker could retire early.[55] The adolescents are in a somewhat different but fundamentally analogous situation. Some of them will be self-consciously biding their time in factories until they can afford to return to school. Encouraged by the leisure-time industry to think that they are on a lifelong consumption trip, the rest may have no clear ideas about their future work at all. But when these latter do seriously consider how they will spend their working lives, they too think of leaving the factories, be it to return to school, to go to work directly in the service sector, to set up a small business, or to work at home. The irony of the situation is that, as in the case of the peasant, artisan, housewife, or retiree, the only source of income necessary to accomplish the adolescents' ends is industrial work.

These unskilled workers view industrial work from a vantage point outside it. They have what can be called an instrumental relation to factory work: They see themselves using it solely as a short-term means to what they hope will be a long-term end.[56] If work is defined as an activity expressive of the meaning of one's life, then inside the factory, these workers do not work at all: They toil or exert themselves. The sooner they save the requisite amount, the sooner they can go back to or begin doing what they consider their *real* work. Hence they want to exchange their effort for the highest possible short-term wage. Because many of the workers who hold this view of industrial work have been farmers, or (as is often the case in Europe) actually continue to farm small plots part time while they hold factory jobs, I will call all workers of this type, regardless of their origins or ultimate intentions, "peasant workers."[57]

A second type of unskilled worker wants out of his job, but not necessarily out of the factory. Think of a young man, perhaps the son of an immigrant, stuck on an assembly line. He has recently become a father. He takes his family responsibilities seriously. He wants to be promoted to a steady job that pays well. But promotion is also a matter of pride. Most of the others who work on his assembly line are immigrants. He has nothing in common with them; they seem as backward, as awkward in his society, as his father. He feels he can do more than they, understands more than they about the factory world. He wants to be accepted by the men who count in that world, and the way to get such acceptance is to prove to them that he has the kind of skills they have. So he will take any kind of promotion he can get; but above all, he wants to become a skilled worker. I will call unskilled workers of this type "would-be craftsmen."[58]

A third type of unskilled worker just wants out. He has hope neither of returning to some Arcadia outside the factory nor of advancing within it. Imagine the younger brother of the would-be craftsman, an adolescent quick-tempered and easily discouraged. He gets stuck in a dead-end job and quickly becomes demoralized. He hates what he is doing; at the same time he accepts society's judgment that no one who is capable of anything better does the work he does. His frustration finds voice in a stormy temper; a stormy temper gets him in trouble, convincing him that he is no exception to the general rule. He moves from job to job, sometimes pulled by the attraction of slightly higher wages (because he is learning nothing that pays off in the future, he thinks of the present), sometimes pushed by layoffs. All his friends are in the same situation: None of them has any long-term plans. No sooner is he married than he is embarrassed before his wife by his incapacity to be the steady breadwinner which society and his own conscience demand that he be. Failure at home and failure at work echo and amplify one another. Fatalism gets the upper hand. He sees himself trapped in a world where *all* human relationships are provisional and fragile. Trusting no one's steadfastness more than his own, he gives up the search for a better job. He does just as much work as necessary to scrape by. His passivity becomes a lesson for his son, who follows his father in anticipating failure even in those rare cases where he might in fact succeed. I will call workers trapped in this cycle of despair "ghetto workers."[59]

These different types of unskilled workers tend to gravitate to different parts of the labor market: Would-be craftsmen, for example, tend to fill unskilled jobs in the stable sector; ghetto workers have corresponding jobs in the unstable sector. Even when they are working side by side, moreover, these types of workers have quite different attitudes toward their bosses and work. Yet at the same time all three types are intimately related: In the course of a generation or two, the peasant worker can become a would-be craftsman or ghetto worker; a would-be craftsman can turn into a peasant worker, and a ghetto worker into a would-be craftsman. This section explores the characteristics of each type, its labor-market location and behavior; and the typical route that leads from one type to another.

Peasant workers

Peasant workers are appealing to employers for two reasons. First, they are not out for promotion: They want to get off the career ladder as soon as possible, not to climb it. Hence they are willing to accept dead-end, boring jobs with low hourly rates of pay, something employers in both the stable and unstable sectors have in abundance. Often these are jobs which natives simply will not take at anything like the going wage. As a Malian working for the Paris Métro put it, "The last thing I worry about is losing my job to a Frenchman. No Frenchman would do what I do for what I get paid."[60]

Second, they are willing to accept unsteady employment, a factor that makes them extremely attractive to unstable-sector employers. Peasant workers can tolerate spells of unemployment, because they are doubly defended against it. Their first line of defense is the diversification of their revenues. Families of peasant workers tend to combine income from several sources (the son's work as an agricultural laborer, the wife's as a homeworker, the uncle's as a factory worker, etc.) to reach a target sum that guarantees their social place.[61] Shortfalls from one activity can be offset if another family member works longer hours at something else.

If this first line of defense fails, the peasant worker falls back to a second one. During business downturns peasants and artisans can return to their original occupations and survive by working extremely hard under subsistence conditions or by relying on relatives and friends in their home community. When the depression hit Flint, Michigan, for example, Southerners who had migrated north to work in the automobile industry during the boom years of the 1920s returned to the rural counties from which they had come: Between 1930 and 1934, the population of Southern whites in Flint decreased by 35.1 percent and that of Southern blacks by 18.9 percent, whereas the population of the city as a whole sank by only 7.7 percent.[62] Similarly, an out-of-work adolescent can go on living in the same place he often lives when he has a job: his parents' home; an older worker can accept the company's offer of early retirement at a shade less than full retirement pay; and so on.

This mesh of job characteristics and attitudes toward work explains the concentration of peasant workers in some parts of the economy over long periods of time. In New York City during the early twentieth century, for example, Italian immigrants crowded into jobs in construction, on the docks, and in the garment industry – three notoriously unsteady kinds of work. Thomas Kessner found that the overwhelming majority of these immigrants were single men of peasant origin, aged fourteen to forty-four; and more detailed studies of the immigrants' origins show that they tended to be small landowners, sharecroppers, or artisans determined to earn abroad the money needed to put themselves on a firm economic footing at home.[63] This goal determined their attitudes to work in the United States:

Transiency narrowed the newcomer's sights to short-range goals. He generally neglected to learn the language or to make other long-term commitments to his new surroundings. Instead, with little specific training, he entered the lowest levels of the job market. Business and petty enterprise, which required investment and promised only gradual progress, were largely ignored. Similarly, the transient spurned clerical work because such higher-status jobs often did not offer better wages than day labor and only paid off in the long run as stepping stones to white-collar careers. The "bird of passage" kept his eye firmly trained on maximizing immediate rewards and eventually returning to Europe.[64]

An investment in skills might have protected this transient worker against unemployment, but cheap transatlantic steamship fares made it possible to weather a slack spell at home. Between those who had made their fortune and were leaving the United States for good and those who were temporarily out of a job, 150,000 Italians on the average sailed from the United States to Italy each year between 1907 and 1911 – just short of three-quarters of the annual reverse traffic from Italy to the United States in those years.[65] Turks, Algerians, and Southern Italians working on construction sites and in factories in West Germany, France, or Italy in the 1960s behaved in strikingly similar ways. A study of *Gastarbeiter* who came to West Germany in the 1960s and 1970s, for instance, showed that 78 percent who arrived with fixed ideas of how long they wanted to remain had stayed longer than intended, and only 6 percent of all the immigrants wanted to remain permanently in West Germany.[66]

In the stable sector of the labor market, peasant workers do the least-skilled jobs: They assemble final products or subcomponents, operate simple metal-cutting machines, work in foundries, or feed workpieces to automatic machines. At Renault, immigrants and former agricultural workers are concentrated in the unskilled divisions. Turnover rates in the divisions where they are most numerous are, independent of any differences in the organization of work, extraordinarily high, suggesting that they are interested only in short-term employment. Naville and his coauthors observed a "cleavage between the stable and the unstable parts of the work force . . . This cleavage is directly related to the social characteristics of the workers: instability is associated principally with immigrant workers in the plants near Paris (Billancourt and Flins) and with workers drawn from agriculture to the provincial plants (notably Cléon and Sandouville)."[67]

In West Germany the situation is similar. A large majority of assembly-line workers in the automobile industry are either foreign migrants or recruits from agriculture, and it is they who bear the brunt of fluctuations in employment levels of the industry as a whole.[68] In Italy the situation was the same until the late 1960s, with the bulk of the work force being migrants from the South of the country. In the United States, farmers from the Midwest, miners from Appalachia, foreign immigrants, and black and white migrants from the South have all been crucial to Detroit's success in the past. Today, with the northern automobile plants dominated by men who do not think of themselves as peasant workers, the industry has begun to migrate south in search of a new labor force.[69] In all these countries women make up a very large part of the production-line work force in the home appliance, electronic parts, textile, and garment industries: Recall the composition of the unskilled work force in the factories in the Bavarian Oberpfalz.[70] On the extremely conservative assumption that only the *Gastarbeiter*, or foreign workers, in Europe and their homologues, the undocumented aliens in the United States, should be counted as peasant workers, a rough estimate would be that the least desirable 10 percent of the jobs, steady and unsteady, in the advanced industrial societies are done by workers who reject the idea of a life at industrial work.[71]

But for all the overlap between the peasant workers' attitudes and the industrialists' requirements, it would be wrong to conceive of the former merely as the tools of the latter. If peasant workers' designs encourage them to collaborate with industry, they also impose important limits on this collaboration; and these limits hint at the potentially subversive role of such workers in industrial society.

In the first place, the peasant worker has no pride of accomplishment in factory work. He has agreed to exchange his effort for a wage. But when he has no need of extra money or when there is something more important than factory work on hand, he is not likely to show up for his job at all. At harvest time, for instance, factories manned by peasant workers from the surrounding area are likely to be half deserted.[72] Even when the peasant worker does work, furthermore, he is indifferent to what he does. As he conceives it, he is obliged to follow instructions, not to worry about the consequences of his obedience.

According to the Fordist ideas of work frequently held by industrial engineers and managers, this sort of performance ought to be enough. The rules are supposed to be constructed so carefully that following them blindly produces a perfect product every time. But as I argued earlier, in factories as elsewhere, reality is so complex and rapidly changing that no plan can be comprehensive enough to be a completely reliable guide to action. In manufacturing this means that even an officially unskilled worker cannot simply follow orders. If he does not show initiative from time to time in adjusting to the unforeseen, production suffers. So the peasant worker's lack of initiative is an important disadvantage from management's point of view: Because he does not care about what is produced, the peasant worker is unlikely to throw his inventiveness into the breach when the plan fails. In this he is the polar opposite of the downgraded craftsman, who delights in showing off his skills.

The following incident, reported in Philippe Bernoux's study of unskilled workers in a French metalworking factory, illustrates the significance of this purely formal participation in factory life.[73] The workers were required to produce a certain number of "minutes" a day, a minute being defined as a given number of workpieces on each of several different machines. In some cases the equation of workpieces to minutes for a particular machine was set so that even the best worker working his hardest could not produce the quota; on other machines anyone could exceed it almost effortlessly. This disparity would have caused more bitterness in the shop than it did but for one circumstance: Workers were seldom penalized for failing to meet their quotas.

One group of workers, nonetheless, took great pride in fulfilling the quota as a proof of their physical stamina and honesty. All of them had been born and raised and, at the time of the study, lived in nearby agricultural villages, where some of them continued to farm small plots. Village life and farm work were the constant, almost the exclusive, themes of their discussions. Of these peasant workers, one was especially intent on producing the norm. When he was assigned to a machine that yielded few minutes he would simply stop what he was doing and, disregarding the consequences of his actions on the whole flow of production, start work at a more favorable post. Consider for a moment how mutually dependent the departments of a modern plant are, and you begin to understand why management must consider a work force that cheerfully executes the letter and never the spirit of industrial law a mixed blessing.[74]

The second kind of defect in the peasant worker's character, from management's point of view, has to do with its fragility: Peasant workers do not stay peasant workers forever. There is no hard-and-fast rule that determines when a peasant worker will give up the idea of himself as a temporary worker. Mere exposure to the practices and artifacts of urban factory life, at any rate, does not produce this result. Instead, in rethinking his relation to factory work, the peasant worker does what we all seem to do when we make complex choices with essentially incalculable results based on insufficient information: He cautiously confronts some of the key presuppositions of his global view of his situation with his best assessment of the relevant facts.

So long as there is a fair fit between expectations and reality – and every group of workers, no less than every group of scientists, will have some common standards for judging which fit counts as fair – the assumptions hold, otherwise they give way to new ones. In practice this means that if peasant workers really have no chance to live up to the standards of dignity implicit in their original world view, they eventually realize the difficulty by themselves or through debate with other groups – and change their view of the world.

Ely Chinoy watched a group of American peasant workers on the verge of this discovery. The ABC automobile factory he studied in the late 1940s was located in a rural midwestern county. About one quarter of the almost three thousand farmers in the county worked more than 250 days a year off the farm; of the roughly twenty-two hundred farms, about seven hundred were less than thirty acres and produced less than eight hundred dollars a year in income. The local labor weekly, perhaps irked at the peasant workers' indifference to the causes of self-conscious industrial workers, reported on their condition in the following half-malicious, half-sympathetic verses:

The odor of the barn yard
Where milk turned into beef
Comes wafting back to me again
Right here at [ABC].

Our country minded workers
Who try to raise their meat
Now come to work with eyes half closed
Too tired to scrape their feet.

And after working here all day,
They till the soil with care.
They think they'll find a pot of gold
Awaiting them out there.

They talk about retiring.
To me it's just a yarn.
We'll have them with us many years
Still talking about their farm.[75]

Typically, the change in attitudes awaits the succession of generations. After the birth of her child, for example, a mother continues working, first to help pay for some home improvements, then to buy a second car, and finally to tide the family over when her husband is laid off or sick. By accident, convinced all the time that she is about to go back to being a full-time housewife, she does a lifetime of factory work. But if her situation is typical of women in her generation, and word gets around that a husband's salary will not support a family, then her daughter may well begin work aware that she will have to stick to it.

Or take the case of fathers who go abroad or to a distant city in their home country in search of work. They may live more than half their lives away from their original home. But they have seen too many of their friends and relatives return home for good – they themselves may have gone back and forth more than once – to be able to give up the idea of doing so themselves. For their children, however, the foreign country, or distant city, *is* home. They can see how farfetched their parents' hopes have become, and they break with their family's past by defining themselves with respect to the factories and streets where they live. Many second-generation Americans have known this experience well. For many of them, home was not just the most familiar but also the most alien spot in the world. Children of the Turks who came to Berlin or Frankfurt in the 1960s are having this experience now.[76]

Sometimes, however, a group of peasant workers virtually colonize a part of town and a cluster of factory jobs. If economic conditions are stable enough, a kind of rustification of industrial life can take place; for a period of several generations, the group will be able to lead some version of its traditional social life in the new setting. Affairs in the factory will be regulated according to the rules that prevailed at home: Many members of the same family will work in a single plant, and promotions will reflect the relations of authority within a given clan, because only superiors with such authority are respected at work. So even though its members are unable to return to the mother country, the group will not be forced to cast off its old self-conception. This situation occurred in some cities in the northeastern United States during the last part of the nineteenth and the first part of the twentieth centuries.[77]

Rustification of factory life is also typical of the early phases of industrialization, in which the owner and workers of a factory are likely to have known one another first as landlord and tenants. An extreme example is imperial Russia, where early factory workers were often serfs still tied to their masters. The Russian state, beginning with the government of Peter I, assigned to the new factories peasants owing quitrents (*obrok*) to the crown, in effect renting its serfs to bourgeois entrepreneurs. Nobles used their serfs in *votchinal* (from *votchina*, a noble's patrimonial estate) factories on their own lands. Or they could take advantage of the *otkhodnichestvo* ("going-away") system, in which peasants were permitted to work outside the village provided they periodically returned home and paid a substantial fraction of their wages as *obrok*. Especially in the Moscow area, these practices kept peasants who were working in factories enmeshed in the affairs of their villages and helped perpetuate rural habits in the city. The emancipation of the serfs in 1861 did not substantially alter these patterns.[78] Peasants working in urban factories married young, unlike workers born in the cities, and often left their wives and families in the home village rather than establishing households in the cities. Sons and daughters succeeded fathers and mothers in the same jobs in the same factories.[79] Under the cover of free-market exchanges, traditional mechanisms of deference have been exploited in one industrializing area after another: in the Silesian mines in the nineteenth century as well as, until recently, in the textile mills of the American South and Brazilian factories.[80]

Another variant of this development can be seen in post–World War II Western Europe and Japan. Here government support of smallholder agriculture, subsidies to firms willing to locate in economically backward areas, and the firms' own desires for cheap land and reservoirs of unskilled labor combine to keep the peasant on the farm and to bring the factories to the country. One result has been to encourage peasants to supplement their income from farming with the proceeds of a factory job not far from home.[81] In the late 1970s, for example, 90 percent of Japan's 5 million farm families farmed only part time, and only about 30 percent of their income came from agriculture.[82] The description given earlier of the behavior of the peasant workers in the French metalworking factory suggests that this combination of incomes can perpetuate the peasant worker's instrumental attitude to work.

But excepting cases such as that of Japan, where the state supports domestic agriculture at almost any cost and crowded cities trap peasants on the land, it is unlikely that relations between peasant workers and industry will remain permanently frozen in these ways.[83] If the peasant workers hold unsteady jobs, sooner or later a downturn in the business cycle coincides with a sharp drop in their other sources of income, and many of them are forced to move to new areas in search of work. If, on the other hand, the peasant workers have jobs in the stable sector, it is likely to be the employer himself who eventually attempts to break their connection with the land.

In the primary sector, everything depends on the coordination of output between divisions, skilled or unskilled. Hence the peasant worker's disruptive work habits – his tendency to skip work at harvest time or his indifference to the substance of his work – can create costly bottlenecks. The employer can counter, as Rolande Trempé's study of peasant miners in the nineteenth century showed, by reverting to all the classic tricks pioneered by British factory owners and used since by all industrialists to crack open the peasants' subsistence economy: imposing penalities for absenteeism, offering bonuses for increased productivity, scheduling work to interfere with the upkeep of a small plot, and enticing the workers to indebt themselves to the point at which they become continuously dependent on their industrial income.[84] The greater the employer's success, the more likely it is that his workers will cease to think of themselves as peasants.

At the opposite extreme, peasants and migrants can enter industrial work eagerly, determined to remain at it. To see how this situation might come about, consider the effect of an immigrant worker, on vacation from a distant factory, on his friends in his home village. His whole ambition may be to buy a small plot of land near the village; but he talks of nothing but big-city adventures, if only to cover the shame of having been forced to emigrate in the first place. A used car and a great deal of pocket money back his boasts, making his fate seem attractive to many of those afraid they will wind up as day laborers at the bottom of the village hierarchy. Under these circumstances, a kind of urbanization of the countryside takes place; agricultural work is scorned as old-fashioned; city ways become fashionable; young women look down on the young men who want to become farmers; young men in search of brides have to go to the city or dress and act as though they already lived there; economically viable farms may even be abandoned because no one is willing to work them. Coming from this kind of community, a young worker who finds an industrial job thinks he has taken a step up. In the early 1970s this was the attitude of many native Puerto Rican youths, on the verge of emigrating to the mainland United States, who distinguished a hipster, or *men* (their pronunciation of "man"), from a *jibaro* ("peasant").[85] Italian and Spanish sociologists noted a similar development among some rural migrants in the 1960s.[86]

There is, to repeat, no ticking sociological clock that determines when the peasant worker's self-conception will break down. Everything depends on the circumstances he faces. But however he comes to realize that, like it or not, he is an industrial worker for good, this realization is likely to have important consequences for the surrounding society.

Would-be craftsmen
So long as the peasant workers hold to their original self-conception, they do not think of comparing themselves with industrial

workers. Either the peasant workers consider themselves to be completely outside the hierarchy of industrial society (an attitude consistent with the notion of an industrial job as dead time) or they think of *any* industrial job, even the most menial, as superior to any job in traditional society (an attitude consistent with the idea of an industrial job as a step up). But once they see themselves as part of industrial society, they realize that they are at the bottom of the dominant hierarchy. Worse yet, just as they discover that they are nobodies, they realize that they are doing jobs that lead nowhere. Neither discovery pleases them; both together seem to produce, within a surprisingly short time, significant changes in their behavior.

In one preliminary reaction to their reappraisal of the situation, these workers become more security-minded. As long as they thought that they had no future in the factory, they were oblivious to the greater security offered by primary-sector unskilled work. Once they realize that they will be permanently dependent on the income from factory work, they begin to migrate to the primary sector in hopes of insuring themselves in a minimal way against economic fluctuations. Such workers might move, for instance, from a small factory or a construction site to a large factory or secure subsidiary.

The peasant worker's heightened need for security is also accompanied by a redefined idea of dignity. He is embarrassed to do the work traditionally reserved for peasant workers precisely because such work is defined in the society at large as beneath the dignity of a truly competent worker. The fact that many employers and fellow workers persist in taking his surname, skin color, accent, or address as signs that he will not object to such work makes him all the more assertive in rejecting it. He becomes, in short, a would-be craftsman, caught between a preindustrial world that he rejects and a factory world that does not yet accept him.

In his study of unskilled metalworkers Bernoux found working side by side with the peasant workers a second group equally low in the plant hierarchy but "completely immersed" in it. From early on, everyone in the group had known some aspect of industrial life. One grew up on a farm, but had been active in the rural trade-union movement. The others had all held factory jobs from an early age. They came from working-class families of more or less recent vintage: One was the son of a railroad worker, another of a Republican refugee from Spain; a third, born in Sicily, had come to France with his family as a young boy. Hence their characteristic dilemma: Having been socialized into a world in which personal worth is determined by place in the hierarchy of skill, they were officially classified as technically incompetent. How could they avoid the conclusion that they were worthless?

Their search for an answer reveals the central elements of the would-be craftsman's labor-market behavior. First, they tried to demonstrate that their cooperation was essential to running the plant. They were critical of the organization of production, the maintenance of the machines, and so on, as if to say that without their expertise nothing would be produced, and that even more could be produced if their advice were respected. But they also systematically restricted output to between 85 and 90 percent of the minutes required. In this way they protected their bargaining position in future negotiations over piece rates; but the slowdown also demonstrated indirectly their importance in the division of labor.

At the same time, they ceaselessly hoped for promotion. Here, too, they pursued one strategy explicitly acknowledging the justice of the prevailing system of classification, and a second denying its validity. Though success was unlikely, they were constantly preparing to take the certifying examination for skilled workers. With the same dedication, they schemed at using higher-ranking friends in other departments or factories to secure promotions, in spite of their lack of formal qualifications. *Promotion, revendication, modernization,* the three demands that Bernoux found to be characteristic of this group, all express the would-be craftsmen's determination to prove that they were more valuable than they had been perceived to be.[87]

Whether would-be craftsmen can fulfill some part of their ambitions individually or must turn instead to collective action depends in a complex way on the labor-market situation and the political ideas and institutions available to help form and express their frustrations. If skilled workers are in short supply, for example, a would-be craftsman can readily find a job at the intermediate skill level, at the very least. From there he may be able to make the jump to craft work. Through the 1920s many second-generation immigrants in this country were integrated in this piecemeal way into the core of the labor force.

But if the labor market is slack and there are no places for the career-minded, the peasant workers must turn to collective solutions. Mass, public action, anticipated and colored by earlier communitarian strikes, replaces or complements private efforts. Through the political parties and in workplace organizations, peasant workers as a group press for reforms that will give them some say in the decisions to hire, fire, and promote that so vitally affect them. Out of this process of collective contractualism can emerge a set of institutions and techniques for regulating industrial conflict that can have serious long-term consequences for the development of the national economy. We will look at this sort of development in Chapter 4. But first I want to take up the case of the unfortunate peasant workers, the ghetto workers who lose the struggle for place and remain at the margins of the industrial work force. What becomes of them?

Ghetto workers

The conventional argument, elaborated by writers like Oscar Lewis and Edward Banfield, is that ghetto workers tumble into a culture of poverty from which it is almost impossible to escape: Failure at work ruins life at home; a ruined home life undermines the will to work; and the result is the economic disasters that start the cycle again.[88] But the type of the ghetto worker differs in two important ways from the image of the urban day laborer that emerges from the culture-of-poverty argument. He is, I argue, a much rarer and less hopeless person than is often assumed.

For one thing, the ghetto-worker category applies to a smaller group than does the standard culture-of-poverty notion. The latter sees all those living in the ghetto as trapped in the same miasma of despair. It is more accurate to say that, at any one time, only a relatively small group of former peasant workers or their offspring – the real losers – are caught in the fatalist trap. Of course, one reason the culture-of-poverty argument has been applied so broadly, and not, as I am suggesting, treated as a residual category, is simply that in any community of peasant workers it is extremely difficult for outsiders to tell the real losers from everyone else.

Suppose, to use an old-fashioned but brutally direct and revealing phrase, I go slumming in a Puerto Rican ghetto in a mainland U.S. city one afternoon. On every street corner I see unemployed men. Because of some similarities in their dress and demeanor, I conclude that they belong to a single social class. In fact, there are, and they themselves know there to be, important differences among them. Some are without a job because, having just arrived from Puerto Rico, they have not had the time to find one. Others just quit work in order to be able to return to the island. Among those who grew up in the United States, some are jobless because they have become picky about the work they will accept. They have had decent jobs and been laid off. Now they insist on having jobs that lead somewhere – and such jobs are hard to come by. Still others of the native-born are in the street because that seems to be where they always wind up. Often these were born into families that were in trouble *before* emigrating to the city.[89] An early reputation as street fighters made it natural to start fights on the job; and a history of fighting on the job did not make it any easier to get hired. By the time they were no longer proud of being street fighters, they had lived up to the family reputation as losers. Getting last crack at the good jobs and being fired for the first mistake only convinced them that they deserved a bad name. It didn't make it easy to support a wife and child, either. Now they work when they have to, and rely on welfare and petty theft for the rest of what they need.

Of all these men, of course, only those in the last group begin to fit the description of the lost souls caught in the culture of poverty. Sometimes the ghetto residents themselves have a special name for them, as in the Dallas barrio of La Bajura, where they are called *los pelados*, "poor, wretched people."[90] The other groups in the ghetto can obviously be described as peasant workers and would-be craftsmen.

Indeed, the evidence suggests that it is more fruitful to see ghettos as way stations for individual peasant workers coming to, departing from, entering, or failing to be admitted into the larger society than as self-renewing centers of moral debility. Implicitly at least, inhabitants of ghettos often see all of these possibilities as simultaneously present: not as stepping-stones in the collective migration of a community, but as so many different ways to lead one's life, each embodied in a particular style of dress and speech. The major styles in the Chicago ghetto that Gerald D. Suttles studied in the 1960s, for example, alluded to the rural origins of new migrants to the city, the middle-class aspirations of some of the city-born, and the urban demimonde of others with no hope of escape: Someone was "country" if he had no idea of city fashions, "Ivy" if he imitated whites in button-down shirts, or a "gauster" if he dressed and walked like a pimp, the archetypal figure in the culture of poverty.[91]

But the available evidence is inconclusive. Exactly how important the culture of poverty is in the life of urban ghettos it is at present impossible to say. As a precondition to fruitful research on the question, however, we must surely drop the assumption that all those without work in the ghetto have a common history and a common psychology.

But the ghetto worker is less common than he is assumed to be. He is neither so resigned as the culture-of-poverty thesis makes him out to be nor so rebellious as some critics of that thesis wish he were. The culture-of-poverty argument is that economic oppression is transformed into psychological self-oppression. In tracing the history of American ghetto blacks, for example, proponents of this theory argue that slavery or the successor sharecropping system created, in John Dollard's words, a "permanent dole which appeal[ed] to the pleasure principle and relieve[d] the Negro of responsibility and the necessity of forethought."[92] The search for pleasure supposedly led men to abandon their wives and children, destroying the nuclear family. Male children then imitated their fathers' irresponsibility, so that any attempt to improve the next generation's condition by an offer of jobs or training was rendered futile. For this school of thought, associated with Stanley M. Elkins's work on slave culture and Daniel P. Moynihan's on the structure of the black family, the slave's original rational adaptation to his servitude has made it impossible for ghetto blacks to take advantage of the opportunities they actually have.[93]

According to many of the critics of this view, oppression succeeds only so long as the balance of terror favors the oppressor. Ghetto workers put up with their lot because they are powerless to change things for the better. Their illegal activities and efforts to secure modest improvements by becoming the clients of powerful patrons, instead of by open, collective political activity, should be understood as the most effective strategy given their situation, not as a sign of venality. Extending Herbert George Gutman's argument that there existed a cohesive slave family and an autonomous slave culture, proponents of this view could argue that even the impression of subservience and acquiescence that the urban poor often make is a sham required by their precarious situation: Because they understand that they are in many ways as vulnerable to oppression in the northern cities as their ancestors were to lynch justice in the rural South, they hide their rage behind a mask of childish irresponsibility.[94]

Both of these positions crumble under the weight of the available evidence. If the first view were accurate, the ghetto worker would remain frozen in despair even when there were alternatives to his situation. But as we will see, ghetto workers singly and in groups sometimes resist working under the conditions normally offered them. If the second explanation were true, ghetto workers would take advantage of every favorable shift in the labor market, or would force an improvement in their condition through collective action. But we will see, too, that urban day laborers sometimes prefer menial jobs even when more challenging work is available. And it is well known that ghetto workers, living in a world in which every social relation is constructed so that minimal damage will be caused when it disintegrates, are reluctant to join together to improve working conditions, even when they face good prospects of success. It is a commonplace among political activists that the sub- or lumpenproletariat is difficult to organize.[95]

It is possible, however, to elaborate the type of the ghetto worker in a way that reconciles these two views and does justice to his fragile combativeness.[96] The central notion is that, as in the second view, there is an autonomous core to the ghetto worker's personality. In the extreme case of the slaves and their offspring, this residual sense of autonomy is kept alive by certain institutions – the church, the family – whose continued existence is itself a sign of the oppressed's determination to sustain an independent identity. But, as Eugene D. Genovese has shown, it is also nurtured, against his will, by the oppressor himself. Even if it were possible to eliminate the slave's discretion at work, it would still prove extremely inconvenient, perhaps impossible, to deny him a certain independent legal personality. To do so would make him an instrument of his master's will, and make his master liable for all his acts. But in fact the slave owner can never simplify work so completely, nor supervise the workers so carefully, that no exercise of discretion is called for; and still less can the factory owner do so. Nor can the slave or factory owner resist the temptation to increase efficiency by bribing the workers to increase output in return for a (not quite proportionate) increase in pay – thus acknowledging the latter's power to control the pace of production. Thus, for reasons having to do with the limits of oppression itself, the spark of autonomy continues to exist; and because it does there is always the hope that ghetto workers will take advantage of opportunities they are provided, even if they cannot provide any for themselves.[97]

But like the first school of thought, this view holds that the ghetto worker (or the slave) does not remain unaffected by his failures. A long experience of insufficiency and impotence, an inseparable part of the life of the slave and the casual laborer, shatters their confidence; they no longer dare to take advantage of those opportunities which, by their own admission, might lead them out of a situation that they themselves acknowledge to be desperate. In this way they come to experience their own hope as an implausible dream.

Recent studies of ethnically diverse American ghetto workers, often conducted in connection with government programs to aid them, bear out the view that like Hegel's slave, they are trapped in a system that forces them to understand the truth of their degradation even as it weakens their power to resist it actively. In his study of the psychology of welfare recipients, for example, Leonard Goodwin found that even women who on the average had been receiving welfare payments for sixteen years continued to value work as a means of self-expression and character development and as an essential source of self-esteem. At the same time, he found that the impossibility of finding steady work ruined the women's confidence in their ability to succeed in realizing their ambitions at work.[98] What emerges from his survey is a portrait of "black welfare women who want to work but who, because of continuing failure in the work world, tend to become more accepting of welfare and less inclined to try again."[99] Elliot Liebow came to similar results in his study of life in a black ghetto in Baltimore. He learned, on the one hand, that the day laborers with whom he spoke were interested in finding steady work—a "security job"—as a means of establishing a more regular existence. At the same time, he found that the men doubted their ability to meet the demands of such jobs:

Each man comes to the job with a long job history characterized by his not being able to support himself and his family. Each man carries this knowledge, born of his experience, with him. He comes to the job flat and stale, wearied by the sameness of it all, convinced of his own incompetence, terrified of responsibility—of being tested still again and found wanting . . . It is the experience of the individual and the group; of their fathers and probably of their sons. Convinced of their inadequacies, not only do they not seek out those few better-paying jobs which test their resources, but they actively avoid them, gravitating in a mass to the menial, routine jobs which offer no challenge—and therefore pose no threat—to the already diminished images they have of themselves.[100]

The experience of work thus ratifies the experience of impermanence that is taken for granted in the rest of social life, and the ghetto worker resigns himself to permanent humiliation. But his resignation includes the knowledge of what he wants but cannot have; and although experience teaches that it is not worth trying to get what he wants, he does not for that reason give up wanting it.

The determination with which former slaves, impoverished and disorganized peasants, and ghetto workers defend rights granted them as the result of revolutionary shifts in the balance of power in the larger society is a further confirmation of these ideas, as is the willingness of these groups to join protest movements organized by others. After the Civil War in the United States, apparently docile slaves left their masters at the first opportunity.[101] In Cuba, after Castro's victory, Oscar Lewis remarked that the dejected inhabitants of a slum he had visited in the late 1940s were well organized and full of optimism, despite their unrelieved poverty.[102] And observers noted a similar reaction among impoverished peasants and workers given new rights over their lands and factories during General Velasco's revolution in Peru from 1968 to 1975.[103] In all these cases it was as though the sudden reversal of fortune, which to its most desperate beneficiaries must at first have appeared as much an act of providence as the result of a political struggle, created new loyalties and tapped buried reservoirs of hope and self-reliance.

In an analogous way, the movements organized by American blacks in the 1960s to press their demands for better jobs drew ghetto workers at least for a time into politics.[104] In Detroit, for example, the growth in demand for cars produced by the economic boom of the Vietnam War years combined with the fear that the unemployed in the ghettos were becoming a significant threat to social order to bring automobile companies to hire ghetto workers normally regarded as unemployable. Once in the plants, these workers were caught up in the march of other work groups; they joined movements to increase black influence in the union and to put an end to implicitly discriminatory company policies such as the concentration of blacks in undesirable shifts and jobs.

But the limits of their activism are as revealing as the fact of their participation. Just as with the similar movements of Slavic Americans in the 1930s and Southern Italians in the 1960s, which we shall look at in detail in Chapter 4, the leadership of the Detroit League of Revolutionary Black Workers was in the hands of would-be craftsmen, workers who as a rule followed their parents into steady, unskilled jobs, with the difference that they were not content to stop there. The ghetto workers with their spotty work records played at best a subaltern role in the organization; and after the downturn in 1969, when many of them were laid off, they disappeared from the political scene, unable to organize an independent defense. In the rare cases in which an organization has tried, as did the American Black Panthers in the same period, to recruit chiefly ghetto workers, the latter's hesitations about collective action have been all the more evident: The Black Panthers were crippled as much by the rank and file's fear (sometimes justified) that the leaders were using their power to private advantage as by the ferocity of the police attacks against them. The rise and decline of such organizations thus reflect both the ghetto worker's indomitable will and his paralyzing heritage of self-doubt and mistrust.

The struggle for place

So far the discussion has focused on the mesh between the characteristics of particular labor markets and the collective personality of certain groups. The underlying scheme is that the economy produces jobs, society produces groups, and the latter find their way to the former via the market. From this perspective, birth is destiny: Membership in a social group leads naturally and inevitably to membership in the corresponding occupational group. In certain extreme cases this may be so: Mining towns, small peasant villages, communities of longshoremen or steelworkers are all examples of self-reproducing worlds in which work and life are so intertwined that becoming a person and becoming a worker of a certain kind are essentially the same thing. But usually young persons do not simply grow into their work; they experience their choice of a job as a choice between alternatives offering substantially different social advantages and possibilities of self-development. To complement and review the preceding analysis, it will therefore be useful to consider some examples indicating how different careers at work look to a single young person trying to make his way in the world.

Take first the situation of the most typical industrial outsider, the male peasant. He faces a double problem. Can he gain by looking for work outside the farm community? If he thinks so, what kind of work should he look for? The answer to the first question concerns his place within the complex and shifting hierarchy of his home village; the answer to the second goes to the range of opportunities that the accessible labor markets provide.

Life in the typical peasant village has never had much to do with romantic notions of primitive egalitarianism or the Burkean image of hierarchies in which everyone is thankful to know his place. Agricultural communities are often egalitarian and hierarchical in turn. In some periods village life becomes more stratified as successful peasants accumulate land and wealth at the expense of unsuccessful ones; in others communitarian practices limiting disparities of wealth are revived in connection with the need to defend the village against outside enemies, be they aristocrats, railroad magnates, military recruiters, or tax collectors.[105] More important, peasants do not accept a particular distribution of wealth and rights as a fact of nature. On the contrary, the historical and ethnographic record reveals a perpetual struggle of whole communities to improve their situation collectively and to advance within the community individually: Think of the way the struggle of the English tenants in the late Middle Ages strengthened the legal position of the peasantry against the aristocracy while encouraging the polarization of the smallholders into *kulaks* and day laborers.[106] The peasant's pursuit of social honor in his home community, different in content but not in kind from the worker's, is the backdrop of his deliberations about work outside agriculture.

His calculations are shaped by the changing balance between egalitarianism and hierarchy within the community and by his position in the village pecking order, not, as study after study shows, by the level of his standard of living per se.[107] If the villagers band together in successful defense of their autonomy, it is unlikely that anyone will hunt for additional work. Nor is there likely to be a large demand for work off the farm in the opposite case, when land is concentrated in the hands of a few families and the rest earn their living as day laborers. Here the evidence is that the latter are reconciled to being landless. Instead of demanding plots to farm, they try to improve their position by organizing unions to push for better wages and working conditions: The leagues of *braccianti*, or day laborers, which made the Po Valley a center of Socialist support at the end of the nineteenth century, are a well-known example.[108]

The situation that pushes the peasant out into the industrial world is the one between these two: when land is widely held but ownership precarious or contested. This might be because population growth and inheritance rules have led to the division of the land into plots too small to support a family. Or it might be that the mass of cultivators are sharecroppers, dependent for credit on a lord who holds formal title to their land. For relatively prosperous peasants in such communities, industrial work means a chance to buy more land or clear title to existing holdings. For those with no plausible chance of winning a place in the ranks of the smallholders, an industrial job means a chance to escape the opprobrium of landless poverty in a society that exalts self-sufficiency. Joseph J. Barton, for example, points to this logic of agricultural pride in explaining the finding that turn-of-the-century immigrants to Cleveland came from rural areas where property was by local standards widely dispersed and income equally distributed.[109]

These are, of course, analytic distinctions. Frequently a smallholder will regard collective and individual action as complementary, not alternative, means of defending his property and social honor. The struggle against debt peonage that succeeded slavery in the American South after the Civil War is an extreme example of these overlapping tendencies. The Reconstruction sharecropping system amounted to a disguised form of serfdom: Tenants borrowed from landlords and fell into arrears; the landlord then forced the tenant to sell the crop and buy seed at manipulated prices, perpetuating the indebtedness. Short-term railroad work, mining, or factory work, however, gave tenants a chance to pay off debts and start the struggle for success within the agrarian community with a clean slate. As a result, as Michael Schwartz reports, "there emerged a pattern of migration back and forth between farm and industry and a general mobility of labor – black and white – into and out of tenant situations."[110] Simultaneously, however, tenants joined yeoman farmers and large landowners in the Farmers' Alliance, a complex and often contradictory association that defended agricultural interests against the power of the railroads and other industrial groups.

If a peasant does begin to look for work off the farm, the job he gets depends chiefly on the vagaries of the labor market. Often an industrial firm in search of unskilled workers will recruit peasants, paying their transportation costs; or, as we have seen, it may locate a subsidiary close to a village of potential peasant workers. In either case, friendship (however casual) and kinship (however distant or fictive) soon replace more formal recruiting methods: Peasants looking for work simply ask an acquaintance, friend, or relative with a factory job to find another in the same plant.[111] Jewish immigrants to North America from one town or village in Eastern Europe formed *landsmanschaftn*; Italians looked to their *paesani*, Russian serfs to their *zemliacki*. For Slavic immigrants working the anthracite coal fields of eastern Pennsylvania around 1900 it was a social obligation to report home on local conditions. Their friends in Europe treated these letters as community property; and by doing so they assured that, regardless of a young man's preferences or capacities, he wound up following the choices of the first from his area to leave home.[112]

But instead of going into factory work, a peasant located in a region full of artisans' shops can become a craftsman. To keep his equipment and buildings in repair, every small peasant must become a jack-of-all-trades. Machine-tool manufacturers desperate for workers with a feel for machinery, no less than the metalworking shops of little construction firms, may therefore find it convenient to hire peasant workers full or part time, giving them a chance to develop their skills and become familiar with the operations of a small business. If farm work or the burden of two jobs becomes oppressive, a peasant worker concentrates more and more of his energies on the craft job; eventually he may sell his land or become a weekend gardener and try to succeed as an artisan.

It has been argued that the peasant worker's choice of job is influenced not only by the availability of work, but also by the way his character was formed on the farm. For example, in a study of Italian artisans in the Adriatic province of the Marche, Massimo Paci showed that sharecropping taught the peasants to husband resources as efficiently as any businessman. An agrarian reform program made it possible for many of the sharecroppers to become small independent farmers. As a shortage of capital took its toll of the new small farmers, they passed to artisanal work, where skilled hands and a well-practiced business sense contributed to their success.[113]

Extensive comparative research may eventually establish some such connection as a general rule. But for the moment, these arguments seem inconclusive attributions of broad significance to what may be details of particular cases. Certainly all sharecropping systems do not produce firms of the type Paci describes; nor are all firms of that type born in the disintegration of sharecropping agriculture. There are examples of sharecropping systems that produced few artisans (as in the American South); and when I visited the small workshops in the areas Paci studied it was easy to find ones founded by the descendants of day laborers and skilled workers, not sharecroppers.[114] For now, it is prudent to assume that many forms of family farming – in which "every meal is a conference on production"[115] – create a psychological matrix that enables peasants to move into almost any activity requiring diligence and calculation. Luck decides which of the available jobs they end up with, as John Waterbury found in his study of the migration of a Berber tribe from the Anti-Atlas to jobs in petty commerce in northern Morocco:

The existential reality of the poverty of their homeland, mediated and intensified by introverted conflicts and struggles for local status and prestige, pushed the Swasa to the north. The commercial savvy of the pioneers . . . did not create their initial success, but rather the fact that they happened to be the right people at the right time. Other Moroccans could just as easily have made the move into commerce . . . And even then a number of Soussi [singular of Swasa] tribes, differing in no significant way from the core tribes, migrated as miners and factory workers. There is nothing magic about commerce; the people of the Ammiln could as easily be working in the Renault plants in France as in the grocery stores of Casablanca.[116]

By contrast, for youngsters who grow up thinking of themselves as part of industrial society, differences in family structure and social position do bear in important ways on the choice of job. These differences operate by coloring the young person's understanding of life and, through that, his view of the educational and career opportunities equally available, at least in theory, to all full members of advanced industrial societies. These differences help account for the paradox that the religion of social mobility and self-improvement preached by these societies is often – though far from always – regarded as mumbo jumbo by those to whom it is addressed.

The way in which family structure affects interpretations of modern youth culture illustrates the connection between social position and understanding of life. At one level, urban youth in the industrialized countries listen to the same music, wear the same clothes, go to the same movies, and take the same drugs. This common culture exalts adventure, love, fantasy, rebellion, action, and tenderhearted toughness. Perhaps its dominant theme is youth's struggle to find its own way in life against the oppressive interference of parents. Because all parents are at least sometimes oppressive, young people regardless of country or class share a common problem and a language to discuss it. During moments of national or international crisis this sense of unity can take on a political coloration as well, the struggle of youth becoming the battle of progress against reaction as well.

But on another level, the young are divided. At one extreme are those who think that adventure, action, and toughness – tender-hearted or not – are the last word about life, its whole meaning. At the other extreme is the idea, summarized in the German notion of *Bildung,* that adventure, fantasy, and rebellion activate and are acti-vated by learning, self-discipline, and technical accomplishment. Each interpretation is linked to the attitudes of a particular social group, and each shapes the attitudes of that group's children toward education and careers at work. Except in extraordinary periods such as the Vietnam War, when the line between generations is more of a barrier than that between social groups, youth culture means differ-ent things to different people.[117]

The idea of life as a tough game of action and adventure is asso-ciated most clearly with urban street gangs; and these in turn are typically a central part of the lives of the children of peasant workers, would-be craftsmen, or ghetto workers: in other words, the children of migrants to the city who have not yet climbed high up the skill hierarchy.

To understand the link between what William F. Whyte, Jr., called "street corner society," a particular view of life, and social position, consider the paradigmatic case of the young son of a peasant worker growing up in a large city with no hope of returning to his father's country. A youth in this situation lives in a no-man's-land between enemy worlds. He is cut off from his father, who, compared with native-born men his age, seems socially incompetent, tongue-tied, long-suffering – a patsy who can't speak right. But he is also cut off from the children of more-established families, to whom he seems shabby and almost foreign, a funny imitation of a normal adoles-cent. The only people who understand him are people like himself, youths whose family life cuts them off from instead of connecting them to the larger society. His society is the street gang, where social place is defined by cunning and toughness because these are the only standards of success. Isolated, misunderstood, oppressed, involuntarily self-reliant, without a future but full of life's energy, he is prone to interpret the youth culture as a description of what life is, and for lack of other models, he models himself on the heroes of this version of the youth culture.[118]

The interpretation of the youth culture as *Bildung* is associated with the children of the professional and intellectual middle classes. These families are often wealthy enough, the parents often so sincerely dedicated to intellectual pursuits or so ashamed of their betrayal of them that the children are encouraged for a time to think that the main business of life is self-exploration. The implicit argument in these circles is that youthful rebelliousness is a necessary step toward the higher end of blending fantasy and rigor: Acid is a trip, but so are Bach and computers.

In a large, urban American high school like the one I attended, for example, these interpretations and social groups form two opposed poles of attraction. Students are pulled toward one or the other according to their family's proximity to one of the two polar social groups, but also according to the particulars of their character: scholastic aptitude, self-confidence, relations with parents and siblings, and so on. There is therefore always a chance to change sides: The bookish son of unskilled workers becomes friends with the intellectuals' children; the black sheep from good families pal around with tough kids. The more homogeneous the social milieu, of course, the less likely the two positions are to be openly juxtaposed; but as both are exemplified at a given moment in particular variants of the youth culture – Hell's Angels and Ken Kesey's acid test in my generation in the United States – almost no one is too isolated to catch wind of the alternatives if he looks.

Furthermore, there are hybrid positions, also rooted in the work experience of certain kinds of families, that mute some of the tension between them and facilitate passage from one to another. An example, typical of craftsmen's families, is the idea that life is *first* about adventure, *then* about discipline and responsibility. The connections between the two epochs are certain activities that require both derring-do and technical prowess – for instance, hot rodding.

These understandings of life affect the young person's choice of work in two ways. First, the interpretations influence behavior at school, and school experience has an important influence on the choice of job. Teachers present themselves as representatives of the adult world. Tough kids at war with the world will be at war with teachers as well; and beleaguered teachers are not likely to help such youths overcome feelings of frustration and incompetence. Adolescents who think they still have things to learn will maintain a residual respect from their teachers that survives all ridicule; and the teachers will encourage even the weakest of such students, if only to demonstrate the triumph of good intention and pedagogic skill over native mediocrity.

These differing interpretations of the world also anticipate and help form different expectations about work: Young people are likely to expect jobs to permit or encourage the sort of behavior implicit in their interpretations of youth culture. Adolescents in gangs will want to roughhouse on the job, and this attitude directs them toward the kinds of jobs reserved for ghetto workers; those who want to develop their talents look for skilled work or go to college.

Paul Willis analyzes these connections in his study of a group of tough kids in Hammertown Boys, a nonselective secondary school with about six hundred students in an overwhelmingly blue-collar region of the English Midlands. From these youths' point of view, the school is divided between themselves – the nonconformist "lads" – and the conformist "ear'oles": Lads see through the sham of school to the rough essentials of life; ear'oles, as their name suggests, are the almost obscenely passive receptors of official claptrap. There is only a rough fit between parents' social position and attitudes toward school and work and their childrens'. Some "respectable" parents who support the school in every way have children "who inexplicably, to them, 'go wrong' and join 'the lads.' " Other parents, typically unskilled workers "indifferent or even hostile to the school," may wind up with ear'ole children, sometimes to their displeasure.[119]

But there is a close fit between the students' attitudes toward life and school and their ideas about work. The lads see life as a running battle between themselves and those in authority. They want adventure, sex, violence; they want to show off their masculine savoir faire whenever possible, because their dignity depends on being able to do just that. The authorities, with the more or less tacit collaboration of the ear'oles, try to stop them, thereby giving the lads an additional chance to impress each other by flouting rules. Work has got to permit the same display of prowess. It has to be a place where a lad can be

open about his desires, his sexual feelings, his liking for "booze" and his aim to "skive off" as much as is reasonably possible. It has to be a place where people can be trusted and will not "creep off" to tell the boss about "foreigners" or "nicking stuff" – in effect where there are the fewest "ear'oles." Indeed it would have to be work where there was a boss, a "them and us" situation, which always carried with it the danger of treacherous intermediaries. The future work situation has to have an essentially masculine ethos. It has to be a situation where you can speak up for yourself, and where you would not be expected to be subservient. The principal visible criterion is that the particular job must pay good money quickly and offer the possibility of "fiddles" and "perks" to support already acquired smoking and drinking habits and to nourish the sense of being "on the inside track," of knowing "how things really work."[120]

Work is supposed to be physically demanding; workplace relations with superiors should be aggressive and those with workmates fraternal. Only a real man can muster the combination of physical stamina, loyalty, and independence required. No one but a comedian, one of the lads remarks, is expected to like his job.[121] In this sense the lads actually want the unskilled manual jobs they get after leaving school.

From the ear'oles' perspective, school is training for work and both are stages in a lifelong process of personal development. As we saw, this attitude is typical of skilled workers, and this is precisely what many of them become. As Nigel, an ear'ole, put it:

I expect it to follow on really, you know, if you enjoy things all your life, just keep on getting on, but if you don't enjoy school, you don't intend to work. I think it just follows on into work, you won't do enough (. . .) [work] is like going to school, after you've left school, say, like I'm goin' to get an apprenticeship, you've got your apprenticeship, you'm qualified, just get, just keep on learning for the rest of your life, that' what I think.[122]

Careers at work are not, of course, determined finally by attitudes toward school or initial experiences on the job. Apprentices can fall back into the ranks of the unskilled; unskilled workers, discovering that they want more out of life than the thrills of street-corner society, may mature into would-be craftsmen, anxious for promotion, eager to learn a trade. They may sometimes succeed, especially if the industrial system, like that in the United States, allows workers to pass from the shop floor to apprenticeship programs. But too often they are already so burdened by family and debt that they cannot find the time to finish the training they once scorned: "Ironically," Willis writes, "as the shopfloor becomes a prison, education is seen retrospectively, and hopelessly, as the only escape."[123]

The closer one is to the bottom of the social heap, the more life is a desperate gamble. For the son of an unskilled worker or an agricultural day laborer, a casual friendship at school can mean a lifetime at a miserable job. The children of the rich have it better. Just as power and wealth make it possible for a national elite to recover from the collective bad guesses of the powerful, wealth and social position enable middle- and upper-class families to repair the botches of their children. The return to the fold of many of the protesters and dropouts of the late 1960s and early 1970s confirms once again that the children of the well-to-do can do almost anything for a time without losing the social places reserved for them.

But good or bad, revocable or not, our solitary choices do not leave us alone. Because there is a structure to the economy and a pattern to individual choices, no matter how we choose, each of us winds up in a boat full of others who have made the same choices. Groups can often have their way in situations in which individuals are powerless. There is therefore always the possibility that persons whose expectations of life have been similarly thwarted by the labor-market choices they made can collectively fight for what they originally wanted. The rest of this book is concerned with the ways such struggles can change the pattern of group expectations and transform the structure of the economy.

4

Interests, conflicts, classes

Conflict between labor and capital pervades contemporary life. Workers struggle to raise their real wages, to protect their jobs, to improve their working conditions, or to get promoted. Most of these struggles are so restricted that they do not come to public attention: The 110,665 grievances entered against management by 89,625 unionized workers in eighteen plants of the General Motors assembly division in 1979 are an example.[1] A few, such as wage settlements in inflationary periods, become matters of public debate. Still more rarely, workers' protests shake governments and states: for example, the *autunno caldo* in Italy and May 1968 in France.

Most explanations of such conflicts draw, deliberately or not, on one of two classic positions in a long-standing debate within social theory. On one side are the moralists. They claim that collective conflict is set off when a group defends an established moral order from outside attack and that it is thus fundamentally conservative or restorative. Their favorite example is the peasant village struggling to defend its tradition against rapacious aristocrats or capitalists. On the other side are the economists.[2] Their claim is that conflict arises from the self-interested pursuit of wealth. For the economist, conflicts are reformative to the extent that they merely redistribute shares of the economic surplus, and revolutionary insofar as they fundamentally change the distribution of rights to the proceeds of economic activity. The economist's examples are industrial workers on strike, peasants seizing a latifundium, or impoverished proletariats expropriating capitalist factories.[3] The view of conflict developed here differs from both these positions, though it is more easily confused with the moralists' position than with the economists'. Its distinctive features will be easier to grasp once the limitations of both sides in the classic debate are brought to mind.

Collective conflicts: restorative or revolutionary?

The preceding chapter suggested the decisive reason for rejecting the unqualified version of the economists' claim. If everyone wanted the same things, it would be easy to understand what it meant to pursue one's economic interest. But as Chapter 3 showed, even within a group as apparently homogeneous as blue-collar workers there are disparate images of social success. These images define and limit ambition; without them, Emile Durkheim argued, we would go mad from infinite, insatiable desires.[4]

To these limits on ambition there correspond limits on the use of the available possibilities for economic activity. How and to what extent we exploit market opportunities depends on our socially acquired ideas of success: Economic activity must be guided by moral ends, and moral ends influence economic means. Recall how the upgraded craftsman's idea of a career at work checked his willingness to compete for jobs against middle-class engineers. Or think of what some historians call the treason of the bourgeoisie: the failure of social groups that in some way resemble the elites of modern capitalist countries to use their economic and political power as these elites would supposedly have done in their place.[5] Thus economically aggressive, upstart social classes like the Equestrian Order in Rome, the merchants of medieval London, or the bourgeois jurists of eighteenth-century France and Prussia battled their way into the established elite.[6] Once there, they were only too willing to turn their backs on the scramble for wealth in favor of the aristocratic pursuits of war, politics, and gentlemanly leisure. Thorstein Veblen and John Maynard Keynes detected similar inclinations in the modern bourgeoisie.[7] Successful assault on the old order can turn the assailants into its defenders: The pursuit of individual interest is as likely to lead to restoration as to revolution.

The moralists' view of collective conflict, on the other hand, has the advantage of placing ideas of social honor at the center of analysis. But the moralists characterize these ideas as more precise and rigid than they are. They ignore the indeterminacy of moral codes and the way conflict can catalyze this indeterminacy, opening the way to radical reinterpretation of what the group is and what it wants. They argue, therefore, that action in the name of these ideas is more backward-looking and defensive than it turns out to be, and they overlook the ways in which the pursuit even of moral claims perceived as traditional can alter the status quo rather than reinforce it.

Take first the incompleteness and ambiguity of any world view.

The moralists conceive of moral ideas as a seamless web, explaining and justifying every aspect of a group's world – hence their romantic visions of past communities in which each was content in his place. But no set of rules can ever anticipate all the world's contingencies. Situations frequently turn up to which the moral code applies equivocally. Even when it generally condones the exercise of power by landlords over tenants or managers over workers, for example, a moral code does not sanctify every application of that power. Only the rarest of cases is so clear-cut as to exclude arguments about extenuating circumstance.

The result is that in social life there is more room for debate over the meaning of moral ideas, and accordingly more jockeying for social position, than the moralists allow. Even in societies where the fit between moral code and social reality is the tightest and social place the most clearly defined, groups exploit gaps in the moral law to realize their ideas of an honorable life. Even in medieval Western Europe there were often violent conflicts between lords and peasants over the terms of leases. "Agrarian revolt," Marc Bloch writes, "is as natural to seigneurial regimes as strikes, let us say, are to large-scale capitalism."[8] Or take as a more modern example of the plasticity of an apparently rigid society the successes of the Viet Minh agitators in the backward areas of Vietnam: The peasants were often willing to experiment with new ways of pooling labor that reduced their dependence on landlords but respected the core values of rural society.[9]

These arguments about peasant communities apply *a fortiori* to industrial society, where social roles are less sharply defined and are often in conflict, and where the background conditions to the moral order can shift rapidly. Thus a worker who is treated like a consumer king when he buys a television is likely to be more sensitive to a foreman's bark than a peasant will be to the authority of a lord with whom he never trades places. And a peasant worker new in a factory is likely to be more perplexed about the value of a fair day's work than a peasant working his forefathers' land.

In most cases, of course, disputes about the detailed application of a moral code remain just that: arguments over details that do not immediately call into question either the fundamental identity of the disputants or the relation between them. Nonetheless, even such routine jockeying for place as the irreducible ambiguity of the moral order encourages can open the door to long-term transformations of group interests.

For one thing, successive incremental extensions of a group's original claims can, if successful, lead to a shift in the balance of power between contestants, and ultimately to a reformulation of the initial claim itself. A classic example is the struggle of the English peasantry against feudal dues. Beginning in the fourteenth century, the serfs took advantage of a labor shortage, caused principally by the plague, to drive progressively better bargains with the lords. First they forced a reduction of their obligations as serfs, converting labor service and rents in kind owed to the lord to money rents. Then they used the power secured by these first victories to insist on an end to serfdom, thereby redefining not only the particulars of their relation to the lords, but the fundamental character of this relation.[10]

A parallel example from industrial society concerns disputes over work rules. Whenever a new machine is introduced there is the question who should operate it, how, and at what rate of pay. Arguing by analogy to existing practices, and backing up its arguments with the willingness to strike, a work group can sometimes establish its claim to operate successive generations of machinery, each time slightly extending the range of its control over the equipment and raising its share of the savings in production costs made possible by the new methods. The more various the machines it presently operates, the more likely it will be to find some analogy between those machines and the ones introduced in the future. The more complex and valuable the future machines are, in comparison with the present ones, the more workers deserve to be paid to operate and safeguard them. Even though the workers may not at first change their ideas about the limited nature of their claims, we will see that the cumulative effect of their successes is to give them a kind of de facto control over the details and proceeds of the reorganization of production – hence over the future of the firm – which they did not have before. Challenges to that control can then drive debate about its nature and justification into the open, forcing the workers to examine the bases of their original claims.

The second transformative effect of conflict goes to the way long-standing definitions of interests can be recast by creation of alliances to pursue them. Even the straightforward defense of a group's clearly vested right frequently requires alliances with other groups judged to have related or compatible interests. These alliances in turn depend on an exchange of pledges, each group undertaking for the sake of the other to make sacrifices in defense of claims against third parties that it might not otherwise have raised. In addition, the allied groups must find ways to reconcile and compose the conflicts of interest that arise between them.

If the alliance endures, this double process of joint defense and mutual conciliation blurs and fuses the originally distinct interests of the two groups. In Wilhelmian Germany, for example, landed and industrial interests merged, to form a group united against the working class; Junker landowners accepted the necessity of industrialization, and the industrialists accepted the costs of political protection of the Junkers' rights. The enduring experience of alliance, which at first may seem no more than a matter of convenience, thus eventually leaves its mark on each group's interpretations of its claims, influencing successive demands and restricting the future choice of additional allies. And, of course, to the extent that this happens, the original defense of an interest can be said to contribute to its redefinition: Through the 1860s the German bourgeoisie had liberal, democratic leanings; by the end of the century, it was monarchist.[11]

The third transformative effect of collective conflict is the reforging of ideas in the intense heat of battle. Readers of modern social science can easily forget how violent, passionate, and unpredictable conflicts – from strikes to revolutions – can be. It is true that the initial distribution of power and interests between contestants sets broad limits on the possible outcomes of a struggle. But given those limits, the ultimate result depends on the contestants' tactical skill and programmatic boldness, as well as on the web of human sympathy or mistrust that binds or separates allies on both sides. This necessity to maneuver makes possible the transformation of interests in the midst of conflict.

Thus, to win new allies or to redouble the efforts of old ones, a group can boldly or desperately increase its customary demands in the heat of battle, stretching old claims far beyond previous limits. The French, American, and Mexican revolutions are full of this kind of trumping and overtrumping. Strikes, we shall see, can set in motion an analogous process. Successful or not, these demands enlarge the scope of debate over what constitutes a legitimate demand and contribute to the long-term transformation of a group's original self-conception.[12]

The upshot is that a group does not necessarily conserve its conception of social honor by defending it. Rather, it may gradually revise its claims by applying them to new circumstances, amalgamating them with those of an ally, or radically extending them in the enthusiasm or desperation of battle. In any event, the ultimate definition of a group's interests cannot simply be deduced from a description of its initial character.

Each of the following discussions of collective conflicts involving a particular work group is, therefore, in two parts. One sets out the ways a group's idea of a career at work leads it to define and defend itself against violations of its rights; the second analyzes the various forms these general strategies can assume, depending on particular economic and social circumstances. The aim is not to present an exhaustive catalog of types of conflict behavior and their associated background conditions, but rather to give a sense of how workers, like the rest of us, can change themselves and the world by defending their interpretation of it.

Revolt against the factory: the struggles of the peasant worker

The peasant worker lives on the margin of the factory world. His ambition is to leave it altogether. His ideas of dignity are certainly no less distinct than those of other workers; but his dealings with more settled workmates are so limited, his ambitions so distant from theirs, that his struggles are more likely to exaggerate than reconcile the differences between them.

In taking a factory job, the peasant worker agrees to do an honest day's work for an honest day's pay, both conventionally defined. So long as he can earn what he needs through hard work, he complies with management's demands and ignores his fellow workers. So long as his expectations are met, therefore, the peasant worker is indifferent to disputes involving other work groups. In the shop studied by Bernoux, for example, the peasant workers would not support a strike planned by the would-be craftsmen in protest against a new foreman's attempt to tighten discipline.[13] A more extreme example comes from Danielle Kergoat's study of immigrant Portuguese working at Bulledor, a factory in the Paris area that produces and bottles mineral water and other beverages. Kergoat reports that, of those immigrants who wanted eventually to return to Portugal, where they had farms and families, fully half left France during the strike of May 1968 to avoid a conflict they regarded as irrelevant.[14]

But suppose that, after he becomes dependent on an industrial income for the maintenance of his social place, the peasant worker finds that the wage for a hard day's work does not cover the difference between his expenses and his other income. The shortfall may result from an increase in the cost of living, a drop in the return from his family's agricultural labor, a devaluation of the currency in which he is paid (which reduces the value of his remittances home), or an intensification of work (which disrupts the established relation between effort and wage). Or suppose that his employer directly affronts his dignity, for example, by dallying about fixing a factory door in winter, leaving the worker to stand in a draft as though he deserved less consideration than he would give animals in a stall, or by commanding youngsters fresh out of school in tones middle-class teachers reserve for delinquents.

At first a group of peasant workers may tolerate what it understands to be breaches of the contract by the employer. But if abuse continues the group reaches an unspoken consensus to suffer no more. The peasant workers are then likely to explode in rage at the slightest additional provocation, belying in an instant their reputation for docility. Unskilled Turks at the Ford plant in Cologne, for example, suddenly stopped work in 1973 in sympathy with a worker who loudly disputed a foreman's order to take on extra work. The incident had been preceded by conflict over wages (held down by the Social Democratic government's incomes policy) and over rights to unpaid leave (of special importance to Turkish immigrants, who spend half their official vacation traveling to and from Anatolia).[15] Similarly, Senegalese, North African, and Portuguese immigrants working at unskilled assembly-line and machine-tending jobs at the Renault factory in Flins spontaneously stopped work in 1973 when a rumor circulated about a fight between a Frenchman and an immigrant. In the background of that strike was the immigrants' anger over devaluation of the franc and complaints about unlivable, expensive housing.[16]

One dominant feature of such conflicts is the contrast they present between the solidarity, combativeness, and determination of the peasant workers, on the one hand, and the absence of any but vague demands for decent treatment and a fair wage on the other. Like eighteenth-century riots against high bread prices, they are protests, outbursts of anger against particular infractions of conventional practice. The object of the anger is clearly enough defined, but the protest itself is not conceived as part of an officially sanctioned negotiating procedure, still less as part of a larger program of reform, as is usually the case with industrial strikes. Implicitly, the demand is for a fair day's pay for a fair day's work – part of the larger web of related ideas of just exchange that E. P. Thompson calls the "moral economy of the poor."[17] It is a potentially far-reaching attack on the meritocratic principle used to justify the wage hierarchy in industrial firms the world over: that pay should be proportional not to the amount of a worker's effort but to its value.[18] Explicitly, and because they are out to escape the factory, not reform it, striking peasant workers rarely derive more from general principle than the demand for egalitarian wages.

Thus the Renault workers formulated no demands at all until two days after the strike began, when they adopted a suggestion from a

French Maoist to call for a flat pay increase for the most poorly paid workers.[19] At the Ford plant the Turks had no clear demands of their own at the beginning of the strike. Eventually, in collaboration with a German worker, they settled on the idea of a one-mark-an-hour increase for all workers.[20]

The second dominant feature of such strikes is that they isolate peasant workers from other work groups. Other workers are often shocked and nonplussed by what they take to be the assertiveness and exclusiveness of a community whose cohesion and extent suddenly become visible. This is especially the case when the peasant workers are in fact workers with rural roots. Communities of such workers, as we have seen, are generally composed of networks of friends and relatives originally from the same territory. The *paesani* and *zemliacki* pool information about jobs, care for new arrivals, and prop up anyone down on his luck. All of this activity goes on out of sight of more established work groups; but once a strike begins, these informal organizations of peasant workers take charge of picket lines and protest marches, guaranteeing complete participation by all members of the community and keeping strikebreakers from other work groups out of the plant: During the strike at Ford, for instance, each gate was controlled by a group of immigrants from a different town in Turkey.[21] Often the immigrants' style of struggle – dancing and fetes in an occupied factory, the participation of wives on picket lines – owes more to traditions of agrarian than of industrial conflict.

Similarly, settled work groups may be confused or antagonized by the peasant workers' willingness to mingle grievances against landlords or local authorities with grievances against employers. As political activists who try to organize them discover, migrants see life inside and outside the plant as a single whole, whereas other work groups normally accept as a precondition to bargaining that management is answerable only for what goes on in the plant.[22]

Finally, egalitarian demands oppose the peasant worker community to workers who define themselves by their place in the wage hierarchy: by what they contribute to production, rather than by the fact that they work hard. Established unions, often out of touch with the new workers and suspicious of their violations of piece-rate norms and their fragile attachment to the factory, are likely to resent both the challenge to their control of the shop floor and the repudiation of a hierarchy they have helped to negotiate. Thus, at the very moment in which the more-established work groups and their representatives see how well organized the peasant workers are, they discover how belligerent and threateningly different they can be.

During the immigrants' work stoppage at Renault, for example, only a few activists of the Confédération Française Démocratique du Travail (CFDT) understood the deep sources of the strikers' despair: During the strike the CFDT showed them *Viva Zapata,* a movie that presents the Mexican Revolution as a peasant uprising.[23] The Communist trade union, the Confédération Général du Travail (CGT), oscillated between restraining immigrants' militancy and encouraging it as a means of securing one of its own ends: a regular system of promotion from unskilled laborer to technician.[24] With two exceptions the reaction of the other work groups on the shop floor was even more reserved. The attitude of the skilled workers was, "You fight for yourselves; afterward, it will be our turn. Everyone in his own corner." There was general talk of a *mouvement des sauvages.*[25] At Ford in Cologne many of the German workers at all skill levels, as well as the union, the Internationale Gewerkschaft Metall (IGM), were openly hostile to the Turks' strike and cooperated with management to break it by force.[26]

Just as those work groups that in some sense embrace the factory hierarchy are antagonized by the factory workers' militancy, groups that themselves repudiate the hierarchy see this militancy as an expression of their own resentments. Of the two exceptional groups that sympathized with the strikers at Renault, for example, one was itself made up of a type of peasant worker, as ill at ease in the factory as the foreign immigrants: young, unskilled Frenchmen, just out of school. They felt like the recruits in the French joke who "raise their hands when the master sergeant asks who speaks German – and are told to clean the latrines. There are hundreds of them who learned at school to look down on unskilled labor, and who then wind up as unskilled workers without a professional future."[27] The other group was a clique of older, unskilled French Communists without hope or possibility of promotion: For them every position in a capitalist factory is as honorable or demeaning as any other. But despite their general sympathies for the protest, both groups were so cut off from each other, from the mass of the French workers, and from the day-to-day life of the immigrants that no alliance was born of the enthusiasm for the strikers' courage.[28]

Successful or not, strikes by peasant workers thus usually remain episodes, isolated from the rest of the life of the factory and further isolating the peasant workers themselves from other workers. Still, those outbursts have two side effects that produce long-term consequences more important than the immediate results of the conflicts. First, they alert fellow workers that peasant workers are not as docile as they appear – that they may be allies in a future fight. Second, they bring some few peasant workers into contact with the outside society in the person of a union militant, a sympathetic native worker, or a representative of management. Typically, younger peasant workers, tempted by the idea of remaining in the factory and more open to the language and customs of the new society than their elders, are drawn to such relations: Think of them as peasant workers becoming would-be craftsmen. To the extent that some of these contacts endure, they can shape the course of later conflict. For the more uncertain the peasant community as a whole becomes about its chances of returning to some work outside the factory, the more dependent it becomes, for advice on how to behave inside, on those peasant workers who already have one foot in the surrounding society. These mediators' previous political experience influences the kind of advice they give. The next section sets out the choices they face.

Between the powerful and the weak: the dilemma of the would-be craftsman

Though the would-be craftsman is sure that he wants a decent place in the factory, he is not automatically sure how to get it. His is the classic dilemma of those caught between the powerful and the weak: to curry favor with those higher up and turn one's back on the other unskilled workers, or to lead the latter in protest against the former. Either course is dangerous: Superiors may not reward deference and betrayal; the unskilled may be defeated in their struggles for better, more secure jobs. Alternatively, either course might succeed; and so the would-be craftsman is left to wonder how he wants to advance in the world. This section briefly outlines some of the factors that bear on his choices.

At one pole are situations in which there are clearly marked paths leading to craft jobs, and the number of candidates for promotion is small relative to the number of unskilled peasant workers intent on leaving the factory as soon as possible. In that case the would-be craftsmen take pains to distinguish themselves from the other unskilled workers and to establish their community with the skilled at every turn.

Under these circumstances, conflicts are opportunities for would-be craftsmen to demonstrate their knowledge of the dos and don'ts of industrial etiquette as much as a chance for them to make a claim to the craft status. To the extent that demands of this sort are fulfilled, of course, the would-be craftsman comes to be treated like a craftsman *tout court*. So whereas conflict separates the peasant worker from the factory routines, it ties this kind of worker more securely to them.

During the strike at the Renault plant in Flins, for example, one group of immigrants did not participate in the strike: the young Portuguese, intent on becoming part of French society, who had established themselves with their families in government-subsidized housing. This group was also marginally more skilled than the other immigrants, presumably a first result of its ambition for a career in the factory. The group abstained from the strike, however, not because it was unwilling to risk its privileges, but rather because it had its own ideas of what demands were worth fighting for. A month before the peasant workers walked out, the Portuguese immigrants joined the French workers of their skill level in a strike for a more favorable job classification.[29]

Bernoux's study provides a second example of the would-be craftsmen's compulsion to phrase their demands in the officially recognized language of the shop. Recall the incident of the plans, dropped for want of the peasant workers' support, to protest tighter discipline. Instead of justifying their protest as a self-explanatory response to injustice, as peasant workers might have done, the would-be craftsmen tried to assimilate their grievances to demands that the union recognized as legitimate: a premium for assembly-line work and a pay raise. When the shop steward refused to support the idea, the would-be craftsmen were thrown into confusion. On the one hand, they wanted to defend their autonomy on the job; on the other, they insisted on doing so in a way that connected their complaints to the broader concerns of the rest of the workers, whose esteem they valued. "You, you're the delegate," one worker said to the union steward. "O.K., it's up to you to find the demands to make to management. Us, we don't know how to say it to them, but we have had it working with that pig of a foreman."[30]

Now consider the opposite case: that in which chances for steady work or promotion to skilled jobs are negligible in relation to the number of applicants, and most of the unskilled are would-be craftsmen in search of more dignified work. In this case, the would-be craftsmen may try to fight for a change in their collective status, say by winning some guarantee of job security, or by the creation of promotion ladders. The greater the chance of using general political considerations as a means of putting pressure on employers outside the factory, the more likely they are to take the risk of a struggle. Collective conflict under these conditions could thus become a means of changing the factory hierarchy rather than affirming and reinforcing the would-be craftsman's allegiance to it.

The unionization of the American automobile industry in the 1930s illustrates this possibility. Since before World War I, the industry had relied on various groups of peasant workers, employing farm hands from the rural counties near Detroit, blacks from southern farms, Appalachian migrants from the coal fields, and successive generations of Slavic immigrants. Hourly wages were high for manufacturing industry.

Employment, however, was extremely unsteady because of periodic slumps and because annual model changes required closing the plant for at least two weeks and perhaps several months in a year. In a good year a worker might be employed for forty-six weeks. But over a period of years he might find himself in the position of one Archie King, whose work history is recorded only because he became a party in a dispute before an administrative agency: In the 1920s King was laid off five times from the same Fisher Body plant in Cleveland in less than seven years, during which time he was unemployed for roughly twenty-five months and worked roughly fifty. Frequently workers were rehired at lower rates after layoffs, and older workers had no guarantee that they would be rehired at all.[31] Craft jobs were under the control of workers of English, Scottish, Irish, or German origin who were willing neither to open their unions to the unskilled nor to let the latter organize themselves independently.[32]

This system was durable so long as there were alternative employment opportunities for the peasant workers and a large majority of them were uninterested in an industrial career. But by the 1930s many of the unskilled were would-be craftsmen, not peasant workers. Some of the southern blacks and Appalachian migrants who had come north during and after World War I, for example, had settled permanently in the industrial cities.[33] Similarly, the legislation that put an end to mass immigration from Eastern Europe in 1924 cut the Slavic immigrants off from their home communities, convincing the immigrants' children, as we will see in a moment, that their only future was in the American factories.

When the depression created mass unemployment in industry, therefore, many of these workers did not try to retreat permanently to agricultural or artisanal work, difficult as that would have been. If they could, they went back home to "live off Mom and Dad and off the land"[34] when they were laid off. But those who left rejoined those who stayed; and together they fought to preserve their jobs, sweeping aside the craftsmen's objections to an independent union and organizing the United Automobile Workers (UAW) to press their claims.

Accordingly, the UAW's principal national demand concerned job security. The leaders of the automobile-workers organizing campaign wanted to negotiate an annual wage to "provide a standard of health, decency and comfort."[35] What they got was a seniority system which assured that older workers would be the last fired during layoffs and the first rehired afterward. The union forced employers to pay high supplements for overtime work in the hope that they would be required to hire new workers. In some cases, the union required that new workers meet a residency requirement, thereby discouraging further immigration.[36] Everywhere these demands were intertwined with the aim of limiting both the power of overbearing foremen in the plants and that of the automobile firms in the affairs of company towns.[37]

Peter Friedlander's study of the unionization of a Ford plant in Hamtramck, Michigan, clearly demonstrates the role of would-be craftsmen in the formation of the UAW. The union's most determined advocates in the plant were second-generation Polish welders with families to support. All had left the world of street-corner gangs behind. They had worked their way up from unskilled jobs to become the elite of the production workers, partly out of a sense of responsibility to their families, partly out of pride in their talents. But they had little chance of learning any of the skilled metalworking trades dominated by the Irish- and German-American craftsmen. For these welders, the creation of the union was thus a means both of defending their jobs and of challenging the craftsmen's moral authority over the plant: To do one, they had to do the other. For instance, to eliminate the craftsmen as a source of opposition to the new union, semi- and unskilled activists were encouraged to apply for places in the company apprenticeship program, and as their leader recalled, they "colonized" the tool room.[38]

The view that would-be craftsmen were at the center of the organizing drive is confirmed as much by those who did not support the union wholeheartedly as by those who did. Older, first-generation Slavs, for example, did not become union activists. Many of them were peasant workers in the strict sense: They were of peasant origin. They seem to have arrived in the United States with no fixed idea of remaining. Almost none had become interested in either American life or the prospect of a factory career. They remained spectators throughout the entire period. As long as the union seemed to have little chance of succeeding, they were cowed by management. Once the union's prospects improved, they showed a certain confused sympathy for it, but no more.[39]

Nor did all the second-generation Slavs fit the picture just described. Some remained caught in the street-corner society described in the last chapter, suspended between the world of the peasant worker and the world of the would-be craftsman, with neither families nor skill. They supported the union out of loyalty to their kind and out of a spirit of adventure. But they were often more enthusiastic about the fights unionization provoked than about the politics of the union. For them the union seemed "something of a bigger and better gang."[40]

A similar picture of this kind of would-be craftsman emerges from Kergoat's studies of strikes in the late 1960s and early 1970s by immigrants at Bulledor and young unskilled French workers at the SAVIEM truck factory near Caen. At Bulledor, she reports, Portuguese immigrants determined to remain in France were the most active supporters of the strike. Some of these were political refugees from the Salazar regime who thought they could never return to Portugal; others were young men who refused to fight in the colonial war in Angola. They were interested in learning French and acquiring skills. Eventually, they hoped for better jobs than any they were likely to get at Bulledor. For the moment they were particularly concerned with stability of employment: During the slack winter months the work force was reduced from 250 to 180. Immigrants – hired on three-month contracts – had only the personnel director's word that they would be rehired after a layoff. For immigrants with wives, children, and plots of land in Portugal, the winter was a good time to return home. For the others, a winter layoff was a threat to their livelihood. The workers intending to stay in France were also especially sensitive to insults to their dignity, particularly to any measure that seemed to draw a distinction between themselves, the production workers, and the French craftsmen and white-collar workers. A sign of their touchiness was their familiarity with all their formal rights and their insistence that those be respected. "The Portuguese who get into French life," one supervisor complained, "are not easy to order around. The others think only of money." These workers looked to the unions to defend their interests and their pride; and they looked on the strike as a way of insisting on decent treatment, as well as a way of extending other contacts with French workers.[41] Similarly, at SAVIEM the most combative workers were of working-class origin and convinced that they were unlikely to leave the plant or to be promoted.[42]

Conversely, as at the Hamtramck plant, unskilled peasant workers did not become strong partisans of either strike. I mentioned earlier that half the immigrants at Bulledor intending to return to Portugal actually left France during the conflict. The half that stayed followed the lead of those who had broken with home, but chiefly because the latter, given their interest in France and French life, had become the natural leaders of the group. The peasant workers never became thoroughly involved in the strike.[43] At SAVIEM the peasant workers from the Calvados region, many of whom owned small plots of land, frequently stayed away from work to tend to farm chores; but they would go on strike, as one worker put it, only if they were forced to.[44]

A last parallel between the Americans who organized the UAW and the activists in the French strikes regards politics. For all its disruptiveness, May 1968 obviously had a less pervasive effect on industrial relations in general and on the place of the immigrant unskilled in the factory in particular than did the New Deal in the United States. There have been unions in mass-production industries in France since the 1930s, providing a minimum of protection for unskilled workers on the job. Hence, in many regions, the French unskilled workers felt no urgent need to join with the immigrants to create new institutions. Furthermore, the massive use of immigrant and agricultural labor in post–World War II French industry had only begun in the early 1960s. Though it is hard to say for sure, the ratio of would-be craftsmen to peasant workers among the unskilled was probably higher in the United States during the New Deal – and the pressure for job security and promotion correspondingly greater – than in France during the 1960s. But for all that, the two movements touched would-be craftsmen in similar ways, drawing them into the political world beyond the factory.

In both cases a sense of moving with the tide of history encouraged activists to take extraordinary risks in challenging the authority of managers and other work groups, and inspired more cautious workers to follow the activists' lead. American workers in the automobile industry saw Roosevelt's victory over Landon in 1936 as a victory over the automobile magnates as well: Alfred P. Sloan, Jr., the head of General Motors, had been a prominent supporter of the American Liberty League, which played an important role in the Republican campaign. "You voted New Deal at the polls, and defeated the Auto Barons – Now get a New Deal in the shop" was the lesson the UAW exhorted workers to draw from the election results.[45] The passage in 1935 of the National Labor Relations Act, which protected the rights of union organizers, was an even more direct demonstration to workers that they could offset management's authority in the plant with their own political power outside.

In France, the nationwide strikes of May 1968 so emboldened the Portuguese activists at Bulledor that they were able to disagree with the French, to whom they had previously deferred. Instead of continuing an experiment in self-management that appealed to the French militants for a combination of political motives, the Portuguese insisted on stopping work entirely to force management to make economic concessions of immediate interest to themselves.[46] At SAVIEM the effect of national events was to make the workers forget their defeats in recent strikes and to press their demand to be treated on a par with other workers in the company's parent firm, Renault.[47]

Finally, in both cases the loyalties and plans formed in struggle led the workers on crisscrossing paths into the broader circle of national life. Some blacks were drawn into the whirlpool of infighting between Communists and other groups during the early years of the UAW; some of the Poles who colonized the tool room at the Hamtramck parts plant joined the Socialist Party; and some of the Portuguese in Bulledor later came to share the political ideals that had seemed distant to them in May 1968.[48]

The examples so far, to repeat, approximate the polar cases that mark the limits of the would-be craftsmen's behavior. In this sense the illustrations are like high-speed photographs, freezing the evolution of factory life at the points where groups are formed and conflict clarifies the division between them. At one extreme the would-be craftsmen join with the official plant hierarchy against the inchoate protest of the peasant workers; in the second the would-be craftsmen lead or participate in a communitarian protest that for a time substitutes for that hierarchy.

But for the single worker the alternatives are seldom so clear-cut, and his choice between them is rarely such a foregone conclusion. Typically, hierarchy and communitarian vision coexist in the form of officially sanctioned rules and careers on the one hand and various kinds of trade-union pressure for reform on the other. Both are indisputably part of the factory world. During the long periods that stand between a moment of massive disruption of management's control and management's complete victory over worker resistance, a would-be craftsman faces a choice between joining those who want to rise in the hierarchy and joining those fighting to change it. To make sense of his deliberations and to review the conclusions drawn thus far, I will take up a theme introduced at the end of Chapter 3 and examine the possibilities typically available to a young worker, this time with no rural roots, as he awakens to the fact that he is in a large factory to stay.

The story that emerges from Huw Beynon's study of the Ford automobile plant at Halewood, near Liverpool, or from Kergoat's study of the SAVIEM truck factory, is brutally straightforward. The prelude is familiar: At first the young recruits are peasant workers unable to believe that they are going to stay at their jobs. They are likely to hate their foreman and the time clock, but to tolerate both. Time in the factory seems less important than and a precondition for adventure outside, and there is always the hope that something better will turn up. The passing of the years corrodes the illusion: Hopes can be disappointed only so many times before hope itself becomes a shameful whimsy, rather than a spring to action. At SAVIEM, for example, young men who leave the factory to fulfill their military service obligation and can find no better jobs upon returning have a good idea of what is in store for them.[49] At Halewood, as at the ABC plant studied by Chinoy, it is the acid sense of futility, the results of uncounted failed escapes, and often the new responsibilities of married life that together make future attempts to break out improbable.[50]

As the truth begins to press on him the worker implicitly faces three choices. The first is familiar from the previous discussion: to aim for promotion to foreman or machine setter. Kergoat calls the workers who take this path "integrated," because they accept the legitimacy of the firm hierarchy.[51]

The second choice is to flee not from the factory, but from all conscious recognition that flight is impossible. This means either a desperate belief in providence, in the possibility of a miraculous escape from a hopeless situation, or an attempt to batter the mind to numbness. Most of the men Beynon interviewed were " 'waiting for something better to turn up.' None of them wanted to be working for Ford when he was forty, yet they all became slightly hesitant when asked what job they'd be doing in ten years' time." But they knew. One of them asked Beynon what *he* would be doing after completing his studies. When he replied that he had no idea, the man looked at him for thirty seconds and said, "It must be great, that . . . not knowing."[52] The situation at SAVIEM was similar, except that the men had discovered tranquilizers as a means of taking the edge off their knowledge. A plant doctor suggested that Hoffman-LaRoche, the maker of Valium, commemorate its loyal customers at SAVIEM with a statue.[53]

The third possibility is resistance: taking stock of the situation and trying to change it. The shop stewards at Halewood, for instance, were men who could say straight out that they were still going to be at their jobs in ten years. "It's all very well saying that you don't want to be at Ford's when you're forty," one of them said, "but you may have no choice. It's your job to make this a place where you can work when you're forty."[54] Here, too, there is a clear parallel with

SAVIEM: The difference between the angry young peasant workers – the *révoltés*, as Kergoat calls them – and the older militants is precisely the latter's capacity to conceive of conflict with management as part of a long-term struggle presupposing a steady relation to factory work.[55]

What determines the course of action a worker chooses? As in the discussion of youth cultures in Chapter 3, it is useful to think of these positions as poles of attraction to which workers are drawn depending on their temperaments and a complex mixture of experiences at home, in school, and at work. In some cases the connections are obvious. The shop stewards at Halewood, for example, were all the sons of manual workers who had grown up familiar with trade unions. Their view of the company and work had been fixed during the conflicts that broke out in the plant's early years.[56] Similarly, to recall an earlier example, the militants in the UAW were often Kentuckians who had grown up in families loyal to the United Mine Workers, blacks who had worked with the Communists organizing tenant farmers, or Poles whose families followed Piłsudsky's socialism.[57] Even so, they were by temperament a special lot: Not every son of a trade unionist can stomach the arguments and tension that are the steward's stock-in-trade. Often the relation between experience and choice is more indirect still. Because the choices shade off into one another and the opportunities for a comprehensive calculation of strategies are so limited, single events take on an undue significance as symbols of what is and is not possible and legitimate. A quarrel with a foreman, a shot of heroin, a fight with a fellow worker, a weekend drunk, a meeting with a courageous trade unionist can shape ambition for years. But for the same reason, choices made on the basis of such incomplete experience can always be reversed by the weight of new events – a successful strike that encourages hope of change, an unsuccessful one that discourages it. Thus the workers at SAVIEM were constantly switching from escapism to opposition to dejection as the synergy of personal and collective experience suggested.[58]

There is yet another perspective from which to view the situation of would-be craftsmen. Instead of looking at it from above as a set of groups with fixed ideas or from below as a set of alternatives available to individuals, we can consider the way groups themselves come to be formed historically, creating the framework within which single workers make their choices. This is the perspective of the next section. It focuses on the historical development of relations between a large group of would-be craftsmen and the rest of the labor force. The subject is the most powerful and sustained mass movement of workers to emerge in the West since the the end of World War II: the movement of Italian migrants who entered factories in the North and allied with the craftsmen already there to challenge the established wage and skill hierarchies. The aim is to demonstrate in a more detailed way how industrial conflict shapes and is shaped by the would-be craftsman's politics.

The *autunno caldo* and the *delegati*

During the 1950s it would have taken utopian vision to imagine that an alliance of unskilled migrants and Northern craftsmen would soon become a major force in Italian politics. The trade unions were weak and divided along political lines. If they protected anyone at all, it was almost exclusively Northern craftsmen.[59] The migrants, arriving in Milan or Turin from the provinces, uncertain of their ambition to begin with, were further bewildered by their new surroundings and repulsed by the Northerners' hostility to their culture. Neither group seemed able to defend itself or willing to ally with the other.

The Christian Democrats and the complex alliance of big industry and large landowners that they brokered seemed in contrast invincible. Their strength rested on the deflationary program of economic recovery established in the late 1940s, a program that appeared to promise continuous economic growth, to conciliate the conflicting interests of the party's clients, and even to hold its enemies on the Left permanently in check.

The defining features of the postwar recovery program were tight credit and a reduction of government spending. By reducing demand and the state subsidies available to marginal producers, these measures bankrupted many small firms and farms, driving up unemployment and marginal employment, and forcing wages down. Low wages made Italian goods more competitive in world markets and thus encouraged investment in industry. Industrial expansion created new jobs; but it also enlarged the supply of potential workers: The spread of mass-produced goods threw traditional artisans out of work, while the spread of cheap farm machinery drove agricultural day laborers off the land. By the late 1950s the rate of emigration from the rural South to the North began to increase, a first sign of the strategy's transformation of the economy. By the end of the decade, its success was openly celebrated as the Italian "economic miracle."[60]

So long as labor reserves could be pressed out of the economy, the system seemed to be self-reproducing. It was politically durable as well. Whenever necessary, the proceeds of growth could be redistributed to the Christian Democrats' economically weaker clients in government bureaucracies and some sectors of small business and smallholder agriculture.

A precondition of this model of development was a labor movement with little influence in parliament or on the shop floor. Labor's opposition in parliament had to be crushed to cut the budget and reduce demand; opposition on the shop floor, which began to form as early as 1942 and would have prevented reorganization of the factories and kept wages up despite the pressure of unemployment, had to be overcome.[61] Step by step in the late 1940s this precondition was met. The election of April 14, 1948, gave the Christian Democrats an absolute majority in parliament and reduced the Left to ineffectual opposition in parliament soon afterward. In July an attempt was made on Togliatti's life. Thousands of Communists and partisans swarmed into the streets, thinking the hour of revolution had come. When the Communist leaders announced that it had not, the bankruptcy of the party's revolutionary extraparliamentary pretensions was revealed.

In the same period, political disputes led to schisms that eventually resulted in the creation of three separate trade-union confederations, each owing allegiance to a different political master: the Confederazione Generale Italiana del Lavoro (CGIL), associated with the Communist (PCI) and Socialist (PSI) parties; the Confederazione Italiana Sindacati Lavoratori (CISL), associated with the Christian Democrats (DC); and the Unione Italiana del Lavoro (UIL), associated with the Republican (PRI) and Social Democratic parties (PSDI).[62]

At the same time, the shop-floor organizations that had grown up covertly during the war and emerged to challenge the authority of management were dismantled. After the defeat of fascism, it had seemed as though the *commissione interna*, a consultative board elected by all workers in the plant, would become the unions' instrument for extending their control of the plant. Instead, the Left's failures in parliament and the splintering of the union confederations encouraged the employers to bribe and browbeat the *commissioni* into docility. At FIAT during the early 1950s at least two thousand workers were fired for reasons having to do with political and trade-union activity; the reorganization of work that accompanied the introduction of modern machines, many from the United States, provided ample possibilities for scattering groups of troublemakers and obstructing political friendships; and still other activists were exiled to undesirable departments, such as the Officina Sussidiaria Ricambi, nicknamed the Red Star. These punishments were combined with enticements to good behavior such as a premium for regular attendance – not paid, of course, to strikers.[63] Deflation redoubled the Left's debility: Unemployment was added to repression inside and outside the factories as a means of disciplining the workers and demonstrating the labor movement's incapacity to defend its interests.

The decline of the labor movement soon became manifest. It became more and more difficult even to find workers willing to stand for election to the *commissioni interne*. By 1955, when Communist and also Socialist candidates for the *commissioni interne* did not win a majority among even the blue-collar workers at FIAT, one of the Left's strongholds, the conviction was widespread that the Northern workers' opposition to capitalist authority in the factories was definitively broken. The migrants moving into the factories were more docile still. Support for the Communist and Socialist unions dropped precipitously: In 1951, 52.2 percent of all metalworkers were affiliated with the CGIL; in 1956 the number was down to 21.9 percent; and in 1960 the figure was 13.8 percent. An obvious sign that management had the whip hand in the 1950s and early 1960s was its power to lengthen and shorten the working day, declare layoffs, and schedule vacations according to market conditions.[64] It seemed as though the Christian Democrats and their allies were in the saddle for good.

To see why these expectations were disappointed, we will look in more detail first at the labor-market situation and the self-conception of the migrants and Northerners. Then we will examine how common struggle changed both elements in ways that expedited an alliance between them.

Consider first the peasants and artisans who moved to the Northern cities from the South, the Veneto, or poorer areas in Tuscany, Lombardy, or Piedmont in search of factory jobs. Some were pushed by fear: Their economic situation was so desperate that they had to look for work in the Northern cities. Others were pulled by hope: They might have been able to survive for a time where they were, but the prospect of relatively stable and well-paying jobs in the city was more appealing to them than a continuous struggle to meet expenses by combining the small and fluctuating incomes of many family members.[65] Either way, they left their homes by the hundreds of thousands to face an uncertain future as unskilled workers. During the peak years of migration, 1960–2, an average of seventy-six thousand migrants arrived and twenty-eight thousand departed annually from Turin alone.[66] Between 1958 and 1963, just under 1 million persons moved from Southern Italy, including Sicily and Sardinia, to the North;[67] and this is to say nothing of the emigration to other Common Market countries in this period.

The migrants' progress through the labor markets of the North traced a pattern familiar from Chapters 2 and 3. A few men from one village would establish a beachhead, doing unskilled work in the unstable sector of the economy. As they advanced to unskilled but stable jobs, friends and relatives from home took their places. Generally the first arrivals started at jobs that appeared attractive by comparison with opportunities in less-developed areas, but counted as unstable or demeaning by Northern standards: menial work in restaurants or hotels; unskilled, often dirty and hazardous jobs in small factories; seasonal jobs on construction sites. But, in search of more security, they quickly worked their way from smaller plants and artisans' shops to large factories, arriving finally at the foundries and assembly lines of the largest firms, for example, the FIAT Mirafiori works in Turin.[68]

At first their position in the large plants was tenuous. Migrants were the first to be laid off for any reason: During the downturn from 1963 to 1965, twenty-seven thousand more migrants left Turin than arrived. But those who lost their jobs often returned to the factory at the first opportunity, working in the meantime at the unskilled jobs they had held previously, retreating to their homes, or taking temporary jobs abroad. By the late 1960s the migrants had thus become an indispensable part of the steadily employed production workers in the largest plants.

For the Northern workers, this new wave of industrialization was more a danger than an opportunity. The slow introduction of mass-production techniques disrupted established patterns of work, unpredictably foreclosing traditional craft careers even if it subsequently created others. The speeding of assembly lines taxed the physical capacity of workers past their primes, encouraging management to replace them with the younger, physically fit recruits.[69] Divisions between the unions and the employers' determined attempts to prevent their reinvigoration left the weak and displaced with no protection: Only those workers with marketable skills could bargain with management.[70]

The fears and hopes of the two groups in this period were revealed most clearly in the ideas each held of the other. Thus the Northerners, pressed on the labor market by capital as well as by the migrants, scorned the newcomers as ignorant of factory life and servile to management. They took the migrants' indifference to trade unions and willingness to accept menial noxious work as justification of their scorn. This antagonism could turn violent when the newcomers, like the southern blacks who arrived in the American North during World War II, got their first jobs as strikebreakers. And professional disdain for the migrants mingled with long-standing mistrust of Southerners. Here the Northerners could point to the new slums, the *Coreas*, into which the migrants crowded as proof that the latter were unsuited to urban life. Economic and cultural resentments reinforced each other, and in 1956 a political movement in Turin called for a limitation on migration. In this period advertisements for apartments there frequently read "for Piedmontese only."[71]

The migrants' relation to the Northerners was in comparison more ambiguous, reflecting differences in the newcomers' experiences and uncertainties in their ideas about the future. Some migrants corresponded to the type of the peasant: A study done at FIAT in the early 1960s showed that 40 percent of those who had done farm work preferred it to a factory job that paid the same.[72] But by the end of the 1950s, and no doubt partly as a consequence of the steady flow of population to the cities during the decade, it seems that the process to which I referred earlier as the urbanization of the countryside had begun. To judge by anecdotal evidence as well as certain inconclusive surveys done at the time, many of the later migrants had broken in some way with their home society before leaving it.[73] Like the Puerto Rican immigrants discussed in the preceding chapter, they came to the cities prepared to stay, attracted by the promise of a world that seemed both more exciting and more inclined to reward effort than the villages and small towns from which they came.

Many of the later migrants, furthermore, were unusual by the standards of their home communities in that they had some experience of industrial life before taking factory jobs in the North. There is also some evidence that the migrants were more likely to belong to leftist parties than were others from the same areas who stayed behind.[74] For all these reasons, the migrants were drawn to underscore the similarities between themselves and the Northern workers, despite the latter's emphasis on the differences.

But even those migrants with more experience at industrial work and politics were usually not prepared for life in the North, and their attachments to their home communities were often more profound than they normally admitted. Often they arrived in the North alone, their wives and children remaining behind, ready to come only if and when the head of the family found steady work.[75] In many cases the desire to become like the Northern workers was no more than the smooth surface of the migrants' turbulent and often confused ideas about their ambitions and capabilities. The same study that demonstrated the openness to change even of these migrants from rural areas also showed that in the North the migrants often preferred to live close to their own kind, knew little about local politics, and remained outside sport, cultural, and political groups, as well as unions.[76] In this sense, Luchino Visconti's *Rocco e i suoi fratelli*, a movie about the profound confusion over what is good, what bad, in Southern culture, captures the central theme of the migrants' life during the whole period.

Even by the early 1970s, when the South was more industrialized than it had been before and unions were far more powerful, the son of a leftist worker could arrive in Turin from a small Southern village after his first train ride, speaking only dialect, unfamiliar with street cars, his fascination with the Left matched by embarrassed ignorance of strikes, unions, leftist parties, and newspapers. His desire to prove himself as a worker and enjoy the freedom of a large city was undercut by a sense of loneliness and rage that a social hierarchy existed in the North as well as the South, with the difference being that in some places in Turin it was as offensive to be a Southerner as to be poor. In his frequent moments of despair, he thought of returning to his family in the village. So although the migrants as a group were not hostile to Northern society, they were neither at ease in it nor completely convinced that they had come to stay.[77]

At the start of the 1960s, therefore, an alliance between the migrants and the Northern working class was not a foregone conclusion. Even leftists, who were critical of migrants' treatment in the factories and the slums, were often more impressed by the newcomers' apparent apathy and disorientation than by their vocation for political activity and self-organization.[78] To many observers, the Northerners' resentment of the migrants seemed invincible. Conceivably the natives' rejection of the newcomers might have shattered the latter's determination to stay in the North, moving them to retreat into an isolation that would have further burdened relations between the two groups. Instead the Northern workers and the migrants combined forces, each defending the dignity of the other. How did they come together?

The decisive factor was the impotence of the trade unions and the corresponding weakness of the Northern workers in the plants. Had the Northerners had strong unions, they might have been tempted to strike a bargain with management. They might, for instance, have ceded certain unskilled jobs to the migrants in return for guaranteed control over the rest. Had they been able to rely on strong parties, they might have secured legislative protection of their interests. In either case, the result would have been to create a permanent, ethnically distinct underclass, as in modern South Africa and post–Civil War Alabama,[79] or, in an attenuated way, in France or West Germany. But without strong unions or parties, the Northerners were in no position to impose such a bargain. Weak as they were, their best chance lay in allying with the migrants against management according to the old maxim that those who do not hang together hang separately.

A similar argument applies to the leftist parties, the PCI and the PSI, and the unions. Had these organizations been strong, they might have been tempted to keep the newcomers at arm's length, treating them as dependent clients rather than taking a chance on their uncertain loyalty to the values of Northern life. But because the parties and unions were excluded from power, they had little to lose and much to gain by actively recruiting the migrants and gambling on their allegiance. The weakness of the unions and leftist parties therefore worked to cement the spontaneous contacts between migrants and Northern craftsmen on the shop floor. And once the two groups formed an alliance, they redefined their interests and forced changes in the institutions representing them.

The actual creation of the alliance and the transformation of the institutions were not, of course, inevitable results of these favorable preconditions. They involved hundreds of chance encounters, acts of trusting generosity and, as we shall see, political daring. Nor were they the result of the slow convergence of the ideas of each group. Northerners and migrants came to trust each other during a series of factory conflicts that transformed both groups, redefining the socialist politics of the Northern workers and recasting the migrants' ambition to join industrial society as an affirmation of political militancy.

Two strike waves, in 1962 and 1969, decisively shaped the final synthesis of political views. The first was preceded by an upsurge of demand in 1960 that led to tight labor markets the following year.[80] One consequence was to force big firms to recruit large numbers of migrants directly from rural areas in the South, rather than hiring them after a period of trial in small firms locally. Another was to encourage demands for higher wages and better working conditions. Strikes organized by the union then gave migrants, angered by the absence of decent housing and still not resigned to industrial work in the North, a chance to protest their condition. The newest recruits, who lived under the worst conditions and had the least experience in the factory, were the most combative. The cumulative result was the *torrido luglio torinese*, the torrid Turin July: a month of official and unofficial strikes whose violence and unpredictability at times alarmed the trade unions and the Communist party almost as much as managers and Christian Democrats.[81]

The strikes revealed diverse groups of migrants familiar from the earlier discussion of peasant workers and would-be craftsmen. At one extreme were peasant rebels, to whom Northern industrial life had remained foreign. There must have been many peasants of this type in Turin in 1962. The strikes broke out first in the small factories, where the concentration of recent immigrants was greatest, and not at FIAT, where they were still a small minority of the work force.[82] But even there it was they who took the lead in the conflict. And according to one observer, the organization of the street demonstrations of July was "very reminiscent of the struggles for land in the South."[83]

At the opposite extreme were migrants who pursued one of the typical strategies of the would-be craftsman: complete identification with the ideas of the skilled. At times such imitation of the Northerner could result in a theatrical reversal of roles. Goffredo Fofi, for example, reports a scene in which a young Southerner picketing at Mirafiori reviled an old Northern strikebreaker, calling him a *napuli* and *marocchino* – two traditional Northern epithets for Southerners.[84]

Between these two groups was a third which, rather than ignoring or faithfully copying Northern values, reinterpreted them in the act of assimilating them. The appearance of this group in the early 1960s was significant in that it prefigured the transformation of identity that was to become widespread by the end of the decade. Workers in this group tended to be political activists, for whom participation in trade unions and parties was often a step toward joining Northern society. The self-conscious attempt to make politics the cornerstone of a new identity meant, however, that these migrants took political ideas more seriously than all but the most dedicated Northern militants. It meant, too, that they tried to express in political categories a series of hopes and frustrations particular to their own experience and foreign even to the native militants. Thus their admiration for Northern values was a precondition for their redefining them, and their determined imitation of Northerners provided them with a language for expressing and conserving parts of their own past. A representative figure is Sante Notarnicola, a Southerner who came to Turin in 1953, became a Communist, participated in the most violent demonstrations of 1963 in Turin, and then became a bank robber in the cause of revolution.

From his own point of view, Notarnicola was only applying faithfully the political lessons he learned as an adolescent in the Bonfo section of the Communist Party in the Barriera di Milano, a proletarian quarter of Turin. There, he writes in his autobiography,

a rage grew inside me, the desire for justice, a kind of rebelliousness. Slowly the revolutionary, the Communist, ripened in me. I learned to live, to think, to speak like someone from Turin. There are some Southerners who come North and after a few years are still closed in their group, squeezed in, limited by their dialect. They are like an isolated tribe. With me it is different. My uncle was a Turiner in his behavior and his mentality. He had come to Turin as a small child. For my part I began at once to integrate myself in Bonfo and in the workshops. In the Via Cuneo more Turin dialect was spoken than Italian. In the street there were no differences: we were all poor and we were all workers. My friends were people from Turin, or they were completely Turinized – not like the other immigrants.[85]

But if his political activity had roots in Communist doctrines, his career as a revolutionary bank robber also reflected influences characteristic of preindustrial societies. The decisions to abandon the party and wage a private war against the rich were prompted partly by impatience with the party's inactivity in the years after 1955. But like the rural bandits described by E. J. Hobsbawm, he also acted to right individual wrongs.[86] "The plant guards at FIAT, together with everything that was boiling inside us," he writes, "were the main reasons for deciding to act."[87] Thus, like Robin Hood, he stole from the rich to do right by the poor. But like a modern revolutionary, he wanted to use the money to pay for revolution, rather than distributing it directly to the needy.

By bringing to light these developments in the migrants' self-conception, the strikes of 1962 helped create bonds of trust between them and Northerners on the shop floor. Apparently shiftless and passive, the migrants surprised Northern workers, union organizers, politicians, and intellectuals by their courage and solidarity. In this sense the Northerners' applause for the Southerner who vilified a strikebreaker was a first sign of the respect that later led to joint action.

The indirect, longer-term, and ultimately more profound effect of the strikes was to provoke complex and interrelated changes in the strategies of Italian capital and labor. In combination, these changes helped drive the migrants and natives together and allowed them to institutionalize their alliance.

The strikes were unsettling on two counts. First, they accelerated the rate of wage increases, already high because of tight labor markets: Hourly wages went up 15.3 percent in 1962, 16.8 percent in 1963, and 11.3 percent in 1964, whereas the hourly productivity of industrial workers went up by an average of about 7 percent in those years.[88] This development obviously threatened to undermine the foundation of the postwar economy: cheap labor. Second, and more ominous, the strikes suggested the possibility of a widespread dissatisfaction with the existing Christian Democratic monopoly of political power.

Industrialists responded to these threats in one of two ways, depending on their political allegiances and investment strategies. Roughly speaking, smaller firms that were producing for the domestic market and that had ties to the more conservative wing of the Christian Democratic Party tended simply to ignore the problem of political disorder. They tried to recoup wage increases by speeding up assembly lines and paring down work crews. They opposed concessions to the unions whose power they wanted to check by the repressive measures tested in the 1950s: mass firings of activists, bonuses to workers who refused to strike, and the like.

On the other hand, larger firms such as FIAT and Olivetti, which operated in international markets and faced constant pressure to modernize production, pursued a strategy of compromise with the unions and the non-Communist leftist parties. Their general aim was to trade rights to participate in decision making for assurances that the new participants would not challenge the existing distribution of power. In the plant this meant changes in the unions' rights to bargain about the reorganization and pace of work, but only within the broad limits set by national labor contracts favorable to industry; in parliament it meant opening the government to the Socialists on the condition that the latter distance themselves from the Communists and agree to an incomes policy restricting wage increases.[89] The transformation of the economy that these firms judged inevitable would thus take place in a foreseeable, controlled way with no political risk.

Had either strategy been applied with constancy and determination, the changes in relations between natives and Northerners might have been retarded or interrupted and the subsequent growth of the unions impeded. Judicious concessions to the skilled Northern workers and minimal guarantees to the unskilled migrants might have created islands of privilege resistant to further changes. Alternatively, ruthless and well-coordinated repression might have forestalled organization of a more powerful labor movement by keeping potential leaders out of the plants.

But, in fact, the Christian Democrats were undecided about the need to make concessions to the Left; the Socialists were divided on the question whether to abandon the Communists; and the managers of the large public and private firms who favored a new coalition were opposed by others who supported a restoration of the system of the 1950s. In politics these conflicts produced a series of half-hearted and ineffective center–left governments in the mid-1960s. In the factories they sent managers down a zigzagging course, in which the unions were alternately bribed and browbeaten.

Where single-mindedness might have achieved the industrialists' ends, this vacillation achieved the opposite: Labor was given a foretaste of power and a chance to experiment with new representative institutions at the plant level, but put on guard against the dangers of compromise with an unreliable partner. At the same time, the reorganization of the plants drove workers together and closer to the unions.

Take the problems of speedups and the rationalization of work. Both created dissatisfaction on the shop floor: the first because it pressed migrant assembly-line workers closer to the limits of physical exhaustion, the second because it exacerbated the Northern craftsmen's uncertainty about the future. By the mid-1960s the discontent had become serious enough to persuade managers in the firms competing in world markets that some kind of plant-level bargaining was necessary to resolve the conflicts provoked by reorganization. The managers, however, were caught in a dilemma that reflected perfectly the difficulty with their larger plans for a new alliance: The point to establishing new representative institutions was to regulate conflict; but once in place, the new institutions might become instruments for encouraging it. Most managers temporized; a few signed agreements with the unions establishing narrowly defined committees to regulate disputes arising from rationalization. By themselves these agreements solved nothing: Power still rested with management. But they did focus the unions' attention on two questions whose full importance became clear only at the end of the decade: How could the union take part in plant-level bargaining without becoming so implicated in management's decisions that it lost the workers' allegiance; and what was to be the relation of new institutions created to serve this purpose to the vestigial commissions that continued, however ineffectively, to represent workers in the large factories? In short, by toying with conflicting answers to this problem, management helped prepare the union to settle the issue on its own terms once the balance of power changed in its favor.[90]

Political conflict worked in analogous ways. The Christian Democrats were paralyzed. On one side was a reform-minded wing with close ties to likeminded parts of big capital. This branch was convinced of the need to appeal to and divide working-class groups by improving social services, limiting some of the internal migration, and redistributing income. On the other side was the traditional petty bourgeois and artisan wing of the party, which feared that concessions would come at its own expense. The Christian Democrats' paralysis meant that no significant reforms were raised, and the political situation was left as unsettled and threatening as before.[91] Confusion among the Christian Democrats in turn exacerbated debate within the Socialist Party on the questions whether and under what conditions to ally with the Christian Democrats, with the Social Democrats, and with Republicans. Debate on this matter eventually led to a schism, with a radical minority breaking off to found the independent Partito Socialista di Unità Proletaria (PSIUP) in January 1964, a little less than a month after the Socialists entered the first center–left government.[92] Unencumbered by further obligations to the majority Socialists, the militants in the PSIUP were free to exploit the discontent of Socialist skilled workers alarmed by the rationalization program: In Turin, for instance, the PSIUP won many craftsmen at FIAT to a plan for introducing factory councils composed of shop stewards, or *delegati*. In 1969 these workers would play an important part in introducing the idea of *delegati* to the unskilled migrants.[93]

The strikes of 1962 and the attempts to reestablish order through a center–left coalition also contributed to the explosion of the late 1960s by directing the attention of the emergent student movement away from parliamentary politics and toward the factories. As in France, West Germany, the United States, and Japan, the student movement that developed in Italy had complex roots in the dissatisfaction of the generations coming of age in the 1960s with the political, social, and cultural stagnation of their societies, as well as with their uncertain place in those societies: American troops in Vietnam were the symbol of the world the activists did not want and could not defend. But the Italian student movement stands out from the other student movements in that, almost from the first anti-Vietnam rallies in 1967, its leaders were eager to ally with the workers. At the most general level this precocious enthusiasm for an alliance with the factories was an instance of the populism that often characterizes the young elites of nations struggling to meet the dominant standards of economic efficiency: the idea that together educated youth and the people can push aside the traditional ruling cliques whose selfishness and subservience to foreign interests impede progress. But the precise shape of this general idea became visible only in the light of the political maneuvering of the 1960s, and especially the effort to draw the Socialist Party into the government.

The political tensions that ultimately led to the creation of the PSIUP were accompanied by a division among non-Communist leftist intellectuals: Progressive technocrats believed that a center–left government could create the basis for efficient economic planning, whereas a group of dissidents considered this idea only a pretext and thought that the real goal was to control the dissatisfaction that capitalist development, in their view, inevitably produces. This latter group, whose leaders often published in *Quaderni Rossi,* sought proof for its ideas and allies for its revolutionary plans in the factories: By involving the workers in research projects (*conricerca*) they tried to discover the facts required to formulate a transformative strategy and to create a new, politically applicable model of relations between intellectuals and workers. The strikes of 1962 encouraged their efforts; the Socialist Party's flirtation with power, the entrapment of the Communist Party in its domestic ghetto, and the debilities of the union made their ideas attractive to a discontented generation on the lookout for ways to churn up the established order. Hence, by the mid-1960s there were numerous contacts between workers and students, especially in Turin and in the factory towns along the Tuscan coast. Whereas student movements in other countries were at first isolated from the workers and preoccupied with visions of utopian counterculture, in Italy these contacts suggested the notion of an alliance between workers and students and made it realizable.[94]

The upshot of all these developments was that underneath the tide of economic recession, industrial reorganization, and attempts at political restabilization, Italian society was taking on a new shape. The mass of factory workers, parts of the labor movement, and the emergent intellectual elite were moving closer together and further away from the control of the dominant institutions. The reorganization of work antagonized the skilled Northerners and unskilled migrants, reinforcing the trust between them that had begun to develop during the strikes of 1962. Efforts to contain the discontent in the plants through the creation of new bargaining institutions gave the unions an apprenticeship in institution building without roping them into a defense of the status quo; attempts at political restabilization helped produce a corps of dissidents who brought new ideas to the factories and took what they learned there back to the universities. When the tide of recession, reorganization, and restabilization receded in the late 1960s, drawn back by the recovery of the economy, all these changes were revealed. The migrants suddenly stood at the center of a vast project of reform that, though realized only in part, was to bring them into the center of Northern factory life and to complete the transformation of their self-conception.

As in the early 1960s, the changes at this point were cast into the open and accelerated by a series of strikes. Also as in the earlier period, the prelude to the strikes of 1969 was rising demand and tight labor markets that encouraged workers and unions to be especially aggressive in negotiating with the industrialists.[95] And again as in 1962, FIAT was the center of events, for all the defining elements of the situation were observable there in their starkest form: a large mass of unskilled migrants (in just the six months before the strikes broke out in 1969, FIAT had hired fifteen thousand workers directly from the South, many of them youngsters straight from school with no experience of factory work or clear idea of the future);[96] politically militant skilled workers with only weak unions to protect them; unions ready to take any gamble to win the loyalty of the workers and establish themselves as representatives of the production workers; and a well-prepared student movement determined to join with the workers. Developments at FIAT in the years 1968–70 are therefore a kind of magnifying glass with which to examine the transformative elements of conflict I mentioned earlier: impromptu attempts to elaborate half-formed ideas to meet new situations; forward plunges in the midst of battle; and the creation of enduring alliances that reshape the ideas of the allies.

For analytic purposes, the epoch can be divided into three periods, though these overlap and events characteristic of one can be found in the others. The trade unions and skilled workers are the protagonists of the first, the migrants of the second, and both migrants and skilled workers of the third, in which they allied to re-form the trade unions.[97]

During the first period, which ran from roughly March 1968 to June 1969, the workers became progressively more assertive. The most aggressive were the skilled workers, aggravated by continuing reorganization of work and new wage scales, a product of the tight labor market, which meant that new recruits could receive more than old hands. They demonstrated the techniques of strike organization to tens of thousands of new workers with little or no knowledge of industrial conflict, often soliciting their support by putting forward egalitarian demands: For example, eight thousand craftsmen at the Officina Ausiliaria at FIAT struck for equal pay increases for workers in all wage groups.[98] There was also a drumfire of less spectacular disputes involving less-skilled groups with more particular demands for better work conditions, better food, and so on: From the start of 1968 through the first month of 1969, at FIAT alone, there were eighty-four incidents serious enough to call for protracted bargaining between the unions and management.[99]

The unions were uncertain how to put this unrest to the best use in bargaining with management. Their general program was to use the renewed militancy to realize the plans for the reconquest of factories, vague as they were, which had emerged during the preceding years. Where the unions were relatively strong and controlled the *commissione interna*, as was often the case in the metalworkers' factories in Lombardy, for instance, the unions used the disputes to strengthen the *commissioni*, forcing management to grant them the power to police disputes involving the speed of assembly lines and the reorganization of work. Where the unions were weak and the *commissione interna* subservient to management, as at FIAT, the unions tried to create an independent network of shop stewards tied to the unions and empowered to bargain with the firm.[100]

The problem was that what the unions hoped would be a controlled mobilization of the workers soon got out of control. The example of the craftsmen's militancy; the unions' solicitations to select leaders in anticipation of formal recognition of shop stewards; the exhortations of student activists, many of whom helped in the organization of *comitati unitari di base* (rank-and-file unity committees that ignored the divisions between rival unions and hence helped undermine their authority);[101] the exhilaration of successful defiance of the bosses after years of subjugation; the unexpected chance to express all their resentments at the world of the factory and Northern society in which they found themselves – all these acted violently upon the migrants, precipitating out of the mass of their ideas a series of demands for recognition of their dignity and place in the factory that, vague as they were, still went far beyond the reforms planned by the unions.[102]

In June, for example, FIAT agreed to the creation of a system of shop stewards (but on the condition that they be subordinated to the firm's docile *commissione interna*). The unions, convinced that no better compromise was possible, declared a great victory and an end to strikes for the summer. But on the very day the agreement was signed, the unskilled migrants in the paint division, who had taken part fitfully in the strikes of the preceding weeks, struck spontaneously for an eight-hour day.[103] If the migrants' growing militancy and autonomy had until then passed unnoticed amidst the general confusion, from that day on it was unmistakable.

The central theme in the second period, which covers the *autunno caldo* of 1969, is the migrants' emergence as an enduring, often decisive, force in the Italian labor movement: their sudden discovery of the capacity to make claims in their own name, using and redefining a set of political categories comprehensible to other workers and the unions. But the migrants were no more a homogeneous mass than they had been in the early 1960s. As at the beginning of the decade, groups of unskilled workers reacted to the strikes in ways that reflected their different experiences in the North.

Thus, as in 1962, some of the migrants were peasant workers, either straight off the farm or just out of school. They understood the strikes as a kind of Jacquerie: an occasion to disrupt Northern society and avenge accumulated humiliations. The young Southerners who blocked train lines near the Autobianchi plant at Desio are an example.[104] No doubt there were also a few migrants so thoroughly integrated into Northern life as to be indistinguishable from the natives; but for that very reason nothing is heard of them. In between these two groups were a large number of migrants who resembled the Portuguese would-be craftsmen at the Bulledor plant and the second-generation Slavs in Hamtramck: young, with experience in the factories, wanting to participate in them and in Northern life, but excluded from both. In another sense, however, these workers recall Notarnicola: However different from his their political views ultimately were in substance, they too were a synthesis of Northern political doctrines and communitarian ideas forged outside the factory. It was these workers who, together with the students, suddenly took charge of the strikes, determining their rhythms and aims and teaching themselves about industrial conflict by inventing new forms of it. Again, events at FIAT were paradigmatic.

Beginning in March, a few students began to meet with workers outside the Mirafiori works. Week by week the numbers on both sides grew. The discussions of conditions in the factory, the organization of strikes, and larger political questions turned into long and crowded meetings at a local bar. When it became necessary to coordinate the spontaneous strikes in different departments, the meetings became a weekly assembly of workers and students. In the next six months this assembly and other, less regular ones served as a vast school of politics: They produced a new set of shop-floor leaders, a rough program of reform for the factory, and a distinctive, if jumbled, theory of political organization.

The strikes and assemblies brought forth new leaders in the way tumultuous popular movements that shake established hierarchies frequently do. Migrants who took the lead in spontaneous strikes or in arguments with foremen suddenly had the courage to speak out in assemblies of their fellows; success there encouraged militancy on the shop floor and the self-assurance to bargain with representatives of management and the unions. Imagine a semiliterate Southerner dictating an incisive flyer in heavily accented Italian to a Northern student. Compare this picture with the incident reported by Bernoux of the disconsolate would-be craftsmen left in the lurch by their shop steward, and you begin to realize the extraordinary character of Italian developments.[105]

The program of reform that emerged under the leadership of these new men and the tactics they used to realize it reflected the sense of community that bound the migrants together. One typical demand was equal wage increases for all workers, which of course flattened the wage hierarchy. A second and related demand was for abolition of all piece-rate systems, for control over working conditions, and generally for an end to any connection between wages and productivity: This was an explicit version of the peasant workers' challenge to the meritocratic system of rewards. A third was an attack on the skill hierarchy. Frequently the migrants demanded collective upgrading and guaranteed promotion to higher skill levels. Assembly-line workers at FIAT, Alfa Romeo, and the Innocenti plant at Lambrate demanded collective promotion.[106] It is as though the workers in the Hamtramck plant studied by Friedlander had decided to colonize the tool room en masse.

The migrants' tactics also reflected and depended on their solidarity. Their principal innovation was the checkerboard strike, a system by which departments stop work at times and in an order that will inflict maximum cost on the company and the minimum losses in forgone wages on the workers. Without detailed knowledge of the plant and intimate cooperation between its divisions, such strikes fail. With them they succeed, reinforcing the solidarity that made them possible in the first place and demonstrating the possibility of the increased control of the pace and conditions of work that was often their ultimate aim. The idea of *una lotta che pratica l'obiettivo*, a struggle that prefigures its objective, was itself central to the workers' strategy.[107]

The political program that accompanied and justified these struggles was little more than the enthusiasm of struggle writ large: *operaismo*, or workerism. The central idea, which had roots in Socialist maximalism and the experience with factory councils after World War I, was simply that by themselves the workers would bring down capitalism and replace it by a society of their own devising.[108]

Paradoxically, the students' collaboration encouraged the workers to make a doctrine of self-reliance. For, isolated as they were from the other political forces in Italian society, the students were only too willing to believe in the irrelevance of these latter and the self-sufficiency of the movement to which they were attached. Thus Lotta Continua, the student group most influential among the workers in this period, rejected the discipline of traditional parties and celebrated the inventiveness of spontaneous struggle. As a consequence, the students were no help at all when by early 1970 the enthusiasm of the first acts of defiance began to fade. The workers, realizing that they had no serviceable strategy for comprehensive reform of the factories – let alone global social transformation – had nowhere else to look for leadership but to the unions.[109]

The dominant theme of the third and longest period, from the first months of 1970 through at least the end of 1972, is the amalgamation of the new movement of migrants into the unions and, through the unions, the unification of the migrants and the skilled workers. Consolidation of the two groups took place in a haphazard, unpremeditated way, at first more out of a sense of mutual dependence and a general allegiance to a common cause than through joint affirmation of a detailed plan of cooperation.[110]

Each side had reason to be wary of the other, but also to solicit its help. The migrants feared the loss of their autonomy and a renewal of the craftsmen's tutelage. The craftsmen feared that the migrants would level the skill and wage hierarchies, destroying craft pride and economic privilege. But other considerations more than offset these suspicions. It was clear to many migrants, for example, that the informal system of shop stewards that was the custodian of their power could survive only if it was somehow integrated into the official system of plant-level bargaining. But because the recently signed contracts gave the union the right to designate its representatives in negotiations with management, their cooperation was essential. Conversely, it was clear to many skilled workers that the only way to protect their remaining rights was to ally with the migrants, which meant in effect recognizing their representatives' place in the union and accepting at least some flattening of the factory hierarchy. And for their part, many labor leaders had come to see that to challenge the legitimacy of the rank-and-file delegates was to risk losing the trust of the production workers, which the unions had sought for more than a decade.

Nor was it only the calculus of interest that brought the parties together. Northern workers believed deeply in the unity of the working class (if they were Communists or Socialists) or in the solidarity of the community of workers (if they were Catholics). If the strikes of the preceding months had alarmed the traditionally militant craftsmen, they had also recalled to them the revolutionary hopes of the first postwar years. Not only that, but the most politically active among them were themselves displeased with the unions' caution: The craftsmen at the Officina Ausiliaria at FIAT, for example, had been as disappointed as the production workers in the compromise between the union and the firm on the question of the shop stewards.[111] And there were migrants who recognized the need to collaborate with the Northerners in the elaboration of a program of transformation that went beyond *operaismo*. Finally, there were many leftists in the trade unions who saw the emergence of the *delegati* as a first indication of the hopes for workplace democracy that had drawn them to the labor movement to begin with.[112]

The compromise that emerged in late 1970 was thus a mixture of calculation and idealism. The unions agreed to recognize as their representatives in the plant the *delegati* elected by all the workers of a given production unit, not just by union members. The old *commissione interna* was to be replaced by a *consiglio di fabbrica*, defined as the assembly of *delegati*, an arrangement that would guarantee the latter's role in plant life. At the same time the migrants tacitly agreed to allow the unions to gerrymander electoral districts on the shop floor so as to protect their organizational interests. In this way the three union confederations, each with its own political allegiances, secured the election of factory councils that assured their survival in factories where they were previously represented. By 1972 a million workers had elected fifty thousand officially recognized delegates, almost all in plants in North and Central Italy.[113]

These intricate compromises of program and organizational form of course disappointed some on both sides. At Innocenti in 1972, for instance, migrants wanted to reduce the number of skill grades to two, with automatic passage between them, whereas the craftsmen fought to maintain some approximation of the old ideas of promotion. Elsewhere large numbers of migrants, some close to the extraparliamentary groups, quit positions as *delegati*, convinced that their cause had been betrayed or (like some of the second-generation Poles at Hamtramck) that union work was less adventurous than they had imagined.[114] But the compromise held: By 1972 the model of the *delegati* elected by all and the *consiglio di fabbrica* composed of the *delegati* was extended, plant by plant, contract by contract, throughout Italy.

This compromise and the series of strikes preceding it completed the incorporation of the migrants into Northern factory life in two ways. First, the unions' successes against the employers and the migrants' successes within the unions frequently guaranteed the latter steady jobs and promotions as well. Throughout the 1970s mass firings in major firms became a rarity. Employers feared that the threatened workers would occupy the plants: The government was so chary of the political repercussions of plant closings that it often

subsidized troubled firms in order to protect jobs; and because promotion under the new arrangements often came to depend only on
the duration of employment with the firm, widespread job security
meant that large numbers of unskilled migrants began to move into
skilled job categories. Often, of course, promotion was only a legal
fiction that justified a wage increase without changing the workers'
activity. But there were many cases – at Alfa Romeo at Arese, for
example – where supplemental agreements obliged the firm to employ many unskilled workers at craft jobs, for which they often
lacked the training.[115] Further, the workers' new power allowed
them to exercise subtle but pervasive power on the shop floor. The
speed of the assembly line, the prerogatives of the foreman, and the
length of the coffee break all became subjects for almost constant
negotiation between the formerly helpless unskilled workers and
management.[116]

The migrants thus took possession of the factories, making a kind
of substitute home for themselves there before finally joining Northern society outside the plant.[117] For example, in their reminiscences,
workers at FIAT often recall that during those years they felt more at
home in the plant than they did in a city they still found alien.

The second element in the final incorporation of the migrants into
Northern factory life was the fact that these years were a watershed
that separated the migrants from their original culture. Many of the
migrants, as I said earlier, had already broken with their home culture before arriving in the North. Nonetheless, before the *autunno
caldo* even such migrants often continued to think of their home
villages as a last refuge, a sanctuary in case of defeat in the North.
Afterward this last connection, too, was broken: Success or failure
was to be lived out in the North; home villages became, in the light
of recent experiences, alien territory.

This transformation was particularly evident among the younger
political activists. Recall, for instance, the Southerner mentioned earlier, the young man from a leftist family who came North in the early
1970s and very nearly returned home. By 1973 he had joined Lotta
Continua and gone to work at FIAT; the more involved in politics he
got, the more distant he felt from his companions at home. "I used to
go home during vacations," he said in an interview,

with the idea of getting a lot closer to my tradition, my village, to the people
I used to know. But the last time I went there it was different. The last time
I went there the newspaper in my pocket was *Lotta Continua*. A year before
maybe it was *Corriere dello Sport*. Going there with *Lotta Continua* in my hand
meant a lot. For example at that point in my thinking there was a mile-wide
gap between me, the militant of Lotta Continua, and the kids in my village.

Before then I could talk of certain things. After that it was all over, because if I talked about the Communists in the government, of the working class at Mirafiori, or union demonstrations, nobody gave a damn – any more than I did when I lived in the village.[118]

To be sure, not all connections to the past were broken. It is common enough to find political militants who speak the language of class struggle and profess no interest in the affairs of their home villages, but who passionately study its history, cook its characteristic dishes, dance its dances, or paint its scenes from childhood recollections. More complicated still are those for whom provincial past and metropolitan present have run together to the point that factory life seems an extension of the village and life in the village becomes unthinkable without connection to the factory. Fantasy becomes a bridge between places, epochs, and generations. One of the most prominent of the FIAT *delegati,* for example, writes in his short autobiography of plans to retire in six or seven years to his native village in the South. Nostalgia for Turin will be no problem for him.

The big city doesn't exist. There are places here in Turin where we have meetings, and that's all. I live here as though I were in a little village with the characteristics of the one where I come from. I could care less about Turin. My children feel more like Turinese, and I think they will stay here. My dream would be that one day one of them manages to get a house with a room where I could stay now and then – for a month or two at a time, no more. Back in the village I would like to keep up the contacts I've made with the FIAT workers from the factory of Grottaminarda.[119]

The strikes and the compromise had contradictory effects on the great mass of Northern craftsmen. In the short term, as we saw, the reorganization of the trade unions brought them closer to the migrants: Despite the opposition of some groups, the craftsmen did by and large support the flattening of wage and skill hierarchies that association with the unskilled implied.[120] But by the mid-1970s the craftsmen began to reassert their autonomy and search for ways to protect both skill and wage differentials. Two related developments prompted this change.

The first was the successful regrouping of the Christian Democrats, who during the 1970s outmaneuvered the Left and prevented it from coming to power at the national level. An egalitarian alliance with the unskilled was far more appealing to the craftsmen when it seemed that the joint power of both groups would increase than when alliance simply meant sharing the burdens of defending the status quo. The second development had to do with the reorganization of the factory. If at first it had seemed that the workers would collectively impose a new division of labor on management, overcoming some of the distinctions between skilled and unskilled and justifying mass promotions, by the mid-1970s it became clear that, at least for the immediate future, management had found ways to counter the workers' power. One was simply to freeze hiring, allowing the work force to decline by attrition. Between 1975 and 1978 firms employing more than a thousand workers stopped hiring almost completely.[121] To expand, they decentralized work, establishing small factories, outside union control, to carry out new assignments or to evade regulations imposed by the workers in central plants.[122] Yet another countermove was plant reorganization, which, as often after 1962, destroyed the small nuclei of workers who had come to trust each other after the *autunno caldo*.

The stalemate between labor and capital gave skilled workers both the motive and the opportunity to jump ship. On the one hand, their dignity was insulted and their pocketbooks were lightened by the mass promotion of the unskilled: Conflicts between skilled and unskilled workers reemerged in the form of disputes over demands for automatic advancement and egalitarian pay scales.[123] On the other hand, the decentralization of production created many well-paid craft jobs in small shops. Throughout the 1970s, therefore, there was a steady flow of skilled workers out of the large factories and into the new, smaller ones. The alliance between skilled and unskilled, in other words, began to dissolve.

But the story of the *autunno caldo* and the integration of the migrants into the trade unions is far from over. The ambitions of the late 1960s have been disappointed, not abandoned. If circumstances were to become more favorable to the Left, significant numbers of migrants and craftsmen would probably become politically active again. In the meantime, the years of conflict have provoked changes in work organization that are affecting the various groups in the work force and relations among them.

Inside the large factories, the unions' demands for mass promotions, job rotation (the circulation of unskilled workers to a variety of posts), and job enrichment (enlargement of their jobs to include maintenance or supervisory tasks) are all blurring the distinction between skilled and unskilled workers.[124] Outside the large factories, in the thousands of small shops created by decentralization, the *decentramento produttivo*, craftsmen are free to develop their skills in previously impossible ways. In Chapter 5 I argue that these developments, catalyzed by changes in the structure of world markets, are producing new, post-Fordist forms of the division of labor within and between firms. But to understand how the craftsmen could get to these small firms in the first place – how they could be tempted by the idea of an egalitarian alliance one moment but walk away from it the next – it is necessary to draw together in a systematic way the observations made so far about the conflict behavior of skilled workers.

Craftsmen: revolutionaries or labor aristocrats?

The discussion to this point has suggested two conflicting images of the craftsman. In Chapter 3 he appeared solitary and pliant; he seemed to accept changes in the division of labor as inevitable and to abandon claims to promotion rather than face competition from the middle class. In this chapter he has been shown as willing to join broad collective movements to defend his rights and to contest threatening changes in the division of labor, but also as fickle in his allegiances: now siding with the unskilled against management, now abandoning them to advance the narrow interests of his immediate peers. This section shows how the craftsman can be both docile and militant – out for himself but capable of solidarity, disposed to lead broad movements against management but also to defend narrow privileges. The key to understanding the unity of these two sides of the craftsman's personality, I argue, is his recognition that he must permanently guard against management's attempts to usurp his skill. But why should management have it in for the craftsman's skill in the first place? And how does the craftsman's self-defense lead to apparently contradictory behavior?

The opposition between craftsmen and management is rooted in the contradiction between the idea of a craft as an ensemble of skills and Fordist principles of routinized mass production of standard goods. Recall the earlier description of the ideal typical craftsman as a kind of subcontractor with the power to pace work and choose tools and materials. The craftsman, we saw, performs a service. His job is to solve problems – for example, to put a particular machine in running order.

But – here is the contradiction – if a factory could be perfectly modeled on the Fordist principles outlined in Chapter 2, there would be no problems left to solve. To any given level of stable demand there would correspond a uniquely efficient set of technical procedures and work routines. The routines would become progressively simpler as productivity was raised through the subdivision of labor, together with the use of ever-more-specialized machines. Preventive maintenance could eliminate even the craft skills associated with repair work: As the wear and tear on machines became more predictable, parts could be replaced just before they were scheduled to

wear out. The closer a factory approached the Fordist ideal, therefore, the less room there would be for the ideal typical craftsman.

The opposition of principle very quickly becomes a real struggle
for control of production. For once management begins to apply
Fordist principles in even a halting way, it quickly discovers advantages to extending their application by further attacking the
craftsmen's autonomy. This was exactly the experience of American
industrialists in the nineteenth century. They began supplying
mass markets with no clear plans to replace craftsmen systematically by less-skilled workers tending specialized machines. But they
soon had motives to start this replacement. One was the need to
overcome bottlenecks in production caused by shortages of skilled
labor (whence the introduction of sewing machines in the shoe
industry);[125] another was the need to cut the costs of assembling
new products and repairing old ones (whence the use of precision,
special-purpose machines to guarantee interchangeability of parts
in the sewing-machine industry);[126] and a third was the need to
take advantage of the new technology that created mass markets
by cheapening traditional products (whence the conversion to the
Bessemer process in steelmaking).[127] Once mechanization was begun in any industry for any of these reasons, it set efficiency standards that led to corresponding changes in the whole chain of
manufacturing operations.

The more self-consciously industrialists drew general lessons from
these early experiences, the more they conceived of product and
production process in a unified way, simultaneously designing a
standard product to be made by special machine tools and unskilled
workers, and special machine tools to make the standard product.
Ford knew what he was doing when he offered customers one
model, the Model T, painted any color so long as it was black, and
produced with "farm tools": specialized machine tools so automatic
that they could be used by workers fresh off the farm.[128]

But, to recall one more set of arguments from Chapter 2, the
industrialists' intentions are not the end of the story. Partly because
Fordist principles could not always be rigorously applied, partly
because of the unintended results of applying them, craft skills are
still required in mass-production industries. For one thing, markets
are seldom stable enough to allow thoroughgoing routinization of
procedures. General Motors, for instance, successfully competed
with Ford by offering its customers many models each year, and
new models every year.[129] But the price of success was annual retooling by a corps of craftsmen. Another factor is that successive generations of machines are more complex. They require more and more

generally trained maintenance crews able to understand the interplay of mechanical, hydraulic, and electronic systems.

Even where the technology seemed permanent and predictable enough to permit preventive maintenance, unexpected problems cropped up. Cataloging all the parts that needed periodic replacement was more costly than anyone had imagined. Extracting various pieces of equipment from the guts of huge, integrated machines required, to the managers' surprise, considerable skill. Disrupting operations to meet a rigid maintenance schedule that ignored production deadlines imposed by customers' needs was prohibitively expensive. Thus, in the steel industry, one of the few in which management actually tried to carry the Fordist program to the limit, preventive maintenance is now regarded as at best a limited success. For reasons explained in Chapter 5, as machinery has become more complex and the mix of products more varied, development has been in the opposite direction, toward the diffusion of maintenance skills to production workers in order that they may better respond to emergencies.[130]

Skilled workers, therefore, live a perpetual cliff-hanger. The impossibility of carrying through the radical program of Fordist rationalization is no guarantee to any particular group of craftsmen that its skills are relatively safe. For there is always the chance that some of the ceaseless changes in materials and tools or in the fundamental definition of the product itself will undermine the market value of their skills. The end can come suddenly, as it did for the glass-blowers shoved aside by the introduction of automatic bottle-making machines in the late nineteenth century, or for the stevedores and watchmakers displaced by containerization and digital watches in the twentieth.[131] More likely, however, the value of skills will decline slowly as, for example, plastics are substituted for metals (or vice versa), electronic devices for mechanical ones, machines that etch and erode metals for machines that cut them, homes made of prefabricated modules for homes built wholly on the spot, and so on. Either way, the fact that some new group of workers with craft or intermediate-level skills is apt to profit from the changes is no consolation to the losers. Hence the problem that has come to preoccupy craftsmen in one country after another ever since the pace of technological change began to increase perceptibly in Great Britain at the start of the nineteenth century: How can they protect themselves against dangerously uncertain changes in the division of labor?

The common element in their answers is a two-step strategy: Claim favored jobs in the present; use the advantages accruing from those jobs to claim the most favored ones in the future. Craftsmen take the market power they have at any moment, use it to secure rights to do certain jobs in a certain way, and then, when work is reorganized, exchange the right to go on working the old way for the right to perform the most valued of the new jobs. Failing that, they settle for a lump-sum settlement to use for a new start in life or as a patrimony for their children. In other words, the craftsmen cling to current practices in the short term, but only to transform their relation to the industry from a market trade of skill for money to a historical relation between social groups: employers who specialize in certain kinds of products, and craftsmen who do whatever demanding work is needed to make them.[132]

The strategy is analogous to the one that keeps the upper classes in any industrial society on top: Use power in the present to take advantage of new opportunities for exercising it as they begin to open up. But the craftsman's variant of the strategy requires collective action, whereas the banker's does not. Barring a threat to the existing order that demands a common defense of the propertied classes, the banker can fend for himself. He simply converts income to wealth and uses his perch above the economy to spot the best investment opportunities, be they up-and-coming companies or good professional schools for his children.

The single craftsman, by contrast, will never make the money or have the information necessary to succeed as an investor in the narrow sense. His investment possibilities are limited at best to the range of jobs in his industry; and his investable income depends on the solidarity of his work group. His insurance for the future depends on collective action in the present: strikes and strike threats to secure recognition both of the right to work according to certain rules in the first place and, for reasons we will consider in a moment, of collective enforcement of the rules once they have been conceded.

The craftsmen's application of this strategy is self-evident in some countries, obscured by thickets of complex collective-bargaining institutions in others. In Great Britain and the United States, where unions of craft workers emerged early, gained power at the workplace, and set the pattern for the rest of the labor movement, workers and managers often make no bones about the fact that work rules are made to be traded for money wages or new rules. The principle is that each group in the work force makes the best rules it can for itself, and management "buys back the rule book" when it has to.[133]

Strategic moves tend to be less direct in countries like France or West Germany, where workers quickly became part of industrial unions including many unskilled groups, unions in general have less power on the shop floor, and plant-level bargaining is carried out by some variety of works council created by national legislation and representing all the work force. Particular groups of craft workers are not organized to bargain explicitly with management over detailed work rules. Instead, they protect their positions in the division of labor by making sure that the national unions and the works council, both of which they influence through informal caucuses, respect their long-term interests in negotiation.[134] In the exceptional cases where craft workers in these countries have preponderant power in a national union, however, they openly pursue the strategy of lifting their relations with management out of the market by contractual agreement and keeping them out through collective enforcement. Thus, in the craft unions in the Communist CGT, Dennis Segrestin writes:

> Everything transpires as if the CGT federations of seamen, longshoremen and typographers were led to use professional solidarity to create a space between the economic and social orders. This effort manifests itself primarily in two kinds of union practices: the first consist in "fixing" a profession by means of collective bargaining contracts or legislation which produces the result that the profession is defined by reference to the texts and not to the economic realities. The second consist in using professional solidarities to counteract the tendency towards increased integration of the worker in the plant insofar as this implies his increasing dependence on the logic of economic forces.[135]

The thread with which this strategic pattern is woven is the solidarity of the work group. Without such solidarity, management cannot be forced to concede advantageous work rules; without solidarity, management can bribe individual workers to break the rules that do exist, rewarding them for setting standards of performance that others must follow or for betraying the group's accumulated knowledge about machines and processes. Even when the craftsmen's bargaining strategy is informally organized, the imperative of solidarity textures every aspect of the craftsmen's group life: the way they teach things to each other and to apprentices, their dealings with management, the way they share work and wages, and even their jokes and pranks. And, of course, in the Anglo-American world solidarity often gives structure to their official workplace organizations as well. In the paradigmatic case, the pursuit of solidarity imposed by the craftsmen's long-term strategy turns their workplace organization into a kind of little Geneva, an egalitarian republic held together by its rectitude and its rules.

The chapels of the English printers are an example of such a craft organization. The modern chapels grew out of early benevolent societies, organizations by which workers insured themselves against unemployment, sickness, and burial costs. In its present form a chapel includes all members of a single printing-craft union in one plant, seldom as many as a hundred men.[136]

The chapel's formal procedures and the substance of its decisions are meant to conserve the unity of the group. Solidarity, A. J. M. Sykes reports in his study of the Glasgow printing trades, was "a constant theme among men, whose first concern on hearing of new developments was often to wonder what their effects on unity would be."[137]

Procedurally, the chapel as a collective body has the exclusive right to decide matters regarding work. Overtime, piece rates, premiums for shift work, and supplements to industry-wide wage agreements are all established in negotiations between the chapel and management. Individual workers do not bargain for themselves. The rule is that no member discusses these matters with his superior except in the presence of the "father" of the chapel, its chief executive and senior judge. Conversely – and this underscores the connection between the craftsmen's solidarity and their need to limit what management can know about them – the chapel does not disclose any worker's production record or allow the installation of devices that would keep track of his performance. Decisions are by plurality vote and bind all members. As in the Renaissance Italian communes, the members guard against the usurpation of power by making it a custom that their chief official, the father of the chapel, not hold office for long.

Substantively, the decisions must maintain rough equality among the chapel's members. Once negotiations with management are completed, therefore, the chapel allocates the work to satisfy prevailing notions of the proper income for a worker of a given skill grade and seniority.[138] The chapel's legislative and administrative activity in turn depend on and reinforce deep-seated and widely shared sentiments of social justice and mutual dependence. Without a consensus on the proper distribution of work or the inviolability of collective decisions, the chapel's combination of egalitarian substance and democratic procedure would not endure. Without sure standards for the interpretation and administration of collective agreements, every decision by the father of the chapel could provoke a political crisis; or his failure to act for fear of provoking a crisis could lead to slow erosion first of de facto equality, then of belief in equality as a principle.[139]

The social consensus that underpins the chapel's actions is expressed and confirmed by two kinds of practices and rituals. The first show the chapel as a community: initiation rites for apprentices, printshop excursions, and "pass-rounds," or collections, for members who are ill or leaving the chapel. The second kind demonstrate to each printer his vulnerability to the others. This is the deeper significance of many workplace pranks played especially on younger and newer members: "Particular enjoyment is derived by encouraging people to lose their equanimity: 'getting him out' or 'having him,' as it is called. This kind of activity serves a valuable function of 'levelling' by preventing men from showing arrogance, conceit, or straying too far from the accepted code of behavior or even from a way of life – to do so will invite comment and sarcasm sufficiently friendly to be heeded."[140]

If such pranks fail to bring results, Ralph, the workshop ghost, begins to spirit away the delinquent's tools. In extreme cases the worker can be drummed out of the union, an event that, given the latter's control over the job market, amounts to exclusion from the trade. Similarly, anyone who abuses the members' tolerance can be excluded by vote from the chapel's beneficial society and so denied his pension.[141]

Historically, this form of organization has helped preserve the printers' professional status from the consequences of the increasing mechanization of their trade. During each round of technological innovation the printers have used the chapel's collective strength and the employers' weaknesses – newspapers cannot make up for sales lost during a strike by extra production later – to secure rights over the use and manning of new machines. The classic example is the transition to Linotype at the end of the nineteenth century. By skillful application of the craftsmen's general strategy, successive generations of English printers have defined themselves as members of a continuously regenerated community of producers, and have forced management to accept that definition.[142] Keith Sisson, for example, writes in his study of present-day Fleet Street, the center of the London newspaper industry:

The management exercises little or no executive control in the production and maintenance departments in Fleet Street. The first-line managers who are most closely involved with the chapels are not in practice responsible for the management in their departments. In effect theirs is a technical role only. Put simply, the industrial relations manager manages by negotiation, or, more specifically, through the payment system. The chapels, for their part, undertake to perform a number of tasks in the manufacturing process. As the preamble to one typical comprehensive agreement states: "The purpose of this agreement, which covers hours, payments and working arrangements, is to provide a comprehensive production service."[143]

The clearest measure of the vitality of these organizations is their capacity to control the introduction of new, electronic typesetting technology. In 1978, for example, the Times Newspapers Ltd., publisher of the *London Times, Sunday Times,* and their three supplements, tried to introduce "single-stroke keyboarding." Under this system journalists and personnel in the advertising department type copy directly into a typesetting computer rather than passing it to a Linotype operator. When the NGA, the National Graphics Association, the federation of chapels that represents compositors and other skilled print workers, refused to accept the plan and other proposed changes, Times Newspapers locked them out. But the Fleet Street chapels found jobs at other newspapers for many of those laid off, and paid meager but regular strike benefits to those with no work. Half a year later, threatened by huge losses and the prospect of an irreversible loss of market, management abandoned its insistence on single-stroke keyboarding. "Chapel power, in Fleet Street," the labor editor at the *Times* wrote, had been "confirmed and consolidated: the final deals were struck with chapel leaders." The outcome of the dispute "lends credence to the NGA view that the union is 'winning the war of the new technology.' " Single-stroke keyboarding, he estimated, would be introduced "only if NGA retains the lion's share of printing and correcting of copy."[144]

Nor, to repeat, is there anything peculiarly British about this pattern of self-defense. Even without an independent workplace organization, French craft workers, for example, succeed in maintaining their solidarity against outsiders by converting their skills into a series of secrets passed from initiate to initiate. Maintenance workers in a factory Michel Crozier studied

keep their skill as a rule-of-thumb. They completely disregard all blueprints and maintenance directions, and have been able to make them disappear from the plants. They believe in individual settings exclusively, and they are the only ones to know these settings. These and all the other tricks of the trade are learned through companionship on the job. Every job is done individually, but there is a great deal of solidarity for learning purposes and whenever there is a difficult problem. However, no explanations are ever given, and the learning process is therefore painful. It is an old handicraft apprenticeship, the harshness of which explains the impatient reactions of the newly arrived men. But these practices are necessary for preserving the group's absolute control over machine stoppages.[145]

Now I want to return to the opening questions concerning the unity of the craftsman's personality, rephrasing them in the light of this account of his strategy. First, what is the relation between the craftsman's career in the factory hierarchy and his participation in the collective defense of the craft's position in the division of labor? Second, how can craftsmen's general strategy of self-defense permit them to side now with, now against, the unskilled?

The connection between the craftsman's views about his own struggle for place in the factory and his group's self-defense is the idea of the craft as an unending series of technical challenges and the craftsman as a problem solver. The single craftsman, we know, sees his career at work not as a fixed set of activities, but as a potentially unlimited succession of jobs, each requiring an extension of his technical prowess and preparing him for the next. The craftsmen's self-defense can be seen as a collective, long-term application of the same view: Each generation claims the right to grapple with the demanding and rewarding tasks of its day, different though these may be from the problems that preceded them. The individual and the group both follow an old maxim of British craftsmen: Follow the work to the machines.

But if the strategies of the individual and the group are ultimately in harmony, they are not always so. At any moment the group, for strategic reasons, stakes a claim to a particular set of jobs, implicitly abandoning the others to its potential competitors. The career of any single craftsman, however, does not automatically respect these conventional limits: Talent and drive can carry him up to the boundary of the territory clearly defined as the group's. If he crosses it, accepting promotion, for example, to a job normally held by a college-trained engineer, it may seem that he is betraying the group, putting its secrets at management's disposal in return for advancement; if he forfeits the promotion, then it is the group that in a sense betrays its obligation to the individual, checking the development of his powers rather than fostering them.

Craftsmen are well aware of these tensions and have found a number of devices for reconciling them. One is to create a kind of double morality based on the distinction between work in large factories and work in small shops. Ambition must yield to the commands of solidarity in the large factory, but not in the small shop. This dichotomy is often expressed in conflicting views of unions: Workers who are union militants whenever they work in large factories can be indifferent to the union, even deprecate it, when they work in small shops. Italian, German, or American craftsmen, for example, often willingly enforce more or less formal limits on work loads and job assignments in large factories so as to share the available jobs. In small shops they seldom think of restricting themselves in this way; on the contrary, they are likely to feel free to earn and learn whatever they can.

A second device for keeping ambition in its place is to treat the official qualifying procedures for promotion in large firms as a kind of rebirth. As long as the craftsman is part of the group, he obeys its rules. If he qualifies for promotion by passing a series of difficult tests, often requiring years of night school and having little to do with the actual requirements of his new job, no one begrudges the successful candidate his success. Though his sacrifices may in fact have gained him nothing in the way of practical knowledge, they justify the belief that superior character and skill have been rewarded. In this way the ambitious craftsman can transcend the group without betraying it and, as we saw in the case of skilled German workers in high positions, continue to respect and be respected by it. The group's defense of decent jobs for all its members thus leaves space for the most energetic to seek their fortune, and the same worker can be in turn loyal to the group and self-interested without fundamentally changing his idea of a craft career at work.[146]

This leaves the riddle of the craftsmen's wavering loyalties. How can they be bargaining for privileges for themselves at one moment and rallying other groups against the management of a single plant, or even capitalism in general, at the next? The answer lies in a central ambiguity of the craftsmen's strategy of self-defense. The attempt to fix contractually the existing division of labor and the corresponding social relations between the craftsmen and the firm has a double significance. It limits management's discretion by opposing the workers' veto power, a rudimentary form of control over production, to established authority.[147] It also gives added weight to the privileges the craftsmen already enjoy with respect to other groups, fusing their preferential rights with their self-definition – for instance, making an advantageous place in the wage hierarchy a symbol of their social position in the plant.[148] Depending on which aspect of the strategy is thrust forward, the craftsmen seem more or less politically radical, the shield of the less skilled against management's aggression or the passive beneficiaries, if not the agents, of the aggressor. But so long as craftsmen defend their interests by fortifying positions within the existing division of labor, both elements are necessarily present. Neglect of the underlying connection between them accounts for much of the confusion in the old debate among sociologists and political activists over the craftsmen's fundamental political predisposition.

Thus, at one extreme, the skilled workers' resistance to managerial control of the factory and to the political authority of a government acting against their interests has made them seem to some the most class conscious of proletarians: victimized by capitalism but, because of their experience of workplace autonomy, capable of taking command of production and turning the machines to better use. At the other extreme, craft defense of privilege has seemed to justify the view, associated with some strands of Lenin's and Engels's thought, of skilled workers as labor aristocrats, tied to a defense of the existing order for fear of losing the advantages it provides.[149] There is historical evidence for both views, but it is always contaminated by facts that suggest that each is incomplete and connected at bottom to the other.

The best evidence for the view of the craftsman as revolutionary is the shop-floor movements led by skilled workers against the militarization of factory life and the rationalization of work that emerged in varying degrees among the major belligerent powers toward the end of World War I.

Typically, the national unions supported the war effort out of a mixture of sincere patriotism, fear of government coercion, and self-interest: They traded assent to the war for recognition of their rights to be consulted by the government on important questions, to organize workers in the factories, and to bargain with industry. In the short run this left managers in war-related industries with a free hand to meet the vast demand for rigidly standardized products by routinizing work in the best Fordist tradition: introducing specialized machines, downgrading craftsmen, and flooding the factories with new, unskilled workers. As fear for the future of their crafts coalesced with resentments at the prospect of military service and anger at high prices caused by wartime shortages, the craftsmen broke free of the national leaders, organized local alliances of different work groups who shared at least some of the grievances, and began to strike and demonstrate in their own name: The strikes led by the *Obleute*, skilled shop stewards in the Berlin armaments industry, are the clearest example. Where the national government and the industrialists were discredited by defeat, these protest movements could become the nuclei of factory soviets that took charge of production at the war's end, as happened in Berlin in 1918 and in St. Petersburg, where unions had been especially weak even before 1914, the year before.[150]

Some aspects of these movements are revolutionary by any standard. The workers' capacity to maintain production certainly cast doubt on middle-class ideas about management's indispensability; and the improvised redistribution of tasks among different work groups that occurred in and between factories under worker control called in question the efficiency of the prevailing hierarchies. During the occupation of the Turin factories in September 1920, for example, the unions and the local chamber of labor established an elaborate system for exchanging products, raw materials, and technical, legal, and political information between plants.[151]

But even at the height of these movements, the craftsmen never made a deliberate effort to overcome the distinction between themselves and the unskilled by training the latter and systematically redistributing tasks to level differences in degrees of discretion. And as the prospects for worker control of the factories in the postwar period worsened, what seemed an oversight rapidly became a conscious choice: With the regrouping of bourgeois authority in the state and factory in Germany in the 1920s, for example, the skilled workers found themselves in opposition to the unskilled, trying as best they could to defend their special interests against capital's reorganization of the factories. Kurt Brigl-Matthiass's description of the factory-council politics in large German plants in this period suggests the intensity of the struggles between the skilled and their unskilled competitors:

Especially in the large plants it is not infrequently the case that, despite the intention of the law, certain categories of workers are represented insufficiently or not all in the factory council. As a rule the underrepresented groups are skilled workers. Either the craftsmen are too few in number to be successful in elections, or else they refuse to stand as candidates because of their dislike for the office. It can also often be observed that the radical mass of unskilled workers refuses to vote for the skilled, whom they regard as a plant aristocracy.[152]

Less extreme but analogous conflicts, as we saw, began to emerge in Italy after the hottest part of the *autunno caldo*.

Conversely, the evidence for the view of the craftsman as labor aristocrat is undercut by signs of a deeply rooted and general opposition to capitalism that goes beyond the requirements of immediate self-interest. Craft workers not directly threatened by changes in work organization frequently continue to support, by their contributions and their votes, leftist parties dedicated to some kind of social transformation. The compositors in the chapels studied by I. C. Cannon, for one example, were loyal supporters of the Labor Party, their comfortable position at the top of the national blue-collar wage hierarchy notwithstanding.[153] The skilled workers who left the large Italian factories for the new small ones in the 1970s, for a second example, are often dedicated members of the Italian Communist Party. Even if one doubts that either the British Labor Party or the Italian Communist Party has any serious revolutionary intentions at all, it is hard to see how such association with pseudo-transformative movements is a cover for selfish interest in either of these cases. A more plausible explanation is that, directly threatened or not, craftsmen experience day by day a series of conflicts with management that make it difficult for them to forget the systematic opposition between craft organization and Fordism even at the best of times, and easy for them to recall it the moment things turn sour.

For these reasons, to debate whether the craftsman is a labor aristocrat or a revolutionary misses the point. He resembles both in turn because he is neither. His strategy of self-defense shapes his view of his work, his relations to managers and other work groups, and his jokes; but it does not unambiguously determine his political views. The same thing is true of the conflict strategies of workers with plant-specific skills, to which I turn next.

Producers and parasites

The worker with intermediate-level skills, I argued earlier, is drawn in contrary directions. His facility with the plant's production techniques affords a degree of autonomy translatable into privileges denied unskilled workers. But his assertiveness is checked by fear, for changes in the division of labor can make his extremely specialized knowledge useless to his employer, the only one who values it. By neglecting the second half of the story, theorists of the new working class convinced themselves that workers with intermediate-level skills, especially the process workers whom they studied most attentively, were more self-assured and demanding than they proved to be. This section argues that, despite their differences, the theorists of the new working class all jumbled the essentials of the half of the story they did tell.

We saw earlier that Blauner, Mallet, and Popitz and Bahrdt agreed that the new worker saw himself as a producer. They also agreed that, because he did, certain demands would necessarily follow. Their disagreements went to what those demands would be. The argument here is that the claims which special workers derive from their responsibility for safeguarding production depend on their relation to other work groups on the job and through politics. Just as the craftsmen's struggle for autonomy leads in different directions, depending on their political experience and possibilities of alliance, so affronts to the special worker's dignity as a producer become actionable only in connection with other aspects of his experience.

The theorists' own disagreements about the substantive relation between work experience and politics should have alerted them to the central difficulty with establishing the connection in the first place: the ambiguity of the distinction between producers and parasites. Blauner thought that the market was rational and that capitalist managers contributed to human happiness by using the technical apparatus to pursue profits. Rational process workers would, accordingly, discover their community of interests with management. Mallet and the others, influenced by the idea of a socialist-planned economy, thought the capitalist market irrational. They were sure that worker producers would arrive at the same conclusion as well and band together against the parasitic managers. If the theorists could disagree on who was a producer and who not, what ensured that the workers would not disagree among themselves as well?

The history of the European labor movement suggests in fact that workers are no more certain of the political upshot of the distinction between producers and parasites than are the intellectuals. Syndicalist, corporatist, and fascist movements all claimed to rally the producers against the exploiters: the first according to an interpretation of the distinction similar to Mallet's; the latter two according to an antimarket (but also antiplanning) variant of Blauner's.

Conversely, because they are all rooted in the same analytic distinction, syndicalist, corporatist, and fascist doctrines shade off into one another. In France, for example, Nicos Poulantzas writes,

the corporatist ideology can, under certain circumstances . . . express "proletarian aspirations" – and not inauthentic ones. By means of the illusion of the factory as an economic cell closed off from the world of political authority, this corporatism expresses the aspiration of the conquest of power and the elimination of authority, property, and control. Corporatism has in this sense the meaning of a rejection of power and authority by means of the exercise of workers' control in the factory, and thereby the imposition of their will on management. This conception is thus linked directly to the tradition of revolutionary syndicalism: one finds in Proudhon's approval of the "corporatist" projects of Napoleon III an illustrious precedent.[154]

The period between the two world wars is also full of examples of passages, individual and collective, from one kind of movement against exploitation to another: Mussolini's switch from socialism to fascism and the German trade unions' flirtation with left-wing Nazism are two of the most notorious.[155]

Still, historical examples can always be dismissed as no more than that. The new working class was supposed to be something new. Though the argument was not made explicitly, the new class was presumably proof against the old confusion. In what follows, therefore, I draw on case studies of special workers to show that even when they do demand rights as producers, their notion of rights is no more politically determinate than was the sense of entitlement of previous generations of workers in different positions in the division of labor.

Take first the workers with intermediate-level skills who correspond most closely to the type of the new worker: process workers on the same shift in an oil refinery. They must cooperate in an articulated way. Even on the day shift, when management is present, they are allowed a substantial measure of autonomy. When it is their turn to work nights they are still freer: No manager is likely to be present except if called in the case of an emergency. Cut off from the world outside and left to themselves, the workers during these hours control the factory. If a single experience can teach that management is dispensable, this is likely to be it.

In a study of technologically comparable pairs of refineries in France and Great Britain, Gallie found, however, that shift workers learned not one lesson from their job, but several.[156] To make things more complicated still, the lessons they learned were not always the same.

Workers in both countries quickly discovered something that theorists of the new working class had overlooked: Shift work disrupts family life, friendships, and digestion. This disruption alone was enough to make them realize the limits of their privileges with respect to other work groups and to give them a chronic grievance against management.

This grievance, however, gave rise to different demands in the two countries. In part the diversity reflected differences in the shift schedules. The morning shift in the French plants started at 5:00 a.m., the afternoon shift at 1:00 p.m., and the night shift at 9:00 p.m. Shifts at the British plants started an hour or two later. A French worker, therefore, almost never had the whole evening free: To get up for the morning shift he had to be in bed by about 8:00 p.m.; he did not arrive home from the afternoon shift until 9:30 or 10:00 p.m.; and to make the night shift he had to be out of the house by 8:00 or 8:30 p.m. If his wife had a daytime job, he scarcely saw her. The British system, on the other hand, allowed the worker on the morning and night shifts to spend most of the evening at home. But the diversity of demands was also a result of important differences in the countries' labor movements and patterns of work organization. Both of these, in turn, were related to the patterns of relation among work groups in the refineries.

In Great Britain the shift workers' demands were influenced by the British style of militant trade unionism examined in the preceding section. Craft and process workers were organized in separate unions, each of which used particular grievances to win itself more money or greater control over work conditions from management. Every demand was therefore narrowly formulated to avoid the impression of asking for general concessions, and was compensable in either money or privileges; and every victory in negotiations with management added new, politically divisive particulars to the shift workers' situation.

The result was that British shift workers drew no general lessons from the disruptiveness of their jobs. After years of passivity, they began in the early 1970s to demand a shift allowance in return for the sacrifice of family and social life. Nor, for that matter, did the experience of part-time freedom from supervision awaken any general sympathy for other workers' defense of workplace autonomy. The process workers were resentful of the maintenance workers' rights to pace their work – rights, they felt, that put process workers as well as management at the mercy of the craftsmen and jeopardized the plant's efficiency.

In France, shift workers' demands were shaped by the style of the two dominant unions in the refineries: the Communist CGT and the Socialist CFDT. Despite their differences, both unions were convinced that a capitalist society could never do justice to workers, and that labor organizations therefore had a double task. They had to seek partial redress for the workers' most pressing grievances; but at the same time they had to use the struggle for reform pedagogically to illustrate the limits of mere reformism and to reinforce the unity of all workers. There were, as we saw, conflicts between skilled and semiskilled workers in France, too. But these tended to be muted because the CGT and CFDT organized both groups in their respective industry-wide unions. Moreover, and no doubt in part because they had no separate representatives, the skilled workers were as ruthlessly antagonistic toward management as were the semiskilled.

The grievances of the French shift workers were consequently interpreted in an extremely general, even symbolic, way and linked to broad issues affecting all workers. During the 1960s the union constantly and successfully called attention to the disruptiveness of shift life as a way of demonstrating to the process workers that they were no exception to capital's oppressiveness. The union's campaign of reform aimed at establishing the substantive equality of the shift workers' with that of the rest of the working class. Process workers were to have warm meals at night, vacations during the national holiday periods, and the right to transfer to day work. Manning levels were to be increased to reduce the possibility that anyone would be unexpectedly called to work to replace a missing workmate. The more management gave in to these demands, the more the experiences of the process workers overlapped with those of other workers. Finally, instead of asking for a shift allowance, which might have caused friction between skilled and process workers within each union, the CGT and the CFDT demanded early retirement for the latter. Although they were much more militant than the British shift workers (the combined result of union agitation and their inherently more onerous schedule), the French refinery operators bore no closer resemblance to the new working class.

Two further and extreme examples suggest the variety of shift-worker behavior possible within each national labor movement. Neither attests the kind of relation between place in the division of labor and politics that is at the heart of the theories of the new working class. Both demonstrate again the importance of politics in- and outside the workplace in shaping process workers' relations to work and other work groups.

The first study, by Dorothy Wedderburn and Rosemary Crompton, is of five chemical plants of a single firm located in a "heavily working class" area of northeast England.[157] It shows that in Great Britain under unusually favorable conditions special workers can begin to regard themselves as a distinct group of producers, but in a way that combines traditional craft pride with the special worker's reliance on his current employer.

Works A produced starting materials for manufacturing operations carried out elsewhere in the concern. Because the output was marketed internally, planning could be long-term. Management thus had few occasions to intervene in day-to-day operations, especially because the highly automatic production apparatus made frequent consultation between workers and supervisors unnecessary. Nor did Works A workers, unlike the process workers in the studies discussed in Chapter 3, fear that their jobs would be redefined or abolished.

Under these conditions the special workers developed a sense of collective responsibility for a particular production area requiring a range of related skills. Because the workers determined their work rhythms, they found time for vocational study on the job. Some had learned enough to qualify for twelve jobs in the area; and their extraordinary diligence was only one sign of a widely felt, incipient professionalism that the men associated with integration into the craft world, whose values are especially conspicuous in their part of Great Britain. The Works A men "appeared more conscious of their identity as chemical workers than the men on other works. They were interested in the idea of a chemical workers' union because, as they put it, 'each trade should have its own unions.' They also emphasized the importance of adequate training for the job, which suggested that they took pride in their technical competence."[158]

Unlike craftsmen in the strict sense, however, the Works A men did not stress their independence from their current employer. On the contrary, there was evidence that they were even *more* willing to identify themselves with a particular workplace than were the other special workers included in the study. For the time being, and thoroughly in keeping with the emergent character of their skills (and their ultimate vulnerability in the labor market), this group of special workers aimed at establishing themselves as a hybrid type: plant craftsmen.[159]

The second example is taken from Christiane Barrier's study of a French nuclear power station.[160] It suggests what can happen when the French labor movement's strategy of arousing the special workers' resentments goes awry. The operating crews' complaints about conditions in the power plant were the familiar ones: Though they were well paid and essentially could not be fired, they found the rigid conditions imposed by their work intolerable. As one of them put it: "We in the continuous sections, we have to put up with a lot more than the discontinuous workers. Holidays, Saturdays, Sundays – smooth operations have to be guaranteed. *We can't have any family life, or, if it comes to that, any life at all.* For us it's either work or sleep."[161] But the workers, Barrier found, directed their anger not just against the supervisors or the government but also against the public at large, obviously not excepting other workers. The operating crews no longer felt part of a broad movement of social transformation. Their view was not that the social hierarchy should be flattened or abolished, but rather that its summit should be occupied "by those immediately responsible for assuring security – production (and capable as well of calling forth a situation of danger or deprivation, of which they too would be victims, but which would not perhaps be less tolerable for them than war or revolution – or quite simply their absurd lives cut off from all natural and cultural rhythms)."[162]

Gallie found signs of potentially similar developments among the French refinery workers he studied. The shift workers' sense of injustice had been aroused by trade-union agitation, but left unsatisfied by the meager short-term results of a strategy that subordinated particular interests to general ones. Hence they were, for instance, tempted to join militant splinter unions interested only in Gompers's "more, more, more."[163] At all events the bitterness of the disappointed French shift workers seems to have led no more in the direction of the new working class than did the satisfied pride of their successful British counterparts.

Next consider the case of conflicts involving the other type of workers with intermediate-level skills: workers with the special kinds of dexterity invaluable in plants where pieces are worked on a succession of machines. To underscore the influence of politics on the ambitions of special workers, I again juxtapose examples of workers doing comparable jobs in different circumstances. But this time, instead of taking contemporaneous examples from different countries, the illustrations are from different periods in the same countries.

The first concerns welders in the United States. We saw from Friedlander's study of a UAW local in Hamtramck that young, second-generation Polish welders had an important part in organizing the union. We saw, too, how the struggle to organize the union local politicized the welders in two ways. It drew them and the immigrant communities in Pittsburgh, Cleveland, Youngstown, Chicago, Buffalo, and Detroit into the larger world of union and national politics, fixing their and their children's allegiance to the Democratic Party for decades: After 1936 Hamtramck gave more than 90 percent of its votes to Roosevelt.[164] And it made the welders the center of a reform movement on the shop floor aimed at limiting management's discretion and opening new career opportunities to the skilled. Thus the welders in the Hamtramck plant represented broad interests even while they advanced their own: "We wanted to have ears, influence all over the shop," one of their leaders recalled. "No part of the shop should be able to say, 'We were not represented.' "[165]

About twenty-five years later, Leonard B. Sayles studied another group of welders and metal polishers in an American plant. He does not report on their family history or their life outside the plant. But from what he does say of their behavior at work it is clear that they used their shop-floor power to advance the narrow interests of their group, not to reform work organization, let alone influence national debate. They affected other work groups only insofar as their struggles with management disrupted established customs and wage differentials, whose readjustment often profited other kinds of workers. Groups like the welders and metal polishers, Sayles writes, "use collective bargaining tactics, the whole range, in fact, to obtain benefits for themselves quite apart from any inequitable management action. In the process they come to set new standards for the plant as a whole for such matters as appropriate work loads, idle time, incentive earnings, and countless non-economic working conditions."[166]

Kergoat's account of the political transformation of the truck drivers at Bulledor provides an example of the reverse development:

a group of special workers that came, through political experience, to see fundamental connections between its interests and those of other workers. The truck drivers' job was to deliver the beverages bottled at the plant to its customers. Before May 1968, they were isolated from the rest of the work force. They regarded their detailed knowledge of delivery routes and customers' quirks as indispensable to the success of the plant. That neither management nor other workers acknowledged their special role was a source of resentment and a justification for any strategic move that furthered the group's particular interest.

The truck drivers' participation in the events of May 1968 began to change all that. Recall that workers occupied the factory during the strike, but continued to produce and deliver mineral water needed by hospitals. Suddenly the established division of labor was overthrown, and the one that temporarily replaced it corresponded to the truck drivers' stylized image of their true place in the factory. They organized the delivery routes themselves; skilled workers accompanied them on the delivery runs.

This experience of solidarity, and indispensability, seconded by a subsequent strike, had a double effect on the truck drivers. It made them more assertive as a group, and especially more willing to demand more autonomy on the job. But it also made them more willing to harmonize their claims with those of other work groups. A newfound interest in the union was an expression of both tendencies. Some of the truck drivers became *delegués du personnel*, a kind of shop steward; and the group as a whole, Kergoat writes, tended "to abandon job actions of a sectional nature and to raise instead more general problems regarding the plant as a whole."[167]

Thus struggle and politics count in the definition of the interests of special workers in these kinds of plants just as much as in continuous-process industries, and just as much for special workers of all kinds as for other work groups. Everywhere we have looked the story has been the same: The idea of a career at work is the starting point, not the end station, of a work group's understanding of its relation to other workers and management. The next section sets out what it is that we do and do not know when we know that much.

The ambiguities of class and the possibilities of politics

Assuming they are not widely off the mark, the last two chapters are bad news for those who hold any version of what I earlier called the reductionist view: the idea that place in the division of labor precisely determines a worker's immediate claims to material rewards and autonomy at the workplace, as well as his vision of a just society – in short, his politics. If a class is defined in the Marxist sense as a group of persons who share a position in the division of labor, and who *for that reason* share political views, then another way to make the same point is to say that blue-collar workers do not form a class.[168]

Thus we saw in Chapter 3 that workers standing side by side in a factory do not necessarily view their work in the same way: Ghetto workers, would-be craftsmen, and peasant workers, each with their own set of aspirations, might be working on the same assembly line. In the same factory craftsmen with downgraded skills and would-be craftsmen climbing the skill hierarchy might be adjusting the same machines, but judging the job in the light of diverse ideas of a career at work.

Worse still for the reductionist, even when workers doing the same work view it in the same way, this agreement alone does not exclude large differences in their attitudes toward other workers, management, and the significance of the factory hierarchy in general. This chapter has showed that workers who think of themselves as would-be craftsmen can try to enter industrial society as individuals, acknowledging the legitimacy of the existing lines of promotion, or can fight for mass, collective admission, and attempt to redefine the hierarchy as they scale it. The craftsmen's assertion of workplace autonomy leads sometimes to a defense of privileges against other work groups' claims to equality, sometimes to a defense of equality against management's authority. Workers with plant-specific skills can see their situation as analogous to the craftsmen's (ambiguous as this latter's may be), or as fundamentally incommensurate with any other kind of blue-collar experience.

Conversely, in cases like the Italian *autunno caldo*, where different work groups did begin to act like a class in that they viewed work and politics in convergent ways, the convergence was not simply the reflection in thought of an increasing homogeneity of jobs. Even the emergence of a (temporarily) unified working class depended on a coincidence of events – the mass migration to the North, the changes in the strategies of parties, unions, and students – that were not simply reflexes of changes in the division of labor.

The findings of the preceding two chapters suggest a positive conclusion as well – that a work group's precise aspirations, its reactions to changes in the division of labor, and even its views about the possibilities of comprehensive social transformations are shaped by its relations to other groups, both inside the blue-collar work force and beyond. The examples of the Italian migrants, the Portuguese at Bulledor, the second-generation Slavic immigrants in Hamtramck, the revolutionary *Obleute,* and the refinery workers in France and Great Britain all tell the same story: Experiences of collaboration and conflict with other groups determine what strategic conclusions a work group ultimately draws from its idea of a career at work.

To put the point another way, the members of the work group learn through collective experience how to realize their ambitions; and it is only as they begin to realize their ambitions that they discover what they really want. In the simplest case a group starts out with general aims – for example, to find a permanent place in the factory or defend a craft. How in fact it begins to pursue this goal depends on an amalgam of objective and subjective factors. By objective factors I mean anything that bears on the balance of forces between a work group and its antagonists: the strength of its organizations and its opponents', the state of the economy, the availability of allies, and so on. Subjective factors refer to the group's convictions about the range of plausible strategies at any moment.

These two kinds of factors are easily confused, and no amount of theoretical discussion will completely eliminate the temptation to reduce subjective to objective features of situation. But the two are distinguishable, and there is no intellectually defensible way to deduce the former from the latter. In the end, more or less confused political debate over choices counts in shaping a group's course of action.

It is difficult to distinguish subjective from objective factors simply because in any concrete situation the two are likely to be tightly intertwined. The more allies one has, for instance, the more plausible certain strategies become; but in order to win allies it is often necessary to have a tentative joint strategy in the first place. Thus the leftist traditions of the Northern skilled workers and students expedited alliance with the unskilled migrants; and the alliance encouraged pursuit of a kind of transformative strategy. To see that ideas played an important part in the outcome, you need only compare Italian developments with the American New Deal, where the ideological traditions of craft workers obstructed cooperation with the unskilled, driving them into opposition to the established labor movement and limiting the range of strategic choices available to either group.[169]

The lingering temptation to reduce subjective to objective factors arises from the indisputable fact that ideas have histories. Before they become relevant in politics, someone had to have and disseminate them. Because the originators and disseminators of ideas are enmeshed in the life of their times, there is always the temptation to see the ideas as nothing but the reflections of the times. The ideas that win out, in this view, win out because they have to: Political debate is just the objective world talking to itself. But the more seriously this claim is pursued, the clearer it becomes that it can be made good only at the price of trivializing the original conception: denaturing any theory that defines in a general way the relation between particular material developments and the evolution of thought.

Ask, for example, why under comparable conditions Swedish Social Democrats risked an alliance with the farmers and experiments with a version of Keynesianism, whereas the German Social Democrats dismissed a plan for demand stimulation devised by trade-union leaders as a theoretical monstrosity, and you discover heterogeneous motives connected loosely at best to differences in social structure. The Swedes, it has been argued, were more attentive to the possibilities of reforming a capitalist economy because of their electoral alliances with liberal industrialists and their familiarity, itself a result of the alliance, with the progressive ideas of early twentieth-century English liberalism. The German Social Democrats were cut off from liberal allies and liberal ideas. Another factor may have been a difference in the balance of power between grain-consuming dairy farmers and grain-growing estate owners in the two countries. In Sweden a preponderance of dairy farmers over grain growers may have facilitated an alliance between the farmers and the grain-consuming workers; in Germany the situation was the reverse.

But no one disputes that imagination, daring, and political instinct were also crucial. Part of the shift in power within the agricultural sector in Sweden can be attributed to the boldness of the insurgents who took control from the conservatives and pushed for an alliance with the Social Democrats. Part of the openness of the Swedish Social Democrats and the insularity of the Germans stemmed from differences in their leaders: the imaginative Wigfoss, who saw political and theoretical considerations as inseparable, compared with the adamantine Hilferding, who at crucial moments deduced his politics from Marxist theory. Try to trace these differences back to underlying differences in social structure, and you end by confusing the idea of an explanation with the assertion that everything has antecedents.[170]

To argue that debate and ideas count in group choices, however, is not to say that everything is always possible. Early choices naturally constrain later ones. Alliances create patterns of trust, fuse interests, reinforce or undermine organizations, and provoke counterreactions by those they exclude – all events that limit the allies' possibilities for action in the future. In this sense a group's politics become set in time. Its choices become habitual, not debatable; its programs become slogans, not plans of action; its theories about society, taught by its newspapers, lobbyists, and intellectuals, become catechisms, not hypotheses pointing the way to political decisions; its human cement becomes personal loyalty and clientelism, not conviction and principle; its votes become signs of gratitude, fealty, or indifference, not mandates to leaders bent on solving problems.[171] In these periods the group's own interpretation of its place in the division of labor is so matter-of-fact that its members easily believe that their experiences reflect a basic truth about the association between interests and economic activity.

But over still longer stretches of time, established patterns of cooperation will be disrupted by shocks to the existing organization of work and authority. Unless everything is frozen solid everywhere, jockeying for advantage between labor and management and the struggle for place in the world order sooner or later lead to a major disruption of patterns of coexistence. The shock can come from outside the factory, as when new, low-wage foreign competitors or radical innovations in product design or production techniques so unsettle existing markets that firms must reorganize to survive. Or the shocks can come from within, as when peasant workers decide to climb skill hierarchies. In either case, disruption can reopen debate inside the competing groups about strategies and alliances, and it reminds the observer of the plasticity of the original situation. Because the politics of social groups are relational, not positional, when relations between them come unstuck, so do their politics. Groups so mired in habit that they cannot see what is happening or change their ways rapidly enough to adjust to the new situation are no more likely to survive than nations that cannot keep up with changes in the conditions of international competition.

With its ideas recast in this way, this chapter becomes an illustration of a broad theme, the ambiguity of interests in relation to the division of labor, rather than an analysis of the peculiarities of blue-collar groups. For the more we look at blue-collar groups, the clearer it becomes that they are alike not in the substance of their interests, but in the way in which the ambiguous significance of their workplace activity is fixed through experience and conflict. Surely in this they are like other groups in society.

Peasants, white-collar workers, upper-level managers, shopkeepers, intellectuals, soldiers – leaving aside the great capitalist magnates and their immediate political and intellectual allies, it is hard to find a social group or caste whose interest in defending capitalism does not at times waver as much as the craftsman's or special worker's. Some of the German white-collar workers who supported the Nazis in the late 1920s had sympathized with the November Revolution ten years before.[172] In countries with a self-assertive industrial bourgeoisie, the role of the intellectuals is often to tend to administrative chores or, in Justice Holmes's words, to "tell the comfortable classes that everything is all right." In countries and zones struggling to find their place in the world order, the intellectuals can become what they became in the nineteenth century in Eastern Europe or are today in parts of the Middle East: an intelligentsia, a corps of self-appointed but widely respected architects of renovation.[173] The army, which can be a dictator's bodyguard or the extrapolitical sword of a democracy, can itself fuse with the intelligentsia and, thrusting aside the possessing classes, try in all seriousness to impose its vision of utopia on the nation: This by Alfred Stepan's account was the project of General Velasco's failed revolution in Peru.[174] The more precisely each group in society is defined, the easier it becomes to find examples of comparable groups proceeding down different political paths.

Factory workers often have dirtier, more exhausting, less healthy jobs than these other social groups; they often bear a disproportionate share of the costs of economic fluctuations. But if they suffer more than others, in the long run their suffering is no more likely than the trials of other groups to lead to particular, uniform views.

At this point some readers may begin to feel uncomfortable. They were glad to see the boulder of reductionism roll into the abyss, clearing the way for detailed analysis of work groups. But with every addition to the list of incongruities between place in the division of labor and career at work, between career at work and politics, they worry more that the rock of science on which they themselves stand may also topple into the pit: that instead of providing more refined categories for analysis, the preceding discussion has merely demonstrated the fruitlessness of categorization, at least of the kind proposed. Assuming that there are no significantly better categories for capturing the differences between work groups attested by the sources, is the burden of the foregoing that the sociology of work and class must be replaced by the history of particular work groups? If this is your worry (and surely it is not everyone's), I think it is misplaced for two reasons suggested by the preceding discussion.

First, so long as tasks and authority over work organization are divided roughly as they are in the advanced industrial societies, the behavior of work groups will vary, but within the limits outlined by these last two chapters. Each kind of work group faces a characteristic problem, to which there are, under prevailing conditions, a limited number of answers. Would-be craftsmen, for instance, want secure, dignified jobs. They can try to get them as individuals, scaling the skill hierarchy one by one; or they can struggle collectively for better places. In the latter case they face the problem of relations with the craftsmen. Should they try to push them aside, or ally with them to change the skill hierarchy? Their answers will depend on the particulars of their experience with other work groups, with political parties, with the opportunities afforded by the labor market – in short, their history. But the possible choices are themselves fixed by, on the one hand, the combination of labor-market position and world view that defines the would-be craftsman as a type and, on the other, the continued existence of factory hierarchies and economic segmentation as we know them.

Second, discussion of the experiences that bear on a work group's choices can be refined. The settling of group interests can itself facilitate their investigation. The more settled a group's interests, the more constant the background conditions of its choices. Find two groups with many comparable background conditions, and it is possible to investigate with precision the effect of the remaining differences on their behavior.

Ideally, the researcher would like to match cases so that, aside from the variations in the workers' behavior, they are alike in all things but one. The presence or absence of this one thing would then account for the differences in behavior, and a historical case study would be transformed into a theory. Of course the world does not provide ideally matched cases; background conditions always diverge enough to raise the question whether they might influence the behavior under investigation. Nonetheless, the comparative method does allow systematic discussion of historical experience. Much of what has gone before has drawn on such comparisons to suggest, as a first approximation, why work groups choose particular strategies. Further refinement is certainly possible.[175]

Passion for this kind of refinement, however, makes it easy to forget that background conditions *do* change, often as the result of the very conflicts under investigation, and makes it easy to conceive of contingent developments as universally valid truths about the nature of craftsmen, unskilled workers, proletarians, or consumers – easy, in sum, to think that the observed regularities and their associated background conditions are necessarily as they are. Just as Fordism appears the inevitable outcome of mechanization so long as its political preconditions are ignored, so the self-conceptions and interests of groups seem natural and inevitable until the genealogy of the conflicts and experiences that produced them is brought to light.

To see through this illusion of necessity it helps to study a period in which conflict is so pervasive that everything – markets, hierarchies, technologies – is in flux, each element disrupting by its mutability the others; a period in which it is impossible to separate foreground from background or pretend that the fundamentals of the situation are fixed, the range of outcomes, let alone the outcome in a particular case, foreordained. The period I have in mind to study is the present.

5
The end of Fordism?

There are new things under the sun. At a time when more and more people find the traditional programs of the Left and the Right primitive, impractical, or dangerous; when society seems immobilized by conflicting interests and politics nothing but a mask covering the pursuit of selfish advantage; at a time when nothing new seems imaginable, let alone realizable, factory work is being revolutionized.

Many signs suggest that the Fordist model of organization is being challenged by new forms of the division of labor. International competition and overlapping domestic conflicts between producers and consumers, and between workers and capitalists, are driving many large firms out of mass markets for standardized goods. To survive this challenge manufacturers often have no choice but to produce more-specialized, higher-quality products. The new products must be made in new ways. Mass markets are the precondition for the Fordist organization of production; when they begin to disintegrate, Fordism begins to lose its appeal inside the factory. Where Fordism calls for the separation of conception from execution, the substitution of unskilled for skilled labor and special-purpose for universal machines, I will argue that specialization often demands the reverse: collaboration between designers and skilled producers to make a variety of goods with general-purpose machines.

What different forms this collaboration can take, whom it will benefit, and the extent to which it replaces Fordism as an explicit model of factory organization and provokes broader debate about our fundamental ideas of hierarchy are all open questions. By modifying currently existing technologies, shop-floor organization, and managerial hierarchies, existing Fordist firms may be able to meet the changing demand without sacrificing their fundamental operating principles. But it is also conceivable that the changes under way could lead to drastic redefinitions of prevailing ideas of organizational and techno-

194

logical efficiency: new types of firms and new types of workers whose activities and self-conceptions cut across the boundaries discussed before. What finally happens will depend on the eventual volatility of demand in the industrialized countries and the stability of the international economic order. It will depend, too, as we will see, on the outcome of workplace struggles – some already under way – between work groups and managers, but also among the work groups themselves, over the costs and benefits of reorganization. Because it builds on so many imponderables, the following discussion is necessarily speculative. Its purpose is to define possibilities, not to predict results. One thing, though, is sure: Practical experience in productive association is racing far ahead of existing ideas of organizational efficiency, all more or less rooted in Fordism.

The breakup of mass markets

Stable demand for large numbers of standard products is the cornerstone of Fordism. It makes possible long-term investment in product-specific machines, which encourages the constant, if only partially successful, attempt to decompose skill. Anything that unsettles prospects of manufacturing a certain product in a fixed way and selling it in predictably large numbers for a foreseeable price undermines the propensity to invest in the Fordist strategy. Paradoxically, events of the last decade have shown that Fordism's own successes set in motion disruptive forces that undermine the system's foundation: market certainty.

Consider the way mass-production industry in the core industrial countries is being crowded out of markets by pressure from formerly or currently low-wage competitors on the periphery, such as South Korea, Taiwan, Brazil, Mexico, and Eastern Europe. The industrialization of these countries is doubly linked to the triumph of Fordism in the United States and elsewhere. For breakthroughs in mass-production techniques in some countries not only make industrialization an urgent matter for the others, but provoke successful competition with the leaders as well.

Industrially backward nations, we saw in Chapter 1, must meet the prevailing standards of economic efficiency by imitating successful innovators if they are to defend their political integrity. The more standardized the product and routinized the production process, the easier it is for unsophisticated managers, engineers, and workers to copy; therefore the imitator first manufactures goods that the innovator makes according to Fordist principles: textiles, basic steel, plastics, and automobile parts.[1]

But imitation implies competition with established producers. The latecomer must often reconquer his domestic market from foreign imports, an undertaking that may require the creation of tariff barriers. And where the output of a technically advanced plant is large relative to potential domestic demand, he must export some of the goods, challenging foreign manufacturers on their home ground or in third markets.[2]

These assaults have good chances of success. Wages for unskilled labor are likely to be much lower in the imitating country, with its reserves of agricultural labor and nascent unions, than in an industrialized innovator with a strong labor movement. Given that the technologies of production and the products are the same in both, this means that the new producer can undersell older competitors, reducing the latter's possibilities for mass production to those products and plants where favorable transportation costs and cheap supplies of raw materials give them an unbeatable edge.

Imitation, of course, is threatening to the leading industries only when it occurs before they have recouped their investment in the product's development and the special equipment needed to produce it. If the lag between innovation and emulation is sufficiently long, the pioneer can take the profits from the sale of one standardized product and invest in the design and production of the next, always keeping one step ahead of the competition. Theories of the product cycle put forward by American economists in the early 1970s, for example, suggested that each good whose production had become easily imitable would be ceded to the industrializing countries; each market lost in this way would be replaced by a new one created by the design of an innovative product that stimulated new wants.[3] But this argument overlooks two fundamental considerations.

First, as the imitators go about their business, they begin to catch up faster. Each round of imitation facilitates the next one by creating skills, institutions, and infrastructures, such as roads or ports, which are at the disposal of later industrialists. The more experience industrializing countries have singly or collectively with mass-production techniques, therefore, the less time it takes before innovative products developed in the core countries are captured by the low-wage periphery. And the slow reduction of the technological gap between the most-advanced countries and the emergent industrial nations makes prospects in the former for recovering investments in specialized machinery progressively less certain.[4]

Sweden's retreat from shipbuilding illustrates the danger to the core countries. In order to minimize the disadvantage of high labor costs, the Swedes concentrated on the construction of relatively unsophisticated large ships in series by automated methods. In the early 1970s Sweden was the second largest shipbuilder in the world. But shipyards in Brazil, Korea, and Spain soon adopted the new techniques, and paid their workers at rates a quarter or less of what Sweden's were earning. When the world market for merchant ships began to collapse (launchings dropped from 35.9 million gross tons in 1975 to 15.4 million in 1978), Sweden was unable to hold its share of the declining orders for standard ships. Beginning in 1977, one major yard after another was taken over by the government. By 1980 there remained only two private shipbuilders, and Sweden ranked eighth in the world league tables of launchings.[5]

Worse yet from the point of view of the advanced countries, the more experience the emergent nations have in copying existing techniques, the less content they are to remain mere imitators. Rather, they insist on becoming innovators in their own right. Just as the emergent nations must become like the advanced countries in order to continue to be themselves, they discover that to catch up to the industrial leaders they must try to surpass them by creating new products and processes that further unsettle existing markets and make future developments less predictable.

As long as their factories merely execute routines established in the core countries, the peripheral nations are still the latter's subordinates. Replacement parts and new ideas continue to come from the advanced countries. The only way to break this dependence is to take full possession of the technology: to learn its intricacies by applying it to new circumstances and varying it to meet local conditions – in short, using it innovatively and challenging the leaders' rights to define future developments. This was the story of Germany and Japan.[6] Today the Brazilian government uses rivalry between multinationals, as well as the ambitions of domestic entrepreneurs, legislation, and administrative rulings, to force foreign investors to set up pharmaceutical and petrochemical plants and train the nation's young scientists, engineers, and managers in the latest techniques. Once local research teams are on their feet, the state helps create efficient, innovative national enterprises competing in world markets.[7] Even without state assistance, some local firms are so successful at adapting products and production technologies to regional needs that they themselves go abroad and set up manufacturing facilities in neighboring countries.[8]

In some industries, in fact, such local adaptations by private or state enterprise have already become a significant source of the new technology used in the advanced economies. In a report on the steel industry published in 1980, for example, the Office of Technology

Assessment of the U.S. Congress noted that "developing countries have produced impressive numbers of innovations that place great emphasis on suiting their fast-growing industries to the efficient use of local resources and conditions." And some of these new techniques are then exported to the highly industrialized nations.[9]

A further source of uncertainty related to international competition concerns sources and prices of raw materials. As more and more countries industrialize, the factories can become the hostages of the producers of raw materials. Available supplies of commodities may be strained by rising demand, which drives up the price; the declining monopsonist's power of the original industrial purchaser may open the way to the formation of producers' cartels. In the case of the most successful of those cartels, the Organization of Petroleum Exporting Countries, most of the raw material is controlled by states without industry of their own that were once subjected to the imperial power of those now dependent on their resources. Hence the temptation is especially great to avenge colonial humiliation and accumulate the wealth needed to break dependence on the advanced countries by restricting supplies until the price skyrockets. But shortages, however caused, set off a frantic search for new products and production processes that allow substitution of cheaper raw materials. Even the prospect of such a scramble deters investment in equipment that cannot easily be adapted to alternative processes.[10]

Within any one society, too, the spread of mass-produced goods slowly undercuts the preconditions of the Fordist model. Consumers, workers, even nature itself all react to the tremendous increase in the production of standardized goods in ways that threaten the stability of mass markets.

Government regulation to protect the environment is a case in point. As increasing amounts of a good are produced, the chance that its production, use, or simply disposal will make the natural environment less hospitable to human life also increases. Whenever insults to the environment come to attention, there is the possibility that the state will regulate the production or use of the offending product in ways that will force its redesign or abandonment.[11] As more countries set separate standards for the performance of a final product, it becomes more difficult to produce a standard, exportable good in mass quantity: In 1974, for example, Renault was having to manufacture several dozen different variants of the R16 for export.[12] And if the political situation within the manufacturer's home country becomes more volatile, he will be less certain of the environmental standards his plant will have to meet.

There is an analogous argument regarding workers in mass-production industries. The more rationalized the work, the faster the machines run, the less time wasted between operations, and the greater the use of new chemicals with untested effects on human health, the greater the chance that in the short or medium term the work force will be palpably injured by its labor. Perceptions of this injury will vary from work group to work group; the willingness to protest against it will depend among other things on the possibilities for finding other jobs. Under conditions favorable to the workers, a national labor movement calls for the imposition of health standards at the work place, forcing reorganization of production that may entail redesign of the product as well. When labor is too weak to protest openly and collectively, rising rates of health-related absenteeism, early retirement, and increases in chronic illness disrupt production and strain social welfare systems that provide for the sick and the disabled.[13]

The final domestic dilemma of Fordism concerns consumers. To the extent that consumers demand a particular good in order to distinguish themselves from those who do not have it, the good becomes less appealing as more of it is sold. Consumers will be increasingly willing to pay a premium for a variant of the good whose possession sets them off from the mass; and as the number of variants competing for attention and encouraging further differentiation of tastes increases, it becomes harder and harder to consolidate production of a standard product.[14] The consumers' increasing attention to variety and fashion, we will see in a moment, has forced giant American shirt manufacturers to change their marketing strategy and introduce new product technology.

Differentiation of taste is a by-product of Fordism's successes for another reason as well. As mass production cheapens the cost of manufactured goods and raises real wages, consumers have the discretionary income to experiment with their tastes. They may discover that they do not like some mass-produced good nearly as much as a slightly more expensive competitor made by artisanal techniques. The more consumers become aware of the possible effects of chemical additives, and the more they rediscover traditional products, the more likely they are, for example, to pay a premium for artisanally produced foods and cosmetics. Production of white pan bread, a mass-consumption good if ever there was one, dropped by 15 percent in the United States between 1972 and 1977, while production of specialty wheat varieties increased by 62 percent.[15]

Firms in the core industrial countries can react to these disturbances in one of two ways. One is to attempt to freeze the existing situation through political and marketing countermeasures. Tariffs, trigger prices, and orderly marketing agreements (which establish a foreign producer's annual contingent of a particular tradable) are all techniques for limiting the potential damage of low-wage, technologically sophisticated foreign competition by controlling the maximum quantity and minimum price of imports. Environmental and health and safety regulations can be gutted by legislators sympathetic to industry or applied half-heartedly by its friends in government. Sophisticated advertising can convince consumers that cosmetic differences between products, requiring negligible changes in their design and manufacture, are significant enough to make one a more prestigious acquisition than another. Reports of the health hazards associated with particular products and production processes can frequently be countered by the claim that, until the etiology of the relevant diseases is perfectly understood, correlations between their incidence and exposure to certain substances or conditions is inconclusive proof of a causal connection.[16]

This strategy of holding the line is risky for two reasons. First, to mount a political defense of industry it is necessary to shape state action through a coalition of business groups, unions, and political factions. Such a coalition is difficult to construct. A single industry is often divided between high-cost producers with older plants who favor protection because they have little chance of meeting world market prices, and a newer, low-cost sector afraid that protection might provoke a trade war and spoil its chances for exporting surplus production. Outputs of industries threatened by imports can be the inputs of other domestic industries, who oppose protection because dependence of high-cost national suppliers would reduce the competitive edge of their final products in the world markets: Automobile makers do not want to pay high prices for domestic steel, nor do garment factories want to pay a premium for locally produced textiles. Labor unions may side with manufacturers when jobs in the industries they organize are threatened. But this attraction is offset by workers' interests as consumers, inhabitants of particular communities, and creatures of flesh and blood. Protection freezes or raises market prices, reducing purchasing power. Unmonitored industrial development has potentially catastrophic effects on workers' health, and it can also lead to substantial reorganization and relocation of plants and jobs, both to the detriment of present union members. Labor leaders and the rank and file will have a hard time seeing where their interest lies. Their loyalty to the probusiness coalition is likely to be limited and conditional.[17]

In the second place, short-term successes of the protectionist strategy can often set the stage for long-term disasters that shake the original coalition. Experience with successive generations of technology facilitates subsequent innovation. Without practical knowledge of how the latest machines work, it is difficult to improve on them. Once overlapping coalitions of those in favor of protection and opposed to regulation are in power, however, tinkering with the production setup may stop or slow down as industrialists sacrifice long-term opportunities for immediate profits. An example is the television industry in the United States, which fell behind the Japanese in adapting solid-state design principles to television, began to lose its domestic market share, arranged for government protection, and transferred its production facilities offshore – only to discover that the Japanese had used the time to develop video recorders, the next generation of product.[18]

The further behind an industry falls in the race for the best equipment, the harder it becomes to catch up. When the gap between its prices and products and the standards set by the world market becomes great enough, its customers jump ship either by paying much higher prices tor imported goods or by demanding an end to protection.

The extreme alternative to a political defense of the status quo is seizing the bull by the horns and promoting innovation. Firms can meet environmental and health standards by modifying products and production processes. They can take refuge from low-wage production of standardized goods by concentrating on the manufacture of specialized products that imitators find impossible or unprofitable to copy. The pieces of the strategy can be complementary: Changes in design required to meet health and safety standards, for instance, can lead to breakthroughs that strengthen the product's overall market position; Honda's stratified charge engine, for example, reduced polluting emissions while improving fuel efficiency.[19]

But if protection freezes current practice at the price of endangering the long-term survival of the sheltered industries, the strategy of bold innovations raises the chances of their long-term survival on the condition that they radically modify, if not completely abandon, the Fordist principles on which they were built: The manufacture of specialized, innovative products requires at least a reinterpretation of Fordist ideas about the nature of markets and the organization of production.

Fordism, to recall the discussion in Chapter 2, rests on the assumption that large numbers of potential customers have essentially identical and well-defined wants for a long list of products. Once a generally acceptable product can be manufactured at a widely accessible price, it sets a standard that defines how the particular want will be satisfied. To permit rationalization of production, the design of the product is fixed. And the more rationalized and product-specific a manufacturing procedure becomes, the less room there is for varying the design of the product. Eventually the constraints on product and production mesh so tightly that both are frozen and the manufactured good resembles a commodity.[20]

Specialized production, in contrast, rests on the idea that, at the outset, customers' wants are vaguely defined and potentially diverse. The presumption is that the customer has no precise need for a particular good. Rather, he has a yearning or problem whose satisfaction or solution will have to reflect many singularities of his situation. The job of the innovative firm is to find a technically and economically feasible way of satisfying this inchoate need, thus creating a new product and defining the customer's wants at the same time. In extreme cases, the latter recognizes his problem only when he sees the producer's solution: In this sense, supply creates its own demand.

This strategy is practicable only if Fordist habits of using labor and machinery are discarded or substantially modified in favor of more flexible forms of organization. Flexibility, the capacity to produce a range of different products at the lowest total cost, will be more important than reducing the cost of any one product to the technically attainable minimum. Because an economy of this type prospers by producing an unforeseeably large variety of products, each in comparatively small numbers, it needs general-purpose machines and an adaptable work force that adjusts quickly to new patterns of organization, rather than special machines and unskilled workers. In the following sections we will see that flexible production can be organized in different ways corresponding to different distributions of discretion between managers and workers and among different work groups. But from the point of view of any firm that has invested in mass-production techniques, all more flexible setups are alike in requiring a costly sacrifice of specialized machines and organizational know-how.

Choice of strategy is further complicated by the imponderables of technological development. Anyone who claims to know reliably what the products and processes of the future will and will not do, and at what cost, is bluffing. Breakthroughs in the uses of computers alone so outrace the capacity to predict them as to make general forecasts about production possibilities no more than judicious guesswork. Yet every strategic move depends crucially on speculations about technological possibilities. However they choose in this regard, firms are in for surprises, pleasant and unpleasant.

The unpleasant surprises are obvious. A mass-production company fighting to reconquer its market by introducing the latest production techniques finds the new process more vulnerable to breakdown and less productive when operating than expected. Or the firm's attempts to open new mass markets by launching a new product miss the mark, perhaps because potential consumers find an alternative technological solution to the problem more appealing: Firms that invested hundreds of millions of dollars in cable TV franchises, for example, may suffer huge losses if cheap ways are found to beam programs over satellites directly into homes. "All of cable could be blown into a cocked hat by a change in technology," an executive in one communications company told *Business Week.*[21] The more innovative a firm, the more likely it is to face such problems; and a single failure can bankrupt a weak company.

The pleasant surprises are the ideas that work better than anyone expected. Often they blur the distinction between mass-production and innovative firms, leading to complex exchanges of technology between them. For example, a technology first developed for small-scale production may prove more efficient per unit output than established mass-production techniques. The possibilities for cost reduction remain hidden so long as efforts at improvement are limited to refinements of the existing large-scale setup. Once the possibilities become apparent, a large firm might simply group a number of small plants under one factory roof, achieving large-volume outputs by aggregating batches of the product. Conversely, innovative firms will occasionally find that the demand for one of their products is larger and more stable than anticipated; in such cases they will be tempted to adopt forms of organization that shade off into those typical of mass production. Or an innovative firm might find that some process pioneered in the large-volume firms but ultimately rejected because of inadequacies at high rates of output suits its needs. Examples will come up in a moment.

Political rearguard action and forward defense through innovation are therefore risky gambles. It is no wonder that established firms are often uncertain where to place their bets. Industries like steel, chemicals, apparel, textiles, consumer electronics, and automobiles in most core countries are divided into loosely defined factions pursuing different strategies. At the extremes are a few firms that have invested so much for so long in the manufacture of either standardized or innovative products that the only imaginable response to changing market conditions is more of the same. In between are the many firms that have some experience of both kinds of production and are capable of choosing either. Their aim is to defer choice and to make do with provisional solutions as long as possible in hopes of deciphering technological development, domestic politics, and a world economy all in flux to begin with and rendered more volatile still by their wavering: Technologists, politicians, and businessmen are all eyeing one another, looking for some clue to suggest where they should concentrate their energies and hopes.

A brief survey of the three strategies open to steel manufacturers in the United States, West Germany, and Japan illustrates the industrialists' general dilemma. One possibility is to produce standard industrial products in large tonnages, modernizing equipment as soon as possible and holding off foreign competition through political protection in the meantime. This strategy allows firms to make the most of existing equipment, to buy time to reestablish a technological lead over foreigners, or, failing that, to use the profits of protection to diversify into new, more promising industries. But as we saw, the protectionist strategy is hard to push through and harder to keep in place without solid results. This choice will thus appeal most to large, established firms with a great deal of old equipment and a great deal of political influence; in the late 1970s the U.S. Steel Corporation, for example, led the fight for protection against imports even as it began to invest heavily in petrochemicals and the extraction of raw materials.[22]

A second strategy is to concentrate on specialty steels and products. Steel is made by reducing the oxygen from iron, oxidizing the impurities in the reduced metal, and adding alloys to give special properties to the final product. New additives and experimentation with the process of purification yield specialty steels with combinations of properties suited to diverse purposes. Similarly, there are frequently new ways to shape steel by casting and milling so that the end product is especially suited to particular industrial needs. A producer of patented new alloys or shapes has little to fear from foreign imitators, in part, however, for reasons that may make him draw back from this strategy himself.[23]

Specialty steels, for example, are produced in small batches, and so they are unsuitable for plants that run efficiently, or at all, only at high volume. Frequent changes in the product require a skilled work force, often difficult to find even in the core countries: Large companies, dreaming of rationalization, have often neglected formal training; and ethnic antagonism between the migrants at the bottom of the skill hierarchy and native workers in the higher grades has obstructed informal transmission of skill on the job.[24] Finally, wild fluctuations in the price of metals such as molybdenum, which are used in alloy steels, can drive successful products off the market in a twinkling.

But for all that, a determined firm with an idea of what it is getting into can prosper making specialty steels. A good example is Thyssen, a Ruhr combine and the largest European steel producer with no major public shareholder. Thyssen's specialty steel production expanded as part of a program of diversification and renovation begun in the early 1970s to meet increased competition, first from Japan and later from Mexico, Brazil, and South Korea. The firm collaborated with Porsche in the mid-1970s to produce galvanized steel for the "long-life auto": Today two of Porsche's three models use the Thyssen product, guaranteed against rust for six years; and other automobile makers such as Volvo, Volkswagen, BMW, and Opel are interested in collaborating in the production of rust-resistant steels. Thyssen also developed a lightweight, durable, and inexpensive stainless* steel substitute for the aluminum beer keg. Another aim is to replace plastic wine casks with steel ones. Total sales of the specialty steel division were $1.5 billion in 1979, and the trend, according to *Fortune*, "is up."[25]

Thyssen's managers, moreover, are well aware that the firm's success depends on specialization and innovation. They refer to the company as a *Tausendfüssler*, a centipede with so many feet everywhere that nothing knocks it off balance. *Fortune* was struck by their consistent descriptions of the firm's strategy: "They talk of the search for *intelligente Produkte* (high-technology items), of *Nischen jagen* (hunting for openings) in world markets . . . Above all, they are constantly reminding themselves to remain *flexibel*."[26] Krupp, another large West German steelmaker, is moving in the same direction: Specialty steels accounted in 1977 for 50 percent of its sales and 30 percent of its tonnage output.[27]

The Japanese, whose competitive position in mass-produced steel is threatened by the rising costs of labor, energy, and transportation, are also following suit. "We realize," the general manager of Kawasaki Steel's international department said in 1978, "that we cannot continue to export large amounts of crude steel."[28] One response has been to shift to the manufacture of specialized products: Japanese production and exports of specialty steels increased fourfold between 1965 and 1967, twice the increase in the production and export of standard products.[29]

Among major steel manufacturers in the United States, Armco is closest to pursuing this strategy in a determined way.[30] But to the extent that current returns on investment and market performance are signs of future developments, other firms are likely to follow. In 1978, a year in which demand for steel was low worldwide, Armco made a 10.4 percent return on invested capital, 4.2 percent more than the average return for the large producers of standard steel, but not quite as much as the average of still more specialized manufacturers of alloys. In the same slack year Armco increased exports of special alloys from 2.9 to 4.6 percent of its output; and, more generally, American alloy makers have had more success than producers of less refined goods against foreign firms in both home and world markets.[31]

The third strategy also depends on specialization. But instead of concentrating on innovative products, firms in this third category use innovative process technologies to produce comparatively light though standard goods faster and in smaller quantities than would be profitable for the larger, or tonnage, mills using the dominant production techniques.

The typical tonnage mill in the United States makes steel by the basic oxygen process. Iron ore is reduced in a giant blast furnace and the molten metal, sometimes mixed with scrap, is fed to a pear-shaped vessel where impurities are removed by blowing a supersonic jet of oxygen onto the surface of the bath. The molten steel is then ladled into ingots, allowed to cool, reheated, and rolled to shape. The system is efficient for more or less continuous production of larger quantities of heavy industrial products, but much less so for smaller volumes and lighter shapes. The smaller modern blast furnaces, for example, run economically only if they produce a minimum of 2 million tons a year; vessels of less than a certain size use energy inefficiently, and reheating after interruptions in production is expensive. Tonnage mills, moreover, like to cast heavy pieces because the lighter the piece, the more cost is added to each ton of the final product by the process of casting into ingots and reheating.[32]

Producers who pick the third strategy avoid these problems by making steel in mini-mills: plants that combine electric-arc furnaces and continuous casting machines to turn out anywhere from 50,000 to 500,000 tons of rod, bar, or wire a year. As their name suggests, electric-arc furnaces melt iron and scrap by striking an arc between the metal charge and two graphite electrodes; oxygen is then injected to purify the bath. Electric-arc furnaces can be charged completely with scrap. Hence the minimum efficient output of blast furnaces no longer establishes a standard for the steelmaking system as a whole. Scrap, moreover, is often much less expensive then iron ore. Costs can be further reduced by the use of a continuous casting machine: a kind of giant Liebig condenser that makes it possible to skip the ingot stage and cast the molten steel directly into slabs, which are then rolled into final shape.

The success of the mini-mills astounds old hands in the steel industry, who have been convinced that the biggest plants are the most efficient. *Iron Age* teased its readers by beginning an article on the situation of the mini-mills in 1980 this way: "The steel industry is in a very dynamic state. New plants are being built and older ones are being expanded. Companies are moving into new products and new locations. New technology is being developed and applied." For example, the expansion in output of two small mini-mill companies, Nucor and Florida Steel, has more than offset the shutdowns of plants in Youngstown, by United States Steel. *Iron Age* calculates that mini-mill capacity will reach 15 million tons a year, or about 10 percent of annual production in the United States, by the time construction now under way is completed. By 1990, the Office of Technology Assessment estimates, mini-mills could double their output and capture at least 25 percent of the market in the United States.[33]

In their own way, however, mini-mills are at the mercy of economic and technological development. As technical advance reduces the per-ton costs of electric furnace production below the levels of even the most efficient of the blast-furnace operations, the major manufacturers are switching to mini-mill methods: Jones and Laughlin Steel in Pittsburgh; Bethlehem Steel in Johnstown, Pennsylvania; and Republic Steel at Warren, Pennsylvania, have all begun to produce tonnage-mill outputs by aggregating the production from electric-arc furnaces placed side by side. Tonnage mills are also introducing continuous-casting machines as old equipment is amortized and new equipment, having proven itself in the mini-mills, wins their and their customers' trust.[34]

As mini-mill techniques spread, the price of scrap might go up, forcing electric-arc producers to charge their furnaces with sponge iron, a solid made by exposing iron pellets directly to a reducing gas. The hitch is that this direct-reduction process requires large amounts of expensive oil or natural gas. However, a process developed by Krupp and, by 1980, in use in six plants worldwide, makes possible the direct reduction of iron by use of cheap coal. Will this SL/RN technique eventually make the price of scrap irrelevant to the operation of mini-mills?[35]

Changes in the markets for steel could threaten the mini-mills as well. Construction of condominiums and shopping centers, two typical destinations of mini-mill products, might slow down. On the other hand, this danger is offset by two opportunities: The mini-mills could move into specialty steels; or an advance in technique could make possible the continuous casting of auto sheet or tinplate, two potentially lucrative products that they cannot presently produce.[36]

In some industries, of course, the choices available to producers in the core countries are even more circumscribed. By the late 1970s, for instance, many of the largest chemical manufacturers were moving away from the production of basic plastics and the simplest artificial fibers. These commodity chemicals were easily produced in Eastern Europe and in the new, often oil-rich industrializing nations in what the industry calls "black boxes": self-contained manufacturing complexes built according to established rules and easily replicated anywhere. Instead, like Thyssen, firms in the core countries have begun to invest in specialty products that are difficult to imitate on short notice and fetch high prices per unit of quantity because of their great utility to the customers whose special needs they meet. Examples are pharmaceuticals, insecticides, and herbicides keyed to the ecological particularities of given regions, high-performance plastics and fibers that can be used as substitutes for metal alloys and ceramics, and microorganisms made by genetic engineering.[37]

This trend was evident first in the United States, where, by the late 1970s, specialty firms were generally recognized to be more profitable than commodity producers.[38] The largest American chemical firm, Du Pont, was chastened earlier in the decade by stagnating sales for some of the artifical fibers it had itself pioneered: nylon, Orlon, Dacron. By 1980 specialty products accounted for one-tenth of the company's sales and one-fifth of its products; and the strategy was to take the proceeds from those parts of the commodity business where Du Pont is still an efficient producer and reinvest them in technologically more sophisticated and specialized products.[39] Dow, the second largest chemical firm, and traditionally more dependent on commodity production than Du Pont, plans to do the same thing. An investment analyst called Dow's decision to concentrate on specialty products "an absolutely necessary strategy; every major chemical company will have to do something like this."[40] It is no surprise, then, that in 1980 W. R. Grace and Co., the world's largest producer of specialty chemicals and the fifth largest chemical company in the United States, was widely held to be on the verge of a golden age.[41]

And it is no wonder, either, that major European firms such as Rhône-Poulenc (France), Solvay (Belgium), and Imperial Chemical (Great Britain) all aimed to follow the lead of the Americans. They announced plans to move into production of high-fashion yarns, engineering plastics, agrichemicals, catalysts, and pharmaceutical intermediaries in the 1980s. "Large chemical companies," *Chemical Week* observed in 1981, seemed to be "tumbling over one another in the rush to get into specialties."[42]

But, again, the choices in the chemical industry are unusually clear-cut. More typically, the range of plausible strategies is greater, the way out of the one dilemma of increased competition and regulation more obscure. Industry by industry, core country by core country, industrialists are speculating on their political and market opportunities, experimenting with contrary strategies even as they experiment with new technologies whose effect is sometimes to undercut the very strategic assumptions that made them appealing in the first place. There is no point piling speculation on speculation by forecasting which strategies in which industries and countries are most likely to predominate. But on the assumption that in some places the strategy of flexibility and innovation will indeed prevail, I want to focus instead on its consequences for the organization of factory work. The next section looks at attempts to make large factories flexible enough to meet the demands of more articulated markets without abandoning the central principles of Fordism; the following one picks up the thread of Italian developments and examines the way even greater flexibility can be achieved by breaking with these principles and decentralizing production to create high-technology cottage industry.

Neo-Fordism

The reorganization now under way in some of the largest factories in the core industrial countries touches every area of production from research to final assembly. Generally the changes occur piecemeal as divisions and shops respond to new developments in markets or elsewhere in the firm's organization. When reorganization involves the introduction of new, computer-based technologies such as numerically controlled machine tools or computer-aided design of parts, managers perceive it as a bold step toward the Fordist ideal of the rationalized factory, even though the new machines often affect established work patterns less dramatically than expected. When reorganization involves changes in work routines such as rearrangements of assembly-line work, it is frequently perceived as a simple adjustment of the existing regime, even though it may have major effects on the skill and wage hierarchies and the uses of manufacturing equipment. But if managers could step back from their work, as only a few of them can do, they would see that the present reorganization reinterprets Fordism as much as it perfects it and, depending on how workers respond to these changes, could perhaps undermine the existing factory hierarchies rather than reinforce them.

Present developments add up to an attempt to respond to market differentiation by increasing the range of products that can be made by a single factory according to some approximation of Fordist techniques. Whether they know it or not, managers are trying to have their cake and eat it too: to meet or create new demands for more varied products while holding fast to familiar principles of command and organization.

The difficulty, anticipated by the preceding discussion, is that there is tension between the principles of Fordism and the goal of flexibility. Fordism, we know, is a method for the efficient production of one thing. It presumes that, once production goals are established, a set of routines and specialized machines can be devised to achieve them at minimum cost. To recall Fox's category, Fordism is a low-trust system that separates conception of tasks from their execution: Once the routines are in place, subordinates are meant only to apply them. Deviations from the routines are more frequent and necessary to the organization's success than management thinks; but the fixity of the goal and the rigidity of the production apparatus keep the need for low-level redefinition of the procedures within bounds, allowing the system to work as well as it does.

Rapid changes in production goals are at odds with this low-trust system on two counts. First, the more frequently products and processes are changed, the less time there is to translate conceptions into reliable, mechanically applicable routines. The more imperfect the routines, of course, the more interpretation and initiative they require from workers at all levels. But, and this is the second clash of principle, workers in low-trust organizations are presumed not to share the organization's goals. They are neither trained to show nor rewarded for initiative. And they know it. Hence they are likely to regard the initiative that they do have to exercise to keep things moving simply as a bargaining chip in their struggles with superiors. The classic example is the strategy of working to rule: stopping production by going by the book.

One way around these problems is through the creation of what Fox calls high-trust organizations, organizations in which conception and execution are combined: These are systems in which those who do the work have also determined what work is to be done and how. Such organizations adapt quickly to shifting goals because each worker is able to elaborate incomplete rules and is willing to do so – able because he understands their connection to the organization's overarching purposes and to other related routines and willing because, having helped establish the goals, he has a stake in their realization. The classic example of a high-trust organization is a commando group in which the soldiers plan their missions together, assign themselves temporary ranks to eliminate confusions about authority during the battle, and singly or collectively vary the plans as combat conditions dictate.

Industrialists, you will have guessed, are not eager to cede wide-ranging authority over product design and manufacture to the workers. Their strategy as it emerges from dozens of experiments in core countries is to use a combination of innovative technologies and organizational devices to increase the flexibility of production while holding to a minimum and sharply circumscribing discretion exercised at the workplace.

Take first the manufacture of workpieces that are eventually combined to make the final product. The fundamental innovation here is flexible automation. The idea is to design numerically controlled machine tools that can be quickly programmed to perform a variety of operations. In this way the advantages of special-purpose, automatic machines can be combined with the flexibility of general-purpose ones: For practical purposes the machines allow batches of different workpieces to be treated as identical elements of a single mass-production run.

In the simplest case flexible automation means replacing a single or stand-alone special machine with a programmable one. From the machine operator's point of view, one piece of automatic equipment is simply being substituted for another. So the effect on work organization is minimal.

The introduction of numerically controlled sewing machines by the Arrow Company, a major manufacturer of shirts, illustrates the industrial strategy behind the substitution. By the 1960s Arrow had adapted mass-production techniques to the manufacture of men's shirts. Pieces of cloth were cut in large numbers by giant presses; crucial stitching operations such as the sewing of collars were performed automatically by sewing machines controlled by metal cams. This system worked well as long as the dies for the presses and cams for the sewing machines paid for themselves before changes in style required their replacement. But in the late 1960s, one of Arrow's executives recalled, "the fashion explosion found its way into the shirt business." Styles changed so quickly that before a cam could be made, let alone pay for itself, it had to be replaced by a new one: A set of replacement cams for a full range of sizes of a given style took from six to eight weeks to produce, and cost $1,800. Had technological advance provided no alternative solution and had Arrow not become accustomed to organizing production by Fordist principles, it might have tried the industry's traditional solution to changing demand: subcontracting. But the development of programmable sewing machines and the habits of mass production made flexible automation seem the obvious answer.[43]

The same logic applies to more complex systems of connected machine tools. In some mass-production industries it has long been economical to automate a series of machining operations by linking a number of special-purpose machines through devices that automatically pass workpieces from one to the next. A line of machines connected in this way is called a transfer; it is frequently used, for example, in the manufacture of automobile engine blocks. If the designers make each work station programmable, devise sensors to tell the machines what kind of workpieces are coming down the line, and write computer programs to control the flow of material and consign the relevant kinds of information to the small, decentralized computers that directly control the individual machines, they have created a flexible manufacturing system. This flexible version of a transfer is already replacing traditional systems for machining engine blocks in the American, West German, and Japanese automobile industries.[44]

In assembly operations, in contrast, there are no such apparently neat technical solutions to the problem of flexibility. Industrial robots will solve part of the managers' problem, especially in welding and spraying operations: It is often possible to program the machines by leading them through a complex motion, which is then recorded and repeated at will. But the robots' awkwardness and their limited capacity to distinguish different objects and manipulate odd shapes, as well as their unreliability (some are enclosed in metal cages to limit the possibility of injury to workers from the capricious sweep of a mechanical arm), will make them of limited use for the near future. Eventually robots may perform a large number of assembly operations, but this will not happen soon. As of 1980 there were about 5,500 programmable robots in use worldwide, 2,500 to 3,000 of them in the automobile industry. Unimation of Danbury, Connecticut, the industry leader, was selling them at the rate of 50 a month. For the time being, therefore, more flexible assembly will require more flexible use of human assemblers; and that raises again the question of the limitations of low-trust organizations.[45]

From the point of view of industrial engineering, the central obstacle to flexible assembly-line production is balancing the line: subdividing tasks and positioning the work force so that with all workers exerting roughly comparable and continuous efforts, production flows smoothly and at a pace that could not be exceeded without more hands. The more frequently the quantity to be produced is varied, workers are absent, or products are changed, the more time is wasted experimenting with different arrangements of the line; the greater the chance that suboptimal, makeshift solutions will be accepted as stopgaps; and the greater, too, the possibility that shifting work assignments will provoke disputes about pay, or grumbling about the unpredictable work load or the additional, unacknowledged responsibility.

It is then no wonder that, from the early 1970s on, the diversification of markets, the greater fluctuations of levels of demand, and the rates of organized and spontaneous worker protest caused managers to experiment with alternatives to traditional assembly methods. In Western Europe and the United States, these experiments were often accompanied by (sometimes sincere) social-psychological speculation about the potential rewards of the humanization of work: Less routine jobs created by combining previously separate tasks (job enrichment) or by allowing workers to circulate from post to post (job rotation) would lead to more contentment and therefore more productive workers.[46] But by the end of the decade it had become clear to observers such as Federico Butera, Benjamin Coriat, and Norbert Altmann that management's experiments had less to do with concern for the workers' contentedness than with the need to reduce the rigidity of existing assembly procedures. "Almost no one measures the effects of the content of work on the workers' well-being," Butera writes, with the bitterness of many who surveyed these developments firsthand, "while instead even the amount of grease consumed is measured with absolute precision."[47]

The attempts at reorganization fall into one of four categories, depending on whether they focus on single workers or on groups and whether they involve modifications of the physical arrangement of the assembly operation or not. In the American garment industry, for example, the introduction of computers has made it practical to devise elaborate incentive schemes that encourage individual workers to learn new jobs. This incentive reduces their reluctance to quit a familiar and lucrative piece-rate post when shifts in production require. Workers are guaranteed their average wage when learning new work, and their cumulative progress toward proficiency in the new job is constantly monitored. Once the appropriate level of output is reached, they can be transferred to an incentive piece-rate payment scheme. Individual workers can thus be shunted about with no change in the physical layout of the plant.[48]

Alternatively, work stations can be designed so that individual workers responsible for a range of closely related operations control the flow of materials and workpieces to and from their stations. Such systems are in use in West German appliance and automobile factories. They increase the individual worker's flexibility, reduce the whole system's vulnerability to absenteeism, and do all this without requiring elaborate modification of existing piece-rate systems.[49]

A third possibility is to hold the technology more or less fixed and form groups of workers who regularly rotate posts, perhaps at a rhythm of their own choosing. This is the basic idea of the quality-of-work-life groups introduced by General Motors in its newer plants, though we will see in a moment that there is more to these groups than just that idea. The last possibility, illustrated by the Volvo factory at Kalmar, is to rearrange assembly work to give the groups the greatest possible autonomy in setting the internal division of labor and the pace of production. At Kalmar the groups form self-contained assembly islands; workpieces rotate among them on computer-guided carts.[50]

All of these schemes can be further embellished by giving the workers, singly or collectively, some responsibility for inspecting their products and setting their machines, thereby reducing the costs of supervision and maintenance. Group leaders, elected by their fellows, may even be substituted for foremen, and the group may be encouraged to take charge of scheduling its work hours, to make small improvements in the procedures, and to care for machines – innovations that are all subject, of course, to management's approval and to the condition that the latter's production goals are met. General Motors' quality-of-work-life groups in the American South approximate this type.[51]

Now the fateful question: Will it work? Will some combination of flexible automation and redesigned assembly procedure make it possible to pursue an innovative production strategy while holding tight to the principles of low-trust, Fordist organization?

The answer is that it depends. Technical difficulties, the resistance of the work force, or economic developments could all bring these schemes to grief. But they need not. Certainly there is no proof that the managers must fail. If they are skillful and lucky, they will create a more flexible neo-Fordism; if they trip themselves up or if fortune betrays them, their experiments could smooth the way to forms of work organization in which they have little, if any, say.

Technical difficulties are most likely to crop up in flexible automation, especially in flexible manufacturing systems. Sensors may need to be developed to recognize oddly shaped parts, and transfer equipment will certainly have to be improved to move such parts from station to station; existing systems handle workpieces that are regularly shaped (as at an Allis-Chalmers plant in Milwaukee, which makes gears) or fabricated to close tolerances (as at Caterpillar Tractor in Peoria, Illinois).[52] Reliability is still a major problem: The systems are so complex that breakdowns, which paralyze production completely, occur frequently and are hard to diagnose and repair.

Programming, too, could become a serious obstacle. No one has sufficient experience with these systems to know whether programming costs might not tip the balance in favor of less-integrated set-ups. The precedents are not reassuring. Writing a program that coordinates machine, tools, transfer equipment, and workpieces is analogous to the difficult job of designing the operating system for a large computer – the master program that manages the execution of all the others, marching each user's data and instructions to the right place at the right time. Operating systems are notoriously complex. Each part fits with the others, and the fit must be exact. No one can intervene to interpret ambiguous commands or take account of new circumstances. As with a flexible manufacturing system, every contingency must be anticipated. If, to assure the necessary precision, a small team designs each part collectively, the job can become hopelessly long. If the task is partitioned to speed up the work, it may, as Frederick Phillips Brooks, Jr., learned from his experience as a project manager for IBM, take even longer.

Aside from the time spent on training the additional programmers, there is the problem of coordinating their efforts. Even if every worker needs to consult only once with each member of the team to see that their ideas mesh, a team of three talks three times as much as a team of two, and a team of four confers six times as much; the extra talk can easily offset the potential productivity gains from subdividing the labor.

Once the program is written, moreover, it is difficult to perfect, let alone to modify for new purposes. Because the fit between pieces is so tight, every adjustment is likely to cause disturbances in some unlikely place. To make major changes the system must be redesigned from scratch. Thus, to the extent that the analogy holds and the programming of flexible manufacturing systems is both lengthy and hard to modify, this new form of automation may prove more rigid than it first seems.[53] If they hit many such snags, managers will face a difficult choice. They can dismiss flexible manufacturing systems as a good idea with limited applications for the future. Or they may try to introduce elementary versions of such systems, only to discover that the less complicated the system, the easier it is for foreign competitors to copy.

Problems with the work force are likely to crop up in the assembly divisions. The introduction of new work rules, job definitions, and pay systems often disrupts established routines, inviting reappraisal of existing disparities and setting off a scramble for an advantageous place in the new system. Where trust is low, change must be negotiated: Because the workers presumably do not share management's goals, they have no reason to think that change will be in their interest. How management fares in these negotiations will vary, of course, from country to country and industry to industry, depending on the local balance of power between labor and capital.

The creation of work groups with some collective discretion is likely to be especially tricky. Blurring the lines between supervisors and subordinates on the one hand, and those between inspectors, machine setters, and unskilled workers on the other, will cause confusion and open the way to jurisdictional disputes of all kinds. Telling workers, or anyone else, that they are a self-determining unit, and then disregarding their decisions whenever these conflict with goals and routines established in ways they cannot influence, is a good way to smother enthusiasm, encourage cynicism, or even provoke open conflict. In the vast literature on the redesign of the assembly line it is easy enough to find instances of work groups disillusioned, embittered, and outraged by a jittery management's decision to reinstate foremen with traditional power: The General Foods experiment in Topeka, Kansas; the work improvement program at the Harman automobile parts plant in Bolivar, Tennessee; and Project D-40 at the pseudonymous Eastern Manufacturing Company are among the best-known cases.

But it is an impossibly long way from the fact that these experiments have sometimes gone awry to the argument that they always and everywhere will. The powerful are skilled in convincing subaltern social groups to accept half a loaf. They have had long experience in denaturing democratic institutions: Think of what mass suffrage might be and what Louis Napoleon, Bismarck, and Disraeli quickly learned to make of it.

And if you are tempted to argue that because partial democratization of the workplace involves face-to-face relations between small numbers, it is harder to control than mass suffrage, remember the theories of the new working class, which saw special workers as proto-revolutionaries, and compare these theories to the vexed reality of the workers' situation: the way their position on the labor market has worked to intimidate them, the way participation in the labor movement has shaped their demands differently from country to country. Chapters 3 and 4 showed that workers' claims depend on their ideas of a career at work, experiences of conflict, and relations to other work groups: They do not automatically regard even the shoddiest treatment as an actionable assault on their rights. Thus Charles Heckscher finds in his review of the experiences of assembly-line groups, including the three mentioned a moment ago, that "even when management has made the worst possible mistakes, raising expectations and then dashing them within . . . a highly skilled and trained work force, the reaction of the workers has not been costly. The period of discontent has been relatively brief, and productivity does not seem to have suffered significantly at any time."[54] Assembly-line work groups may prove inefficient or explosively volatile, but if the idea fails, it will fail not because it necessarily had to, but because it was mismanaged or because the workers in a particular plant or country were strong enough to exploit the possibilities for democratization that the scheme opens.

Finally, even if the technical and managerial problems are solved, economic developments may cut the ground out from under the strategy. Neo-Fordism depends on enlarging the range of mass-produced goods, but within the limits plausibly compatible with the flexible automation systems likely to be available in the near and middle term. Ideally, an industry would like to meet the demands of differentiated markets by designing a range of products composed of a limited set of modules in different combinations and producing these using the new techniques. Once the new line of products was established and production routinized, business would return to normal. The clearest example of this strategy is the General Motors world car: The various models are built on a single chassis and equipped with more or less prestigious trim. Eventually GM cars may be outfitted with one or another version of a single "rubber engine," which can be stretched from three to six cylinders simply by combining two basic engine-head modules, one for two cylinders, the other for three.[55]

But remember the example of Sweden: There is no guarantee that even advanced technologies will not be imitated by the periphery once they have been routinized in the core. If flexible automation spreads too rapidly, the firms in the core countries may have to diversify their products even more, stretching the limits of even the most elastic version of Fordism. General Motors and Chrysler are both hedging against this possibility: Even as they are retooling to produce standardized world cars, they are accelerating development of specialized vans, trucks, electric city cars, and fuel-efficient touring vehicles for the more particular customer of the future.[56]

And do not forget all those fashion-, health-, and quality-conscious consumers who, quite independent of foreign competition, are unsettling the manufacturers of everything from shirts to bread. Will they be content with many different varieties of Arrow shirts, or will they want many altogether different kinds of shirts? The more aggressively manufacturers fight for emergent segments of markets, the more they force their competitors to create space for themselves by encouraging further subdivisions. "After the consumer is introduced to almost endless variations of models and colors," an executive of a men's clothing firm observed, "it is highly unlikely that a manufacturer who continues to produce only basic black sedans will be successful."[57] And as manufacturers experiment more widely with flexible technology, the chances are greater that they will create processes or machines that can be used still more flexibly by competitors willing to relax organizational constraints. No one can say whether the new techniques will satisfy or stimulate the taste for variety, whether they will vindicate the efficiency of low-trust organizations or expose their limits.

New specialty firms, for example, bake high-quality products like French bread, raspberry Danish twist, or sour cream chip-and-nut loaf in huge numbers in the most modern tunnel ovens; but other bakers have tried to meet the fluctuations in taste and the demand for greater variety and traditional quality by returning to artisanal methods of production.[58] In some cases vertically integrated bakeries are forced to decentralize fundamental operations because they can no longer coordinate the flow of materials necessary to produce an ever-larger assortment of breads. As a manager of a Milwaukee bakery explained to the tenth annual meeting of the Association of Cereal Chemists' Milling and Baking Division in Kansas City in 1980:

If you're running a white bread plant, the purchasing agent schedules . . . four cars of white, patent flour a day, and three cars of shortening, and two cars of corn syrup, and sets up the schedule, shipping carload quantities – and he just keeps plugging away . . . Now, suddenly, his marketing and sales people come and say, "We now want to make 13 types of variety bread, and one's going to have some oatmeal in it, and one's going to have cornmeal, and one's going to have some fiber in it, and one's going to have some wheat germ, one cracked wheat," and about that time he throws down his pencil and says, "I'm going to go out and have a three-martini lunch." The other thing he says is, "I can't always obtain the best buy on these because we've got 28 different plants . . . I can't do it efficiently; I can't buy carloads."[59]

The solution is to subcontract to a blender who aggregates demand from different specialty bakeries, buys in bulk, blends the bases, and ships a carload of the desired assortment to the large bakery. But how many different kinds of bread can the large bakery make on its assembly lines? And how will it respond if the blender hits on some tasty base and goes into the bakery business himself?

Computer typesetting illustrates the dilemma still more starkly. On the one hand, sophisticated new machines and programs make it possible to eliminate nearly all the skill from setting newspapers, phone books, or law textbooks. An operator types in the text and selects by a few simple instructions one of the available formats; and a program sets columns to the specified width, justifies the characters, and prints the result in the correct font. But on the other hand, someone who knows the intricacies of formatting programs can use the same machine to vary margins and change fonts and type sizes to produce effects that, could they have been achieved at all by traditional hot-metal methods, would have been prohibitively expensive. The result is that, while the typesetting of standardized products such as phone books is becoming more routine, editors and artists are increasingly tempted to experiment with bold designs that call for close collaboration between layout staffs and skilled typesetters: Publishers now vaunt the pedagogic merits of a textbook's layout rather than its contents.[60]

Neo-Fordism may succeed in some industries, in some core countries. In others, it may be possible to move to more flexible forms of production without fundamentally shaking management's power to control, invest in, and limit changes in the organization of work. The West Germans, because of the features of their high-trust culture examined in Chapter 1, may have less trouble than others with this system: For example, although West German shipbuilders had begun to shift to mass-production techniques in the early 1970s, by 1979, 90 percent of the ships built were technically advanced and customized, and the industry was weathering the downturn at least as well as any of its European competitors.[61] American managers, trained by a vigilant stock market to want to show a profit every quarter, may have particular difficulty in undertaking long-term plans for reorganization that show no short-term results.[62]

In yet other cases, attempts to restore flexibility to the factories may get out of hand, leading to the emergence of forms of work association unanticipated by the managers who set them in motion. It has happened once already, in Italy, producing a form of high-technology, decentralized production that suggests radically new ways of organizing industrial society even as it recalls the earlier variant of small-scale industrialization that gave way in the nineteenth century before the triumph of Fordism. It is to these developments, a sign of future possibilities – but no more than possibilities – that I turn next.

High-technology cottage industry: the unity of conception and execution, the abstract and the concrete

There are small towns near Bologna, along the Adriatic coast near Ancona and Venice, where the number of officially registered factories or artisans' workshops almost equals the number of inhabitants: many residents own more than one, and a few outsiders have set up business there as well.[63] The regions in central and northeastern Italy where these shops cluster have come to be called the Third Italy, defined in contrast to the Industrial Triangle formed by Turin, Milan, and Genoa on the one hand and the South on the other.[64] Within this area each district specializes in the production of a range of related goods: In Tuscany, for instance, cloth is made at Prato, ceramics at Sesto and Montelupo; in Emilia-Romagna, knitwear is made at Carpi, ceramic tiles at Sassuolo, motorcycles and automatic machines at Bologna, farm machinery at Reggio Emilia; in the Marche, shoes are made near Ancona; and in the Venetian hinterland ceramics, plastic furniture, and sport shoes are made.

Most of the shops and factories in these areas employ from 5 to 50 workers, a few as many as 100, and a very few 250 or more. Some recall turn-of-the-century sweatshops: The three or four workers are children scarcely fifteen years old, supervised by an adult or two, perhaps their parents; the tools are simple, the product crude, the hours long, the air full of dust and fumes. But many of the others are spotless; the workers extremely skilled and the distinction between them and their supervisors almost imperceptible; the tools the most advanced numerically controlled equipment of its type; the products, designed in the shop, sophisticated and distinctive enough to capture monopolies in world markets. If you had thought so long about Rousseau's artisan clockmakers at Neuchâtel or Marx's idea of labor as joyful, self-creative association that you had begun to doubt their possibility, then you might, watching these craftsmen at work, forgive yourself the sudden conviction that something more utopian than the present factory system is practical after all.

The emergence of high-technology cottage industry in Italy is the result of two developments, both necessary for the outcome: the industrial conflicts of the 1960s and 1970s discussed in Chapter 4 and the general changes in market conditions discussed earlier in this chapter. These Italian events, then, are circumstantial but compelling proof of my earlier claim that local conflicts over the application of dominant models of organization can combine with global changes in economic conditions to produce novel forms of the division of labor.

We left the story of industrial struggle in Italy in the mid-1970s, when decentralization of production was well under way. As the unions' power over wages, hours, work conditions, and employment levels in the large factories increased, managers tried to regain control by subcontracting work to small producers. Craftsmen, unsettled by the compression of wage and skill hierarchies, began to look for work in small shops. Sometimes the new orders and disaffected craftsmen came together in small factories founded especially to evade union control. Often, however, they met in older shops that had been established during earlier periods of economic and political turmoil: For example, near Modena, in Emilia-Romagna, many beneficiaries of the *decentramento produttivo* were Socialist and Communist artisans who had gone into business for themselves in the early 1950s after a series of bitter strikes at the Officine Meccaniche Reggiane, a large engineering firm; near Turin, many shops were founded by skilled workers expelled from the factories during the political purges of the 1950s.[65]

The upshot was that by the mid-1970s there were in Italy innumerable small firms specializing in virtually every phase of the production of textiles, automatic machines, machine tools, automobiles, buses, and agricultural equipment. In the province of Modena, for instance, there were in 1963, the year after the first strike wave in the large factories, 4,970 officially registered artisans' firms, each employing at most 15 workers. By 1975 the number of registered firms had risen to 21,473, an increase of more than 300 percent, while the population as a whole grew by just over 10 percent, from 521,924 to 576,513.[66] Some of these were sweatshops of the kind described a moment ago. They continued to survive by evading taxes, paying no social welfare benefits, and exploiting to the hilt all the legal exemptions from labor statutes and other regulatory legislation that Italy offers its artisans.[67] But many of the others paid wages higher than those in the large factories (though sometimes still under the table to avoid taxes and social welfare deductions) and had equipment identical to that used in the most modern factories to perform equivalent operations. Following one of the strategies outlined in Chapter 2, they bought modern, high-output machines, aggregated orders from different customers, and prorated the fixed costs of operation among them. In Emilia-Romagna, the center of the small metalworking shops, many firms were unionized, although work rules and regulations regarding overtime were never applied so rigidly as in the large factories.[68]

Economic statistics from this period give an impression of the changes under way. From 1971 to 1973 wages in Emilia-Romagna averaged 93 percent of the national level, whereas wages in the highly industrialized region of Piedmont were 107 percent of the national standard during the same period. Between 1975 and 1977 wages in Emilia-Romagna had risen to 99 percent of the national average for those years, while wages in Piedmont were just 104 percent of the national level. Investment per employee in Emilia-Romagna was just under the average level in Piedmont between 1971 and 1973, but on the average one and a half times greater between 1975 and 1977. A further sign of prosperity was the region's tight labor markets. In 1966 the official unemployment rate was 4.0 percent for Italy as a whole, 4.3 percent in Emilia-Romagna, but just 2.5 percent in Piedmont. In 1976, however, both the Piedmontese and Emilian employment rates were 2.8 percent, well below the national level of 3.7 percent. A dramatic proof of the area's new riches is the ascent of Modena, regarded as the capital of the small-firm economy, in the league tables of provincial wealth: Ranked by per capita income, it was the seventeenth richest province in 1970, the second richest (after a center of luxury tourism) in 1979.[69]

Many of these more prosperous firms were becoming economically more autonomous as well. During the years immediately following 1969, even the larger and more advanced subcontractors, those who were seldom dependent on one or even a few customers, were still subordinate to the big factories. Often the client delivered the blueprints and tools needed to manufacture the part: Like the emergent industrial countries, the subcontractors were dependent on someone else's know-how. Because most of a subcontractor's customers were in closely related fields, moreover, an economic downturn that affected one would be likely to affect all. Although they could bargain over prices in good times, therefore, the subcontractors were still hostage to their customers' good will and prosperity.

To understand how this dependence was broken in the course of the 1970s, and a new system of production created, imagine a small factory producing transmissions for a large manufacturer of tractors. Ambition, the joy of invention, or fear that he and his clients will be devastated by an economic downturn lead the artisan who owns the shop to modify the design of the tractor transmission to suit the needs of a small manufacturer of high-quality seeders. To do this he draws on experiences acquired during years spent in West German factories, when he was unable to find work at home; or perhaps he consults with the young engineers working for his prospective client. But once the new transmission is designed, he discovers that to make it he needs precision parts not easily available on the market.

If he cannot modify his own machines to make these parts, he turns to a friend with a special lathe, who like himself fears being too closely tied to a few large manufacturers of a single product. Soon more and more artisans with different machines and skills are collaborating to make more and more diverse products.

The result is a system of high-technology cottage industry that does in a decentralized way what large innovative companies like the Thyssen specialty steel division do within the framework of huge organizations: create new demand by filling needs that potential customers may have only begun to suspect were there. Where the subcontractor's original customers arrived with a blueprint to execute, his new ones arrive with a problem to solve. They need, for example, a gearshift for a new small tractor, a pump for spreading a new insecticide that must be finely vaporized, or an elaborate container for mounting the cables of a nuclear power station. Even if the customer has a blueprint for his part, it is much more likely to serve as a guide to posing his problem than as a solution to it.

Typically, the small firm's solution will involve modifications of existing technology, which taken one at a time are marginally significant. For example, a conventional automatic packing machine is redesigned to fit the available space in a particular assembly line; a machine that injects one type of plastic into molds is modified to inject another, cheaper plastic; a membrane pump used in automobiles is modified to suit agricultural machinery; a standard loom or cloth-cutting machine is adjusted to work efficiently with particularly fine threads.

Often these modifications concern only the client whose problem inspired them. But as the discussion of machine tools in Chapter 2 suggested, a constant, if small, percentage of the marginal innovations prove generally applicable to a variety of problems: For example, an efficient, low-horsepower diesel engine can be used in a wide variety of agricultural machines, and certain improvements in packing machinery can be applied to a variety of specialized automatic devices. In this way a small firm occasionally succeeds in creating a new, international market, first for itself and then for a series of imitators, greatly enlarging the circle of its customers and freeing itself from any residual dependence on local conditions.[70]

The innovative capacity of this type of firm depends on its flexible use of technology; its close relations with other, similarly innovative firms in the same and adjacent sectors; and above all on the close collaboration of workers with different kinds of expertise. These firms practice boldly and spontaneously the fusion of conception and execution, abstract and practical knowledge, that only a few exceptional giant firms such as Thyssen have so far been able to achieve on a grand scale, and then, as we saw, only by disregarding the rules of Fordism.

The need for collaboration between different kinds of workers and across levels of the official skill hierarchy follows directly from the firm's relation with its clients. No good comes of proposing a solution if the small firm cannot supply the proposed product at an affordable price. Hence the design of the new product is inextricably connected to discussion of its production; and the final blueprint can be drawn only after consultation among technicians of several kinds and production workers of several levels.

The internal division of labor in such firms thus tends to be extremely flexible. The contacts among owners, engineers, technicians, the various heads of production, and skilled workers of various grades are close, and hierarchical distinctions are often treated as formalities. Unskilled workers, however, especially in the larger firms, tend to be excluded from this collaboration, a point to which I will return in a moment.

The boundary between intellectual and manual work in these firms is therefore blurred. No one, it is thought, can design a usable, economically viable product if he does not know at least approximately how to build it; nor can he do a good job of building it if he does not know roughly how to design it.

The founder of the innovative small firm is in fact the proverbial living proof of the efficacy of this fusion of the abstract and the concrete. Typically he starts his career at work as a skilled worker, a builder of prototypes, or a tool and diemaker. Eventually he has a bright idea for a new product, component, or piece closely related to his experience in a large plant, and goes into business for himself. As his market expands, he begins to face design problems involving specialized kinds of knowledge that go beyond his original stock of practical experience. Frequently he attends night-school classes, acquires a degree as a technical designer or engineer, and applies the new knowledge practically as he acquires it.

The explosion of creativity in the small Italian firms thus illustrates the argument from Chapter 3 that it is often social hierarchy and the world views associated with it that restrict the unfolding of human capacity, and not the limitations of natural endowment. We saw earlier that the night-school engineers in large West German plants often sacrificed their chances to develop their technical prowess to their fears and to repudiation of the middle-class world of university-trained engineers. Given the freedom to experiment with their skills outside rigid hierarchies, Italian craftsmen are capable of inventiveness and sophistication that confound middle-class expectations about the possibilities of learning by doing.

The small firm's use of technology follows from its use of skill. The production of ever-new parts and machines requires constant experimentation with the production equipment: To make a new machine at a reasonable price or produce a new weave with an existing loom, it is frequently necessary to modify an existing machine tool or to jimmy rig the loom. The necessity for making this kind of adjustment is completely independent of the sophistication of the equipment: An innovative artisan with a numerically controlled lathe or grinding machine is just as likely to tinker with it – inventing new tools, finding new ways to cut odd-shaped pieces – as an artisan with traditional equipment.

This tinkering, furthermore, constantly spurs and jostles suppliers of machine tools to improve *their* products: By listening to the reports of the men who service his machines in the shops, a maker of machine tools quickly learns what needs to be done and how to do it; and if he does not learn quickly enough, his servicemen will take what they have discovered and go into business for themselves. In this way Italy has become a leading manufacturer of wood-cutting, ceramic, and metal-cutting machinery.

The last cause and effect of the firm's innovative capacity is its relations with other similar firms. Small dependent subcontractors in the same sector compete with each other intensely. The relation among the innovative firms resembles the collegial relation among good doctors, good lawyers, or good university teachers: Each firm is jealous of its autonomy, overly proud of its capacities, but fully conscious that its success and its very survival are linked to the collective efforts of the community to which it belongs and whose prosperity it must defend.

One kind of dependence on related firms is implicit in the firm's innovative activity. At first the firm's comparative advantage derives from intense specialization – the capacity to tailor a particular part or component to special conditions. The disadvantage of this concentration of attention on one particular is that it distracts attention from all the others. The moment the firm begins to expand and move beyond its original speciality it finds itself dependent on the help of neighbors with complementary kinds of specialties; and because the neighbors can never exactly anticipate when they too will need assistance, the help is forthcoming.

The more the system of related, innovative small firms expands and prospers, pressing against its original limits, the more explicit the collective character of the activity becomes. The artisans realize that to expand business they must increase the sophistication and range of their products; and the only means to that end is to increase the range of sophistication of their capital equipment. But investment in exotic equipment is risky. No one is likely to undertake it unless he is confident that his friends will help him utilize the new machine by passing along orders even when there is no immediate profit to them from doing so. Mistrust freezes the technological progress of a whole sector; trust fosters it. The same logic applies to every phase of business: Where invention creates demand and invention is collective, this is a natural result.

This sense of mutual dependence is further reinforced by an appreciation of economies of scale that can sometimes be achieved by explicit collaboration. For most aspects of production, the small firms are not at a disadvantage because of their size; they have found that economies of scale exist at the level of one or a very few machines, not whole factories. Three lathes in each of three shops are at least as efficient as nine lathes under one roof.[71] But firms can seldom maintain white-collar staffs to handle marketing, accounting, or even technical services. An obvious solution, frequently adopted in Italy, is to pool resources and form an association of artisans or small employers who provide the services collectively. Similarly, consortia of small employers can purchase raw materials or secure bank loans at better prices than single firms. Thus narrow economic considerations combine with less precisely calculable ideas of collective advantage to create a sense of professional solidarity that is the backdrop and limit for competition between the firms.

As the story unfolds, it may seem both that dependent subcontractors naturally evolve into innovative small firms and that innovative small firms naturally perpetuate themselves, expanding and multiplying as they invent new demand. Neither is the case. The development of innovative small industry in Italy in the 1970s, in fact, depended on a number of background conditions, some peculiar to that country, some rooted in the general changes in world markets discussed in the preceding sections. If it were not for these background conditions, there would probably have been a few innovative firms in Italy, as there are in all industrial countries, but nothing like the systematic reordering of whole segments of industry that in fact occurred. And the long-term survival of these industrial structures will probably depend on the creation of new institutions to shape the labor and product markets in which the high-technology cottage industries operate. A closer look at the preconditions for the emergence and perpetuation of the innovative small firms will underscore the relation between Italian developments and my overarching theme: the role of ideas about the world, political conceptions in the broadest sense, in shaping economic activity.

Politics again

The rise of advanced cottage industry depended first on the joint expansion and diversification of the international market. A severe economic crisis at the wrong moment might have decimated the small firms before they had accumulated the experience and capital necessary to diversify production and assure their independence. Instead, they learned their lessons in an expanding market, and one that, for reasons not directly connected to Italian capital's motives for decentralizing production, increasingly demanded diversification and innovation.

Second, and this was a peculiarly Italian feature of developments, the innovative small firms did not face substantial competition from established economic powers. Precisely because the large firms were so embattled that they decentralized production in the first place, they were seldom in a position themselves to respond to the demand for new products. In West Germany or the United States, in contrast, the continued vitality of large firms doubly stifles the growth of an innovative small-business sector. First, as we saw, the large firms can supply at least some part of the diversified market through more neo-Fordist techniques. Second, and in part as a means of acquiring the technology necessary for the neo-Fordist strategy, they may simply buy up innovative small firms before their owners are successful enough to resist the temptation of a secure future as pensionaries of giant combines.

The deeper significance of these considerations is that the emergence of the new type of innovative economy depended on the coincidence of several political struggles. The struggle for place in the international order, motivated by each nation's will to political survival and pursued with all the instruments of state power, helped clear room for experiments with new forms of economic association. So did, on the national level, the Italian migrants' struggle to define a place for themselves in the large factories of the North. And as we saw in Chapter 4, the outcome of the migrants' struggles reflected their exchange of ideas with Northern craftsmen as much as underlying economic and social conditions.

The role of politics in shaping the new industrial structures is likely to become still clearer as time goes on. For no sooner were they born than the innovative small firms faced two dilemmas whose resolution, if any is found at all, will depend on the interplay of the political views of trade unions, employers, workers, and political parties.

The first threat to the expansion and reproduction of high-technology cottage industry regards the transmission of skill from one generation to another. As a rule, the medium-size innovative firms, those with fifteen or more workers, are divided into a stratum of skilled and a stratum of less-skilled workers. The skilled workers usually have acquired their knowledge through a combination of experiences in large firms in Italy and elsewhere and night-school education. The collaboration between technical and production workers described earlier develops and extends their skill. But this collaboration does not reach down to the stratum of unskilled workers, and it is therefore difficult for them to take the first steps toward learning a trade. Moreover, firms are reluctant to train workers: Once they possess the generally applicable skills that innovative work requires, nothing prevents the newly minted craftsmen from moving to another firm or going into business for themselves, a problem familiar from the analysis of secondary-sector firms in Chapter 2.

The system as a whole therefore needs skills that no single employer is likely to produce and that can be siphoned off from large firms only under specific historical conditions – as in Italy in the 1970s, for example, when the trade unions pushed egalitarian demands so far that craftsmen could earn more outside the large factory than inside.

The second danger has to do with the possibility of a reduction of the innovative drive of the small firms. Whenever an innovation is applicable to a range of products, a new market is created. To exploit it the firm is tempted to adopt mass-production methods typical of the large factory. The distance between technical personnel and production workers increases; the possibilities for further development of craft skills diminish; and the chances for the unskilled to acquire some technical versatility (chances present both in the very largest plants with their formalized skill ladders and in the traditional artisan's shop) are likely to vanish completely. The longer and more self-contentedly the firm lives from a single successful innovation, and the greater the shortage of skilled workers, the greater is this danger. And once a firm falls into this trap, it is unlikely to get out. Success reduces the entrepreneur's appetite for innovation; the rationalization of production and the stagnation of training reduce his innovative capacity; and by the time the firm needs to innovate again simply to survive, it cannot. Representatives of the Association of Small and Medium Sized Industry acknowledge the severity of both dangers.[72]

Conceivably, both dilemmas could be addressed by creating regional or industry-wide apprenticeship programs. In this way the costs of training could be borne collectively, by all the employers of an industry, for example, or all the taxpayers of a region. And once employers were faced with a steady stream of young workers intent on perfecting newly acquired skills, they would have less incentive to seek a safe market niche and adopt mass-production methods as a hedge against the day when the innovative drive faltered for lack of skills. On the contrary, the logic of the situation would press the other way, because a retreat to routine techniques might anger a technically ambitious work force. Similarly, collective provision of accounting services, advice on new marketing possibilities, and the applicability of new technologies to local needs could all encourage the new firms to grow through innovation rather than settling into a routine out of the fear of overreaching the limits of small, local consortia.[73]

In Emilia-Romagna, for instance, the innovative proprietors, the unions, and the regional government are already so intertwined by common political ideas that the creation of such collective services seems possible. The founders of many of the innovative metalworking firms, as we saw, were Communists or Socialists expelled from the large factories for political reasons; and often they have remained loyal to the leftist parties. In 1980, 55 percent of the 145,725 officially registered artisan enterprises in the region were members of the Confederazionne Nazionale dell'Artigianato, closely affiliated with the Communist and Socialist parties. In the most industrialized and rapidly growing provinces, such as Reggio Emilia, Bologna, and Modena, the average was 66 percent.[74] This loyalty contributes to the Left's preeminence in the regional politics and is in turn reinforced by the extensive aid that town and regional agencies under the Left's control give to small employers: Towns, for example, often construct industrial parks in which tens or even hundreds of artisans can rent space, a practice that recalls the public wheels and "Power to Let" signs of nineteenth-century Sheffield and Birmingham. For its part, the region advises small firms on market strategy and the use of technology.[75] The success of agricultural and industrial producers' cooperatives, owing in some measure to the government's willingness to place orders with local artisans determined to defend their independence against large firms, has popularized the idea of collectively owned enterprise while drawing the state and the labor movement still closer together.[76]

For all these reasons the boundary between the labor movement and the government has become blurred. The Left, proud of its part in the resistance to fascism and determined never again to repeat the mistake of abandoning the organization of the small firms to the Right, tries with some success to be both a party of labor and the party of orderly cooperation with the new firms.[77] And the small firms have come to depend on the services provided by the regional government or the CNA for everything from the balancing of their books to the construction of communal mess halls. Under such conditions, experiments in the collective provision of services from apprenticeship programs to investment counseling are likely. If they succeed, they will create industrial structures and careers at work that will appear more improbable still against the backdrop of Fordist ideas.

In the garment, ceramic tile, shoe, and furniture industries in the Veneto, in contrast, there is less chance of experimentation with collective solutions to the problems of innovative small firms. Here the influence of the church and traditional Catholic culture is still predominant; and as in Japan the government has worked hard to weave industrialization into the fabric of country life. Since 1960 the aim of the regional Christian Democratic Party has been to provide *una fabbrica per campanile*, a factory for every belfry, a slogan that recalls the success of a powerful local industrialist, Alessandro Rossi, who built an empire manufacturing woolens in a rural parish in the late nineteenth century.[78] When they exist, cooperatives are more often agricultural than industrial; and they, as well as the system of cooperative banks, tend to be hostile to much of the labor movement, rather than seeing themselves as a central part of it.[79] Proprietors of small firms, many of them former artisans, often treat their subordinates paternalistically and try to keep trade unions out of the shop. The influence of the CNA, for example, is negligible, and if they are organized at all, artisans join organizations close to the Christian Democrats.[80] Hence, to the extent that the survival of the innovative firms depends on subtle and changing forms of cooperation between labor and capital, between the firms and the state, and among groups of entrepreneurs, decentralization in the Veneto may ultimately result in nothing more than the creation of medium-size firms, each with its own market niche and each organized on traditional principles.

So the future of the innovative firms is as likely to depend on politics as their past. And the political views of the central players, the new entrepreneurs, are no more a direct outgrowth of their place in the division of labor than are the views of peasant workers or would-be craftsmen. Here, too, experience and conflict will shape the ambitions of social groups, and their ambitions will shape the economic structure. The more you look at Italian developments the more you are driven to conclude again that, within the broad limits imposed by competition in world markets, economic structure is fixed by political choices.

By the end of the 1980s it is likely that comparable stories, different in substance but with equally uncertain ends, will be told for each of the advanced industrial countries. The reindustrialization debate in the United States, the wave of neo-liberalism in Great Britain and nationalization in France, and the discussion of the democratization and social ownership of large firms in Sweden are surely just the first signs of an epochal redefinition of markets, technologies, and industrial hierarchies. The outcomes will depend on the daring and imagination of trade unions, industrialists, and politicians, and on the ideas of different social classes about how they want to work and live. But as soon as a new system, however shaky, is in place, the scientific thinkers on the Right will tell you that everything everywhere, down to the last detail, was determined by the pursuit of efficiency. Scientific thinkers on the Left will say that each group's inevitable pursuit of its interest, determined by its place in the division of labor, is the real explanation. Both will agree that ideas of dignity and honor, the political programs they inform, and the conflicts to which they give rise were only foam on the wave of history. If you have been persuaded by the book you have just read, you will not believe them.

Notes

Chapter 1. Workers and world views

1 The best survey of industrial conflict in Europe in the post–World War II period is Alessandro Pizzorno and Colin Crouch, eds., *Conflitti in Europa* (Milan: Etas Libri, 1977).

2 Ferdynand Zweig, *The Worker in an Affluent Society: Family Life and Industry* (London: Heinemann, 1961), pp. 205–12. A related but distinct argument is that the extension of citizenship rights to include provision of a certain minimum level of social welfare is eroding the difference between the working and middle classes. See T. H. Marshall, *Class, Citizenship, and Social Development* (Garden City, N.Y.: Doubleday and Co., 1964), pp. 300–14, for a discussion of the relation between the "affluent society" and the welfare state.

3 " 'The people,' previously the ferment of social change," Marcuse wrote in 1964, "have 'moved up' to become the ferment of social cohesion." Because the "conservative popular base" would not make a revolution, change could come only from the "substratum of outcasts and outsiders, the exploited and persecuted of other races and other colors, the unemployed and the unemployable." See Herbert Marcuse, *One-Dimensional Man: Studies in the Ideology of Advanced Industrial Society* (Boston: Beacon Press, 1964), p. 256. Even in a more optimistic essay, "The Left under the Counterrevolution," in his *Counterrevolution and Revolt* (Boston: Beacon Press, 1972), p. 6, Marcuse argued that the "integration" of the largest part of the working class was not a surface phenomenon. It was rooted in "benefits accorded to the metropolitan working class thanks to surplus profits, neocolonial exploitation, the military budget, the gigantic government subventions."

4 Robert Blauner, *Alienation and Freedom* (Chicago: University of Chicago Press, 1964), pp. 1–57.

5 Serge Mallet, *La nouvelle classe ouvrière* (Paris: Editions du Seuil, 1963), pp. 27–74: On the changes in Mallet's positions after May 1968, see Alessandro Pizzorno, "Ricordo di Serge Mallet," *Problemi del socialismo* 15 (March 1973):394–9.

6 John H. Goldthorpe et al., *The Affluent Worker in the Class Structure* (Cambridge: Cambridge University Press, 1969), pp. 157–95.

7 On the general outlines of these strike waves and their impact on industrial relations in the several countries, see Pizzorno and Crouch, *Conflitti in Europa;* for a good account of the unsettled state of the sociology of work in the wake of these disturbances, see Michael Mann, *Consciousness and Action among the Western Working Classes* (London: Macmillan, 1973).

232

8 Daniel Bell, *The Cultural Contradictions of Capitalism* (New York: Basic Books, 1978).

9 Representative of the neoorthodox position is Sebastian Herkommer, "Conscience et position dans le procès social de reproduction: rapports de médiation," *Sociologie du travail* 20 (January 1978): 69–79. The most influential recent statement of the traditional Marxist claim that only the dependent – those dispossessed economically, subjected to the political authority of others, and subordinated intellectually – can develop a revolutionary consciousness is Nicos Ar Poulantzas, *Pouvoir politique et classes sociales* (Paris: François Maspero, 1968). A clear restatement and (partial) critique of Poulantzas's views is Erik Olin Wright, "Class Boundaries in Advanced Capitalist Societies," *New Left Review*, no. 98 (July 1976), pp. 3–42.

10 See, for example, Alessandro Pizzorno, "Interests and Parties in Pluralism," in Suzanne Berger, ed., *Organizing Interests in Western Europe* (Cambridge: Cambridge University Press, 1981), pp. 247–84.

11 The classic statement of the convergence hypotheses is Clark Kerr et al., *Industrialism and Industrial Man* (Cambridge: Harvard University Press, 1960). For a very brief summary and critique of the vast body of related literature, see Richard Scase, *Social Democracy in Capitalist Society: Working-Class Politics in Britain and Sweden* (London: Croom Helm, 1977), pp. 9–15. A more thorough analysis is Suzanne Berger and Michael J. Piore, *Dualism and Discontinuity in Industrial Societies* (Cambridge: Cambridge University Press, 1980). Where the concept of convergence developed in *Industrialism and Industrial Man* focuses on the constraints that technology supposedly imposes on social structure, a second and complementary variant of the idea sees convergence as the result of a search for optimal economic organization. For a discussion of the presuppositions and shortcomings of this school, associated with the work of Jan Tinbergen, see Michael Ellman, "Against Convergence," *Cambridge Journal of Economics* 4 (September 1980):199–210.

The idea of convergence is deeply rooted in the classics of modern social thought. Thus Durkheim sought to trace the progress of the division of labor and the correlate forms of moral life, Marx the successive modes of class domination in relation to the advancing human capacity to dominate nature, Weber the progressive demystification of the world and the resulting tyranny of instrumental rationality over all of social life. A useful introduction to the works of all three is Anthony Giddens, *Capitalism and Modern Social Theory: An Analysis of the Writings of Marx, Durkheim and Max Weber* (Cambridge: Cambridge University Press, 1971). For an especially clear explanation of the functionalist ideas that underlie both Marxist and non-Marxist arguments connecting human progress and the transformation of institutions, see G. A. Cohen, *Karl Marx's Theory of History: A Defense* (Princeton: Princeton University Press, 1978).

12 A particularly graphic account of the process by which modern society is said to create new desires in traditional peoples is Daniel Lerner, *The Passing of Traditional Society* (New York: Free Press, 1958), pp. 398–412. For a Marxist variant of this argument, see Paul Sweezy's critique of Maurice Dobb's *Studies in Development of Capitalism*, in Rodney Hilton, ed., *The Transition from Feudalism to Capitalism* (London: New Left Books, 1976), pp. 33–56.

13 See Bell's essay "The End of Ideology in the West" in Daniel Bell, *The End of Ideology: On the Exhaustion of Political Ideas in the Fifties*, rev. ed. (New York: Free Press, 1965), pp. 393–407.

14 On the long-standing debate over the determinants of process, see Gernot Müller et al., *Ökonomische Krisentendenzen im gegenwärtigen Kapitalismus* (Frankfurt am Main: Campus Verlag, 1978), pp. 40–51.

15 Blauner, *Alienation and Freedom*, p. 180.

16 Mallet, *La nouvelle classe ouvrière*, p. 64.

17 Zweig, *The Worker in an Affluent Society*, p. 209.

18 See John H. Goldthorpe and David Lockwood, "Affluence and British Class Structure," *Sociological Review* 11 (July 1963):133–63; Goldthorpe et al., *The Affluent Worker*, p. 170; and John H. Goldthorpe, "The Current Inflation: Towards a Sociological Account," in Fred Hirsch and John H. Goldthorpe, eds., *The Political Economy of Inflation* (London: Martin Robertson, 1978), pp. 187–214.

19 W. G. Runciman, *Relative Deprivation and Social Justice: A Study of Attitudes to Social Inequality in Twentieth-Century England* (London: Routledge and Kegan Paul, 1966).

20 Runciman, *Relative Deprivation*, pp. 24–35.

21 Alessandro Pizzorno, "Scambio politico e identità collettiva nel conflitto di classe," *Rivista italiana di scienza politica* 7 (August 1977):165–98.

22 For a comprehensive discussion of the concept of alienation, see István Mészaros, *Marx's Theory of Alienation* (New York: Harper and Row, 1972). A critique of attempts to apply this concept in empirical studies of workers' consciousness is Daniel Vidal, "Un cas de faux concept: la notion d'aliénation," *Sociologie du travail* 11 (January 1969):61–82.

23 On the distinction between class consciousness taken as reflective of objective conditions and "empirically given" consciousness that consists of the "psychologically describable and explicable ideas which men form about their situation in life," see Georg Lukács, *History and Class Consciousness: Studies in Marxist Dialectics*, trans. Rodney Livingstone (Cambridge: MIT Press, 1971), p. 51. Lukács held that class consciousness would prevail against false, empirical consciousness. But the opposite conclusion is prima facie no less compelling. In some of the writings of Marcuse, capitalism's ability to control alienation through ideological manipulation and the promise of material well-being is seen as almost unlimited. See again the despairing conclusion of Marcuse, *One-Dimensional Man*, pp. 247–57.

24 Lukács, *History and Class Consciousness*, pp. 314 ff.; Mallet, *La nouvelle classe ouvrière*, pp. 261–6.

25 See Max Weber, *Gesammelte Aufsätze zur Religionssoziologie*, 3 vols. (Tübingen: J. C. B. Mohr [Paul Siebeck], 1922–3); Clifford Geertz, *The Interpretation of Cultures* (New York: Basic Books, 1973); Pierre Bourdieu, *Outline of a Theory of Practice*, trans. Richard Nice (Cambridge: Cambridge University Press, 1977); idem, *Zur Soziologie der symbolischen Formen*, trans. Wolfgang Fietkau (Frankfurt am Main: Suhrkamp Verlag, 1974); Eugene D. Genovese, *Roll, Jordan, Roll: The World the Slaves Made* (New York: Random House, 1972); and E. P. Thompson, *The Making of the English Working Class* (London: Gollancz, 1963).

26 Bourdieu, *Outline of a Theory of Practice*, pp. 159 ff.

27 This example is from Raymond Boudon, *L'inégalité des chances: la mobilité sociale dans les sociétés industrielles* (Paris: Armand Colin, 1973), pp. 51–74. Disparities of power between cooperating groups can be described as unequal exchange. See Alvin W. Gouldner, "The Norm of Reciprocity: A Preliminary Statement," *American Sociological Review* 25 (April 1960):161–78; and Gianfranco Poggi, "Alcune riflessioni su 'Le organizzazioni, il potere e i conflitti di classe,' di Alessandro Pizzorno," *Quaderni di sociologia* 12 (April 1963):201–15.

28 See for example Bourdieu, *Outline of a Theory of Practice*, pp. 72–95; and the chapter "Religion as a Cultural System" in Geertz, *The Interpretation of Cultures*, pp. 87–125.

29 On the necessary incompleteness and hence conventionality of scientific theories, see Thomas S. Kuhn, *The Structure of Scientific Revolutions* (Chicago: University of Chicago Press, 1962).

30 On the fragmentation of personality in liberal societies, see Roberto Mangabeira Unger, *Knowledge and Politics* (New York: Free Press, 1975), pp. 164–70.

31 Geertz, *The Interpretation of Cultures*, p. 93.

32 Roberto Mangabeira Unger, *Law and Modern Society* (New York: Free Press, 1976), pp. 127–9.

33 Bourdieu, *Outline of a Theory of Practice*, pp. 10–15.

34 The notion that men constitutionally subject themselves to a moral order is common to writers as diverse as Lévi-Strauss and Habermas. See Claude Lévi-Strauss, *La pensée sauvage* (Paris: Librairie Plon, 1962); and Jürgen Habermas, *Legitimationsprobleme im Spätkapitalismus* (Frankfurt am Main: Suhrkamp Verlag, 1973).

35 An important source for the analysis of Italian developments is Alessandro Pizzorno et al., *Lotte operaie e sindacato: il ciclo 1968–1972 in Italia* (Bologna: Il Mulino, 1978).

36 Alessandro Pizzorno, "I sindacati nel sistema politico italiano: aspetti storici," *Rivista trimestrale di diritto pubblico* 21 (October 1971):1522.

37 Geertz, *The Interpretation of Cultures*, pp. 142–69; Bourdieu, *Outline of a Theory of Practice*, pp. 159–71.

38 For a perceptive discussion of the relation between the advanced worker consciousness and economic backwardness, see Michael Mann, *Consciousness and Action*, pp. 34–44.

39 On the importance of radical political parties in shaping worker consciousness see Frank Parkin, *Class Inequality and Political Order: Social Statification in Socialist Societies* (New York: Praeger Publishers, 1971), pp. 79–102; on the failure of socialism to take root in the United States see John M. Laslett and Seymour Martin Lipset, eds., *Failure of a Dream? Essays in the History of American Socialism* (Garden City, N.Y.: Doubleday and Co., Anchor Books, 1974).

40 A pessimist could draw this conclusion from Michel Crozier, *The Bureaucratic Phenomenon* (Chicago: University of Chicago Press, 1964).

41 Crozier, *The Bureaucratic Phenomenon*.

42 Alan Fox, *Beyond Contract: Work, Power and Trust Relations* (London: Faber and Faber, 1974), pp. 13–151.

43 On the importance of master–apprentice relations in German industry, see Alan Fox, "Corporatism," mimeographed (Oxford, 1977). For an account of the ways German craftsmen develop their skills, see Burkart Lutz and Guido Kammerer, *Das Ende des graduierten Ingenieurs? Eine empirische Analyse unerwarteter Nebenfolgen der Bildungsexpansion* (Frankfurt am Main: Europäische Verlagsanstalt, 1975), pp. 93–6.

44 Marc Maurice, François Sellier, and Jean-Jacques Silvestre, "La production de la híerarchie dans l'entreprise: recherche d'un effet sociétal," *Revue française de sociologie* 20 (April 1979):331–80.

45 For the organization of skill acquisition in Japan see Kazuo Koike, "Japan's Industrial Relations: Characteristics and Problems," *Japanese Economic Studies* 7 (Fall 1978):42–90. Robert E. Cole, *Japanese Blue Collar* (Berkeley and Los Angeles: University of California Press, 1971), compares skilled workers in a Tokyo die-cast plant with unskilled peasant workers in an auto-parts factory three hours by train from the capital.

46 Ronald P. Dore, *British Factory–Japanese Factory: The Origins of National Diversity in Industrial Relations* (Berkeley and Los Angeles: University of California Press, 1973).

47 Robert E. Cole, *Work, Mobility, and Participation* (Berkeley and Los Angeles: University of California Press, 1979), pp. 11–32.

48 Ronald P. Dore, "Late Development – or Something Else? Industrial Relations in Britain, Japan, Mexico, Sri Lanka, and Senegal," mimeographed (Sussex, England, 1974).

49 A classic example is the revitalization of Prussia after the defeat at Jena. See Friedrich Meinecke, *The Age of German Liberation, 1795–1815*, trans. Peter Paret (Berkeley and Los Angeles: University of California Press, 1977).

50 Giuseppe Tomasi di Lampedusa, *Il Gattopardo* (Milan: Feltrinelli, 1958), p. 43. Trotsky's remark is cited in Isaac Deutscher, *The Prophet Armed: Trotsky, 1879–1921* (London: Oxford University Press, 1954), p. 483.

51 See for instance Sarmiento's account of Rosas in Domingo Faustino Sarmiento, *Facundo; o, civilización y barberie en las pampas argentinas* (Buenos Aires: Ediciónes Peuser, 1955).

52 Patrick Fridenson, "The Coming of the Assembly Line in Europe," in Wolfgang Krohn, Edwin T. Layton, Jr., and Peter Weingart, eds., *The Dynamics of Science and Technology* (Dordrecht: D. Reidel Publishing Co., 1978), pp. 160–75.

Chapter 2. The structure of the labor market

1 On the production of Singer sewing machines, see David Allen Hounshell, "From the American System to Mass Production: The Development of Manufacturing Technology in the United States, 1850–1920" (Ph.D. diss., University of Delaware, 1978), p. 163; for Pullman see Stanley Buder, *Pullman* (Oxford: Oxford University Press, 1967), p. 17.

2 For the clock, sewing-machine, and bicycle industries in the United States, see Hounshell, "From the American System to Mass Production"; for changes in British light engineering in the nineteenth century, see G. A. Allen, *The Industrial Development of Birmingham and the Black Country, 1860–1927* (London: George Allen and Unwin, 1929); for changes in the steel industry in the two countries, see Bernard Elbaum and Frank Wilkinson, "Industrial Relations and Uneven Development: A Comparative Study of the American and British Steel Industries," *Cambridge Journal of Economics* 3 (September 1979): 275–303; and on the mechanization of the shoe industry, see Alan Dawley, *Class and Community: The Industrial Revolution in Lynn* (Cambridge: Harvard University Press, 1976).

3 Alfred D. Chandler, Jr., *The Visible Hand: The Managerial Revolution in American Business* (Cambridge: Harvard University Press, Belknap Press, 1977).

4 The following paragraphs draw on the exhaustive account in Hounshell, "From the American System to Mass Production," pp. 331–79.

5 The system of mass production might alternatively be called the age of Taylorism, after Frederick Winslow Taylor, the champion of scientific management. Taylor's idea was for management to secure the most efficient possible use of labor by codifying craft knowledge and deciding by scientific means the one right way to do a particular job. Workers were then to be forced to execute this plan exactly through the promise of high wages and the threat of sanctions for disobedience. The extreme routinization of work that Taylorism implied, however, presupposes the fixity of markets and the production process characteristic of mass production: The more frequently tasks change, the more difficult and expensive it becomes to plan the precise execution of any one of them. The Fordist system of special-purpose equipment, furthermore, transferred skill from worker to machine, accomplishing partly by mechanical means what Taylor wanted to do through administrative control. Because Taylorism presupposes Fordism and Fordism implies Taylorism, I associate the age of mass production with the name of the automobile maker, not the industrial engineer. Compare Ford's preoccupation with the connection between mass markets and the routinization of production in Henry Ford, in collaboration with Samuel Crowther, *My Life and Work* (Garden City, N.Y.: Garden City Publishing Co., 1926), pp. 16–18 and 47–50, with Taylor's neglect of the theme in Frederick Winslow Taylor, *The Principles of Scientific Management* (New York: Harper and Brothers, 1915).

6 The figures are from David Brody, "Labor and Small-Scale Enterprise during Industrialization," in Stuart W. Bruchey, ed., *Small Business in American Life* (New York: Columbia University Press, 1980), p. 264. An astute account of the organization and importance of small industry at the begining of the twentieth century is P. Kropotkin, *Fields, Factories, and Workshops*, rev. ed. (London: Thomas Nelson and Sons, 1912).

7 For the stability of value added and percentage of employment by size of firm through 1975, see Bureau of Statistics, *Japan Statistical Yearbook, 1973–74* (Tokyo: Office of the Prime Minister, 1975), pp. 182–3; and Bureau of Statistics, *Japan Statistical Yearbook, 1980* (Tokyo: Office of the Prime Minister, 1980), pp. 170–3.

8 The most influential accounts of the dual structure of modern industrial economies are Robert T. Averitt, *The Dual Economy: The Dynamics of American Industry Structure* (New York: W. W. Norton and Co., 1968); Robin Marris, *The Economic Theory of 'Managerial' Capitalism* (New York: Free Press, 1964); and John Kenneth Galbraith, *The New Industrial State* (Boston: Houghton Mifflin Co., 1967). An elegant attempt to elaborate these early works into a comprehensive alternative to neoclassical theories that assume perfectly competitive markets is Alfred S. Eichner, *The Megacorp and Oligopoly: The Micro Foundations of Macro Dynamics* (Cambridge: Cambridge University Press, 1976). For a neoclassical explanation of dualism see Arthur M. Okun, "Inflation: Its Mechanics and Welfare Costs," *Brookings Papers on Economic Activity*, no. 2 (1975), pp. 351–90. For an interesting *marxisant* view of dualism, see Richard Edwards, *Contested Terrain: The Transformation of the Workplace in the Twentieth Century* (New York: Basic Books, 1979).

9 Michael J. Piore, "The Technological Foundations of Dualism and Discontinuity," in Suzanne Berger and Michael J. Piore, *Dualism and Discontinuity in Industrial Societies* (Cambridge: Cambridge University Press, 1980), pp. 55–81. For Smith's original formulation, see Adam Smith, *The Wealth of Nations*, ed. Edwin Cannan (Chicago: University of Chicago Press, 1976), pp. 7–25.

10 By the 1920s, calculation of fixed costs played a decisive role in the determination of corporate strategies. See, for Germany, Ernst Schmalenbach, *Selbstkostenrechnungen und Preispolitik*, 6th ed. rev. (Leipzig: G. A. Gloeckner, 1934), pp. 57–65. In the United States, Alfred P. Sloan, Jr., first a director and then, for twenty-three years, the chief executive officer at General Motors, played an important part in bringing the connection between fluctuation in demand, fixed costs, and profitability to the attention of big industry. The recessions in the automobile industry in 1920–1 and 1924 convinced Sloan of the need to match production to average expected levels of demand. This meant on the one hand developing forecasting techniques and inventory controls in order to predict market developments and adjust to them as rapidly as possible, and on the other hand trying to augment demand by offering such services as credit (the General Motors Acceptance Corporation) and insurance (General Exchange Insurance Corporation) to potential customers. Prices and target rates of return were calculated on the basis of predicted average rates of plant utilization, the standard volume. See Alfred P. Sloan, Jr., *My Years with General Motors* (Garden City, N.Y.: Doubleday and Co., 1964), pp. 30, 127–58, 301–7.

11 For this argument see Stephen A. Marglin, "What Do Bosses Do? The Origins

and Functions of Hierarchy in Capitalist Production," *Review of Radical Political Economy*, Summer 1974, pp. 60–112.

12 Jan de Vries, *The Economy of Europe in the Age of Crisis, 1600–1675* (Cambridge: Cambridge University Press, 1976).

13 For the contribution of early modern mathematicians and instrument makers to the development of machine tools, see Robert S. Woodbury, *Studies in the History of Machine Tools* (Cambridge: MIT Press, 1972).

14 See David S. Landes, *The Unbound Prometheus* (Cambridge: Cambridge University Press, 1969), pp. 64–5.

15 Merritt Roe Smith, *Harpers Ferry Armory and the New Technology* (Ithaca, N.Y.: Cornell University Press, 1977).

16 Nathan Rosenberg, *Perspectives on Technology* (Cambridge: Cambridge University Press, 1958), pp. 158–9.

17 Joan Thirsk, *Economic Policy and Projects: The Development of a Consumer Society in Early Modern England* (Oxford: Oxford University Press, 1978).

18 See generally on Sheffield G. I. H. Lloyd, *The Cutlery Trades* (London: Longmans, Green and Co., 1913); and Sidney Pollard, *A History of Labour in Sheffield* (Liverpool: Liverpool University Press, 1959). For Birmingham, see Allen, *Industrial Development of Birmingham*.

19 On "public wheels" in Sheffield see Lloyd, *The Cutlery Trades*, pp. 44–5; and Pollard, *History of Labour in Sheffield*, pp. 51, 54–6. The Birmingham advertisements for power to rent are cited in Allen, *Industrial Development of Birmingham*, p. 152.

20 Henry Hamilton, *The English Brass and Copper Industries to 1800* (London: Longmans, Green and Co., 1926), pp. 215–39.

21 On the peasants' tenacious defense of their land see, for example, Emmanuel Le Roy Ladurie, "Les masses profondes: la paysannerie," in Fernand Braudel and Ernest Labrousse, eds., *Histoire économique et sociale de la France* (Paris: Presses Universitaires de France, 1977), vol. 1, pt. 2, pp. 819–59. For the rural, fragmented character of demand in France and Europe generally, as compared to Great Britain, see Landes, *The Unbound Prometheus*, pp. 50–1, 126–7. William H. Sewell, Jr., *Work and Revolution in France* (Cambridge: Cambridge University Press, 1980), discusses the *métiers jurés* and related organizations.

22 This paragraph draws on Patrick O'Brien and Caglar Keyder, *Economic Growth in Britain and France 1780–1914: Two Paths to the Twentieth Century* (London: George Allen and Unwin, 1978), esp. pp. 174–98. Two earlier works in this tradition are Maurice Lévy-Leboyer, "Les processus d'industrialisation: le cas de l'Angleterre et de la France," *Revue historique* 92 (April 1968):281–98; and Richard Roehl, "French Industrialization: A Reconsideration," *Explorations in Economic History* 13 (July 1976):233–81. Where Landes's *The Unbound Prometheus* sees the structure of labor and product markets in France as an obstacle to development, this school regards them as the starting point of a distinctive kind of economic growth.

23 See O'Brien and Keyder, *Economic Growth in Britain and France*, p. 91, tab. 4.3, for the comparison of labor productivity, and pp. 152–68 for a discussion of labor productivity in the workshop sectors of the two countries.

24 See, on the development of the Jacquard loom, Pierre Cayez, *Métiers Jacquard et hauts fourneaux: aux origines de l'industrie lyonnaise* (Lyons: Presses Universitaires de Lyon, 1978), pp. 105–8. The figures for the increase in the number of façonné patterns are taken from E. Pariset, *Histoire de la fabrique lyonnaise* (Lyons: A. Rey, 1901), pp. 301–2.

25 By 1834 the Rue Tolozan in the heart of the Lyons silk district was jammed with 1,427 residents and 678 looms, almost half of them Jacquard. There were 232 master weavers, 227 resident journeymen. Only one master owned as many as eight looms. Two owned seven; nine owned six; thirteen owned five; and all the rest had no more than four. See the description in Robert J. Bezucha, *The Lyon Uprising of 1834* (Cambridge: Harvard University Press, 1974), p. 18.

26 See Allen, *Industrial Development of Birmingham*, pp. 17–19, 43–4; and Pollard, *History of Labour in Sheffield*, pp. 52, 158, 225.

27 J. W. Lozier, "The Forgotten Industry: Small and Medium Sized Cotton Mills South of Boston," *Working Papers from the Regional Economic History Research Center* 2, no. 4 (1979):101–24; and, for references to the differential gear and other related inventions, David J. Jeremy, *Transatlantic Industrial Revolution: The Diffusion of Textile Technologies between Britain and America, 1790–1830's* (Cambridge: MIT Press, 1981), pp. 204–8.

28 Landes, *The Unbound Prometheus*, pp. 138–9.

29 On foreign influences on German machine design, for example, see Kropotkin, *Fields, Factories, and Workshops*, p. 46; and Alfred Schröter and Walter Becker, *Die deutsche Maschinenbauindustrie in der industriellen Revolution* (Berlin: Akademie Verlag, 1962).

30 These paragraphs are based on R. A. Church, "The Effect of the American Export Invasion on the British Boot and Shoe Industry, 1885–1914," *Journal of Economic History* 28 (June 1968):223–54 (the citation is from p. 231).

31 A pioneering study on this topic is Russell I. Fries, "British Response to The American System," *Technology and Culture* 16 (July 1975):377–403. The perspective, however, is close to Landes's.

32 Two good examples of newer studies that show the persistence of artisanal techniques of production are Alastair Reid, "The Division of Labour in the British Shipbuilding Industry, 1880–1920" (Ph.D. diss., Cambridge University, 1980); and Jonathan Zeitlin, "Craft Regulation and the Division of Labor: Engineers and Compositors in Britain, 1890–1914" (Ph.D. diss., University of Warwick, 1981).

33 Michel Laferrère, *Lyon: ville industrielle* (Paris: Presses Universitaires de France, 1960), pp. 217–41.

34 For the Swiss reaction to the spread of mass production, see the discussion of the machine-tool industry in B. Lincke, *Die schweizerische Maschinenindustrie und ihre Entwicklung in wirtschaftlicher Beziehung* (Frauenfeld: Huber and Co., 1911). "Pure mass production," Lincke writes, "cannot be the goal of the Swiss machine tool industry. Its market is too differentiated and home demand is too small for that. Rather its strategy should be to do full justice to the demands of its customers by thoroughly mastering special areas. The strength of the Swiss machine tool industry cannot be in the application of fixed patterns. On the contrary, the road to success lies in providing the most perfect possible solution to an assignment through well-informed accommodation of the particular needs of the individual customer" (p. 194). Even in the large European countries there was, despite the rush to imitation, an undercurrent of similar caution in informed reactions to Fordism and the rationalization of work. A German engineer, commissioned in 1902–3 by the Verein Deutscher Ingenieure to report on American industrial methods, warned, for example, that the techniques were suited to production of standard goods, whereas "flexibility has opened many foreign markets to German producers." See Heidrun Homburg, "Anfänge des Taylorsystems in Deutschland vor dem Erstem Weltkrieg," *Geschichte und Gesellschaft*, 4, no. 2 (1978):174.

35 See, on the Swedish Social Democrats' attempts to shape industrial structure, Andrew Martin, "The Dynamics of Change in a Keynesian Political Economy: The Swedish Case and Its Implications," in Colin Crouch, ed., *State and Economy in Contemporary Capitalism* (London: Croom Helm, 1979), pp. 88–121.

36 See, on the ambiguous relation of the plan and extraplan economies in the Soviet-type states, Gregory Grossman, "The 'Second Economy' of the USSR," *Problems of Communism*, September 1977, pp. 25–40; Dimitri K. Simes, "The Soviet Parallel Market," *Survey* 21 (Summer 1975):42–52; and I. R. Gábor, "The Second (Secondary) Economy," *Acta Oeconomica* 22, nos. 3–4 (1979):291–311.

37 For a review of the theoretical and empirical literaure on secondary-sector unskilled jobs, see David M. Gordon, *Theories of Poverty and Underemployment* (Lexington, Mass.: D. C. Heath and Co., 1972).

38 See Knut Gerlach and Peter Liepmann, "Konjunkturelle Aspekte der Industrialisierung peripherer Regionen – dargestellt am Beispiel des ostbayerischen Regierungsbezirks Oberpfalz," *Jahrbücher für Nationalökonomie und Statistik* 187 (1972):1–16; idem, "Industrialisierung und Siedlungsstruktur: Bemerkungen zum regionalpolitischen Programm einer aktiven Sanierung der bayerischen Rückstandsgebiete," *Jahrbücher für Nationalökonomie und Statistik* 187 (1973):507–21; and Knut Gerlach and Karl-Friedrich Kühner, "Freiwilliger Arbeitsplatzwechsel in Rückstandsregionen," *Zeitschrift für Wirtschafts- und Sozialwissenschaft* 94 (1974):167–82.

39 Gerlach and Liepmann, "Konjunkturelle Aspekte," pp. 20–1.

40 Dietrich Fürst and Klaus Zimmermann, under the direction of Karl-Heinrich Hansmeyer, *Standortwahl industrieller Unternehmen: Ergebnisse einer Unternehmensbefragung*, Schriftenreihe der Gesellschaft für regionale Strukturentwicklung 1 (Bonn: Gesellschaft für regionale Strukturentwicklung, 1973).

41 Friedrich Buttler, Knut Gerlach, and Peter Liepmann, "Funktionsfähige regionale Arbeitsmärkte als Bestandteil ausgewogener Funktionsräume," in Detlev Marx, ed., *Ausgeglichene Funktionsräume*, Veröffentlichungen der Akademie für Raumsforschung – Forschung und Sitzungsbericht 94 (Hannover: Akademie für Raumsforschung, 1975), pp. 84–5.

42 On the tendency for the sophistication of the decision-making techniques to increase with the size of the firm making the investment, see Fürst and Zimmermann, *Standortwahl*, pt. 2, p. 169. European and Japanese firms, as is frequently remarked, have longer payback periods than U.S. companies; so even the shortest payback periods in the sample may strike an American reader as relatively long.

43 Georg Raum, "Die Arbeitsplatzqualifikationsanforderungen der Zweigbetriebe," mimeographed (Regensburg, 1975), p. 65.

44 Gerlach and Liepmann, "Konjunkturelle Aspekte," p. 18.

45 Jürgen Strunz, *Die Industrieansiedlungen in der Oberpfalz in den Jahren 1957 bis 1966*, Regensburger geographische Schriften 4 (Regensburg: Geographisches Institut der Universität Regensburg, 1974), pp. 94, 108.

46 On the connection between the switch to capital-intensive production techniques and the substitution of male for female labor see Otfried Mickler, "Die ökonomischen Bedingungen des Fraueneinsatzes im Bereich der industriellen Produktion," mimeographed (Göttingen, 1975), pp. 24 ff.

47 Fürst and Zimmermann, *Standortwahl*, pt. 2, p. 3.

48 Bayerisches Staatsministerium für Arbeit und soziale Fürsorge, ed., *Probleme des bayerischen Arbeitsmarktes: eine Untersuchung des Arbeitsmarktgeschehens 1966/67* (Munich: Bayerisches Staatsministerium für Arbeit und soziale Fürsorge, n.d.), pp. 67, 150. Of course, as suggested previously, under appropriate conditions – growth in the power of unions or increasingly stringent application of minimum wage laws – small factories producing for the secondary sector can be dissolved in favor of a return to domestic work. See Franco Crespi, Roberto Segatori, and Vinicio Bottachiari, *Il lavoro a domicilio: il caso dell'Umbria* (Bari: De Donato, 1975).

49 On the relation between the uncertain functioning of computer machines and power within organizations, see Michel Crozier, *The Bureaucratic Phenomenon* (Chicago: University of Chicago Press, 1964), pp. 145–74.

50 To use Chomsky's language, they must have a generative grasp of the principles underlying the relevant technology. See Noam Chomsky, *Aspects of the Theory of Syntax* (Cambridge: MIT Press, 1965).

51 See the discussion of this type of job in Edwards, *Contested Terrain*, pp. 171–4.

52 Horst Kern and Michael Schumann, *Industriearbeit und Arbeiterbewusstsein: eine empirische Untersuchung über den Einfluss der aktuellen technischen Entwicklung auf die industrielle Arbeit und auf das Arbeiterbewusstsein,* 2 vols. (Frankfurt am Main: Europäische Verlagsanstalt, 1970), 1:155.

53 Peter Doeringer and Michael J. Piore, *Internal Labor Markets and Manpower Analysis* (Lexington, Mass: D. C. Heath and Co., 1971).

54 Gordon, *Theories of Poverty and Unemployment*, p. 77.

55 Duncan Gallie, *In Search of the New Working Class* (Cambridge: Cambridge University Press, 1978), pp. 213–14.

56 Giuseppe Bonazzi, *In una fabbrica di motori* (Milan: Feltrinelli, 1975).

57 William Kornblum, *Blue Collar Community* (Chicago: University of Chicago Press, 1974), pp. 56–7.

58 See, for an argument regarding the manipulative effects of schooling, Samuel Bowles and Herbert Gintis, *Schooling in Capitalist America* (New York: Basic Books, 1976). For the claim that the struggle to meet artfully set production quotas itself contributes to workers' acceptance of their jobs, see Michael Burawoy, *Manufacturing Consent* (Chicago: University of Chicago Press, 1979).

59 Harry Braverman, *Labor and Monopoly Capital: The Degradation of Work in the Twentieth Century* (New York: Monthly Review Press, 1974), pp. 196–206.

60 David F. Noble, "Social Choice in Machine Design: The Case of Automatically Controlled Machine Tools, and a Challenge to Labor," *Politics and Society* 8, nos. 3–4 (1978):313–47.

61 Braverman, *Labor and Monopoly Capital*, p. 202. For a skeptical view of these claims based on a survey of numerical-control users, see Bryn Jones, "Destruction or Re-distribution of Engineering Skills? The Case of Numerical Control," mimeographed (School of Humanities and Social Sciences, University of Bath, n.d.).

62 Noble, "Social Choice in Machine Design," p. 333.

63 Benjamin Coriat, "Robots et automates dans les industries de serie: esquisse d'une économie de la robotique d'atelier" (paper presented to the Sixtieth National Meeting of the Association pour le Développement des Etudes sur la Firme Industrielle, Chantilly, September 18–19, 1980), pp. 22–6.

64 For Great Britain, see S. K. Bhattacharyya, K. F. Li, B. McMinn, and C. M. Mellors, "Penetration and Utilization of NC/CNC Machine Tools in British Industry," mimeographed (Manufacturing Systems Unit, Department of Engineering Production, University of Birmingham, November 1976). For the United States, see "The American Machinist Inventory of Metalworking Equipment, 1973," *American Machinist*, October 29, 1973, p. 12; and the magazine's twelfth survey, covering the years 1976–8, in *American Machinist*, December 1978, p. 139.

65 Alice M. Greene, "The Subtle Shifts in the NC Market Scene," *Iron Age*, March 3, 1979, p. 35. See also Greene's "NC Technology Has No Time for Tapes," *Iron Age*, May 19, 1980, pp. 55–60.

66 Interview with M. Gouberti, director of ADEPA, June 15, 1980. This and subsequent remarks about the use of numerically controlled machine tools are based principally on visits to almost fifty users by myself (in the United States, Italy, and Great

Britain) and my research assistant, Charles Ferguson (in France, Great Britain, and the United States), from 1979 to 1981.

67 Andrea Saba, *L'industria sommersa: il nuovo modello di sviluppo* (Venice: Marsilio Editori, 1980), pp. 74–7.

68 See Manufacturing Data Systems, Inc., *Annual Report 1978*, pp. 11–14.

69 See also Jones, "Destruction or Re-distribution of Engineering Skills?"; and Eckart Hildebrand, "Im Betrieb überleben mit der neuen Technik: Arbeitserfahrungen eines Drehers," in Otto Jacobi, Eberhard Schmidt, and Walter Müller-Jentsch, eds., *Moderne Zeiten – alte Rezepte: kritisches Gewerkschaftsjahrbuch 1980/81* (Berlin: Rotbuch Verlag, 1980), pp. 24–33.

70 Regione Piemonte, "Le nuove tecnologie e l'organizzazione del lavoro: l'utilizzo del controllo numerico in Piemonte," study conducted by the Centro di Formazione della Regione per Tecnici Informatici orientati all'automazione industriale (Turin: Ufficio Pubbliche Relazioni e Documentazione della Giunta Regionale, 1978), p. 35.

71 *Wall Street Journal*, November 28, 1980., p. 10.

72 Tree Machine Tool Co., Inc., "The Tree 300 Journeyman 3-Axis-CNC Mill," Racine, Wis., 1979.

73 Rosenberg, *Perspectives on Technology*, pp. 22–3.

74 Already in the mid-nineteenth century, for example, a properly set up slide-rest lathe could be used virtually to automate certain jobs. At the same time a skilled worker could employ the lathe to perform a variety of jobs. The first use of the new machines led to speculation about the end of craft skills, the second to the creation of the archetype of the twentieth-century craftsman: the skilled lathe operator. Jeffreys explains the employers' failure to deskill the work force this way: "It was true that the jobs which had required a high degree of skill and experience to produce on a hand lathe or with a chisel and file, were usually comfortably within the ability of a youth or less skilled man on a 'go-cart' or planer. And as long as the demands on the engineering industry were similar, except in number, with those made in the 'handicraft' period, there was some justification for the employers' high hopes. But industry was not to remain satisfied for long with the hand tool standards of quality and speed of production. The new machines were capable of an entirely different range of work, and with the demand for larger jobs, greater accuracy, intricacy and speed, the operator, youth, or unskilled man, had to develop a range of skill to match the capabilities of the machines or be replaced by the man who was so able. Furthermore, these machines, revolutionary as they were in comparison with earlier methods, still left the major portion of the engineering work, from patternmaking to fitting and erecting, in the hands of the skilled worker with hand tools." See James Bavington Jeffreys, *The Story of the Engineers* (London: Lawrence and Wishart, 1946), p. 16. See generally, on the breakdown of the millwright's craft and the rise of new skilled trades, Jonathan H. Zeitlin, "Craft Regulation and the Division of Labor: Engineers and Compositors in Britain, 1890–1914" (Ph.D. diss., University of Warwick, 1981), pp. 38–45.

75 David Montgomery, "Quels standards? Les ouvriers et la réorganisation de la production aux Etats-Unis (1900–1920)," *Annales* 32 (November 1977):107.

76 Noble, "Social Choice in Machine Design," pp. 330–1.

77 For case studies that, despite these shortcomings, generally support the view of skill redistribution given here, see James R. Bright, *Automation and Management* (Boston: Division of Research, Graduate School of Business Administration, Harvard University, n.d.), pp. 170–97; Kern and Schumann, *Industriearbeit und Arbeiterbewusstsein;* 1:138 ff; and the conclusion to the excellent, exhaustive study by Otfried Mickler, Wilma Mohr, and Ulf Kadritzke, with the collaboration of Martin Baethge and Uwe

Neumann, *Produktion und Qualifikation*, 2 vols. (Göttingen: Soziologisches Forschungsinstitut, 1977), 2:485–522.

78 Pierre Naville et al., *L'Etat entrepreneur: le cas de la Régie Renault* (Paris: Editions Anthropos, 1971).

79 Naville et al., *L'état entrepreneur*, pp. 95, 157, 234. For an analysis of the Renault management's tendency to assimilate the business practices of the private sector, see Pierre Dubois, *Mort de l'Etat-patron* (Paris: Editions Ouvrières, 1971).

80 Naville et al., *L'Etat entrepreneur*, pp. 157–9. All figures are from 1969.

81 For the neoclassical economics of "narrow" jobs, see James G. Scoville, "A Theory of Jobs and Training," *Industrial Relations* 9 (October 1969):36–53.

82 Comparable data on the distribution of skills in various divisions of the FIAT Mirafiore works can be found in Gianfranco Guidi, Alberto Bronzino, and Luigi Germanetto, *FIAT: struttura aziendale e organizzazione dello sfruttamento* (Milan: Gabriele Mazzotta Editore, 1974), pp. 131 ff.

83 Table 12 in fact understates the stability of unskilled work, because it excludes a group of workers who have been put on monthly salary as a reward for long service. In the automatic machines division, for instance, such workers amounted to 6.3 percent of the division's employees. Of this group 62 percent were in the lowest skill grade and 99 percent had been at their current jobs for fifteen or more years (Naville et al., *L'Etat entrepreneur*, pp. 196, 201, 205).

84 For Great Britain, see Andrew L. Friedman, *Industry and Labor: Class Struggle at Work and Monopoly Capitalism* (Macmillan, 1970), p. 245.

Chapter 3. Careers at work

1 Thomas Kessner, *The Golden Door: Italian and Jewish Immigrant Mobility in New York City, 1880–1950* (New York, Oxford University Press, 1977), p. 27.

2 Philippe Bernoux, "Les O.S. face à l'organisation industrielle," *Sociologie du travail* 14 (October 1972):415–16.

3 Guido Kammerer, Burkart Lutz, and Christoph Nuber, *Ingenieure im Produktionsprozess – Zum Einfluss von Angebot und Bedarf auf Arbeitsteilung und Arbeitseinsatz am Beispiel des Maschinenbaus* (Frankfurt am Main: Athenäum Verlag, 1973); Burkart Lutz and Guido Kammerer, *Das Ende des graduierten Ingenieurs? eine empirische Analyse unerwarteter Nebenfolgen der Bildungsexpansion* (Frankfurt am Main: Europäische Verlagsanstalt, 1975).

4 Throughout the 1970s, for example, millions of undocumented immigrants in the United States had no trouble finding jobs despite high unemployment rates among native workers.

5 Gary S. Becker, *Human Capital: A Theoretical and Empirical Analysis, with Special Reference to Education*, 2nd ed. (New York: National Bureau of Economic Research, 1975).

6 See Claude Lévi-Strauss, *Le totémisme aujourd'hui* (Paris: Presses Universitaires de France, 1962).

7 Bernard Kayser, *Cyclically Determined Homeward Flows of Migrant Workers and the Effects on Migration* (Paris: OECD, 1972), pp. 42–5. The findings of a study of Italian migrants in the mid-1970s were similar. See Amalia Signorelli, Maria Clara Tiritico, and Sara Rossi, *Scelte senza potere: il ritorno degli emigranti nelle zone dell'esodo*, (Rome: Officina Edizioni, 1977), p. 256.

8 Otto Busch, *Militärsystem und Sozialleben im alten Preussen, 1713–1807* (Berlin: Walter de Gruyter and Co., 1962).

9 See William Brown, *Piecework Bargaining* (London: Heineman Educational

Books, 1973); and Arthur L. Stinchcombe, "Bureaucratic and Craft Administration of Production: A Comparative Study," *Administrative Science Quarterly* 4 (September 1959):168–87.

10 Melvin L. Kohn, *Class and Conformity* (Homewood, Ill.: Dorsey Press, 1969), pp. 165–203; Gavin Mackenzie, *The Aristocracy of Labor: The Position of Skilled Craftsmen in the American Class Structure* (Cambridge: Cambridge University Press, 1973).

11 Lutz and Kammerer, *Das Ende des graduierten Ingenieurs?*

12 For a general survey of the development of job training in Europe and the United States, see Organisation for Economic Co-operation and Development, *Policies for Apprenticeship* (Paris: OECD, 1979). An illustration of the history and workings of apprenticeship is Daniel Quinn Mills's discussion of the U.S. construction industry, in his *Industrial Relations and Manpower in Construction* (Cambridge: MIT Press, 1972), pp. 181 ff.

13 The following paragraphs draw on ideas developed in Siegfried Braun and Jochen Fuhrmann, *Angestelltenmentalität: berufliche Position und gesellschaftliches Denken der Industrieangestellten – Bericht über eine industriesoziologische Untersuchung* (Neuwied am Rhein: Harmann Luchterhand Verlag, 1970); Lutz and Kammerer, *Das Ende des graduierten Ingenieurs?* and Bernard Zarca, "L'ami du trait," *Actes de la recherche en sciences sociales* 29 (September 1979):27–43.

14 In 1956, for example, over half the craftsmen in the American construction industry had fathers in a skilled trade. See F. Ray Marshall and Vernon M. Briggs, Jr., *The Negro and Apprenticeship* (Baltimore: Johns Hopkins Press, 1967), p. 18. A more extreme case is the New York Printing Pressmen's Local Union No. 2. In the late 1970s the local had just over 1,500 members, of whom at least 200 had grandfathers who had worked for New York newspapers. A few were descendants of pressmen who had worked for the *Post* when it was founded in 1801. See A. H. Raskin, "A Reporter at Large: New York Newspaper Strike, Part 1," *New Yorker*, January 22, 1979, p. 47.

15 Braun and Fuhrmann, *Angestelltenmentalität*, pp. 67 ff.

16 Mackenzie, *The Aristocracy of Labor*, pp. 59–60.

17 Lutz and Kammerer, *Das Ende des graduierten Ingenieurs?*

18 Bernard Zarca, "Artisanat et trajectoires sociales," *Actes de la recherche en sciences sociales* 29 (September 1979):3–26.

19 Braun and Fuhrmann, *Angestelltenmentalität*, p. 286.

20 Ibid., p. 423.

21 Zarca, "Artisanat et trajectoires sociales," p. 35.

22 Lutz and Kammerer, *Das Ende des graduierten Ingeniers?* pp. 168–73.

23 Ibid., p. 179.

24 Ibid., pp. 133–40.

25 Ibid., pp. 93 ff.

26 The interviews were conducted in 1972–3 by Friedrich Weltz and others in connection with their studies of continuing education programs for workers. Transcripts of the interviews are on file at the IFS.

27 IFS Interview 7, p. 2.

28 IFS Interview 9, p. 1.

29 IFS Interview 5, p. 2.

30 IFS Interview 15, p. 2. Conversely, sociolinguists find that the upwardly mobile do tend to imitate the speech patterns (at least at the level of pronunciation) of socially respected groups. See William Labov, "The Effect of Social Mobility on Linguistic Behavior," in Stanley Lieberson, ed., *Explorations in Sociolinguistics* (Bloomington: Indiana University Press, 1966), pp. 58–75.

31 Quotations from Friedrich Weltz, Gert Schmidt, and Jürgen Sass, *Facharbeiter im Industriebetrieb: Eine Untersuchung in metallverarbeitenden Betrieben* (Frankfurt am Main: Anthenäum Verlag, 1974), p. 68.

32 See, for instance, interview A105, pp. 12 ff., collected under the supervision of Rainer Zoll, University of Bremen, in connection with his project on *Krisenbetroffenheit*.

33 This point is made explicitly in Lutz and Kammerer, *Das Ende des graduierten Ingenieurs?* p. 76.

34 Kendall E. Bailes, *Technology and Society under Lenin and Stalin* (Princeton: Princeton University Press, 1978), pp. 288–9, 297–336.

35 John R. Low-Beer, *Protest and Participation: The New Working Class in Italy* (Cambridge: Cambridge University Press, 1978), pp. 138–63; Claude Durand and Michelle Durand, *De l'O.S. à l'ingénieur: carrière ou classe sociale* (Paris: Editions Ouvrières, 1971), pp. 213–22.

36 Serge Mallet, *La nouvelle classe ouvrière* (Paris: Editions du Seuil, 1963); Heinrich Popitz et al., *Technik und Industriearbeit: soziologische Untersuchungen in der Hüttenindustrie* (Tübingen: J. C. B. Mohr [Paul Siebeck], 1957); Burkart Lutz, *Krise des Lohnanreizes: ein empirisch-historischer Beitrag zum Wandel der Formen betrieblicher Herrschaft am Beispiel der deutschen Stahlindustrie* (Frankfurt am Main: Europäische Verlagsanstalt, 1975); Claude Durand, Claude Prestat, and Alfred Willener, *Travail, salaire, production*, 2 vols. (Paris: Mouton and Co., 1972).

37 Quotations from Popitz et al., *Technik und Industriearbeit*, pp. 180–1.

38 Ibid., p. 186.

39 Ibid., p. 139.

40 Ibid., p. 211.

41 Durand, Prestat, and Willener, *Travail, salaire, production*, 1:160–218.

42 Lutz, *Krise des Lohnanreizes*, p. 35.

43 Ibid., p. 37.

44 Ultimately, theories of the worker as producer rest on a series of ontological convictions about the centrality of work in social life. See Georg Lukács, *Ontologie-Arbeit* (Neuwied am Rhein: Hermann Luchterhand Verlag, 1973).

45 Heinrich Popitz et al., *Das Gesellschaftsbild des Arbeiters* (Tübingen: J. C. B. Mohr [Paul Siebeck], 1957), p. 40.

46 Mallet, *La nouvelle classe ouvrière*, pp. 56–7.

47 Jürgen Prott, *Industriearbeit bei betrieblichen Umstrukturierungen: soziale Konsequenzen, Interessenvertretung und Bewusstseinsstrukturen* (Cologne: Bund-Verlag, 1975), p. 57.

48 Encouraging job rotation obviously makes economic sense from management's point of view: "The cost of switching workers from job to job decreases in proportion to the number of different jobs each worker is qualified to fill" (Burkart Lutz and Werner Sengenberger, *Arbeitsmarktstrukturen und öffentliche Arbeitsmarktpolitik: eine kritische Analyse von Zielen und Instrumenten* [Göttingen: O. Schwartz, 1974], p. 65).

49 Prott, *Industriearbeit bei betrieblichen Umstrukturierungen*, pp. 55–6.

50 Horst Kern and Michael Schumann, *Industriearbeit und Arbeiterbewusstsein: eine empirische Untersuchung über den Einfluss der aktuellen technischen Entwicklung auf die industrielle Arbeit und auf das Arbeiterbewusstsein*, 2 vols. (Frankfurt am Main: Europaische Verlagsanstalt, 1970), 1:219–20.

51 Michael Mann, *Workers on the Move: The Sociology of Relocation* (Cambridge: Cambridge University Press, 1973), p. 218; cf. pp. 136–41.

52 Konrad Thomas, *Die betriebliche Situation des Arbeiters* (Stuttgart: Enke Verlag, 1964), p. 17.

53 Alfred Sohn-Rethel, *Ökonomie und Klassenstruktur des deutschen Faschismus*

(Frankfurt am Main: Suhrkamp Verlag, 1973), p. 66. Schatz has reported a similar structure of labor relations for the U.S electronics industry before World War II. See Ronald Schatz, "The End of Corporate Liberalism: Class Struggle in the Electrical Manufacturing Industry, 1933–1950," *Radical America* 9 (July 1975):187–205.

54 Company property is here not just a figure of speech. In the neoclassical view, the company owns returns to the worker's skills in proportion to its investment in his training. See Gary S. Becker, *Human Capital: A Theoretical and Empirical Analysis, with Special Reference to Education*, 2nd ed. (New York: National Bureau of Economic Research, 1975), pp. 26–37. On the relation between property in the sense of a possible good (*Eigentum*) and in the sense of a human quality or feature (*Eigenschaft*), see Pierre Naville, *Vers l'automatisme sociale? problèmes du travail et de l'automation* (Paris: Editions Gallimard, 1963), pp. 217 ff.

55 On the peasant's situation see Bernoux, "Les O.S. face à l'organisation industrielle"; on adolescents, see Paul Osterman, *Getting Started: The Youth Labor Market* (Cambridge: MIT Press, 1981); on housewives and unmarried women, see Christel Eckart, Ursula G. Jaerisch, and Helgard Kramer, *Frauenarbeit in Familie und Fabrik* (Frankfurt am Main: Campus Verlag, 1979); on older workers, see Ely Chinoy, *Automobile Workers and the American Dream* (Boston: Beacon Press, 1965), pp. 124–34. The analysis in these sections has been developed in many conversations with Michael J. Piore. See his *Birds of Passage and Promised Lands: Long-Distance Migrants and Industrial Societies* (Cambridge: Cambridge University Press, 1979), which focuses on the economic preconditions and consequences of mass employment of peasant workers in industrial market economies.

56 For an extensive discussion of one variant of the instrumental relation, see John Goldthorpe et al., *The Affluent Worker in the Class Structure* (Cambridge: Cambridge University Press, 1969), pp. 165 ff.

57 The term is ungainly, but it is commonly used in German (*Arbeiterbauer*) and French (*ouvrier-paysan*) writing on factory work. In Yugoslavia, *seljak-radnik* (peasant worker) is an officially recognized category in the system of social stratification.

58 Bernoux, "Les O.S. face à l'organisation industrielle," also treats this type.

59 Eliot Liebow, *Tally's Corner: A Study of Negro Streetcorner Men* (Boston: Little, Brown, 1967).

60 Cited in Philip L. Martin and Mark J. Miller, "Guestworkers: Lessons from Europe," *Industrial and Labor Relations Review* 33 (April 1980):322.

61 On the idea of a target family income, see Michele Salvati, *Sviluppo economico, domanda di lavoro e struttura dell' occupazione* (Bologna: Il Mulino, 1976), pp. 74–6.

62 Erdmann Doane Beynon, "The Southern White Laborer Migrates to Michigan," *American Sociological Review* 3 (June 1938):337. Kayser found that Italian, Greek, Spanish, Portugese, Turkish, and Yugoslav emigrants who left West Germany during the recession of 1966–7 treated their forced return home as "prolonged holidays" (Kayser, *Cyclically Determined Homeward Flows of Migrant Workers*, p. 51).

63 Kessner, *The Golden Door*, p. 30. For a parallel description of Slavic immigrants during the same period, see Victor Greene, *The Slavic Community on Strike: Immigrant Labor in Pennsylvania Anthracite* (Notre Dame, Ind.: University of Notre Dame Press, 1968), pp. 17, 54. For a more detailed discussion of the social conditions that favor emigration, see the section entitled "The Struggle for Place."

64 Kessner, *The Golden Door*, p. 27.

65 Ibid., p. 28.

66 Achim Schrader, Bruno W. Nikles, and Hartmut M. Griese, *Die Zweite Generation: Sozialisation und Akkulturation ausländischer Kinder in der Bundesrepublik* (Kronberg: Athenäum Verlag, 1976), p. 89. On the (often disappointed) ambitions of returned migrants, see, for example, Suzanne Paine, *Exporting Workers: The Turkish Case* (Cambridge: Cambridge University Press, 1974).

67 Pierre Naville et al., *L'Etat entrepreneur: le cas de la Régie Renault* (Paris: Editions Anthropos, 1971), p. 232.

68 In the aftermath of the 1973 recession, for example, one West German automobile maker cut employment of blue-collar workers by an average of 22.8 percent. Employment of German men was reduced 12.1 percent; of German women, 25.9 percent; of foreign women, 39.7 pecent; of foreign men, 57.6 percent. See Rainer Schultz-Wild, *Betriebliche Beschäftigungspolitik in der Krise* (Frankfurt am Main: Campus Verlag, 1978), p. 275.

69 David Friedman, "Workers' Expectations and Labor Relations in the U.S. Auto Industry" (senior honors essay, Harvard College, Mar. 1979). On the role of agricultural migrants in the early development of the British automobile industry, see Jonathan Zeitlin, "The Emergence of Shop Steward Organization and Job Control in the British Car Industry," *History Workshop*, No. 10 (Autumn 1980), pp. 125–7.

70 For a more detailed analysis of the labor-market in this region – one that supports the view that many of the unskilled are peasant workers – see Knut Gerlach and Karl-Friedrich Kühner, "Freiwilliger Arbeitsplatzwechsel in Rückstandsregionen," *Zeitschrift für Wirtschafts- und Sozialwissenschaften* 94 (1974): 167–82.

71 In 1976 foreign workers were 10.9 percent of the economically active population in France and 9.7 percent of the economically active population in West Germany (Martin and Miller, "Guestworkers," p. 322).

72 Managers are well aware of this. In an article discussing the problems of subcontracting in the garment industry, for instance, Roy Cavender, contractor manager and director of product integrity for Levi-Strauss and Co., Sportswear Division, remarks, "Many times during the fall in farm areas, there is an increase in absenteeism due to crop harvest" (Cavender, "Contractors: Quality Evaluation and Performance," *Bobbin*, June 1980, p. 142).

73 Bernoux, "Les O.S. face à l'organisation industrielle."

74 Poppinga has also noted the peasant worker's seemingly contradictory relation to work. On the one hand, employers value the peasant worker because of his "marked sense of responsibility"; but they also criticize his unwillingness to give up his exaggerated sense of independence, to submit to plant discipline, and to adapt to peice work. See Onno Poppinga, "Arbeiterbauern im Industriebetrieb," in Otto Jacobi, Walter Müller-Jentsch, and Eberhard Schmidt, eds., *Gewerkschaften und Klassenkampf: kritisches Jahrbuch 1975* (Frankfurt am Main: Fischer Verlag, 1975), pp. 216–19.

75 Chinoy, *Automobile Workers and the American Dream*, pp. 91–2.

76 A useful study of the situation of second-generation immigrants, with a summary of recent literature, is Schrader, Nikles, and Griese, *Die Zweite Generation*.

77 Virginia Yans-McLaughlin, "A Flexible Tradition: Southern Italian Immigrants Confront a New York Experience," in Richard L. Ehrlich, ed., *Industrial American, 1850–1920* (Charlottesville: University of Virginia Press, 1977), pp. 67–84.

78 Robert Eugene Johnson, *Peasant and Proletarian: The Working Class of Moscow in the Late Nineteenth Century* (Leister: Leister University Press, 1979), pp. 12–13; Reginald E. Zelnik, "The Peasant and the Factory," in Wayne S. Vucinich, ed., *The Peasant in Nineteenth-Century Russia* (Stanford: Stanford University Press, 1968), pp. 11–15, 158–90.

79 Johnson, *Peasant and Proletarian*, pp. 58–66.

80 Lawrence Schofer, *The Formation of a Modern Labor Force: Upper Silesia, 1865–1914* (Berkeley and Los Angeles: University of California Press, 1974); Liston Pope, *Millhands and Preachers: A Study of Gastonia* (New Haven: Yale University Press, 1965);

Detlev Puls, "Ein im ganzen gutartiger Streik: Bemerkungen zu Alltagserfahrungen und Protestverhalten der oberschlesischen Bergarbeiter am Ende des 19. Jahrhunderts," in Detlev Puls, ed., *Wahrnehmungsform und Protestverhalten: Studien zur Lage der Unterschichten im 18. und 19. Jahrhundert* (Frankfurt am Main: Suhrkamp Verlag, 1979), pp. 175–227; Fernando Henrique Cardoso, "Proletariado e mundança social em São Paulo," *Sociologia* 22 (Mar. 1960): 3–11.

81 A good description of the way this has worked in West Germany is Rolf G. Heinze and H. Willy Horn, "Arbeitsmarkt und Politik in strukturschwachen ländlichen Regionen," in Claus Offe, ed., *Opfer des Arbeitsmarktes* (Neuwied: Hermann Luchterhand Verlag, 1977), pp. 151–84. For Italy see Ada Cavazzani, *Il part-time agricolo: ristrutturazione capitalistica e famiglia agricola* (Venice: Marsilio Editori, 1979). For France see the description of the SAVIEM truck factory near Caen in Danièle Kergoat, "La combativité ouvrière dans une usine de construction de camions, mimeographed (Paris: Centre de Sociologie des Organisations, 1977).

82 "Japan Inc. versus the Peasants," *Economist*, February 28, 1981, pp. 66–7; Ronald P. Dore, *Shinohata: A Portrait of a Japanese Village* (New York: Pantheon, 1978), p. 110.

83 The connection between politics and state agricultural policy is especially clear in Japan. Government support for rice production began to rise sharply in 1960, just after a wave of massive migration from the country to the booming urban factories. About 40 percent of all voters had some connection to agriculture, usually rice growing, and their votes went overwhelmingly to the dominant Liberal Democratic Party. The rural electorate is crucially important in Japanese politics because voter turnout is higher in the countryside than in the cities, and because the boundaries of electoral districts give extra weight to rural ballots in elections to the lower house (Michael W. Donnelly, "Setting the Price of Rice: A Study in Political Decisionmaking," in T. J. Pempel, ed., *Policymaking in Contemporary Japan* [Ithaca, N.Y.: Cornell University Press, 1977], p. 159; Dore, *Shinohata*, p. 109–10).

84 See, on the rise of factory discipline in eighteenth-century Great Britain, the pioneering work by Sidney Pollard, *The Genesis of Modern Management: A Study of the Industrial Revolution in Great Britain* (Cambridge: Harvard University Press, 1966), pp. 160–208; and E. P. Thompson, especially his "Time, Work-Discipline and Industrial Capitalism," *Past and Present*, no. 38 (December 1967), pp. 56–97. See also Roland Trempé, *Les mineurs de Carmaux, 1848–1914* (Paris: Editions Ouvrières, 1971).

85 See the unsympathetic account of these adolescents in Eduardo Seda, *Social Change and Personality in a Puerto-Rican Agrarian Reform Community* (Evanston, Ill.: Northwestern University Press, 1973), p. 37.

86 Francesco Alberoni and Guido Baglioni, *L'integrazione dell'immigrato nella società industriale* (Bologna: Il Mulino, 1965), pp. 104 ff.; Víctor Pérez-Díaz, *Emigración y cambio social: procesos migratorios y vita rural en Castilla* (Barcelona: Editiones Ariel, 1971), p. 165. Because workers who anticipate their integration into urban society before leaving the land perceive acquisition of a factory job as a partial fulfillment of their ambitions, they tend to be more optimistic about their chances for promotion than do equally unskilled industrial workers who have not experienced the "success" of transition from farm to factory. See Alain Touraine, "Les ouvriers d'origine agricole," *Sociologie du travail* 1 (July 1960): 230–45.

87 Bernoux, "Les O. S. face à l'organisation industrielle."

88 For the culture-of-poverty view, see Oscar Lewis, *La Vida* (New York: Random House, 1966); and Edward C. Banfield, *The Unheavenly City* (Boston: Little, Brown, 1968), especially p. 126: "Lower-class poverty . . . is inwardly caused (by psychological inabilities to provide for the future and all that this inability implies)."

89 Compare the early histories of two Appalachian migrants to a midwestern city –

one who becomes a skilled worker with a stable family, the other a hard-drinking semiskilled worker who has lost touch with his two children (one of whom may be in trouble with the police) – reported in William E. Fowles, "The Southern Appalachian Migrant: Country Boy Turned Blue-Collarite," in Arthur B. Shostak and William Gomberg, eds., *Blue-Collar World* (Englewood Cliffs, N.J.: Prentice-Hall, 1964), pp. 270–81.

90 Shirley Achor, *Mexican Americans in a Dallas Barrio* (Tucson: University of Arizona Press, 1978), p. 131.

91 Gerald D. Suttles, *The Social Order of the Slum: Ethnicity and Territory in the Inner City* (Chicago: University of Chicago Press, 1963), p. 126.

92 John Dollard, *Caste and Class in a Southern Town*, 3rd ed. (Garden City, N.Y.: Doubleday and Co., Anchor Books, 1957), p. 406.

93 See Stanley M. Elkins, *Slavery: A Problem in American Institutional and Intellectual History* (Chicago: University of Chicago Press, 1959); and Daniel P. Moynihan, *The Negro Family: The Case for National Action* (Washington, D.C.: U.S. Department of Labor, 1965), pp. 30, 47.

94 On the slave family see Herbert George Gutman, *The Black Family in Slavery and Freedom, 1750–1925* (New York: Pantheon Books, 1976). There is no comparably elaborate work on urban blacks in recent times from this point of view; but elements of this interpretation play a central part in the work of, for example, Piven and Cloward on the urban riots of the 1960s. Their position is that blacks were subjected to "near feudal" social controls in the South, that these controls broke down during migration to and in the ghettos of the North, and that without the controls, the blacks dared to express their anger at their oppressors. Their account is like Gutman's in assuming that *at bottom* blacks are always enraged at whites, but it differs from his on an important point. Piven and Cloward see the black family as an extension of, not a refuge from, white control; hence they regard the breakdown of the family as a precondition for black revolt, not a belated victory of the whites over slave culture. See Frances Fox Piven and Richard A. Cloward, *Regulating the Poor: The Functions of Public Welfare* (New York: Random House, 1971), pp. 193, 222–46.

95 See, for instance, the discussion of this problem by John Watson, a black militant active in Detroit in the late 1960s, in James A. Geschwender, *Class, Race and Worker Insurgency: The League of Black Revolutionary Workers* (Cambridge: Cambridge University Press, 1977), pp. 141–42. Marx distinguished proletarians with steady work and the casual laborers here called ghetto workers. See his definition of the Lumpenproletariat in Karl Marx, "Die Klassenkämpfe in Frankreich 1848 bis 1850," in Institut für Marxismus beim Zk der SED, ed., *Marx–Engels Werke*, 39 vols. (Berlin: Dietz Verlag, 1957), 7:26.

96 For a related argument see Charles A. Valentine, *Culture and Poverty: Critique and Counter-Proposals* (Chicago: University of Chicago Press, 1968), pp. 142–7.

97 On these points see Eugene D. Genovese, *Roll, Jordan, Roll: The World the Slaves Made* (New York: Random House, 1972), pp. 3–7, 25–49, 161–8, 280–4, 309–24.

98 See, for example, Leonard Goodwin, *Do the Poor Want to Work? A Social-Psychological Study of Work Orientations* (Washington: Brookings Institution, 1972), pp. 14–29, 32–52.

99 Ibid., p. 113. Goodwin's findings are compatible with the results of Rushing's study of farm laborers (half of them migrants) in Washington. See William A. Rushing, *Class, Culture, and Alienation: A Study of Farmers and Farm Workers* (Lexington, Mass.: D. C. Heath and Co., 1972), pp. 29–30, 159–64.

100 Liebow, *Tally's Corner*, pp. 53–4. See also, on this point, Jan E. Dizard, "Why Should Negroes Work?" in Louis A. Ferman, Joyce L. Kornbluth, and J. A. Miller, eds., *Negroes and Jobs: A Book of Readings* (Ann Arbor: University of Michigan Press, 1963), pp. 401–13.

101 Gutmann, *The Black Family in Slavery and Freedom*, pp. 320–6.

102 Lewis, *La Vida*, p. xlix.

103 Before 1969, McClintock writes, "Peruvian hacienda peasants were cowed and atomized, fitting well into the model image of the peasant presented by anthropologists and scholars of political culture. The Peruvian hacienda peasant did not appear to be a likely candidate for dramatic development into a 'new man.' Yet, with the demise of the hacienda and the emergence of the self-managed enterprise, new orientations of assertiveness and collaboration emerged relatively quickly" (Cynthia McClintock, *Peasant Cooperatives and Political Change in Peru* [Princeton: Princeton University Press, 1981], p. 319). Although the peasants' trust extended only as far as the limits of their home cooperative, the principal reason for this was the government's own failure to create institutions that would have justified broader loyalties (ibid., p. 284).

104 The following paragraphs draw on Geschwender, *Class, Race and Worker Insurgency*, pp. 142–43, 169–173, 180. Leggett's study of class consciousness in Detroit provides some evidence consistent with these views. He finds, for example, that among the *unemployed*, unionized blacks (who tend to have had experience in large plants) are more militant than unorganized blacks (who tend to have worked in smaller shops). But to what extent the out-of-work militants are radicalized peasant workers–a group discussed in Chapter 4–rather than ghetto workers whose hopes have been renewed, then dashed, by experiences in what they thought was the stable sector of the labor market, Leggett's study does not permit us to say. Similarly, we do not know whether the more passive unemployed blacks are acquiescent peasant-workers–first-generation migrants to Detroit still under the illusion that they are not going to remain there–or ghetto workers putting up with their lot. See John Leggett, *Class, Race, and Labor: Working-Class Consciousness in Detroit* (New York: Oxford University Press, 1968), pp. 62–85.

105 On peasant communities, see Joel S. Migdal, *Peasants, Politics, and Revolution* (Princeton: Princeton University Press, 1974).

106 Rodney H. Hilton, *The Decline of Serfdom in Medieval England* (London: Macmillan, 1969).

107 See John S. MacDonald, "Some Socio-Economic Emigration Differentials in Rural Italy, 1902–1913," *Economic Development and Cultural Change* 7 (October 1958): 71–2.

108 See, on this point and more generally on patterns of agrarian conflict, Jeffrey M. Paige, *Agrarian Revolution: Social Movements and Export Agriculture in the Underdeveloped World* (New York: Free Press, 1975), pp. 1–71.

109 Josef J. Barton, *Peasants and Strangers: Italians, Rumanians and Slovaks in an American City, 1890–1950* (Cambridge: Harvard University Press, 1975), pp. 27–47; John W. Briggs, *An Italian Passage: Immigrants to Three American Cities, 1890–1930* (New Haven: Yale University Press, 1978), pp. 1–14; on the attraction of industrial life for agricultural laborers, see Nicole Eizner and Bertrand Hervieu, *Anciens paysans, nouveaux ouvriers* (Paris: Editions l'Harmattan, 1979), pp. 99–104.

110 Michael Schwartz, *Radical Protest and Social Structure* (New York: Academic Press, 1976), p. 12.

111 See, for instance, Beynon, "The Southern White Laborer Migrates to Michigan," p. 339.

112 Greene, *The Slavic Community on Strike*, pp. 27–8. In some cases the idea of emigration as a collective activity extends to the proceeds of work done abroad. Sally

N'Dongo, for instance, reports that in the 1970s Africans from the same village working in France sometimes pooled part of their wages to buy medicines, build schools or mosques, or set up cooperatives whenever the home government proved unable to do these things. See Sally N'Dongo, *Voyage forcé: itinéraire d'un militant* (Paris: François Maspero, 1975), p. 54.

113 Massimo Paci, "Struttura e funzioni della famiglia nello sviluppo industriale 'periferico,' " in Paci, ed., *Famiglia e mercato del lavoro in una economica periferica* (Milan: Franco Angeli, 1980), pp. 9–70.

114 Surveying studies on the origins of entrepreneurs in areas and industries similar to those Paci studied, Bagnasco and Pini conclude that the hypothesis of a strong link between farming and entrepreneurship "will have to be scaled down." Research confirms that the children of workers, artisans, and the middle classes make up the bulk of the entrepreneurs in the new, small firms in a variety of industries and regions. There is no sign that children of sharecroppers are more likely than the children of other groups to start new firms. See Arnaldo Bagnasco and Rosella Pini, *Sviluppo economico e trasformazioni sociopolitiche dei sistemi territoriali a economia diffusa*, Quaderni Fondazione Giangiacomo Feltrinelli, no. 14 (Milan: Feltrinelli, 1981), pp. 31–3.

115 Melville Dalton, "The Industrial 'Rate-Busters': A Characterization," *Applied Anthropology* 7 (Winter 1948): 13–14.

116 John Waterbury, *North for the Trade: The Life and Times of a Berber Merchant* (Berkeley and Los Angeles: University of California Press, 1972), p. 197.

117 Good discussions of youth subculture are Herbert Gans, *The Urban Villagers* (New York: Free Press, 1962), pp. 229–78; and Mike Brake, *The Sociology of Youth Culture and Youth Subcultures* (London: Routledge and Kegan Paul, 1980).

118 William F. Whyte, Jr., *Street Corner Society* (Chicago: University of Chicago Press, 1943).

119 Paul Willis, *Learning to Labour* (Westmead: Saxon House, 1977), p. 73.

120 Ibid., p. 96.

121 Ibid., p. 102.

122 Ibid., p. 99.

123 Ibid., p. 107.

Chapter 4. Interests, conflicts, classes

1 Unpublished statistics, General Motors Assembly Division, 1979.

2 See, for a recent statement of this position, James C. Scott, *The Moral Economy of the Peasant* (New Haven: Yale University Press, 1976).

3 See Samuel L. Popkin, *The Rational Peasant* (Berkeley and Los Angeles: University of California Press, 1979).

4 Emile Durkheim, *De la division du travail social* (Paris: F. Alcan, 1893).

5 For a general discussion of this notion see J. H. Hexter, "The Myth of the Middle Class in Tudor England," in J. H. Hexter, *Reappraisals in History*, 2nd ed. (Chicago: University of Chicago Press, 1979), pp. 71–116.

6 On the merchants of medieval London see Sylvia Thrupp, *The Merchant Class of Medieval London, 1300–1500* (Chicago: University of Chicago Press, 1948); on eighteenth-century France see Franklin L. Ford, *Robe and Sword* (Cambridge: Harvard University Press, 1953); on eighteenth-century Prussia see Hans Rosenberg, *Bureaucracy, Aristocracy, and Autocracy* (Cambridge: Harvard University Press, 1958).

7 On the conversion of major parts of the modern bourgeoisie into a rentier class content to maximize its proceeds from a production system it no longer seeks to control or develop directly, see John Maynard Keynes, "Social Consequences of Changes in the Value of Money," in J. M. Keynes, *Essays in Persuasion* (New York: Harcourt Brace and Co., 1932), pp. 80–104; and Thorstein Veblen, *The Theory of the Leisure Class* (New York: Vanguard Press, 1927).

8 Marc Bloch, *French Rural History*, trans. Janet Sondheimer (Berkeley and Los Angeles: University of California Press, 1960), p. 170.

9 Popkin, *The Rational Peasant*, pp. 184 ff.

10 Good accounts of the way the English peasantry helped create a free market in land and at the same time undermine the security of its own holdings are given in Rodney H. Hilton, *The Decline of Serfdom in Medieval England* (London: Macmillan, 1969); and J. L. Bolton, *The Medieval English Economy, 1150–1500* (London: J. M. Dent and Sons, 1980), esp. pp. 180–245.

11 On the economic underpinnings of the alliance between Junkers and industrialists see Alexander Gerschenkron, *Bread and Democracy in Germany* (Berkeley and Los Angeles: University of California Press, 1943). In the essays on the Prussian bureaucracy and reserve officer corps, Eckart Kehr describes some of the mechanisms by which the aristocracy encouraged the "feudalization" of the middle classes; see Kehr's *Der Primat der Innenpolitik*, ed. Hans-Ulrich Wehler (Berlin: Walter de Gruyter and Co., 1965), pp. 53–86.

12 The way in which politics shapes revolutions is underscored in John Dunn, *Modern Revolutions: An Introduction to the Analysis of a Political Phenomenon* (Cambridge: Cambridge University Press, 1972).

13 Philippe Bernoux, "Les O.S. face à l'organisation industrielle," *Sociologie du travail* 14 (October 1972): 426–9.

14 Danièle Kergoat, *Bulledor* (Paris: Editions du Seuil, 1973), p. 115.

15 Betriebszelle Ford der Gruppe Arbeiterkampf, ed., *Streik bei Ford-Köln* (Erlangen: Politikladen Erlangen, 1973). An analogous situation is described in Pierburg Authors' Collective, *Pierburg-Neuss: Deutsche und ausländische Arbeiter – ein Gegner, ein Kampf* (n.p.: Internationale Sozialistische Publikationen, 1974).

16 Authors' Collective, "Le mouvement des O.S. de Renault-Flins, 26 mars–26 avril 1973," *Les temps modernes* 29 (July 1973): 2163–241.

17 E. P. Thompson, "The Moral Economy of the English Crowd in the Eighteenth Century," *Past and Present*, no. 50 (February 1971), pp. 76–136. See also George Rudé, *Ideology and Popular Protest* (London: Lawrence and Wishart, 1980), pp. 133–45.

18 Claus Offe, *Leistungsprinzip und industrielle Arbeit* (Frankfurt am Main: Europäische Verlagsanstalt, 1973).

19 Authors' Collective, "Le mouvement des O.S. de Renault-Flins," p. 2203.

20 Betriebszelle Ford der Gruppe Arbeiterkampf, *Streik bei Ford-Köln*, pp. 57, 61.

21 Ibid., p. 61.

22 "Rent strikes," the president of the Union Générale des Travailleurs Sénégalais en France writes, "are often the spark, the trigger which makes African workers think that combat pays and that to fight well they have to organize" (Sally N'Dongo, *Exil, connais pas* [Paris: Editions du Cerf, 1976], pp. 86–7).

23 Authors' Collective, "Le mouvement des O.S. de Renault-Flins," p. 2183.

24 Ibid., pp. 2222–3.

25 Ibid., pp. 2195, 2203, 2215.

26 Betriebszelle Ford der Gruppe Arbeiterkampf, *Streik bei Ford-Köln*, pp. 69–71, 180–1.

27 Base Ouvriére, *Revolutionäre Betriebsarbeit bei Renault-Flins*, trans. Dieter Meyer (Berlin: Merve Verlag, 1972), p. 10.

28 Authors' Collective, "Le mouvement des O.S. de Renault-Flins," pp. 2212–16.

29 Ibid., pp. 2206–11.

30 Bernoux, "Les O.S. face à l'organisation industrielle," p. 429.

31 John G. Kruchko, *The Birth of a Union Local: The History of UAW Local 674, Norwood, Ohio, 1933 to 1940* (Ithaca: New York State School of Industrial and Labor Relations, Cornell University, 1972), pp. 3–5.

32 Many automobile tool and diemakers, largely unorganized in the early 1930s, reacted to the depression wage cuts by forming a craft union to protect their interests. See Harry Dahlheimer, *A History of the Mechanics Educational Society of America in Detroit from Its Inception in 1933 through 1937* (Detroit: Wayne State University Press, 1951). In exceptional cases, particularly when craftsmen in mass-production industries were few in number, isolated, and threatened by dequalification, they tried to organize alliances with the semi- and unskilled. See Ronald Schatz, "Union Pioneers, the Founders of Local Unions at General Electric and Westinghouse, 1933–37," *Journal of American History* 66 (December 1979): 586–602. Nationally, the established craft unions in the American Federation of Labor were unwilling to let the assembly-line workers in the automobile industry organize until their conflicting rights to enroll the skilled workers in the industry had been clarified. See Sidney Fine, *Sit-Down* (Ann Arbor: University of Michigan Press, 1969), pp. 63 ff. On the social composition of the skilled, see the description in Peter Friedlander, *The Emergence of a UAW Local, 1936–1939: A Study in Class and Culture.* (Pittsburgh: University of Pittsburgh Press, 1975), pp. 45–6.

33 See, for example, the discussion of young black migrants' determination to stay in the North in Allan H. Spear, *Black Chicago: The Making of a Negro Ghetto, 1890–1920* (Chicago: University of Chicago Press, 1967), pp. 136–8.

34 Kruchko, *Birth of a Union Local*, p. 14.

35 Fine, *Sit-Down*, p. 97.

36 Kruchko, *Birth of a Union Local*, p. 29.

37 See, for example, James F. McDonnell, "The Rise of the CIO in Buffalo, New York, 1936–42" (Ph.D. diss., University of Wisconsin, 1970).

38 Friedlander, *Emergence of a UAW Local*, pp. 26–8, 83–7.

39 Ibid., pp. 4, 46, 97–8.

40 Ibid., pp. 100–1.

41 Kergoat, *Bulledor*, pp. 103–14. The quotation is from p. 107.

42 Danièle Kergoat, "La combativité ouvrière dans une usine de construction de camions," mimeographed (Paris: Centre de Sociologie des Organisations, 1977), pp. 252–4, 277.

43 Kergoat, *Bulledor*, p. 136.

44 Kergoat, "La combativité ouvrière," pp. 253–5, 306.

45 Fine, *Sit-Down*, p. 96.

46 Kergoat, *Bulledor*, p. 122.

47 Kergoat, "La combativité ouvrière," pp. 21–6.

48 See Friedlander, *Emergence of a UAW Local*, pp. 36, 103; Charles Denby, *Indignant Heart: Testimony of a Black American Worker* (Boston: South End Press, 1979); and Kergoat, *Bulledor*, p. 137.

49 Kergoat, "La combativité ouvrière," pp. 276–7.

50 Huw Beynon, *Working for Ford* (London: Allen Lane, 1973), pp. 89–91; Ely Chinoy, *Automobile Workers and the American Dream* (Boston: Beacon Press, 1965), pp. 110–22.

51 Kergoat, "La combativité ouvrière," p. 275.

52 Both citations are from Beynon, *Working for Ford*, p. 121.

53 Kergoat, "La combativité ouvrière," p. 276.

54 Beynon, *Working for Ford*, p. 122.

55 Kergoat, "La combativité ouvrière," pp. 277, 302–3.

56 Beynon, *Working for Ford*, pp. 107, 190.

57 See, for example, Kruchko, *Birth of a Union Local*, p. 14; and Friedlander, *Emergence of a Union Local*, pp. 7–8.

58 Kergoat, "La combativité ouvrière," p. 282.

59 The best account of the weakness, but also the capacity for survival, of the Communist and Socialist unions in the 1950s is Aris Accornero, *Gli anni '50 in fabbrica* (Bari: De Donato, 1973).

60 See Michele Salvati, *Sviluppo economico, domanda di lavoro e struttura dell'-occupazione* (Bologna: Il Mulino, 1976), pp. 7–49, for a discussion of the transformation of the economy from the end of World War II until 1964.

61 The alternative leftist program focused on a Keynesian strategy of stimulation of domestic demand through government spending. But the Left's desire to elaborate an alternative was undercut by its belief that Western capitalism was on the verge of collapse. See Renzo Razzano, "I modelli di sviluppo della CGIL e della CISL," in Aris Accornero, ed., *Problemi del movimento sindacale in Italia, 1943–1973* (Milan: Feltrinelli, 1976), pp. 527–51.

62 B. Salvati, "The Rebirth of Italian Trade Unionism, 1943–54," in S. J. Woolf, ed., *The Rebirth of Italy, 1943–1950* (London: Longman, 1972), pp. 181–211.

63 Emilio Pugno and Sergio Garavini, *Gli anni duri alla FIAT* (Turin: Einaudi, 1974), p. 17; Renzo Gianotti, *Lotte e organizzazione di classe alla FIAT* (Bari: De Donato, 1970), pp. 103–15.

64 Enrollment figures are tabulated in Alessandro Pizzorno et al., *Lotte operaie e sindacato: il ciclo 1968–1972 in Italia* (Bologna: Il Mulino, 1978), p. 295. For the employers' capacity to fix pay scales and work schedules all but unilaterally after 1955, see Gianotti, *Lotte e organizzazione di classe alla FIAT*, pp. 154–9, 205; and Pugno and Garavini, *Gli anni duri alla FIAT*, p. 49.

65 M. Salvati, *Sviluppo economico*, pp. 61–83, discusses the failure of available research to distinguish carefully between these two motives for migration.

66 Goffredo Fofi, *L'immigrazione meridionale a Torino*, expanded ed. (Milan: Feltrinelli, 1976), p. 299.

67 Stefano Passigli, *Emigrazione e comportamento politico* (Bologna: Il Mulino, 1969), pp. 81–2, n. 64, summarizes the literature on the chain of migration to the North.

68 For a study of Italian migrants in the construction and automobile industries, as compared with the situation of foreign workers in the same industries in France, see Henry M. Slater, "Migration and Workers' Conflict in Western Europe" (Ph.D. diss., Massachusetts Institute of Technology, 1977). In the mid-1950s the immigrants generally began working in the artisanal sector; by the early 1960s their jobs were in manufacturing plants, even if small ones (Fofi, *L'immigrazione meridionale a Torino*, p. 152).

69 On the substitution of Southern for Northern labor, see Massimo Paci, "Migrazioni interne e mercato capitalistico del lavoro," in Paolo Leon and Marco Marocchi, eds., *Sviluppo economico italiano e forza-lavoro* (Venice: Marsilio Editori, 1973), pp. 181–96; and Fofi, *L'immigrazione meridionale a Torino*, p. 299.

70 Ida Regalia, "Rappresentanza operaia e sindacato: mutamento di un sistema di relazioni industriali," in Pizzorno et al., *Lotte operaie e sindacato: il ciclo 1968–1972 in Italia*, pp. 185–8.

71 Franco Alasia and Danilo Montaldi, *Milano, Corea*, new expanded ed. (Milan: Feltrinelli, 1975), esp. pp. 33–4. For the analogous experience of the American blacks who migrated north, see Alma Herbst, *The Negro in the Slaughtering and Meat-Packing Industry in Chicago* (Boston: Houghton Mifflin, 1932); and Spear, *Black Chicago*. On the eventual organization of blacks in the industrial unions, see David Brody, "The Emergence of Mass-Production Unionism," in John Braeman, Robert Brenner, and Everett Walters, eds., *Change and Continuity in Twentieth-Century America* (Columbus: Ohio State University Press, 1964), pp. 240–1; and August Meier and Elliott Rudwick, *Black Detroit and the Rise of the UAW* (Oxford: Oxford University Press, 1979), pp. 3–107.

72 Paola Ammassari, "The Italian Blue-Collar Worker," in N. F. Dufty, ed., *The Sociology of the Blue-Collar Worker* (Leiden: E. J. Brill, 1969), p. 13.

73 Francesco Alberoni and Guido Baglioni, *L'integrazione dell'immigrato nella società industriale* (Bologna: Il Mulino, 1965). For a critical discussion of this survey, see Passigli, *Emigrazione e comportamento politico*, pp. 190–8.

74 Massimo Paci, "Mobilitá sociale e partecipazione politica," *Quaderni di sociologia*, July 1966, pp. 387–410. More generally, on the migrants' dissatisfaction with their original homes, see Johan Galtung's study of three Sicilian villages, *Members of Two Worlds* (New York: Columbia University Press, 1971).

75 Fofi, *L'immigrazione meridionale a Torino*, p. 79.

76 Alberoni and Baglioni, *L'integrazione dell'immagrato nella società industriale*, tabs. 24, 25, 36; pp. 171, 179.

77 See the short autobiography of the FIAT worker in Mauro Perino, *Lotta Continua: sei militanti dopo dieci anni* (Turin: Rosenberg e Sellier, 1979), pp. 134–41.

78 See the summary of early views on the migrants in Renato Mannheimer and Giuseppe Micheli, "Alcune ipotesi sul concetto di integrazione degli immigrati," *Quaderni di sociologia* 23 (January 1974):86–7.

79 Stanley B. Greenberg, *Race and State in Capitalist Development* (New Haven: Yale University Press, 1980), pp. 273–380.

80 Ida Regalia, Marino Regini, and Emilio Reyneri, "Conflitti di lavoro e relazioni industriali in Italia, 1968–75," in Alessandro Pizzorno and Colin Crouch, eds., *Conflitti in Europa* (Milan: Etas Libri, 1977), p. 2.

81 Gianotti, *Lotte e organizzazione di classe alla FIAT*, pp. 208–32.

82 Fofi, *L'immigrazione meridionale a Torino*, p. 302.

83 Giannotti, *Lotte e organizzazione di classe alla FIAT*, pp. 209, 228, and, for the remark on street demonstrations, p. 216.

84 Fofi, *L'immigrazione meridionale a Torino*, p. 177.

85 Sante Notarnicola, *L'evasione impossibile* (Milan: Feltrinelli, 1972), pp. 30–1.

86 Although this sort of action is a protest, Hobsbawm writes, "it is a modest and revolutionary protest. It protests not against the fact that peasants are poor and oppressed, but against the fact that they are sometimes excessively poor and oppressed. Bandit-heroes are not expected to make a world of equality. They can only right wrongs and prove that sometimes oppression can be turned upside down" (E. J. Hobsbawm, *Social Bandits and Primitive Forms of Social Movement in the Nineteenth and Twentieth Centuries* [Glencoe, Ill.: Free Press, 1959], p. 24).

87 Notarnicola, *L'evasione impossibile*, p. 51. An analogous figure in German labor history was Max Hoelz. A leader of the anarcho-Communist movement in Weimar Germany, Hoelz used money stolen from rich industrialists to support a revolutionary army. He was known as a "noble robber"; like Notarnicola, he was not born to a family of industrial workers. See Hans Manfred Bock, *Syndikalismus und Linkskommunismus von 1918–1923: zur Geschichte und Soziologie der Freien Arbeiter-Union Deutschlands (Syndikalisten), der Allgemeinen Arbeiter-Union Deutschlands und der Kommunistischen Arbeiter-Partei Deutschlands* (Meisenheim am Glan: Verlag Anton Hain, 1969), pp. 308 ff.

88 Fernando Vianello, "I meccanismi di recupero del profitto: l'esperienza italiana, 1963–73," in Augusto Graziani, ed., *Crisi e ristrutturazione nell'economia italiana* (Turin: Einaudi, 1975), p. 118.

89 Regalia, Regini, and Reyneri, "Conflitti di lavoro e relazioni industriali in Italia," pp. 48–9.

90 Regalia, "Rappresentanza operaia e sindacato," pp. 191–2. Pugno and Garavini, *Gli anni duri alla FIAT*, pp. 142–7, gives examples of some of the early agreements.

91 Gianfranco Pasquino, "Recenti trasformazioni nel sistema di potere della Democrazia Cristiana," in Luigi Graziano and Sidney Tarrow, eds., *Il sistema politico e le istituzioni* (Turin: Einaudi, 1979), pp. 609–56; Alfredo Gigliobianco and Michele Salvati, *Il maggio francese e l'autunno caldo italiano: la risposta di due borghesie* (Bologna: Il Mulino, 1980), pp. 39–42.

92 For the history of the center–left, see Giuseppe Tamburrano, *Storia e cronaca del centro sinistra* (Milan: Feltrinelli, 1971).

93 Luigi Bobbio, *Lotta Continua* (Rome: Savelli, 1979), pp. 27–8.

94 Ibid., pp. 3–26.

95 Regalia, Regini, and Reyneri, "Conflitti di lavoro e relazioni industriali in Italia," p. 2.

96 Fofi, *L'immigrazione meridionale a Torino*, p. 304.

97 The periodization parallels the one in Regalia, Regini, and Reyneri, "Conflitti di lavoro e relazioni industriali in Italia," pp. 51–60.

98 Bobbio, *Lotta Continua*, p. 28. For a general discussion of the activities of skilled workers in this period, see Emilio Reyneri, " 'Maggio strisciante': l'inizio della mobilitazione operaia," in Pizzorno et al., *Lotte operaie e sindacato: il ciclo 1968–1972 in Italia*, pp. 81–92.

99 Gianotti, *Lotte e organizzazione di classe alla FIAT*, pp. 252–3.

100 On union strategy, see Regalia, "Rappresentanza operaia e sindacato," pp. 199–200. Where the unions were strongest during the 1960s, as for example at Alfa Romeo, they were able to achieve their ends with no more than the threat of strikes. See Reyneri, " 'Maggio strisciante,' " p. 85.

101 Regalia, Regini, and Reyneri, "Conflitti di lavoro e relazioni industriali in Italia," p. 50.

102 Regalia, "Rappresentanza operaia e sindacato," pp. 204–9.

103 Bobbio, *Lotta Continua*, pp. 28–30.

104 Laura Luppi, "Autobianchi," in Alessandro Pizzorno, ed., *Lotte operaie e sindacato in Italia (1968–1972)*, 6 vols. (Bologna: Il Mulino, 1974), 1:55.

105 Bobbio, *Lotta Continua*, pp. 29–31.

106 Reyneri, " 'Maggio strisciante,' " p. 85; Regalia, Regini, and Reyneri, "Conflitti di lavoro e relazioni industriali in Italia," pp. 27–33. For a detailed account of Innocenti, see Emilio Reyneri, "Innocenti," in Pizzorno, ed., *Lotte operaie e sindacato in Italia (1968–1972)*, 1:176.

107 Regalia, Regini, and Reyneri, "Conflitti di lavoro e relazioni industriali in Italia," pp. 11–23.

108 On the factory councils and their connection to Socialist ideas, see Martin Clark, *Antonio Gramsci and the Revolution That Failed* (New Haven: Yale University Press, 1977).

109 Bobbio, *Lotta Continua*, pp. 32–3.

110 See generally, on the period, Regalia, "Rappresentanza operaia e sindacato," pp. 211–35.

111 Ibid., p. 204.

112 See the account of the origin of the *delegati* and the transformation of the labor

movement in this period given by Bruno Trentin, then head of the Communist and Socialist Metalworkers' Union: *Il sindacato dei consigli* (Rome: Editori Riuniti, 1980).

113 Regalia, "Rappresentanza operaia e sindacato," pp. 224–8.

114 Reyneri, "Innocenti," p. 176; Regalia, "Rappresentanza operaia e sindacato," pp. 220–2.

115 In memoranda *not* intended for public circulation, the managers at Alfa Romeo note that many of the newly promoted workers do not do well at their jobs, slowing down production and antagonizing the more practiced craftsmen (Progetto di formazione, "Aree professionali," mimeographed [Alfa Romeo, June 1979]).

116 A good example of these restrictions is the agreement signed at FIAT in Turin in 1971 that limited the percentage of the working day during which each assembly-line worker was required actually to be performing his task. To see the wide-reaching effects of such restrictions, imagine an assembly line composed of three workers each reporting to work for 100 minutes a day. Assume further that because of the physical construction of the product the assembly tasks must be divided in such a way that the longest job takes 2 minutes to complete, whereas the remaining operations take 1 minute each. If the contract provided that, on the average, the workers could be on the line up to a maximum of two-thirds of the working day, output would be fifty units: The worker with the longest job would work the full 100 minutes and his two mates 50 minutes each, and the total would be 200 minutes, or two-thirds of the group's total in the plant. But if, as at FIAT, the same ceiling is placed on individual effort, output falls to thirty-three units. Once the worker with the longest job has reached 66 minutes, or two-thirds of his working day, he stops; and unless some elaborate and costly system of job rotation is developed to relieve him, his performance paces the rest of the assembly line. See the detailed analysis of the application and importance of this form of contract, the *saturazione individuale massima*, in FLM, comitato cottimo, off. 76-77-73/cambi, FIAT, Mirafiori, "Ricerca sugli effetti dell'applicazione della saturazione media di gruppo sulle linee meccanizzate al montaggio – motori e cambi – della meccanica Mirafiori," mimeographed (Turin, February 6, 1981).

117 This and the following observations on the situation in the Northern factories and the views of craftsmen and migrants are based on discussions with workers and managers in Milan, Turin, and Modena in spring 1979 and spring 1980.

118 Perino, *Lotta Continua*, p. 148.

119 Domenico Liberato Norcia, with the collaboration of Fausto Tortora, *Io garantito: frammenti di vita e di pensieri di un operaio FIAT*. (Rome: Edizioni Lavoro, 1980), pp. 68–9.

120 In 1973, after the first wave of egalitarian wage demands, a worker in the middle wage category in a large metalworking plant made 112 percent of the wage of a worker in the lowest skill category. The pay of workers at the top of the hierarchy was 124.7 percent of that of the workers at the bottom. By 1981 the figures had sunk to 110.3 and 117.9 percent, respectively, and a much smaller proportion of workers were classed in the lowest categories (Giuseppe Medusa, "Le relazioni industriali a una svolta? L'intreccio produttività-salario nell'accordo aziendale Alfa Romeo," *Impresa e società* 11 [May 15, 1980]:tab. 11, p. 22.

121 On the hiring freeze, see Aviana Bulgarelli, *Crisi e mobilità operaia* (Milan: Mazzotta, 1978), p. 24; on the partial (and temporary) resumption of hiring by the large plants, see Martino Ciatti, "Torino: la FIAT riapre le assunzioni," *Sinistra*, April 1979, pp. 44–51.

122 The most detailed study of decentralization is by the FLM (Federazione Italiana Metalmeccanici), Sindacato Provinciale di Bologna, *Occupazione, sviluppo economico, territorio* (Rome: Edizioni SEUSI, 1977).

123 One expression of these strains was the defeat in November 1978, in an election for the factory council, of a Communist activist who (following the line of his group in the unified metalworkers' union) refused to support automatic promotions of un- and semiskilled workers to craft jobs. See Bruno Ugolini, "Nessuna sconfitta FIOM e PCI ma seri problemi all'Alfa," *L'Unità*, November 3, 1978, pp. 1, 13.

124 A typical agreement is the one between the metalworkers and Alfa Romeo providing for experimental introduction of a new form of assembly line. See "Accordo 17/2/78: sperimentazione 'gruppi di produzione,' " mimeographed (Arese, 1978).

125 Alan Dawley, *Class and Community: The Industrial Revolution in Lynn* (Cambridge: Harvard University Press, 1976), pp. 93–4.

126 David Allen Hounshell, "From the American System to Mass Production: The Development of Manufacturing Technology in the United States, 1850–1920" (Ph.D. diss., University of Delaware, 1978), pp. 86–203.

127 Bernard Elbaum and Frank Wilkinson, "Industrial Relations and Uneven Development: A Comparative Study of the American and British Steel Industries," *Cambridge Journal of Economics* 3 (September 1979):275–303.

128 Hounshell, "From the American System to Mass Production," pp. 331–80.

129 See, for GM's marketing strategy, Alfred P. Sloan, Jr., *My Years with General Motors* (Garden City, N.Y.: Doubleday and Co., 1964), pp. 149–68, 238–47.

130 See, on the development of maintenance work in the West German steel industry, Inge Asendorf-Krings, *Facharbeiter und Rationalisierung* (Frankfurt am Main: Campus Verlag, 1979); and Otfried Mickler, Wilma Mohr, and Ulf Kadritzke, with the collaboration of Martin Baethge and Uwe Neumann, *Produktion und Qualifikation*, 2 vols. (Göttingen: Soziologisches Forschungsinstitut, 1977), 1:570–666, 2: 414–84. It is difficult to estimate the degree to which the complex reskilling of maintenance crews described in these reports is the result of the partial abandonment of Fordism discussed in the next chapter, rather than of the limits of Fordism per se.

131 See, for instance, Joan Scott, *The Glassmakers of Carmaux: French Craftsmen and Political Action in the Nineteenth Century* (Cambridge: Harvard University Press, 1974).

132 Good discussions of this strategy are Ivar Berg and James W. Kuhn, "The Assumptions of Featherbedding," *Labor Law Journal* 13 (April 1962):227–83; and Margaret K. Chandler, "Craft Bargaining," in John T. Dunlop and Neil W. Chamberlain, eds. *Frontiers of Collective Bargaining* (New York: Harper & Row, 1967), pp. 50–75. On the creation and formalization of customary rights in industrial plants, see William Brown, *Piecework Bargaining* (London: Heinemann Educational Books, 1973); and idem, "A Consideration of Custom and Practice," *British Journal of Industrial Relations* 10 (March 1972):42–61.

133 Allen Flanders, *The Fawley Productivity Agreements* (London: Faber and Faber, 1964).

134 In West Germany, for instance, craftsmen generally control the inner circles of the factory council; and the most powerful factory councillors are also members of local and regional committees that set union bargaining strategy. See Gernot Müller et al., *Ökonomische Krisentendenzen im gegenwärtigen Kapitalismus* (Frankfurt am Main: Campus Verlag, 1978), pp. 279–321.

135 Denis Segrestin, "Du syndicalisme de métier au syndicalisme de classe: pour une sociologie de la CGT," *Sociologie du travail* 17 (April 1975):165.

136 On the history of the chapel and the British typographers' union, see Albert Edward Musson, *The Typographical Association: Origins and History up to 1949* (London: Oxford University Press, 1954); for a discussion of the organization of American typographers, see Seymour Martin Lipset, Martin A. Trow, and James S. Coleman, *Union Democracy: The Internal Politics of the International Typographical Union* (Glencoe,

Ill.: Free Press, 1956). On the current practices of the chapel, see A. J. M. Sykes, "Trade-Union Workshop Organization in the Printing Industry: The Chapel," *Human Relations* 13 (February 1960):49–65; and I. C. Cannon, "Ideology and Occupational Community: A Study of Compositors," *Sociology* 1 (May 1967):165–85. Mancur Olson, Jr., *The Logic of Collective Action: Public Goods and the Theory of Groups* (Cambridge: Harvard University Press, 1965), offers an explanation of why unions are often founded by small groups of craftsmen.

137 Sykes, "Trade-Union Workshop Organization in the Printing Industry," p. 64.

138 Note that, Michels's allegedly Iron Law of Oligarchy notwithstanding, the bureaucratic power of the father of the chapel does not lead him to subvert the organization's democracy. See A. J. M. Sykes, "The Cohesion of a Trade-Union Workshop Organization," *Sociology* 1 (May 1967):141–63. The same thing is generally true of the business agents in the U.S. building trades' locals studied by Strauss. See George Strauss, "Control by Membership in Building Trades Unions," *American Journal of Sociology* 61 (May 1956):527–35; but compare the discussion of democracy in industrial unions in Leonard R. Sayles and George Strauss, *The Local Union*, rev. ed. (New York: Harcourt, Brace and World, 1967).

139 Looked at in this way, the chapel resembles an archaic society that periodically redistributes wealth in order to prevent the emergence of disruptive inequalities. See Frank Cancian, *Economics of Prestige in a Maya Community: The Religious Cargo System in Zincantan* (Stanford: Stanford University Press, 1965); and more generally, on the subordination of economic to social relations in archaic societies, Karl Polanyi, *The Livelihood of Man* (New York: Academic Press, 1977), pp. 47–62.

140 Cannon, "Ideology and Occupational Community," p. 171.

141 On the workshop ghost see Sykes, "Cohesion of a Trade-Union Workshop Organization," p. 150; on the need to solicit votes for election to the Printers' Pension Corporation, see Cannon, "Ideology and Occupational Community," p. 172.

142 Jonathan Zeitlin, "Craft Control and the Division of Labour: Engineers and Compositors in Britain, 1890–1930" *Cambridge Journal of Economics* 3 (September 1979):263–74.

143 Keith Sisson, *Industrial Relations in Fleet Street: A Study in Pay Structure* (Oxford: Blackwell, 1975), p. 165.

144 Paul Routledge, "The Dispute at Times Newspapers Ltd.: A View from the Inside," *Industrial Relations Journal* (Winter 1979–80):7, 9. The chief long-term threat to the union comes not from the change in skills required by computerization but from the sharp reduction in the number of print-shop jobs at newspapers that it makes possible. Compare the experience of the New York typographers since 1974 reported in Theresa F. Rogers and Nathalie S. Friedman, *Printers Face Automation* (Lexington, Mass.: D.C. Heath and Co., 1980).

145 Michel Crozier, *The Bureaucratic Phenomenon* (Chicago: University of Chicago Press, 1964), p. 153.

146 These observations are based on numerous discussions with skilled metalworkers in Italy, the United States, and West Germany between 1978 and 1980.

147 See Carter Goodrich, *The Frontier of Control* (London: G. Bell and Sons, 1920).

148 On the symbolic importance of the wage hierarchy for skilled workers, see Richard Hyman and Ian Brough, *Social Values and Industrial Relations: A Study of Fairness and Equality* (Oxford: Blackwell, 1975), pp. 47 ff. An excellent general discussion of the importance of comparisons in wage determination is William Brown and Keith Sisson, "The Use of Comparisons in Workplace Wage Determination," *British Journal of Industrial Relations* 13 (March 1975):23–51. For the tendency of skilled workers to freeze existing privileges, see Leonard R. Sayles, *Behavior of Industrial Work*

Groups: Prediction and Control (New York: Wiley, 1958), p. 58; and the case study of work group relations in a British shipyard reported in R. K. Brown et al., "The Contours of Solidarity: Social Stratification and Industrial Relations in Shipbuilding," *British Journal of Industrial Relations* 10 (March 1972):12–41.

149 On the intellectual pedigree of the concept of the labor aristocracy, see Eric J. Hobsbawm, "Lenin and the 'Aristocracy of Labor,' " in Eric J. Hobsbawm, *Revolutionaries: Contemporary Essays* (London: Weidenfeld and Nicolson, 1973), pp. 121–9. A recent statement of the extreme positions in this debate is Jean Monds, "Worker Control and the New Historians: A New Economism," *New Left Review*, no. 97 (May 1976), pp. 81–100. Monds sides with Lenin in seeing the craftsmen as conservative labor aristocrats. James Hinton's "Rejoinder," published in the same issue, pp. 100–4, points toward the resolution presented here.

150 On the British shop-stewards' movement, see James Hinton, *The First Shop Stewards' Movement* (London: Allen and Unwin, 1973). For the German factory council or *Betriebsräte* movement, see Fritz Opel, *Der Deutsche Metallarbeiterverband während des ersten Weltkrieges und der Revolution* (Hannover: Norddeutsche Verlagsanstalt Gödel, 1957); and Peter von Oertzen, *Betriebsräte in der Novemberrevolution: eine politikwissenschaftliche Untersuchung über Ideengehalt und Struktur der betrieblichen und wirtschaftlichen Arbeiterräte in der deutschen Revolution, 1918–1919* (Düsseldorf: Droste, 1963). For Italy, see Clark, *Antonio Gramsci;* and for Russia, see Paul Averich, "The Bolshevik Revolution and Workers' Control in Russian Industry," *Slavic Review* 22 (March 1963):47–63. In France and the United States, too, wartime rationalization measures had brought skilled and unskilled workers at least temporarily closer together in the factories, uniting them in opposition to national leaders seen as in league with the government. But in these countries the result of the dissatisfaction was a series of strikes, primarily in the metalworking industry, rather than factory occupation. For France see Bertrand Abhervé, "Les origines de la grève des métallurgistes parisiens, juin 1919," *Le mouvement social*, no. 93 (October 1975), pp. 75–85. For the United States see David Montgomery, "The 'New Unionism' and the Transformation of Workers' Consciousness in America, 1909–1922," *Journal of Social History* 7 (Summer 1974):509–29; and David Brody, *Labor in Crisis: The Steel Strike of 1919* (Philadelphia: Lippincott, 1965). The best general account of these movements is Carmen J. Siriani, "Workers' Control in the Era of the First World War: A Comparative Analysis of the European Experience," *Theory and Society* 9 (January 1980):29–88.

It seems likely, however, that the picture that emerges from these studies will be modified at least in part by the results of research in progress. One element of the emergent view is that the wartime reorganization of production was less dramatic and thoroughgoing than it seemed. The second is that the state in the belligerent countries was so dependent on the cooperation of the work force that it granted significant powers to the labor movement, often intervened in labor's favor in industrial disputes, and willy-nilly demonstrated some of the potential benefits to the work force of state control of the economy. In this view it seems improbable that by war's end the craftsmen were in such a desperate position politically and inside the factories that they had no choice but to strike. Rather, the argument runs, they were alarmed by the rationalization of work, with its unforeseeable consequences, yet not in fact thrown into disorganization by it. At the same time the prospect of a successful appeal to the state emboldened the craftsmen not just to counter a threat to their shop-floor powers, but to press through strikes and demonstrations for the socialization of industry and an extension of their powers in the factories. Like the dominant interpretation, therefore, this alternative view points to the importance of craft community as a locus of collective action; but unlike the established account, it emphasizes the promise of political transformation, rather than the overwhelming threat of a change in the division of labor, as the spring of action. See, for a detailed analysis of British developments from this perspective, Alastair Reid, "The Division of Labour in the British Shipbuilding Industry, 1880–1920" (Ph.D. diss., Cambridge University, 1980).

151 Clark, *Antonio Gramsci*, pp. 158–60.

152 Kurt Brigl-Matthiass, *Das Betriebsräteproblem* (Berlin: Walter de Gruyter and Co., 1926), p. 140.

153 Cannon, "Ideology and Occupational Community," pp. 170. Also see Gavin Mackenzie, *The Aristocracy of Labor: The Position of Skilled Craftsmen in the American Class Structure* (Cambridge: Cambridge University Press, 1973), pp. 95–115, which challenges the idea that affluence and upward mobility undermine allegiance to the party of the workingman.

154 Nicos Ar Poulantzas, *Fascisme et dictature: la IIIe Internationale face au fascisme* (Paris: François Maspero, 1970), pp. 178–9.

155 On the German unions' political vacillation see Michael Schneider, *Das Arbeits-beschaffungsprogramm des ADGB* (Bonn-Bad Godesberg: Verlag Neue Gesellschaft, 1975), pp. 105–65.

156 The following paragraphs rely on Duncan Gallie, *In Search of the New Working Class* (Cambridge: Cambridge University Press, 1978). Gallie's results are consistent with the results of a study by Cotgrove and Vamplew of workers doing comparable jobs in five chemical or oil processing plants in South Wales, Severnside, Grange-mouth, Manchester, and East London. They found that the "workers' degree of support for unions, their perceptions of industrial relations and of the effort-wage bargain as basically a conflict situation are heavily colored by the orientations and frames of reference which they bring with them from outside the factory gates" (Stephen Cotgrove and Clive Vamplew, "Technology, Class, and Politics: The Case of the Process Workers," *Sociology* 6 [May 1972]:182).

157 The following discussion draws on Dorothy Wedderburn and Rosemary Crompton, *Workers' Attitudes and Technology* (Cambridge: Cambridge University Press, 1972), esp. pp. 26–36, 76–80, 135.

158 Ibid., p. 80. On the analogous professionalization of English printing-press operators, see Philip Sadler, "Sociological Aspects of Skill," *British Journal of Industrial Relations* 8 (March 1970):26–31.

159 Wedderburn and Crompton, *Workers' Attitudes and Technology*, p. 76.

160 Christiane Barrier, *Le combat ouvrier dans une entreprise de pointe* (Paris: Editions Ouvrières, 1975), pp. 67–178.

161 Ibid., p. 150.

162 Ibid., p. 178.

163 Gallie, *In Search of the New Working Class*, p. 285–8.

164 Friedlander, *Emergence of a UAW Local*, p. 9; Edgar Eugene Robinson, *They Voted for Roosevelt: The Presidential Vote, 1932–1944* (Stanford: Stanford University Press, 1947). Andersen's study of the New Deal electoral majority shows that the allegiance of new voters, especially the second-generation immigrants who came of political age during the depression, was crucial to the Democrats' success. See Kristi Andersen, *The Creation of the Democratic Majority, 1928–1936* (Chicago: University of Chicago Press, 1979), pp. 83–120.

165 Friedlander, *Emergence of a UAW Local*, p. 95.

166 See Sayles, *Behavior of Industrial Work Groups*, pp. 33, 78, and (for the citation) p. 98.

167 Kergoat, *Bulledor*, p. 162.

168 A good elaboration and defense of Marxist ideas of class is Erik Olin Wright, *Class, Crisis, and the State* (London: New Left Review Books, 1978).

169 A good synthesis of contemporary studies of the various groups within the American labor movement and the relation between those groups on the one hand and the political parties and state on the other is Mike Davis, "The Barren Marriage of American Labor and the New Deal," *New Left Review*, No. 124 (November 1980), pp. 43–84.

170 For a thoughtful review of the literature on Sweden that deliberately pushes the determinist view to its limits, see Peter Alexis Gourevitch, "The Politics of Economic Policy in the Great Depression of 1929: Some Comparative Observations" (paper presented at the annual meeting of the American Political Science Association, Washington, D.C., August 27–31, 1980), pp. 6–10. The arguments against this position and for the one present in the body of the text are developed in Mary Nolan and Charles F. Sabel, "Class Conflict and the Social Democratic Reform Cycle in Germany," forthcoming in Gøsta Esping-Andersen and Roger Friedland, eds., *Power and Society*, vol. 3 (Los Altos, Calif.: Geron-X).

171 Burnham's work on critical elections in which new coalitions emerge to tackle accumulating problems is one of the few pieces of contemporary American political science to capture this oscillation between periods of fermentation, during which consequential workplace issues are decided by national political debate, and more routine stretches, during which, whatever the pretensions of the political elite, there are few opportunities to influence economic developments through mass politics and little desire to do so. See Walter Dean Burnham, *Critical Elections and the Mainsprings of American Politics* (New York: W. W. Norton and Co., 1970).

172 Jürgen Kocka, *Klassengesellschaft im Krieg, 1914–1918*, (Göttingen: Vandenhoeck und Ruprecht, 1973), p. 82.

173 George Konrád and Ivan Szelény, *The Intellectuals on the Road to Class Power*, trans. Andrew Arato and Richard E. Allen (New York: Harcourt Brace Jovanovich, 1979); Eliezer Be'eri, "The Self-Image of the Arab Officer Politician," in Amos Perlmutter and Valerie Plave Bennett, eds., *The Political Influence of the Military* (New Haven: Yale University Press, 1980), pp. 299–307.

174 Alfred Stepan, *The State and Society: Peru in Comparative Perspective* (Princeton: Princeton University Press, 1978), pp. 117 ff.

175 The explanatory possibilities of this comparative method are discussed in Theda Skocpol, *States and Social Revolutions* (Cambridge: Cambridge University Press, 1979), pp. 33–40.

Chapter 5. The end of Fordism?

1 For evidence of the growth of mass production in some developing countries, see, for example, Frank Dietmar Weiss, *Electrical Engineering in West Germany: Adjusting to Imports from Less Developed Countries*, Kieler studien 155, (Tübingen: J.C.B. Mohr [Paul Siebeck], 1978), which refers to the already large body of international-trade literature on this point.

2 On the problems of the early stages of industrialization and especially the struggle to substitute domestically produced goods for imports, see Albert O. Hirschmann, *The Strategy of Economic Development* (New Haven: Yale University Press, 1958).

3 The best concise statement of the theory of the product cycle is Louis T. Wells, Jr., "International Trade: The Product Cycle Approach," in Wells, ed., *The Product Life Cycle and International Trade* (Boston: Division of Research, Graduate School of Business Administration, Harvard University, 1972), pp. 3–33.

4 In 1979 a study by the OECD concluded: "Although no hard evidence is available, it seems likely that since the early 1960s there has been a gradual acceleration of the product cycle due to a more rapid transfer of technology. This was facilitated by a reduction in transport and information costs, the faster growth and enlarged range of exports of machinery and equipment embodying modern technologies as well as of know how itself. These developments stemmed in part from the activities of transnational enterprises" (*The Impact of the Newly Developing Countries on Production and Trade in Manufactures* [Paris: OECD, 1979], p. 33).

5 For a general analysis of Swedish shipbuilding from this perspective, see Boston Consulting Group, "A Framework for Swedish Industrial Policy," mimeographed (Boston, 1978). A detailed survey of the industry in the late 1970s is Nicholas Blenkey, "Scandinavian Shipbuilding," *Marine Engineering/Log*, April, 1980, pp. 51–8.

6 See, for Japanese strategies for technological independence, Terutomo Ozawa, *Japan's Technological Challenge to the West, 1950–1974* (Cambridge: MIT Press, 1974).

7 Peter Evans, *Dependent Development* (Princeton: Princeton University Press, 1979).

8 For examples and further discussion, see Louis T. Wells, Jr., "The Internationalization of Firms from Developing Countries," in Tamir Agmon and Charles P. Kindelberger, eds., *Multinationals from Small Countries* (Cambridge: MIT Press, 1977), pp. 138–43.

9 Office of Technology Assessment, *Technology and Steel Industry Competitiveness* (Washington D.C.: Office of Technology Assessment, Congress of the United States, June 1980), p. 80.

10 For an indication of the sensitivity of production technologies to fluctuations of commodity prices, see the report on new alloys developed by the American firm Colt Industries, Inc., in response to sharp increases in the price of tungsten and cobalt, in Agis Salpukas, "Mixing Metals in Special Steel," *New York Times*, January 29, 1981, p. D2. Similarly, because managers of the Union Twist Drill Co., another American firm, believe that "an OPEC-like cartel" will be formed by the suppliers of alloying materials, they are experimenting with a process for making cutting tools out of powdered metal. See Richard T. Dann, "Machine Tools on the Move," *Machine Design*, March 12, 1981, p. 722.

11 A classic example is the regulation of air pollution caused by automobile emissions. For a discussion of the history of the relevant debate and legislation in the United States, see Alan Altshuler, *The Urban Transportation System* (Cambridge: MIT Press, 1979), pp. 172–209.

12 Benjamin Coriat, *L'atelier et le chronomètre* (Paris: Christian Bourgois, 1979), p. 253.

13 See, on government regulation of workplace health and safety, Steven Kellman, *Regulating America, Regulating Sweden: A Comparaive Study of Occupational Safety and Health Policy* (Cambridge: MIT Press, 1981).

14 On positional goods, which are valued because few possess them, see Fred Hirsch, *The Social Limits to Growth* (Cambridge: Harvard University Press, 1978), pp. 27–54.

15 "1977 Breadstuffs Census," *Milling and Baking News*, August 26, 1980, p. 10-c.

16 For an example of this grim *pas de deux*, see the reply of the National Coffee Association to a study at the Harvard Medical School linking coffee to pancreatic cancer, reported in the *New York Times*, March 12, 1981, p. B15.

17 Michael Borrus, "The Case of the U.S. Steel Industry," and James E. Millstein, "The Problem of Consumer Electronics: The Case of the U.S. Television Industry," both in Laura Tyson and John Zysman, eds. *American Industry in International Competi-*

tion (forthcoming), are full of examples of the fragility of and limited effectiveness of protectionist measures. It is easy to find implicit attacks on employers' neglect of health and safety and offers to ally with employers to defend jobs against imports on successive pages of U.S. union publications. See, for instance, "Death Rate Demonstrates Need for OSHA," and "UAW Presses Washington for Quick Import Action," *Solidarity,* December 16–31, 1980, pp. 4 and 5, respectively.

18 Millstein, "The Problem of Consumer Electronics," pp. 43–7.

19 William J. Abernathy and Larry Ronan, "Honda Motor Company's CVCC Engine" (Report DOT-TSC-NHTSA-80-3, prepared for U.S. Department of Transportation, National Highway Traffic Safety Administration, July 1980).

20 This argument is developed with examples from the American automobile industry in William J. Abernathy, *The Productivity Dilemma* (Baltimore: Johns Hopkins University Press, 1978).

21 "The Race to Plug In," *Business Week,* December 8, 1980, p. 62.

22 Borrus, "The Case of the U.S. Steel Industry," p. 50.

23 Whereas my definition of specialty steels focuses on the firm's strategy, especially the relation between manufacturer, technology, and customer, the standard definitions of the term turn on the character of the product. Because some alloy products, such as tool and stainless steels, can be mass produced, and some shapes of standard carbon steel are uncommon enough to count as specialty items, available statistics give only an imprecise idea of market structure in the steel industry. To complicate the picture further, it is often difficult to ascertain the combination of alloys and standard steels of various types that any one company makes. Figures given in the subsequent discussion are therefore only indicative of broad trends. For a discussion along these lines of this and related difficulties in the analysis of changes in steel production, see Office of Technology Assessment, *Technology and Steel Industry Competitiveness,* pp. 248–50, 258.

24 See Ingrid Drexel and Christoph Nuber, *Qualifizierung für Industrie im Umbruch* (Frankfurt am Main: Campus Verlag, 1979); and Inge Asendorf-Krings, *Facharbeiter und Rationalisierung* (Frankfurt am Main: Campus Verlag, 1979), for the general movement toward the use of more skilled labor in the West German steel industry, which has resulted at least in part from the switch to higher-quality, more specialized production.

25 David B. Tinnin, "Reforging an Old Steelmaker," *Fortune,* June 16, 1980, pp. 113–18.

26 Ibid., p. 114.

27 For Krupp see Tom Walsh, "Evolutionary Changes," *American Metal Market: International Steel Supplement,* October 7, 1977, p. 6A.

28 Cited in Tracy Dahlby, "Japan Seeks a Long-Term Strategy for Prosperity," *Far Eastern Economic Review,* August 25, 1978, p. 45.

29 Office of Technology Assessment, *Technology and Steel Industry Competitiveness,* p. 261. Another part of the Japanese strategy is to switch from the export of steel to the sale of steel technology to such developing countries as Brazil, China, Indonesia, and those in Southeast Asia and the Middle East. The Japanese do not believe, however, that they will be able to maintain a technological lead into the distant future; and the export of basic steel technology seems to be conceived as one aspect of an orderly retreat from this sector of the industry. See Dahlby, "Japan Seeks a Long-Term Strategy for Prosperity," p. 45; and Office of Technology Assessment, *Technology and Steel Industry Competitiveness,* pp. 302–3.

30 For Armco, see Borrus, "The Case of the U.S. Steel Industry," p. 52.

31 For returns on investment by industry segment, see Office of Technology Assessment, *Technology and Steel Industry Competitiveness*, tab. 24, p. 122; and for Armco's export successes, see ibid., p. 261. Although imports of almost all kinds of steel are increasing in the United States in the aggregate, specialized products are still substantially more competitive than standard goods. In 1978 U.S. exports were 9.3 percent of imports in standard carbon steel, compared with 65.6 percent of imports in true specialty markets. Though distorted by the complex system of tariff regulations in effect at the time, these figures indicate the general pattern. See ibid., tab. 103, p. 260.

32 A concise survey of established and emergent steelmaking technologies and their significance is Julian Szekely, "Radically Innovative Steelmaking Technologies," *Metallurigical Transactions (B)* 11B (September 1980):353–71.

33 George J. McManus, "Mini-Mills Begin to Make Noises in a Big Way," *Iron Age*, May 5, 1980, p. mp-5. On the spread of continuous casting, see Wayne Loewe, "Day for Combined Processes Nears," *American Metal Market: Steelmaking Today Supplement*, September 25, 1978, p. 8A. For the estimates of the mini-mill market share in 1990, see Office of Technology Assessment, *Technology and Steel Industry Competitiveness*, p. 256. In the late 1970s mini-mills in the United States were even more profitable than alloy producers: On the average the former returned 12.3 percent on investment in 1978, 1.2 percent more than the latter. See ibid, tab. 24, p. 122.

34 George J. McManus, "Electric Furnace Succeeds in Technology and Profit," *Iron Age*, Feb. 4, 1980, p. mp-7; Tom Stundza, "Capitalizing on Flexibility," *American Metal Market: Steelmaking Today Supplement*, September 25, 1978, p. 4A.

35 McManus, "Electric Furnace Succeeds," p. mp-18. For the development and diffusion of direct reduction technology, see "Iron Producers Foresee a Golden Future," *World Business Weekly* August 18, 1980, p. 10; and Office of Technology Assessment, *Technology and Steel Industry Competitiveness*, pp. 194–5.

36 This move into more sophisticated products is already under way and will likely be accelerated by introduction of the Steckel rolling mill: Whereas the normal method of flattening steel is to pass it along a line of paired rollers, the Steckel mill does the job by passing the hot strand of metal repeatedly through a single stand. The method appears to be especially suited to the needs of smaller producers. See, for a discussion of this matter and the capacity of the mini-mills to produce alloys and large-diameter pipe, Office of Technology Assessment, *Technology and Steel Industry Competitiveness*, p. 252–4.

37 For general discussion of the chemical industry at this turning point, see the survey article by Iain Carson, "Middle-aged Spread," *Economist*, April 7, 1979, pp. survey 3–survey 30. For a detailed analysis of the growth prospects of a typical specialty product, thermoplastics, see "Engineering Plastics: European Outlook Bright," *Chemical Engineering News*, November 10, 1980, pp. 19–20.

As in the case of steel, the definition of specialty markets for chemicals overlaps with but is not identical to many standard definitions of specialty products. The best classification from the present point of view is the one used in *Kline Guide to Chemical Industry*. The *Guide* distinguishes *true commodities* (high-volume products produced according to generally accepted specifications), *fine chemicals* (infrequently produced commodity chemicals), *specialty chemicals* (low-volume custom products), and *pseudo commodities* (high-volume specialty chemicals). But the ambiguities of publicly available company data make it impossible for even the editors of this trade publication to apply their classifactory scheme rigorously to the analysis of the industry's segments. See *Kline Guide to Chemical Products*, 3rd ed., ed. Mary K. Meegan (Fairfield, N.J.: Charles H. Kline, 1977), pp. 20–2. As with the steel industry, therefore, statistics on the trends in the chemical industry are intended only to suggest broad developments.

38 Referring to the *Kline Guide's* classifications, Hickel writes that specialty chemicals "tend to give more consistent and higher rates of return on capital than commodities and pseudo commodities." Returns to equity in ten U.S. specialty firms with sales between $100 million and $999 million in 1977 ranged from 28.5 to 14.5 percent, with six of the firms earning 20 percent or more on investment. In a group of large commodity and pseudo commodity producers, only one earned more than 20 percent on equity, one earned 16.7 percent, and the rest earned less than 13 percent on invested capital. See James R. Hickey, "Performance Chemicals: An Overview," in *Trends in Performance Chemicals: Papers Presented at the February, 1979 Meeting of the Chemical Marketing Research Association, San Francisco* (Staten Island, N.Y.: Chemical Marketing Research Association, 1979), pp. 6–7 and tab. 3 and 4, p. 16.

39 "DuPont: Seeking a Future in Biosciences," *Business Week*, November 24, 1980, pp. 86–98; Lee Smith, "Dow vs. DuPont: Rival Formulas for Leadership," *Fortune*, September 10, 1979, pp. 74–84.

40 Winston Williams, "Dow Broadens Product Lines," *New York Times*, February 11, 1981, p. D1.

41 John C. Bolen, "Amazing Grace," *Barron's*, December 8, 1980, pp. 41–5.

42 For the plans of the European firms, see "Overseas, the Switch to Specialties Is Growing," *Chemical Week*, October 14, 1981, pp. 40–2. For the citation, see "Beware the Specialties Fad," ibid., p. 3.

43 Manuel Gaetan, "Complete Report on Gerber's Numerically Controlled Stitcher in Operation at the Arrow Company," *Bobbin*, July 1971, pp. 45–6. For case studies of the responses of U.S. apparel firms to the rapid increase of imports from 1960 on, see José de la Torre et al., *Corporate Responses to Import Competition in the U.S. Apparel Industry*, Research Monograph no. 74 (Atlanta: Publishing Services Division, College of Business Administration, Georgia State University, 1978).

44 A good survey of the origins, economic appeal, and diffusion of flexible manufacturing systems is Comptroller General of the United States, "Manufacturing Technology: A Changing Challenge to Improved Productivity," General Accounting Office of the United States, LCD-75-436, June 1976.

45 See, generally, Benjamin Coriat, "Robots et automates dans les industries de serie: esquisse d'une économie de la robotique d'atelier" (paper presented to the Sixtieth National Meeting of the Association pour le Développement des Etudes sur la Firme Industrielle, Chantilly, September 18–19, 1980). For production estimates and a survey of the current and near-term use of programmable industrial robots, see the interview with Joseph F. Engelberger, president of Unimation, in *Production*, May 1980, p. 81.

46 For a survey of the literature on job reform, see Ivar Berg, Marcia Freedman, and Michael Freeman, *Managers and Work Reform: A Limited Engagement* (New York: Free Press, 1978). My review of this book in *Challenge*, July 1979, pp. 64–6, which is based on interviews with automobile workers in the American South who are familiar with the new experiments, points in the same direction as the European research cited next.

47 See N. Altmann, P. Binkelmann, K. Düll, R. Mendolia, and H. Stück, "Bedingungen und Probleme betrieblich initiierter Humanisierungsmassnahmen," mimeographed (Institut für Sozialwissenschaftliche Forschung, Munich, 1980); Coriat, *L'atelier et le chronomètre*, pp. 237–61; and Federico Butera, "La linea di montaggio: la sua logica e il suo futuro," *Politica ed economia* 11 (January 1980):43.

48 Mara Havinovsky, "The Transfer Allowance Program," *Bobbin*, March 1980, p. 142.

49 N. Altmann et al., "Bedingungen und Probleme betrieblich initiierter Humanisierungsmassnahmen," gives detailed descriptions of experiments of this type.

50 See Stefan Agurén, Rene Hansson, and K. G. Karlsson, *The Volvo Kalmar Plant,* trans. David Jenkins (Stockholm: Rationalization Council, SAF-LO, 1976).

51 For descriptions, see my review of Berg, Freedman, and Freeman, *Managers and Work Reform;* and Richard E. Walton, "Work Innovations in the United States," *Harvard Business Review,* July 1979, pp. 91–2. The quality-of-work-life teams in the South were set up in the middle and late 1970s, before unionization of many of the new plants. GM's experiments in work redesign in the North, where the union is of course well established, have been much more hesitant. See, for an example of the latter, Robert H. Guest, "Quality of Work Life: Learning from Tarrytown," *Harvard Business Review,* July 1979, pp. 76–87.

52 These remarks are based on conversations with several visitors to these plants.

53 Frederick Phillips Brooks, Jr., *The Mythical Man-Month: Essays on Software Engineering* (Reading, Mass.: Addison-Wesley, 1975), pp. 18–19, 122–3. Software engineers are becoming increasingly aware of these problems and correspondingly more attentive to the possibilities for both simplifying the design of large-scale systems and modifying them as changed circumstances require. See Charles Rich, Howard E. Shrobe, and Richard C. Waters, "Computer Aided Evolutionary Design for Software Engineering," mimeographed (Massachusetts Institute of Technology, Artificial Intelligence Laboratory, A.I. Memo 506, January 1979).

54 Charles Chevreux Heckscher, "Democracy at Work: In Whose Interests? The Politics of Worker Participation" (Ph.D. diss., Harvard University, 1981), pp. 119–22.

55 For the new GM engines, an in-line 3-cyclinder, a V-4, a V-5, a V-6, and a V-8, see *Ward's Engine Update,* July 15, 1980, p. 6. The new development is clearly linked to the experience of the late 1970s, when GM found itself unable to adapt existing equipment to meet the surge in demand for smaller, more fuel-efficient cars. "We couldn't even convert our V-8 engine capacity to making V-6s without spending millions and taking 18 months to do it," a company representative reported. See Robert L. Simison, "Agony Now May Mean a Brighter Tomorrow for U.S. Auto Makers," *Wall Street Journal,* February 3, 1981, p. 1. But there are formidable technical difficulties. Each size engine must be balanced with respect to the chassis on which it is mounted. This can require modification of the latter, especially when, to improve fuel efficiency, the engine is parallel rather than at right angles to the axles. In such cases a modular engine may do little to further and could even complicate the achievement of a modular car.

56 For Chrysler's plan to build specialty vans and a new, small Imperial to compete with GM's two-seat Cadillac, see Robert Irwin, "Iacocca Lifts the Veil on Models to Follow K-Car," *Automotive News,* July 7, 1980, pp. 1, 40. For a description of the way vehicle markets are being segmented to take account of local circumstance, see the account of the Brazilian firm founded by João Conrado do Amaral Gurgel in Warren Hodge, "Brazil Car Maker Finds a Niche," *New York Times,* September 9, 1980, p. D1. The firm makes eight different kinds of jeeps and a range of specialized vehicles for hospitals, fire departments, the army, and the police. Big firms, according to Gurgel, regard these products as *abacaxis* – pineapples, or particularly thorny problems. For conflicting views on the future of the electric car in the core industrial countries, see Leonard M. Apcar, "GM and Ford Split on Future of Electric Car," *Wall Street Journal,* February 11, 1981, pp. 30, 42.

57 Ron Margel, "The Human Approach," *Bobbin,* October 1980, pp. 123–4.

58 See, for instance, the description of Gnome Bakers, a Manhattan firm that uses automated equipment to produce French rolls and bread, in *Business Week,* October 14, 1972, p. 58; and the report on the Entenmann pastry bakeries in *Fortune,* March 15, 1977, p. 48.

59 *Milling and Baking News,* July 8, 1980, p. 27.

60 Interview with Barbara Kirk, purchaser of phototypesetting, Addison-Wesley, Reading, Mass., October 24, 1980.

61 Nicholas Blenkey, "West German Expertise Expands Shipbuilding Growth," *Marine Engineering/Log,* September, 1980, p. 105.

62 On the paralyzing effects of managing American businesses as short-term assets, see Robert H. Hayes and William J. Abernathy, "Managing Our Way to Economic Decline," *Harvard Business Review,* July 1980, pp. 67–77. One indication of the rigidity of American business is that many managers of mini–steel mills are former employees of the large companies who were discouraged by the bureaucratic obstacles to the renovation of the tonnage mills (interview with Gordon Forward, Chaparral Steel Co., Midlothian, Tex., March 23, 1981).

63 This section is based on numerous interviews and discussions with workers, employers, and trade unionists in Emilia-Romagna, the Marche, and the Veneto in 1979 and 1980. Without the help of Vittorio Capecchi, Adele Pesce, and Donata Menegelli, all of the metalworkers' union, the Federazione Lavoratori Metalmeccanici (FLM) of Bologna, this work would have been impossible.

The large literature on the *decentramento produttivo* is summarized in two clearly written books. Work done in the first half of the 1970s is reviewed in Arnaldo Bagnasco, *Tre Italie: la problematica territoriale dello sviluppo italiano* (Bologna: Il Mulino, 1977), pp. 114–38. A central tendency during this period was to regard the spread of small shops as the result of either the capitalists' efforts to evade union controls or Italy's peripheral place in the international division of labor, or both: Small shops were thought to be the ideal refuge for beleaguered entrepreneurs making fashionable consumer goods for foreign markets. Research done in the second half of the decade is discussed at length in Arnaldo Bagnasco and Rosella Pini, *Sviluppo economico e trasformazioni sociopolitiche dei sistemi territoriali a economia diffusa,* Quaderni Fondazione Giangiacomo Feltrinelli, no. 14 (Milan: Feltrinelli, 1981). During this second period, and largely as a result of the continual reorganization of the industrial structure, the workshop economy gradually came to be seen as a distinct system of production capable of adapting technology to its own purposes and producing goods, such as sophisticated machine tools, that cannot be dismissed as peripheral to the advanced economies. See ibid, pp. 99–116. Examples of the newer interpretation, from the entrepreneurs' point of view, are Gianni Lorenzoni, "Una tipologia di produzioni in conto terzi nel settore metalmeccanico," in Riccardo Varaldo, ed., *Ristrutturazioni industriali e rapporti fra imprese* (Milan: Franco Angeli, 1979), pp. 181–208; and Lorenzoni, *Una politica innovativa nelle piccole medie imprese* (Milan: Etas Libri, 1979). A similar account from a Socialist perspective is Andrea Saba, *L'industria sommersa: un nuovo modello di sviluppo* (Venice: Marsilio Editori, 1980).

64 The phrase and territorial definition come, plainly, from Bagnasco, *Tre Italie.*

65 See, for instance, B. Melossi et al., *Restaurazione capitalistica e piano del lavoro* (Rome: Editrice Sindacale Italiana, 1977).

66 According to the law of July 25, 1956, no. 860, an artisanal firm is defined as one with no more than ten fully qualified employees, including members of the proprietor's family, and up to five apprentices. The text of the law is in Regione Emilia-Romagna, *Le imprese artigiane dell'Emilia-Romagna nel 1975* (Bologna: Regione Emilia-Romagna, 1977), p. XXVII. For the figures on artisans' shops in Modena, see ibid., p. 240. By 1980 the number of officially registered firms had increased to 26,925. See the CNA pamphlet *Una moderna organizzazione per costruire il progetto di qualificazione dell'artigianato degli anni '80* (Bologna: Confederazione Nazionale dell'Artigianato, Comitato Regionale Emilia-Romagna, 1980), p. 11.

Population figures for Modena in 1963 are from ISTAT, *Popolazione e circonscrizioni amministrative dei comuni, 1964* (Rome: Istituto Centrale di Statistica, 1964), p. 4; figures for 1975 are from ISTAT, *Popolazione e movimento anagrafico dei comuni, 1976*, tab. 7, p. 8. The population in 1979 was 590,547, an increase of under 3 percent compared to the roughly 25 percent increase in the number of artisanal firms. See ISTAT, *Popolazione e movimento anagrafico dei comuni 1980*, tab. 2, p. 4.

67 For a full discussion of the legal privileges and liabilities of artisanal firms in Italy, see Marco Ricolfo, "Legislazione economica e piccole imprese," in F. Ferrero and S. Scamuzzi, eds., *L'industria in Italia: la piccola impresa* (Rome: Editori Riuniti, 1979), pp. 119–86. The single most important piece of labor legislation, the Statuto dei lavoratori passed in 1970 to protect the unions' rights to organize in the factories and to increase employment security, exempts firms with fewer than fifteen employees. See generally, on the Statuto dei lavoratori, Tiziano Treu, ed., *L'uso politico dello Statuto dei lavoratori*, 2 vols. (Bologna: Il Mulino, 1975).

68 The best of the scanty research on unionization in the small firms is a survey by Capecchi of metalworking firms in the province of Bologna in 1975. He found that there was an official union representative in only about 25 percent of the firms with fewer than fifty employees (which accounted for just under half the 80,000 workers covered in the survey). In contrast, there was a union representative in 90 percent of the firms with fifty or more employees. See Vittorio Capecchi and Enrico Pugliese, "Due città a confronto: Bologna e Napoli," *Inchiesta* 9 (September 1978):tab. 4, p. 10. The significance of this finding, however, is difficult to establish. On the one hand, the absence of an official shop steward is by no means proof of the complete absence of union influence. There are national contracts signed by the artisans' associations and the trade unions that fix minimum wages by skill category; and these wages lists are often displayed in the small firms. Acting through their allies in local governments, moreover, the unions can obtain administrative rulings that, for example, close down primitive foundries and other dirty and dangerous small shops. Finally, social pressure may not be an effective way to control large entrepreneurs, but it does shape the behavior of small proprietors in tiny communities in which workers and employers are both thoroughly familiar with trade-union practices, have known each other since birth, and may be related by blood or marriage. On the other hand, informal forms of control often leave room for substantial abuse of single workers, and they offer no protection to workers collectively if proprietors choose to disregard customary obligations in times of crisis. The labor movement may ultimately come to play a more prominent and explicit role in the system of small-scale production, for reasons developed later in the body of the text; but this result is far from certain. See also Bagnasco and Pini, *Sviluppo economico e trasformazioni sociopolitiche*, p. 11; they speak of the "growing unionized sector" in the small firms.

69 Bagnasco and Pini, *Sviluppo economico e trasformazioni sociopolitiche*, report wage (tab. 4.16, p. 105), unemployment (tab. 4.10, p. 92), and investment data (tab. 3.9, p. 54). For income ranks, see Luigi Pieraccioni, ed., *Il reddito prodotto nelle province italiane nel 1979* (Rome: Unione Italiana delle Camere di Commercio Industria, Artigianato e Agricoltura, 1981), tab. 4, p. 22, and tab. 8, p. 39.

During the period of these transformations, growth in the small-firm sector more than offset the generally acknowledged stagnation in areas dominated by large firms. According to OECD figures, from 1970 through 1980 the uncompounded average annual increase in the Italian Gross Domestic Product was 3.4 percent, compared to 2.6 percent in the United States and 3.1 percent in West Germany. See *OECD Economic Outlook* 29 (July 1981), tab. H1, p. 132.

Changes indicated by these aggregate data are also confirmed by detailed studies of technological innovation in the small firms. An excellent description of the reorganization of the ceramic-tile industry, for instance, is Margherita Russo, "La natura e le implicazioni del progresso tecnico: una verifica empirica," mimeographed (Modena, December 1980).

Another well-documented example is the machine-tool industry, which combines technological sophistication and pronounced decentralization. In 1977, 40 percent of the Italians in the industry worked in firms employing up to 100 workers, compared with 12 percent in West Germany and 23 percent in the United States. See Anna Maria Gaibisso, "Ruolo e struttura dell'industria italiana delle macchine utensili," *Bollettino CERIS* 5 (September 1980):29. Italy is now the second largest producer of numerically controlled machine tools in Europe, after West Germany, and well ahead of France and Great Britain. As of 1975, 20 percent of numerically controlled machines in use in Italy were located in shops employing between 20 and 49 workers, and their use in small firms was increasing rapidly. See Secondo Rolfo, "La diffusione del controllo numerico nella produzione italiana di macchine utensili." *Bollettino CERIS* 5 (September 1980):126–9. For detailed evidence of the technological sophistication of the industry, see Roberto Taranto, Mariella Franchini, and Vittorio Maglia, *L'industria italiana della macchina utensile* (Bologna: Il Mulino, 1979), pp. 163–87.

70 Statistics on foreign trade compiled by the Italian chamber of commerce, the Unione Italiana delle Camere di Commercio, Industria, Artigianato e Agricoltura, suggest a crude measure of the growing autonomy of the small firms. The method of accounting is simply to credit exports and debit imports to the province in which the firm making the transaction is legally registered, regardless of the ultimate origin or destination of the traded goods: Grain imported by a firm in Ravenna, for instance, counts as an import to that province, no matter where it is finally consumed, and a car exported by FIAT in Turin counts as a plus in the Turinese balance of trade even if most of the parts of the vehicle were produced elsewhere. Assuming that the sources of imported consumer and producers' goods are likely to remain relatively fixed for long periods of time, and leaving aside problems of exchange-rate fluctuation and changes in the terms of trade, an increase in the provincial balance of trade indicates an increase in the capacity of local firms to market their products directly to foreign customers. Changes in the provincial balances of trade, therefore, can be used as rough indicators of changes in industrial autonomy, especially because autonomous expansion into comparatively inaccessible foreign markets is likely to be at least matched by increasing independence for firms operating only in the domestic economy.

Interpreted in this way, the statistics show a striking increase in economic independence in areas dominated by small firms. Again, the eight provinces that make up the region of Emilia-Romagna are a good example. In 1969, a good year for the economy there as elsewhere in Italy, exports amounted to 147 percent of imports. In 1979, another good year locally and nationally, exports came to 232 percent of imports. See Unione Italiana delle Camere di Commercio, Industria, Artigianato e Agricoltura, *Statistiche provinciali dei movimenti valutari inerenti alle importazione ed alle esportazione* (Rome: Unione Italiana delle Camere di Commercio, Industria, Artigianato e Agricoltura, January–December 1970, 1980), p. XIV (1970), and p. XV (1980). These volumes contain the corrected figures for 1969 and 1979, respectively.

Other trade statistics support this view. Italy's share of manufactured exports from 14 major industrial countries rose from about 7 percent in 1969–70 to about 8 percent in 1979–80 (unpublished statistics, U.S. Department of Commerce). Emilia-Romagna's share of all Italian exports rose from about 6 to 7 percent during the 1960s, and to 9.2 percent in 1979. See, for the period up to 1976, Dipartimento Bilancio e Programmazione, *Primo rapporto sull'industria dell'Emilia-Romagna* (Bologna: Dipartimento Bilancio e

Programmazione della Regione Emilia-Romagna, 1979), tab. 1, p. 143; and for the years through 1979, Unione Regionale delle Camere di Commercio dell'Emilia-Romagna–CERES, *Il commersio con l'estero dell'Emilia-Romagna: serie storica*, 1975–9 (Bologna: Unione Regionale delle Camere di Commercio dell'Emilia-Romagna–CERES, 1981), tab. 10, p. 35. The composition of Emilia-Romagna's exports, moreover, shifted during this twenty-year period from agricultural and nondurable consumer products to consumer durables and producers' goods. In 1963 the two leading exports were sweaters and fruits. Together they accounted for 42.7 percent of regional exports, whereas the shares of machinery and vehicles of all kinds came to only 23.5 percent. By 1976 the latter two categories contributed 34.3 percent of regional exports, and the share of sweaters and fruits had dropped to 19.5 percent. The share of ceramic products, used principally as building materials, rose from 1.5 percent in 1963 to 9 percent in 1976 (Dipartimento Bilancio e Programmazione, *Primo rapporto sull'industria dell'Emilia-Romagna*, tab. 4, p. 146).

71 Sebastiano Brusco, "Economie di scala e livello tecnologico nelle piccole imprese," in Augusto Graziani, ed., *Crisi e ristrutturazione nell'economia italiana* (Turin: Einaudi Editore, 1975), pp. 530–59.

72 These ideas are based on discussions with Lucio Brevini, president of the Associazione Piccole e Medie Industrie of Reggio Emilia, in June and July 1980.

73 A proposal along these lines is elaborated in Adele Pesce and Charles F. Sabel, "Taylorismo: una stella in declino," *I consigli*, n.s. 1 (April 1980):57–64.

74 The figures are from CNA, *Una moderna organizzazione per costruire il progetto di qualificazione dell'artigianato degli anni '80*, p. 11.

75 An example of the kind of service provided by the government is the detailed report on the American shoe market published in 1978 by an agency responsible for encouraging economic development in the relatively backward areas of the region. The study clearly documents Italy's retreat from the low end of the market in the face of new competition from the Far East and recommends that local makers who have not already done so move to more specialized and sophisticated goods. See ERVET, *Indagine sul mercato delle calzature negli Stati Uniti d'America* (Bologna: Ente Regionale per la Valorizzazione Economica del Territorio, 1978).

76 On the origins and diffusion of the cooperative movement in Italy in general and in Emilia-Romagna in particular, see Maurizio Degl'Innocenti, "Geografia e strutture della cooperazione in Italia," in Giulio Sapelli, ed., *Il movimento cooperativo in Italia* (Turin: Einaudi, 1981), pp. 3–87.

77 On the Communist Party's alliance strategy, see Stephen Hellman, "The PCI's Alliance Strategy and the Case of the Middle Classes," in Donald L. M. Blackmer and Sidney Tarrow, eds., *Communism in Italy and France* (Princeton: Princeton University Press, 1975), pp. 373–419.

78 On the Christian Democrats' strategy and the "modello Rossi" in the Veneto, see Mino Monicelli, *La follia veneta: come una regione bianca diviene culla del terrorismo* (Rome: Editori Riuniti, 1981), esp. pp. 43–9, 110–11.

79 For the history of the Catholic political movement's efforts to counter the rise of socialism by organizing its own agrarian leagues, producers' cooperatives, and cooperative banks, see Mario G. Rossi, *Le origini del partito cattolico: movimento cattolico e lotta di classe nell'Italia liberale* (Rome: Editori Riuniti, 1977).

80 Even in the Veneto, however, small firms frequently form cooperatives to export their products. See Giancarlo Marcato, "Imprese esportatrici e organismi associativi per l'esportazione nel Veneto," in *La rivista veneta* 13 (May 1979):103–43.

Bibliography

Abernathy, William J. *The Productivity Dilemma*. Baltimore: Johns Hopkins University Press, 1978.

Abernathy, William J., and Ronan, Larry. "Honda Motor Company's CVCC Engine." Report DOT-TSC-NHTSA-80-3, prepared for U.S. Department of Transportation, National Highway Traffic Safety Administration. July 1980.

Abhervé, Bertrand. "Les origines de la grève des métallurgistes parisiens, juin 1919." *Le mouvement social*, no. 93 (October 1975), pp. 75–85.

Accornero, Aris. *Gli anni '50 in fabbrica*. Bari: De Donato, 1973.

Achor, Shirley. *Mexican Americans in a Dallas Barrio*. Tucson: University of Arizona Press, 1978.

Agurén, Stefan; Hansson, Rene; and Karlsson, K. G. *The Volvo Kalmar Plant*. Translated by David Jenkins. Stockholm: Rationalization Council, SAF-LO, 1976.

Alasia, Franco, and Montaldi, Danilo. *Milano, Corea*. New expanded ed. Milan: Feltrinelli, 1975.

Alberoni, Francesco, and Baglioni, Guido. *L'integrazione dell'immigrato nella società industriale*. Bologna: Il Mulino, 1965.

Alfa Romeo. "Accordo 17/2/78: sperimentazione 'gruppi di produzione.' " Mimeographed. 1978.

Alfa Romeo. "Aree professionali." Mimeographed. June 1979.

Allen, G. A. *The Industrial Development of Birmingham and the Black Country, 1860–1927*. London: George Allen and Unwin, 1929.

Altmann, N.; Binkelmann, P.; Düll, K.; Mendolia, R.; and Stück, H. "Bedingungen und Probleme betrieblich initiierter Humanisierungsmassnahmen." Mimeographed. Institut für Sozialwissenschaftliche Forschung. Munich, 1980.

Altschuler, Alan. *The Urban Transportation System*. Cambridge: MIT Press, 1979.

Ammassari, Paola. "The Italian Blue-Collar Worker." In *The Sociology of the Blue-Collar Worker*, edited by N. F. Dufty, pp. 3–21. Leiden: E. J. Brill, 1969.

Andersen, Kristi. *The Creation of the Democratic Majority, 1928–1936*. Chicago: University of Chicago Press, 1979.

Asendorf-Krings, Inge. *Facharbeiter und Rationalisierung*. Frankfurt am Main: Campus Verlag, 1979.

Authors' Collective. "Le mouvement des O.S. de Renault-Flins, 26 mars–26 avril 1973." *Les temps modernes* 29 (July 1973):2163–241.

Averich, Paul. "The Bolshevik Revolution and Workers' Control in Russian Industry." *Slavic Review* 22 (March 1963):47–63.

Averitt, Robert T. *The Dual Economy: The Economics of American Industry Structure.* New York: W. W. Norton and Co., 1968.

Bagnasco, Arnaldo, and Pini, Rosella. *Sviluppo economico e trasformazioni sociopolitiche dei sistemi territoriali a economia diffusa.* Quaderni Fondazione Giangiacomo Feltrinelli, no. 14. Milan: Feltrinelli, 1981.

Bailes, Kendall E. *Technology and Society under Lenin and Stalin.* Princeton: Princeton University Press, 1978.

Banfield, Edward C. *The Unheavenly City.* Boston: Little, Brown, 1968.

Barrier, Christiane. *Le combat ouvrier dans une entreprise de pointe.* Paris: Editions Ouvrières, 1975.

Barton, Josef J. *Peasants and Strangers: Italians, Rumanians and Slovaks in an American City, 1890–1950.* Cambridge: Harvard University Press, 1975.

Base Ouvrière. *Revolutionäre Betriebsarbeit bei Renault-Flins.* Translated by Dieter Meyer. Berlin: Merve Verlag, 1972.

Bassoul, René; Bernard, Pierre; and Touraine, Alain. "Retrait, conflit, participation." *Sociologie du travail* 1 (October 1960):314–29.

Bayerisches Staatsministerium für Arbeit und soziale Fürsorge, ed. *Probleme des bayerischen Arbeitsmarktes: eine Untersuchung des Arbeitsmarktgeschehens 1966/1967.* Munich: Bayerisches Staatsministerium für Arbeit und soziale Fürsorge, n.d.

Becker, Gary S. *Human Capital: A Theoretical and Empirical Analysis, with Special Reference to Education.* 2nd ed. New York: National Bureau of Economic Research, 1975.

Be'eri, Eliezer. "The Self-Image of the Arab Officer Politician." In *The Political Influence of the Military,* edited by Amos Perlmutter and Valerie Plave Bennett, pp. 299–307. New Haven: Yale University Press, 1980.

Bell, Daniel. *The Cultural Contradictions of Capitalism.* New York: Basic Books, 1978.

Bell, Daniel. "The End of Ideology in the West." In Daniel Bell, *The End of Ideology: On the Exhaustion of Political Ideas in the Fifties,* pp. 393–407. Rev. ed. New York: Free Press, 1965.

Berg, Ivar, and Kuhn, James W. "The Assumptions of Featherbedding." *Labor Law Journal* 13 (April 1962):227–83.

Berg, Ivar; Freedman, Marcia; and Freeman, Michael. *Managers and Work Reform: A Limited Engagement.* New York: Free Press, 1978.

Berger, Suzanne, and Piore, Michael J. *Dualism and Discontinuity in Industrial Societies.* Cambridge: Cambridge University Press, 1980.

Bernoux, Philippe. "Les O.S. face à l'organisation industrielle." *Sociologie du travail* 14 (October 1972):410–36.

Betriebszelle Ford der Gruppe Arbeiterkampf, ed. *Streik bei Ford-Köln.* Erlangen: Politikladen Erlangen, 1973.

Beynon, Erdmann Doane. "The Southern White Laborer Migrates to Michigan." *American Sociological Review* 3 (June 1938):pp. 333–43.

Beynon, Huw. *Working for Ford.* London: Allen Lane, 1973.

Bezucha, Robert J. *The Lyon Uprising of 1834.* Cambridge: Harvard University Press, 1974.

Bhattacharyya, S. K.; Li, K. F.; McMinn, B.; and Mellors, C. M. "Penetration and Utilization of NC/CNC Machine Tools in British Industry." Mimeographed. Manufacturing Systems Unit, Department of Engineering Production, University of Birmingham, November 1976.

Blauner, Robert. *Alienation and Freedom.* Chicago: University of Chicago Press, 1964.

Blenkey, Nicholas. "Scandinavian Shipbuilding." *Marine Engineering/Log,* Apr. 1980, pp. 51–8.

Blenkey, Nicholas. "West German Expertise Expands Shipbuilding Growth." *Marine Engineering/Log*, September 1980, p. 105.

Bloch, Marc. *French Rural History*. Translated by Janet Sandheimer. Berkeley and Los Angeles: University of California Press, 1960.

Bobbio, Luigi. *Lotta Continua*. Rome: Savelli, 1979.

Bock, Hans Manfred. *Syndikalismus und Linkskommunismus von 1918–1923: zur Geschichte und Soziologie der Freien Arbeiter-Union Deutschlands (Syndikalisten), der Allgemeinen Arbeiter-Union Deutschlands und der Kommunistischen Arbeiter-Partei Deutschlands*. Meisenheim am Glan: Verlag Anton Hain, 1969.

Bolen, John C. "Amazing Grace." *Barron's*, December 8, 1980, pp. 41–5.

Bolton, J. L. *The Medieval English Economy, 1150–1500*. London: J. M. Dent and Sons, 1980.

Bonazzi, Giuseppe. *In una fabbrica di motori*. Milan: Feltrinelli, 1975.

Borrus, Michael. "The Case of the U.S. Steel Industry." In *American Industry in International Competition*, edited by Laura Tyson and John Zysman. Forthcoming.

Boston Consulting Group. "A Framework for Swedish Industrial Policy." Mimeographed. Boston, 1978.

Boudon, Raymond. *L'inégalité des chances: la mobilité sociale dans les sociétés industrielles*. Paris: Armand Colin, 1973.

Bourdieu, Pierre. *Outline of a Theory of Practice*. Translated by Richard Nice. Cambridge: Cambridge University Press, 1977.

Bourdieu, Pierre. *Zur Soziologie der symbolischen Formen*. Translated by Wolfgang Fietkau. Frankfurt am Main: Suhrkamp Verlag, 1974.

Bowles, Samuel, and Gintis, Herbert. *Schooling in Capitalist America*. New York: Basic Books, 1976.

Brake, Mike. *The Sociology of Youth Culture and Youth Subcultures*. London: Routledge and Kegan Paul, 1980.

Braun, Siegfried, and Fuhrmann, Jochen. *Angestelltenmentalität: Berufliche Position und gesellschaftliches Denken der Industrieangestellten – Bericht über eine industriesoziologische Untersuchung*. Neuwied am Rhein: Hermann Luchterhand Verlag, 1970.

Braverman, Harry. *Labor and Monopoly Capital: The Degradation of Work in the Twentieth Century*. New York: Monthly Review Press, 1974.

Briggs, John W. *An Italian Passage: Immigrants to Three American Cities, 1890–1930*. New Haven: Yale University Press, 1978.

Bright, James R. *Automation and Management*. Boston: Division of Research, Graduate School of Business Administration, Harvard University, n.d.

Brigl-Matthiass, Kurt. *Das Betriebsräteproblem*. Berlin: Walter de Gruyter and Co., 1926.

Brody, David. "The Emergence of Mass-Production Unionism." In *Change and Continuity in Twentieth-Century America*, edited by John Braeman, Robert Brenner, and Everett Walters, pp. 221–62. Columbus: Ohio State University Press, 1964.

Brody, David. "Labor and Small-Scale Enterprise during Industrialization." In *Small Business in American Life*, edited by Stuart W. Bruchey, pp. 263–79. New York: Columbia University Press, 1980.

Brody, David. *Labor in Crisis: The Steel Strike of 1919*. Philadelphia: Lippincott, 1965.

Brooks, Frederick Phillips, Jr. *The Mythical Man-Month: Essays on Software Engineering*. Reading, Mass.: Addison-Wesley, 1975.

Brown, R. K.; Brannen, P.; Cousins, J. M.; and Samphier, M. L. "The Contours of Solidarity: Social Stratification and Industrial Relations in Shipbuilding." *British Journal of Industrial Relations* 10 (March 1972): 12–41.

Brown, William, "A Consideration of Custom and Practice." *British Journal of Industrial Relations* 10 (March 1972):42–61.

Brown, William. *Piecework Bargaining.* London: Heinemann Educational Books, 1973.

Brown, William, and Sisson, Keith. "The Use of Comparisons in Workplace Wage Determination." *British Journal of Industrial Relations* 13 (March 1975):23–51.

Brusco, Sebastiano. "Economie di scala e livello tecnologico nelle piccole impresse." In *Crisi e ristrutturazione nell'economica Italia,* edited by Augusto Graziani, pp. 530–59. Turin: Einaudi, 1975.

Buder, Stanley. *Pullman.* Oxford: Oxford University Press, 1967.

Bulgarelli, Aviana. *Crisi e mobilità operaia.* Milan: Gabriele Mazzotta, 1978.

Burawoy, Michael. *Manufacturing Consent.* Chicago: University of Chicago Press, 1979.

Burnham, Walter Dean. *Critical Elections and the Mainsprings of American Politics.* New York: W. W. Norton and Co., 1970.

Busch, Otto. *Militärsystem und Sozialleben im alten Preussen, 1713–1807.* Berlin: Walter de Gruyter and Co., 1962.

Butera, Federico. "La linea di montaggio: la sua logica e il suo futuro." *Politica ed economia* 11 (January 1980):41–8.

Buttler, Friedrich; Gerlach, Knut; and Liepmann, Peter. "Funktionsfähige regionale Arbeitsmärkte als Bestandteil ausgewogener Funktionsräume." In *Ausgeglichene Funktionsräume,* edited by Detlev Marx, pp. 72–93. Veröffentlichungen der Akademie für Raumsforschung–Forschung und Sitzungsbericht 94. Hannover: Akademie für Raumsforschung, 1975.

Cancian, Frank. *Economics of Prestige in a Maya Community: The Religious Cargo System in Zincantan.* Stanford: Stanford University Press, 1965.

Cannon, I. C. "Ideology and Occupational Community: A Study of Compositors." *Sociology* 1 (May 1967):165–85.

Capecchi, Vittorio, and Pugliese, Enrico. "Due città a confronto: Bologna e Napoli." *Inchiesta* 8 (September 1978):3–54.

Cardoso, Fernando Henrique. "Proletariado e mudança social em São Paulo." *Sociologia* 22 (March 1960):3–11.

Cavazzani, Ada. *Il part-time agricolo: ristrutturazione capitalistica e famiglia agricola.* Venice: Marsilio Editori, 1979.

Cavender, Roy. "Contractors: Quality Evaluation and Performance." *Bobbin,* June 1980, p. 142.

Cayez, Pierre. *Métiers jacquard et hauts fourneaux: aux origines de l'industrie lyonnaise.* Lyons: Presses Universitaires de Lyon, 1978.

Chandler, Alfred D., Jr. *The Visible Hand: The Managerial Revolution in American Business.* Cambridge: Harvard University Press, Belknap Press, 1977.

Chandler, Margaret K. "Craft Bargaining." In *Frontiers of Collective Bargaining,* edited by John T. Dunlop and Neil W. Chamberlain, pp. 50–75. New York: Harper and Row, 1967.

Chinoy, Ely. *Automobile Workers and the American Dream.* Boston: Beacon Press, 1965.

Chomsky, Noam. *Aspects of the Theory of Syntax.* Cambridge: MIT Press, 1965.

Church, R. A. "The Effect of the American Export Invasion on the British Boot and Shoe Industry, 1885–1914." *Journal of Economic History* 28 (June 1968):223–54.

Ciatti, Martino. "Torino: la FIAT riapre le assunzioni." *Sinistra,* April 1979, pp. 44–51.

Clark, Martin. *Antonio Gramsci and the Revolution That Failed.* New Haven: Yale University Press, 1977.

Cohen, G. A. *Karl Marx's Theory of History: A Defense.* Princeton: Princeton University Press, 1978.

Cole, Robert E. *Japanese Blue Collar.* Berkeley and Los Angeles: University of California Press, 1971.

Cole, Robert E. *Work, Mobility, and Participation.* Berkeley and Los Angeles: University of California Press, 1979.

Comptroller General of the United States. "Manufacturing Technology – A Changing Challenge to Improved Productivity." General Accounting Office of the United States, LCD-75-436. June 1976.

Coriat, Benjamin. *L'atelier et le chronomètre.* Paris: Christian Bourgois, 1979.

Coriat, Benjamin. "Robots et automates dans les industries de série: esquisse d'une économie de la robotique d'atelier," pp. 22–6. Paper presented to the Sixtieth National Meeting of the Association pour le Développement des Etudes sur la Firme Industrielle, Chantilly. September 1980.

Cotgrove, Stephen, and Vamplew, Clive. "Technology, Class, and Politics: The Case of the Process Workers." *Sociology* 6 (May 1972):169–85.

Crespi, Franco; Segatori, Roberto; and Bottachiari, Vinicio. *Il lavoro a domicilio: il caso dell'Umbria.* Bari: De Donato, 1975.

Crozier, Michel. *The Bureaucratic Phenomenon.* Chicago: University of Chicago Press, 1964.

Dahlheimer, Harry. *A History of the Mechanics Educational Society of America in Detroit from Its Inception in 1933 through 1937.* Detroit: Wayne State University Press, 1951.

Dalton, Melville. "The Industrial 'Rate-Busters': A Characterization." *Applied Anthropology* 7 (Winter 1948):13–14.

Dann, Richard T. "Machine Tools on the Move." *Machine Design,* March 12, 1981, p. 722.

Davis, Mike. "The Barren Marriage of American Labor and the New Deal." *New Left Review,* no. 124 (November 1980), pp. 43–84.

Dawley, Alan. *Class and Community: The Industrial Revolution in Lynn.* Cambridge: Harvard University Press, 1976.

De la Torre, José; Jedel, Michael Jay; Arpan, Jeffrey S.; Ogram, E. William; and Toyne, Brian. *Corporate Responses to Import Competition in the U.S. Apparel Industry.* Research Monograph no. 74. Atlanta: Publishing Services Division, College of Business Administration, Georgia State University, 1978.

Denby, Charles. *Indignant Heart: Testimony of a Black American Worker.* Boston: South End Press, 1979.

Deutscher, Isaac. *The Prophet Armed: Trotsky, 1879–1921.* London: Oxford University Press, 1954.

de Vries, Jan. *The Economy of Europe in the Age of Crisis, 1600–1675.* Cambridge: Cambridge University Press, 1976.

Dipartimento Bilancio e Programmazione. *Primo rapporto sull'industria dell'Emilia-Romagna.* Bologna: Dipartimento Bilancio e Programmazione della Regione Emilia-Romagna, 1979.

Dizzard, Jan E. "Why Should Negroes Work?" In *Negroes and Jobs: A Book of Readings,* edited by Louis A. Ferman, Joyce L. Kornbluth, and J. A. Miller, pp. 401–13. Ann Arbor: University of Michigan Press, 1963.

Doeringer, Peter, and Piore, Michael J. *Internal Labor Markets and Manpower Analysis.* Lexington, Mass.: D. C. Heath and Co., 1971.

Dollard, John. *Caste and Class in a Southern Town.* 3rd ed. Garden City, N.Y.: Doubleday and Co., Anchor Books, 1957.

Donnelly, Michael W. "Setting the Price of Rice: A Study in Political Decisionmaking." In *Policymaking in Contemporary Japan,* edited by T. J. Pempel, pp. 143–200. Ithaca, N.Y.: Cornell University Press, 1979.

Dore, Ronald P. *British Factory–Japanese Factory: The Origins of National Diversity in Industrial Relations.* Berkeley and Los Angeles: University of California Press, 1973.

Dore, Ronald P. "Late Development – or Something Else? Industrial Relations in Britain, Japan, Mexico, Sri Lanka, and Senegal." Mimeographed. Sussex, England, 1974.

Dore, Ronald P. *Shinohata: A Portrait of a Japanese Village.* New York: Pantheon, 1978.

Drexel, Ingrid, and Nuber, Christopher. *Qualifizierung für Industrie im Umbruch.* Frankfurt am Main: Campus Verlag, 1979.

Dubois, Pierre. *Mort de l'Etat-patron.* Paris: Editions Ouvrières, 1971.

Dunn, John. *Modern Revolutions: An Introduction to the Analysis of a Political Phenomenon.* Cambridge: Cambridge University Press, 1972.

Durand, Claude, and Durand, Michelle. *De l'O.S. à l'ingénieur: carrière ou classe sociale.* Paris: Editions Ouvrières, 1971.

Durand, Claude; Prestat, Claude; and Willener, Alfred. *Travail, salaire, production.* 2 vols. Paris: Mouton and Co., 1972.

Durkheim, Emile. *De la division du travail social.* Paris: F. Alcan, 1893.

Eckart, Christel; Jaerisch, Ursula G.; and Kramer, Helgard. *Frauenarbeit in Familie und Fabrik.* Frankfurt am Main: Campus Verlag, 1979.

Edwards, Richard. *Contested Terrain: The Transformation of the Workplace in the Twentieth Century.* New York: Basic Books, 1979.

Eichner, Alfred S. *The Megacorp and Oligopoly: The Micro Foundations of Macro Dynamics.* Cambridge: Cambridge University Press, 1976.

Eizner, Nicole, and Hervieu. Bertrand. *Anciens paysans, nouveaux ouvriers.* Paris: Editions l'Harmattan, 1979.

Elbaum, Bernard, and Wilkinson, Frank. "Industrial Relations and Uneven Development: A Comparative Study of the American and British Steel Industries." *Cambridge Journal of Economics* 3 (September 1979):275–303.

Elkins, Stanley M. *Slavery: A Problem in American Institutional and Intellectual History.* Chicago: University of Chicago Press, 1959.

Ellman, Michael. "Against Convergence." *Cambridge Journal of Economics* 4 (September 1980):199–210.

ERVET. *Indagine sul mercato delle calzature negli Stati Uniti d'America.* Bologna: Ente Regionale per la Valorizzazione Economica del Territorio, 1978.

Evans, Peter. *Dependent Development.* Princeton: Princeton University Press, 1979.

Fine, Sidney. *Sit-Down.* Ann Arbor: University of Michigan Press, 1969.

Flanders, Allen. *The Fawley Productivity Agreements.* London: Faber and Faber, 1964.

FLM (Federazione Italiana Metalmeccanici), comitato cottimo, off. 76-77-73/cambi, FIAT, Mirafiori."Ricerca sugli effetti dell'applicazione della saturazione media di gruppo sulle linee meccanizzate al montaggio – motori e cambi – della meccanica Mirafiore." Mimeographed. Turin, February 6, 1981.

FLM, Sindacato provinciale di Bologna. *Occupazione, sviluppo economico, territorio.* Rome: Edizione SEUSI, 1977.

Fofi, Goffredo. *L'immigrazione meridionale a Torino.* Expanded ed. Milan: Feltrinelli, 1976.

Ford, Franklin L. *Robe and Sword.* Cambridge: Harvard University Press, 1953.

Ford, Henry, in colloboration with Samuel Crowther. *My Life and Work.* Garden City, N.Y.: Garden City Publishing Co., 1926.

Fowles, William E. "The Southern Appalachian Migrant: Country Boy Turned Blue-Collarite." In *Blue-Collar World,* edited by Arthur B. Shostak and William Gomberg, pp. 270–81. Englewood Cliffs, N.J.: Prentice-Hall, 1964.

Fox, Alan. *Beyond Contract: Work, Power and Trust Relations.* London: Faber and Faber, 1974.

Fox, Alan. "Corporatism." Mimeographed. Oxford, 1977.

Freyssenet, Michel. *La division capitaliste du travail*. Paris: Editions Savelli, 1977.

Fridenson, Patrick. "The Coming of the Assembly Line in Europe." In *The Dynamics of Science and Technology*, edited by Wolfgang Krohn, Edwin T. Layton, Jr., and Peter Weingart, pp. 160–75. Dordrecht: D. Reidel Publishing Co., 1978.

Friedlander, Peter. *The Emergence of a UAW Local, 1936–1939: A Study in Class and Culture*. Pittsburgh: University of Pittsburgh Press, 1975.

Friedman, Andrew L. *Industry and Labor: Class Struggle at Work and Monopoly Capitalism*. London: Macmillan, 1970.

Friedman, David. "Workers' Expectations and Labor Relations in the U.S. Auto Industry." Senior Honors Essay, Harvard University, March 1979.

Fries, Russell I. "British Response to the American System." *Technology and Culture* 16 (July 1975):377–403.

Fürst, Dietrich, and Zimmermann, Klaus, under the direction of Karl-Heinrich Hansmeyer. *Standortwahl industrieller Unternehmen: Ergebnisse einer Unternehmensbefragung*. Schriftenreihe der Gesellschaft für regionale Strukturentwicklung 1. Bonn: Gesellschaft für regionale Strukturentwicklung, 1973.

Gábor, I. R. "The Second (Secondary) Economy." *Acta Oeconomica* 22, nos. 3–4 (1979):291–311.

Gaetan, Manuel. "Complete Report on Gerber's Numerically Controlled Stitcher in Operation at the Arrow Company." *Bobbin*, July 1971, pp. 44–68.

Gaibisso, Anna Maria. "Ruolo e struttura dell'industria italiana delle macchine utensili." *Bollettino CERIS* 5 (September 1980):9–48.

Galbraith, John Kenneth. *The New Industrial State*. Boston: Houghton Mifflin Co., 1967.

Gallie, Duncan. *In Search of the New Working Class*. Cambridge: Cambridge University Press, 1978.

Galtung, Johan. *Members of Two Worlds*. New York: Columbia University Press, 1971.

Gans, Herbert. *The Urban Villagers*. New York: Free Press, 1962.

Geertz, Clifford. *The Interpretation of Cultures*. New York: Basic Books, 1973.

Genovese, Eugene D. *Roll, Jordan, Roll: The World the Slaves Made*. New York: Random House, 1972.

Gerlach, Knut, and Kühner, Karl-Friedrich. "Freiwilliger Arbeitsplatzwechsel in Rückstandsregionen." *Zeitschrift für Wirtschafts- und Sozialwissenschaft* 94 (1974):167–82.

Gerlach, Knut, and Liepmann, Peter. "Industrialisierung und Siedlungsstruktur: Bemerkungen zum regionalpolitischen Programm einer aktiven Sanierung der bayerischen Rückstandsgebiete." *Jahrbücher für Nationalökonomie und Statistik* 187 (1973):507–21.

Gerlach, Knut, and Liepmann, Peter. "Konjunkturelle Aspekte der Industrialisierung peripherer Regionen – dargestellt am Beispiel des ostbayerischen Regierungsbezirks Oberpfalz." *Jahrbücher für Nationalökonomie und Statistik* 187 (1972):1–21.

Gerschenkron, Alexander. *Bread and Democracy in Germany*. Berkeley and Los Angeles: University of California Press, 1943.

Gerwin, Donald, and Tarondeau, Jean Claude. "Uncertainty and the Innovation Process for Computer Integrated Manufacturing Systems: Four Case Studies." Mimeographed. Cergy, France: Ecole Supérieure des Sciences Economiques et Commerciales, March 1981.

Geschwender, James A. *Class, Race and Worker Insurgency: The League of Black Revolutionary Workers*. Cambridge: Cambridge University Press, 1977.

Gianotti, Renzo. *Lotte e organizzazione di classe alla FIAT*. Bari: De Donato, 1970.

Giddens, Anthony. *Capitalism and Modern Social Theory: An Analysis of the Writings of Marx, Durkheim and Max Weber.* Cambridge: Cambridge University Press, 1971.

Gigliobianco, Alfredo, and Salvati, Michele. *Il maggio francese e l'autunno caldo italiano: la risposta di due borghesie.* Bologna: Il Mulino, 1980.

Goldthorpe, John H. "The Current Inflation: Towards a Sociological Account." In *The Political Economy of Inflation,* edited by Fred Hirsch and John H. Goldthorpe, pp. 187–214. London: Martin Robertson, 1978.

Goldthorpe, John H., and Lockwood, David. "Affluence and British Class Structure." *Sociological Review* 11 (July 1963):133–63.

Goldthorpe, John H.; Lockwood, David; Bechhofer, Frank; and Platt, Jennifer. *The Affluent Worker in the Class Structure.* Cambridge: Cambridge University Press, 1969.

Goodrich, Carter. *The Frontier of Control.* London: G. Bell and Sons, 1920.

Goodwin, Leonard. *Do the Poor Want to Work? A Social-Psychological Study of Work Orientations.* Washington: Brookings Institution, 1972.

Gordon, David M. *Theories of Poverty and Underemployment.* Lexington, Mass.: D. C. Heath and Co., 1972.

Gouldner, Alvin W. "The Norm of Reciprocity: A Preliminary Statement." *American Sociological Review* 25 (April 1960):161–78.

Greenberg, Stanley B. *Race and State in Capitalist Development.* New Haven: Yale University Press, 1980.

Greene, Alice M. "NC Technology Has No Time for Tapes." *Iron Age,* May 19, 1980, pp. 55–62.

Greene, Alice M. "The Subtle Shifts in the NC Market Scene." *Iron Age,* March 5, 1979, pp. 35–9.

Greene, Victor. *The Slavic Community on Strike: Immigrant Labor in Pennsylvania Anthracite.* Notre Dame: University of Notre Dame Press, 1968.

Grossman, Gregory. "The 'Second Economy' of the USSR." *Problems of Communism,* September 1, 1977, pp. 25–40.

Gourevitch, Peter Alexis. "The Politics of Economic Policy in the Great Depression of 1929: Some Comparative Observations." Paper presented at the annual meeting of the American Political Science Association, Washington, D.C., August 27–31, 1980.

Guest, Robert H. "Quality of Work Life: Learning from Tarrytown." *Harvard Business Review,* July 1979, pp. 76–87.

Guidi, Gianfranco; Bronzino, Alberto; and Germanetto, Luigi. *FIAT: struttura aziendale e organizzazione dello sfruttamento.* Milan: Gabriele Mazzotta Editore, 1974.

Gutman, Herbert George. *The Black Family in Slavery and Freedom, 1750–1925.* New York: Pantheon Books, 1976.

Habermas, Jürgen. *Legitimationsprobleme im Spätkapitalismus.* Frankfurt am Main: Suhrkamp Verlag, 1973.

Hamilton, Henry. *The English Brass and Copper Industries to 1800.* London: Longmans, Green and Co., 1926.

Hayes, Robert H., and Abernathy, William J. "Managing Our Way to Economic Decline." *Harvard Business Review,* July 1980, pp. 67–77.

Heckscher, Charles Chevreux. "Democracy at Work: In Whose Interests? The Politics of Worker Participation." Ph.D. dissertation, Harvard University, 1981.

Heinze, Rolf G., and Horn, H. Willy. "Arbeitsmarkt und Politik in strukturschwachen ländlichen Regionen." In *Opfer des Arbeitsmarktes,* edited by Claus Offe, pp. 151–84. Neuwied: Hermann Luchterhand Verlag, 1977.

Hellman, Stephen. "The PCI's Alliance Strategy and the Case of the Middle Classes."

In *Communism in Italy and France*, edited by Donald L. M. Blackmer and Sidney Tarrow, pp. 373–419. Princeton: Princeton University Press, 1975.

Herbst, Alma. *The Negro in the Slaughtering and Meat-Packing Industry in Chicago*. Boston: Houghton Mifflin, 1932.

Herding, Richard. *Job Control and Union Structure: A Study on Plant-Level Conflict in the United States with a Comparative Perspective on West Germany*. Rotterdam: Rotterdam University Press, 1972.

Herkommer, Sebastian. "Conscience et position dans le procès social de reproduction: rapports de médiation." *Sociologie du travail* 20 (January 1978):69–79.

Hexter, J. H. "The Myth of the Middle Class in Tudor England." In *Reappraisals in History*, edited by J. H. Hexter, pp. 71–116. 2nd ed. Chicago: University of Chicago Press, 1979.

Hickey, James R. "Performance Chemicals: An Overview." In *Trends in Performance Chemicals: Papers Presented at the February, 1979 Meeting of the Chemical Marketing Research Association, San Francisco*, pp. 1–19. Staten Island, N.Y.: Chemical Marketing Research Association, 1979.

Hildebrand, Eckart. "Im Betrieb überleben mit der neuen Technik: Arbeitserfahrungen eines Drehers." In *Moderne Zeiten – alte Rezepte: kritisches Gewerkschaftsjahrbuch 1980/81*, edited by Otto Jacobi, Eberhard Schmidt, and Walter Müller-Jentsch, pp. 24–33. Berlin: Rotbuch Verlag, 1980.

Hilton, Rodney H. *The Decline of Serfdom in Medieval England*. London: Macmillan, 1969.

Hinton, James. *The First Shop Stewards' Movement*. London: Allen and Unwin, 1973.

Hinton, James. "Rejoinder." *New Left Review*, no. 97 (May 1976), pp. 100–4.

Hirsch, Fred. *The Social Limits to Growth*. Cambridge: Harvard University Press, 1978.

Hirschmann, Albert O. *The Strategy of Economic Development*. New Haven: Yale University Press, 1958.

Hobsbawm, E. J. *Revolutionaries: Contemporary Essays*. London: Weidenfeld and Nicolson, 1973.

Hobsbawn, E. J. *Social Bandits and Primitive Forms of Social Movement in the Nineteenth and Twentieth Centuries*. Glencoe, Ill.: Free Press, 1959.

Homburg, Heidrun. "Anfänge des Taylorsystems in Deutschland vor dem Ersten Weltkrieg." *Geschichte und Gesellschaft* 4, no. 2 (1978):170–94.

Hounshell, David Allen. "From the American System to Mass Production: The Development of Manufacturing Technology in the United States, 1850–1920." Ph.D. dissertation, University of Delaware, 1978.

Hyman, Richard, and Brough, Ian. *Social Values and Industrial Relations: A Study of Fairness and Equality*. Oxford: Blackwell, 1975.

Jeffreys, James Bavington. *The Story of the Engineers*. London: Lawrence and Wishart, 1946.

Jeremy, David J. *Transatlantic Industrial Revolution: The Diffusion of Textile Technologies between Britain and America, 1790–1830's*. Cambridge: MIT Press, 1981.

Johnson, Robert Eugene. *Peasant and Proletarian: The Working Class of Moscow in the Late Nineteenth Century*. Leister: Leister University Press, 1979.

Jones, Bryn. "Destruction or Re-distribution of Engineering Skills? The Case of Numerical Control." Mimeographed. School of Humanities and Social Sciences, University of Bath, n.d.

Kadritzke, Ulf, and Ostendorp, Dieter. "Beweglich sein fürs Kapital; Das 'Stuttgarter Modell' der Rationalisierung und Arbeitsplatzvernichtung in der Zeitungsindustrie." In *Gewerkschaftspolitik in der Krise: kritisches Gewerkschaftsjahrbuch 1977/78*, edited by Otto Jacobi, Walter Müller-Jentsch, and Eberhard Schmidt. Berlin: Rotbuch Verlag, 1978.

Kammerer, Guido; Lutz, Burkart; and Nuber, Christoph. *Ingenieure im Produktionsprozess: zum Einfluss von Angebot und Bedarf auf Arbeitsteilung und Arbeitseinsatz am Beispiel des Maschinenbaus.* Frankfurt am Main: Athenäum Verlag, 1973.

Kayser, Bernard. *Cyclically Determined Homeward Flows of Migrant Workers and the Effects on Migration.* Paris: OECD, 1972.

Kehr, Eckart. *Der Primat der Innenpolitik.* Edited by Hans-Ulrich Wehler. Berlin: Walter de Gruyter and Co., 1965.

Kellman, Steven. *Regulating America, Regulating Sweden: A Comparative Study of Occupational Safety and Health Policy.* Cambridge: MIT Press, 1981.

Kergoat, Danièle. *Bulledor.* Paris: Editions du Seuil, 1973.

Kergoat, Danièle. "La combativité ouvrière dans une usine de construction de camions." Mimeographed. Paris: Centre de Sociologie des Organisations, 1977.

Kern, Horst, and Schumann, Michael. *Industriearbeit und Arbeiterbewusstsein: eine empirische Untersuchung über den Einfluss der aktuellen technischen Entwicklung auf die industrielle Arbeit und das Arbeiterbewusstsein.* 2 vols. Frankfurt am Main: Europäische Verlagsanstalt, 1970.

Kerr, Clark; Dunlop, John T.; Harbison, Frederick H.; and Myers, Charles A. *Industrialism and Industrial Man.* Cambridge: Harvard University Press, 1960.

Kessner, Thomas. *The Golden Door: Italian and Jewish Immigrant Mobility in New York City, 1800–1950.* New York: Oxford University Press, 1977.

Keynes, John Maynard. "Social Consequences of Changes in the Value of Money." In J. M. Keynes, *Essays in Persuasion,* pp. 80–104. New York: Harcourt Brace and Co., 1932.

Kocka, Jürgen. *Klassengesellschaft im Krieg, 1914–1918.* Göttingen: Vandenhoeck and Ruprecht, 1973.

Kohn, Melvin L. *Class and Conformity.* Homewood, Ill.: Dorsey Press, 1969.

Koike, Kazuo. "Japan's Industrial Relations: Characteristics and Problems." *Japanese Economic Studies* 7 (Fall 1978):42–90.

Konrád, George, and Szelény, Ivan. *The Intellectuals on the Road to Class Power.* Translated by Andrew Arato and Richard E. Allen. New York: Harcourt Brace Jovanovich, 1979.

Kornblum, William. *Blue Collar Community.* Chicago: University of Chicago Press, 1974.

Kropotkin, P. *Fields, Factories, and Workshops.* Rev. ed. London: Thomas Nelson and Sons, 1912.

Kruchko, John G. *The Birth of a Union Local: The History of UAW Local 674, Norwood, Ohio, 1933 to 1940.* Ithaca: New York State School of Industrial and Labor Relations, Cornell University, 1972.

Kuhn, Thomas S. *The Structure of Scientific Revolutions.* Chicago: University of Chicago Press, 1962.

Labov, William. "The Effect of Social Mobility on Linguistic Behavior." In *Explorations in Sociolinguistics,* edited by Stanley Lieberson, pp. 58–75. Bloomington: Indiana University Press, 1966.

Laferrère, Michel. *Lyon: ville industrielle.* Paris: Presses Universitaires de France, 1960.

Landes, David S. *The Unbound Prometheus.* Cambridge: Cambridge University Press, 1969.

Laslett, John M., and Lipset, Seymour Martin, eds. *Failure of a Dream? Essays in the History of American Socialism.* Garden City, N.Y.: Doubleday and Co., Anchor Books, 1974.

Leggett, John. *Class, Race and Labor: Working-Class Consciousness in Detroit.* New York: Oxford University Press, 1968.

Lerner, Daniel. *The Passing of Traditional Society.* New York: Free Press, 1958.

Le Roy Ladurie, Emmanuel. "Les masses profondes: la paysannerie." In *Histoire économique et sociale de la France,* edited by Fernand Braudel and Ernest Labrousse, vol. 1, pt. 2, pp. 483–685. Paris: Presses Universitaires de France, 1977.

Lévi-Strauss, Claude. *La pensée sauvage.* Paris: Librairie Plon, 1962.

Lévi-Strauss, Claude. *Le totémisme aujourd'hui.* Paris: Presses Universitaires de France, 1962.

Lévy-Leboyer, Maurice. "Les processus d'industrialisation: le cas de l'Angleterre et de la France." *Revue historique* 92 (April 1968), pp. 281–98.

Lewis, Oscar. *La Vida.* New York: Random House, 1966.

Liebow, Elliot. *Tally's Corner: A Study of Negro Streetcorner Men.* Boston: Little, Brown, 1967.

Lincke, B. *Die schweizerische Maschinenindustrie und ihre Entwicklung in wirtschaftlicher Beziehung.* Frauenfeld: Huber and Co., 1911

Lipset, Seymour Martin; Trow, Martin A.; and Coleman, James S. *Union Democracy: The Internal Politics of the International Typographical Union.* Glencoe, Ill.: Free Press, 1956.

Lloyd, G. I. H. *The Cutlery Trades.* London: Longmans, Green and Co., 1913.

Lopreato, Joseph. *Peasants No More: Social Class and Social Change in an Underdeveloped Society.* San Francisco: Chandler Publishing Co., 1967.

Lorenzoni, Gianni. *Una politica innovativa nelle piccole-medie imprese.* Milan: Etas Libri, 1979.

Lorenzoni, Gianni. "Una tipologia di produzioni in conto terzi nel settore metalmeccanico." In *Ristrutturazioni industriali e rapporti fra imprese,* edited by Riccardo Varaldo, pp. 181–208. Milan: Franco Angeli, 1979.

Low-Beer, John R. *Protest and Participation: The New Working Class in Italy.* Cambridge: Cambridge University Press, 1978.

Lozier, J. W. "The Forgotten Industry: Small and Medium Sized Cotton Mills South of Boston." *Working Papers from the Regional Economic History Research Center* 2, no. 4 (1979):101–24.

Lukács, Georg. *History and Class Consciousness: Studies in Marxist Dialectics.* Translated by Rodney Livingstone. Cambridge: MIT Press, 1971.

Lukács, Georg. *Ontologie-Arbeit.* Neuwied am Rhein: Hermann Luchterhand Verlag, 1973.

Luppi, Laura. "Autobianchi." In *Lotte operaie e sindacato in Italia (1968–1972),* edited by Alessandro Pizzorno, 6 vols., 1:29–112. Bologna: Il Mulino, 1974.

Lutz, Burkart. *Krise des Lohnanreizes: ein empirisch-historischer Beitrag zum Wandel der Formen betrieblicher Herrschaft am Beispiel der deutschen Stahlindustrie.* Frankfurt am Main: Europäische Verlagsanstalt, 1975.

Lutz, Burkart, and Kammerer, Guido. *Das Ende des graduierten Ingenieurs? eine empirische Analyse unerwarteter Nebenfolgen der Bildungsexpansion.* Frankfurt am Main: Europäische Verlagsanstalt, 1975.

Lutz, Burkart, and Sengenberger, Werner. *Arbeitsmarktstrukturen und öffentliche Arbeitsmarktpolitik: eine kritische Analyse von Zielen und Instrumenten.* Göttingen: O. Schwartz, 1974.

McClintock, Cynthia. *Peasant Cooperatives and Political Change in Peru.* Princeton: Princeton University Press, 1981.

MacDonald, John S. "Some Socio-Economic Emigration Differentials in Rural Italy, 1902–1913." *Economic Development and Cultural Change* 7 (October 1958):71–2.

McDonnell, James F. "The Rise of the CIO in Buffalo, New York, 1936–1942." Ph.D. dissertation, University of Wisconsin, 1970.

Mackenzie, Gavin. *The Aristocracy of Labor: The Position of Skilled Craftsmen in the American Class Structure.* Cambridge: Cambridge University Press, 1973.

McManus, George J. "Electric Furnace Succeeds in Technology and Profit." *Iron Age,* February 4, 1980, pp. mp-7–mp-18.

McManus, George J. "Mini-Mills Begin to Make Noises in a Big Way." *Iron Age,* May 5, 1980, pp. mp-5–mp-15.

Mallet, Serge. *La nouvelle classe ouvrière.* Paris: Editions du Seuil, 1963.

Mann, Michael. *Consciousness and Action among the Western Working Classes.* London: Macmillan, 1973.

Mann, Michael. *Workers on the Move: The Sociology of Relocation.* Cambridge: Cambridge University Press, 1973.

Mannheimer, Renato, and Micheli, Giuseppe. "Alcune ipotesi sul concetto di integrazione degli immigrati." *Quaderni di sociologia* 23 (January 1974):82–113.

Marcato, Giancarlo. "Imprese esportatrici e organismi associative per l'esportazione nel Veneto." *La rivista veneta* 13 (May 1979):103–43.

Marcuse, Herbert. *Counterrevolution and Revolt.* Boston: Beacon Press, 1972.

Marcuse, Herbert. *One-Dimensional Man: Studies in the Ideology of Advanced Industrial Society.* Boston: Beacon Press, 1964.

Marglin, Stephen A. "What Do Bosses Do? The Origins and Functions of Hierarchy in Capitalist Production." *Review of Radical Political Economy,* Summer 1974, pp. 60–112.

Marris, Robin. *The Economic Theory of 'Managerial' Capitalism.* New York: Free Press, 1964.

Marshall, F. Ray, and Briggs, Vernon M., Jr. *The Negro and Apprenticeship.* Baltimore: Johns Hopkins Press, 1967.

Marshall, T. H. *Class, Citizenship, and Social Development.* Garden City, N.Y.: Doubleday and Co., 1964.

Martin, Andrew. "The Dynamics of Change in a Keynesian Political Economy: The Swedish Case and Its Implications." In *State and Economy in Contemporary Capitalism,* edited by Colin Crouch, pp. 88–121. London: Croom Helm, 1979.

Martin, Philip L., and Miller, Mark J. "Guestworkers: Lessons from Europe." *Industrial and Labor Relations Review* 33 (April 1980):315–30.

Marx, Karl. "Die Klassenkämpfe in Frankreich 1848 bis 1850." In *Marx–Engels Werke,* edited by Institut für Marxismus beim ZK der SED, 39 vols., 7:9–107. Berlin: Dietz Verlag, 1957.

Maurice, Marc; Sellier, François; and Silvestre, Jean-Jacques. "La production de la hiérarchie dans l'entreprise: recherche d'un effet sociétal." *Revue française de sociologie* 20 (April 1979):331–80.

Medusa, Giuseppe. "Le relazioni industriali a una svolta? L'intreccio produttività-salario nell'accordo aziendale Alfa Romeo." *Impresa e società* 11 (May 15, 1981):10–22.

Meier, August, and Rudwick, Elliott. *Black Detroit and the Rise of the UAW.* Oxford: Oxford Univerity Press, 1979.

Meinecke, Friedrich. *The Age of German Liberation, 1795–1815.* Translated by Peter Paret. Berkeley and Los Angeles: University of California Press, 1977.

Melossi, B.; Rugerini, M. G.; Versace, L.; Iora, A.; and Ligarbue, G. *Restaurazione capitalistica e piano del lavoro.* Rome: Editrice Sindacale Italiana, 1977.

Mészaros, István. *Marx's Theory of Alienation.* New York: Harper and Row, 1972.

Mickler, Otfried. "Die ökonomischen Bedingungen des Fraueneinsatzes im Bereich der industriellen Produktion." Mimeographed. Göttingen, 1975.

Mickler, Otfried; Mohr, Wilma; and Kadritzke, Ulf, with the collaboration of Martin Baethge and Uwe Neumann. *Produktion und Qualifikation.* 2 vols. Göttingen: Soziologisches Forschungsinstitut, 1977.

Migdal, Joel S. *Peasants, Politics, and Revolution.* Princeton: Princeton University Press, 1974.

Mills, Daniel Quinn. *Industrial Relations and Manpower in Construction.* Cambridge: MIT Press, 1972.

Millstein, James E. "The Case of the U.S. Television Industry." In *American Industry in International Competition,* edited by Laura Tyson and John Zysman. Forthcoming.

Monds, Jean. "Worker Control and the New Historians: A New Economism." *New Left Review,* no. 97 (May 1976), pp. 81–100.

Monicelli, Mino. *La follia veneta: come una regione bianca diviene culla del terrorismo.* Rome: Editori Riuniti, 1981.

Montgomery, David. "The 'New Unionism' and the Transformation of Workers' Consciousness in America 1909–1922." *Journal of Social History* 7 (Summer 1974):509–29.

Montgomery, David. "Quels standards? Les ouvriers et la réorganisation de la production aux Etats-Unis (1900–1920)." *Annales* 32 (November 1977):101–27.

Moynihan, Daniel P. *The Negro Family: The Case for National Action.* Washington, D.C.: U.S. Department of Labor, 1965.

Müller, Gernot; Rödell, Ulrich; Sabel, Charles F.; Stille, Frank; and Vogt, Winfried. *Ökonomische Krisentendenzen im gegenwärtigen Kapitalismus.* Frankfurt am Main: Campus Verlag, 1978.

Musson, Albert Edward. *The Typographical Association: Origins and History up to 1949.* London: Oxford University Press, 1954.

Naville, Pierre. *Vers l'automatisme social? problèmes du travail et de l'automation.* Paris: Editions Gallimard, 1963.

Naville, Pierre; Bardou, Jean-Pierre; Brachet, Philippe; and Lévy, Catherine. *L'Etat entrepreneur: le cas de la Régie Renault.* Paris: Editions Anthropos, 1971.

N'Dongo, Sally. *Exil, connais pas.* Paris: Editions du Cerf, 1976.

N'Dongo. *Voyage forcé: itinéraire d'un militant.* Paris: François Maspero, 1975.

Noble, David F. "Social Choice in Machine Design: The Case of Automatically Controlled Machine Tools, and a Challenge to Labor." *Politics and Society* 8, nos. 3–4 (1978):313–47.

Nolan, Mary, and Sabel, Charles F. "Class Conflict and the Social Democratic Reform Cycle in Germany." In *Power and Society,* edited by Gøsta Esping-Andersen and Roger Friedland. Los Altos, Calif.: Geron-X, forthcoming.

Norcia, Domenico Liberato, with the collaboration of Fausto Tortora. *Io garantito: frammenti di vita e di pensieri di un operaio FIAT.* Rome: Edizioni Lavoro, 1980.

Notarnicola, Sante. *L'evasione impossibile.* Milan: Feltrinelli, 1972.

O'Brien, Patrick, and Keyder, Caglar. *Economic Growth in Britain and France, 1780–1914: Two Paths to the Twentieth Century.* London: George Allen and Unwin, 1978.

Oertzen, Peter von. *Betriebsräte in der Novemberrevolution: eine politikwissenschaftliche Untersuchung über Ideengehalt und struktur der betrieblichen und wirtschaftlichen Arbeiterräte in der deutschen Revolution, 1918–1919.* Düsseldorf: Droste, 1963.

Offe, Claus. *Leistungsprinzip und industrielle Arbeit.* Frankfurt am Main: Europäische Verlagsanstalt, 1973.

Office of Technology Assessment. *Technology and Steel Industry Competitiveness.* Washington, D.C.: Office of Technology Assessment, Congress of the United States, June 1980.

Okun, Arthur M. "Inflation: Its Mechanics and Welfare Costs." *Brookings Papers on Economic Activity*, no. 2 (1975), pp. 351–90.

Olson, Mancur, Jr. *The Logic of Collective Action: Public Goods and the Theory of Groups.* Cambridge: Harvard University Press, 1965.

Opel, Fritz. *Der Deutsche Metallarbeiterverband während des Ersten Weltkrieges und der Revolution.* Hannover: Norddeutsche Verlagsanstalt Gödel, 1957.

Organisation for Economic Co-operation and Development. *The Impact of the Newly Developed Countries on Production and Trade in Manufactures.* Paris: OECD, 1979.

Organisation for Economic Cooperation and Development. *Policies for Apprenticeship.* Paris: OECD, 1979.

Osterman, Paul. *Getting Started: The Youth Labor Market.* Cambridge: MIT Press, 1981.

Ozawa, Terutomo. *Japan's Technological Challenge to the West, 1950–1974.* Cambridge: MIT Press, 1974.

Paci, Massimo. "Migrazioni interne e mercato capitalistico del lavoro." In *Sviluppo economico italiano e forza-lavoro*, edited by Paolo Leon and Marco Marocchi, pp. 181–96. Venice: Marsilio Editori, 1973.

Paci, Massimo. "Mobilità sociale e partecipazione politica." *Quaderni di sociologia*, July 1966, pp. 387–410.

Paci, Massimo. "Struttura e funzioni della famiglia nello sviluppo industriale 'periferico.' " In *Famiglia e mercato del lavoro in una economia periferica*, edited by Massimo Paci, pp. 9–70. Milan: Franco Angeli, 1980.

Paige, Jeffrey M. *Agrarian Revolution: Social Movements and Export Agriculture in the Underdeveloped World.* New York: Free Press, 1975.

Paine, Suzanne. *Exporting Workers: The Turkish Case.* Cambridge: Cambridge University Press, 1974.

Pariset, E. *Histoire de la fabrique lyonnaise.* Lyons: A. Rey, 1901.

Parkin, Frank. *Class Inequality and Political Order: Social Stratification in Socialist Societies.* New York: Praeger Publishers, 1971.

Pasquino, Gianfranco. "Recenti trasformazioni nel sistema di potere della Democrazia Cristiana." In *Il sistema politico e le istituzioni*, edited by Luigi Graziano and Sidney Tarrow, pp. 609–56. Turin: Einaudi, 1979.

Passigli, Stefano. *Emigrazione e comportamento politico.* Bologna: Il Mulino, 1969.

Pérez-Díaz, Víctor. *Emigración y cambio social: procesos migratorios y vita rural en Castilla.* Barcelona: Editiones Ariel, 1971.

Perino, Mauro. *Lotta Continua: sei militanti dopo dieci anni.* Turin: Rosenberg e Sellier, 1979.

Pesce, Adele, and Sabel, Charles F.. "Taylorismo: una stella in declino." *I consigli*, n.s. 1 (April 1980):57–64.

Pierburg Authors' Collective. *Pierburg-Neuss: Deutsche und ausländische Arbeiter – ein Gegner, ein Kampf.* N.p.: Internationale Sozialistische Publikationen, 1974.

Piore, Michael J. *Birds of Passage and Promised Lands: Long-Distance Migrants and Industrial Societies.* Cambridge: Cambridge University Press, 1979.

Piore, Michael J. "The Technological Foundations of Dualism and Discontinuity." In Suzanne Berger and Michael J. Piore, *Dualism and Discontinuity in Industrial Societies*, pp. 55–81. Cambridge: Cambridge University Press, 1980.

Piven, Frances Fox, and Cloward, Richard A. *Regulating the Poor: The Functions of Public Welfare.* New York: Random House, 1971.

Pizzorno, Alessandro. "Interests and Parties in Pluralism." In Suzanne Berger, ed., *Organizing Interests in Western Europe*, pp. 247–84. Cambridge: Cambridge University Press, 1981.

Pizzorno, Alessandro. "I sindacati nel sistema politico italiano: aspetti storici." *Rivista trimestrale di diritto pubblico* 21 (October 1971):1510–59.

Pizzorno, Alessandro. "Ricordo di Serge Mallet." *Problemi del socialismo* 15 (March 1973):394–9.

Pizzorno, Alessandro. "Scambio politico e identità collettiva nel conflitto di classe." *Rivista italiana di scienza politica* 7 (August 1977):165–98.

Pizzorno, Alessandro, and Crouch, Colin, eds. *Conflitti in Europa*. Milan: Etas Libri, 1977.

Pizzorno, Alessandro; Reyneri, Emilio; Regini, Marino; and Regalia, Ida. *Lotte operaie e sindacato: il ciclo 1968–1972 in Italia*. Bologna: Il Mulino, 1978.

Poggi, Gianfranco. "Alcune riflessioni su 'Le organizzazioni, il potere e i conflitti di classe,' di Alessandro Pizzorno." *Quaderni di sociologia* 12 (April 1963):201–15.

Polanyi, Karl. *The Livelihood of Man*. New York: Academic Press, 1977.

Pollard, Sidney. *The Genesis of Modern Management: A Study of the Industrial Revolution in Great Britain*. Cambridge: Harvard University Press, 1966.

Pollard, Sidney. *A History of Labour in Sheffield*. Liverpool: Liverpool University Press, 1959.

Pope, Liston. *Millhands and Preachers: A Study of Gastonia*. New Haven: Yale University Press, 1965.

Popitz, Heinrich; Bahrdt, Hans Paul; Jüres, Ernst August; and Kesting, Hanno. *Das Gesellschaftsbild des Arbeiters*. Tübingen: J. C. B. Mohr [Paul Siebeck], 1957.

Popitz, Heinrich, Bahrdt, Hans Paul, Jures, Ernst August, and Kesting, Hanno. *Technik und Industriearbeit: soziologische Untersuchungen in der Hüttenindustrie*. Tübingen: J. C. B. Mohr [Paul Siebeck], 1957.

Popkin, Samuel. *The Rational Peasant*. Berkeley and Los Angeles: University of California Press, 1979.

Poppinga, Onno. "Arbeiterbauern im Industriebetrieb." In *Gewerkschaften und Klassenkampf: kritisches Jahrbuch 1975*, edited by Otto Jacobi, Walter Müller-Jentsch, and Eberhard Schmidt, pp. 212–24. Frnkfurt am Main: Fischer Verlag, 1975.

Poulantzas, Nicos Ar. *Fascisme et dictature: la IIIe Internationale face au fascisme*. Paris: Maspero, 1970.

Poulantzas, Nicos Ar. *Pouvoir politique et classes sociales*. Paris: François Maspero, 1968.

Prott, Jürgen. *Industriearbeit bei betrieblichen Umstrukturierungen: soziale Konsequenzen, Interessenvertretung und Bewusstseinsstrukturen*. Cologne: Bund-Verlag, 1975.

Pugno, Emilio, and Garavini, Sergio. *Gli anni duri alla FIAT*. Turin: Einaudi, 1974.

Puls, Detlev. "Ein im ganzen gutartiger Streik: Bemerkungen zu Alltagserfahrungen und Protestverhalten der oberschlesischen Bergarbeiter am Ende des 19. Jahrhunderts." In *Wahrnehmungsform und Protestverhalten: Studien zur Lage der Unterschichten im 18. und 19. Jahrhundert*, edited by Detlev Puls, pp. 175–227. Frankfurt am Main: Suhrkamp Verlag, 1979.

Raskin, A. H. "A Reporter at Large: New York Newspaper Strike, Part I." *New Yorker*, January 22, 1979, pp. 41–87.

Raum, Georg. "Die Arbeitsplatzqualifikationsanforderungen der Zweigbetriebe." Mimeographed. Regensburg, 1975.

Razzano, Renzo. "I modelli di sviluppo della CGIL e della CISL." *Problemi del movimento sindacale in Italia, 1943–1973*, edited by Aris Accornero, pp. 527–51. Milan: Feltrinelli, 1976.

Regalia, Ida. "Rappresentanza operaia e sindacato: mutamento di un sistema di relazioni industriali." In Alessandro Pizzorno, Emilio Reyneri, Marino Regini, and Ida Regalia, *Lotte operaie e sindacato: il ciclo 1968–1972 in Italia*, pp. 177–287. Bologna: Il Mulino, 1978.

Regalia, Ida; Regini, Marino; and Reyneri, Emilio. "Conflitti di lavoro e relazioni industriali in Italia, 1968–75." in *Conflitti In Europa*, edited by Alessandro Pizzorno and Colin Crouch, pp. 1–73. Milan: Etas Libri, 1977.

Regione Piemonte. "Le nuove tecnologie e l'organizzazione del lavoro: l'utilizzo del controllo numerico in Piemonte." Study conducted by the Centro di Formazione della Regione per Tecnici Informatici orientati all'automazione industriale. Turin: Ufficio Pubbliche Relazioni e Documentazione della Giunta Regionale, 1978.

Reid, Alastair. "The Division of Labour in the British Shipbuilding Industry, 1880–1920." Ph.D. Dissertation, University of Cambridge, 1980.

Reyneri, Emilio. "Innocenti." In *Lotte operaie e sindacato in Italia (1968–1972)*, edited by Alessandro Pizzorno, 6 vols., 1:113–209. Bologna: Il Mulino, 1974.

Reyneri, Emilio. " 'Maggio strisciante': l'inizio della mobilitazione operaia." In Alessandro Pizzorno, Emilio Reyneri, Marino Regini, and Ida Regalia, *Lotte operaie e sindacato: il ciclo 1968–1972 in Italia*, pp. 48–107. Bologna: Il Mulino, 1978.

Rich, Charles; Shrobe, Howard E.; and Waters, Richard C. "Computer Aided Evolutionary Design for Software Engineering." Mimeographed. Massachusetts Institute of Technology, Artifical Intelligence Laboratory, A.I. Memo. 506, January 1979.

Ricolfi, Marco. "Legislazione economica e piccole imprese." In *L'industria in Italia: la piccola impresa*, edited by F. Ferrero and S. Scamuzzi, pp. 119–86. Rome: Editori Riuniti, 1979.

Robinson, Edgar Eugene. *They Voted for Roosevelt: The Presidential Vote, 1932–1944*. Stanford: Stanford University Press, 1947.

Roehl, Richard. "French Industrialization: A Reconsideration." *Explorations in Economic History* 13 (July 1976), pp. 233–81.

Rogers, Theresa F., and Friedman, Nathalie S. *Printers Face Automation*. Lexington, Mass.: D.C. Heath and Co., 1980.

Rolfo, Secondo. "La diffusione del controllo numerico nella produzione italiana di macchine utensili." *Bollettino CERIS* 5 (September 1980):125–36.

Rosenberg, Hans. *Bureaucracy, Aristocracy, and Autocracy*. Cambridge: Harvard University Press, 1958.

Rosenberg, Nathan. *Perspectives of Technology*. Cambridge: Cambridge University Press, 1976.

Rossi, Mario G. *Le origini del partito cattolico: movimento cattolico e lotta di classe nell'Italia liberale*. Rome: Editori Riuniti, 1977.

Routledge, Paul. "The Dispute at Times Newspapers Ltd.: A View from the Inside." *Industrial Relations Journal*, Winter 1979–80, pp. 5–9.

Rudé, George. *Ideology and Popular Protest*. London: Lawrence and Wishart, 1980.

Runciman, W. G. *Relative Deprivation and Social Justice: A Study of Attitudes to Social Inequality in Twentieth-Century England*. London: Routledge and Kegan Paul, 1966.

Rushing, William A. *Class, Culture, and Alienation: A Study of Farmers and Farm Workers*. Lexington, Mass.: D. C. Heath and Co., 1972.

Russo, Margherita. "La natura e le implicazioni del progresso tecnico: una verifica empirica." Mimeographed. Modena, December 1980.

Saba, Andrea. *L'industria sommersa: il nuovo modello di sviluppo*. Venice: Marsilio Editori, 1980.

Sabel, Charles F. Review of Ivar Berg, Marcia Freedman, and Michael Freeman, *Managers and Work Reform: A Limited Engagement* (New York: Free Press, 1978), in *Challenge*, July 1979, pp. 64–6.

Sadler, Philip. "Sociological Aspects of Skill." *British Journal of Industrial Relations* 8 (March 1970):22–31.

Salvati, B. "The Rebirth of Italian Trade Unionism, 1943–54." In *The Rebirth of Italy, 1943–1950,* edited by S. J. Woolf, pp. 181–211. London: Longman, 1972.

Salvati, Michele. *Sviluppo economico, domanda di lavoro e struttura dell'occupazione.* Bologna: Il Mulino, 1976.

Sarmiento, Domingo Faustino. *Facundo; o, civilización y barberie en las pampas argentinas.* Buenos Aires: Ediciónes Peuser, 1955.

Sayles, Leonard R. *Behavior of Industrial Work Groups: Prediction and Control.* New York: Wiley, 1958.

Sayles, Leonard R., and Strauss, George. *The Local Union.* Rev. ed. New York: Harcourt, Brace and World, 1967.

Scase, Richard. *Social Democracy in Capitalist Society: Working-Class Politics in Britain and Sweden.* London: Croom Helm, 1977.

Schatz, Ronald. "The End of Corporate Liberalism: Class Struggle in the Electrical Manufacturing Industry, 1933–1950." *Radical America* 9 (July 1975):187–205.

Schatz, Ronald. "Union Pioneers, the Founders of Local Unions at General Electric and Westinghouse, 1933–37." *Journal of American History* 66 (December 1979):586–602.

Schmalenbach, Ernst. *Selbstkostenrechnungen und Preispolitik.* 6th ed. rev. Leipzig: G. A. Gloeckner, 1934.

Schneider, Michael. *Das Arbeitsbeschaffungsprogramm des ADGB.* Bonn-Bad Godesberg: Verlag Neue Gesellschaft, 1975.

Schofer, Lawrence. *The Formation of a Modern Labor Force: Upper Silesia, 1865–1914.* Berkeley and Los Angeles: University of California Press, 1974.

Schrader, Achim; Nikles, Bruno W.; and Griese, Hartmut M. *Die Zweite Generation: Sozialisation und Akkulturation ausländischer Kinder in der Bundesrepublik.* Kronberg: Athenäum Verlag, 1976.Schröter, Alfred, and Becker, Walter. *Die deutsche Maschinenbauindustrie in der industriellen Revolution.* Berlin: Akademie Verlag, 1962.

Schultz-Wild, Rainer. *Betriebliche Beschäftigungspolitik in der Krise.* Frankfurt am Main: Campus Verlag, 1978.

Schwartz, Michael. *Radical Protest and Social Structure.* New York: Academic Press, 1976.

Scoville, James G. "A Theory of Jobs and Training." *Industrial Relations* 9 (October 1969):36–53.

Scott, James C. *The Moral Economy of the Peasant.* New Haven: Yale University Press, 1976.

Scott, Joan. *The Glassmakers of Carmaux: French Craftsmen and Political Action in the Nineteenth Century.* Cambridge: Harvard University Press, 1974.

Seda, Eduardo. *Social Change and Personality in a Puerto-Rican Agrarian Reform Community.* Evanston, Ill.: Northwestern University Press, 1973.

Segrestin, Denis. "Du syndicalisme de métier au syndicalisme de classe: pour une sociologie de la CGT." *Sociologie du travail* 17 (April 1975):152–73.

Sewell, William H., Jr. *Work and Revolution in France.* Cambridge: Cambridge University Press, 1980.

Signorelli, Amalia; Tiritico, Maria Clara; and Rossi, Sara. *Scelte senza potere: il ritorno degli emigranti nelle zone dell'esodo.* Rome: Officina Edizioni, 1977.

Simes, Dimitri K. "The Soviet Parallel Market." *Survey* 21 (Summer 1975):42–52.

Siriani, Carmen J. "Workers' Control in the Era of the First World War: A Comparative Analysis of the European Experience." *Theory and Society* 9 (January 1980):29–88.

Sisson, Keith. *Industrial Relations in Fleet Street: A Study in Pay Structure.* Oxford: Blackwell, 1975.

Skocpol, Theda. *States and Social Revolutions*. Cambridge: Cambridge University Press, 1979.

Slater, Henry M. "Migration and Workers' Conflict in Western Europe." Ph.D. dissertation, Massachusetts Institute of Technology, 1977.

Sloan, Alfred P., Jr. *My Years with General Motors*. Garden City, N.Y.: Doubleday and Co., 1964.

Smith, Adam. *The Wealth of Nations*, edited by Edwin Cannan. Chicago: University of Chicago Press, 1976.

Smith, Merritt Roe. *Harpers Ferry Armory and the New Technology*. Ithaca, N.Y.: Cornell University Press, 1977.

Sohn-Rethel, Alfred. *Ökonomie und Klassenstruktur des deutschen Faschismus*. Frankfurt am Main: Suhrkamp Verlag, 1973.

Spear, Allan H. *Black Chicago: The Making of a Negro Ghetto, 1890–1920*. Chicago: University of Chicago Press, 1967.

Stepan, Alfred. *The State and Society: Peru in Comparative Perspective*. Princeton: Princeton University Press, 1978.

Stinchcombe, Arthur L. "Bureaucratic and Craft Administration of Production: A Comparative Study." *Administrative Science Quarterly* 4 (September 1959):168–87.

Strauss, George. "Control by Membership in Building Trades Unions." *American Journal of Sociology* 61 (May 1956):527–35.

Strunz, Jürgen. *Die Industrieansiedlungen in der Oberpfalz in den Jahren 1957 bis 1966*. Regensburger geographische Schriften 4. Regensburg: Geographisches Institut der Universität Regensburg, 1974.

Suttles, Gerald D. *The Social Order of the Slum: Ethnicity and Territory in the Inner City*. Chicago: University of Chicago Press, 1963.

Sweezy, Paul. "A Critique." In *The Transition from Feudalism to Capitalism*, edited by Rodney Hilton, pp. 33–56. London: New Left Books, 1976.

Sykes, A. J. M. "The Cohesion of a Trade-Union Workshop Organization." *Sociology* 1 (May 1967):141–63.

Sykes, A. J. M. "Trade-Union Workshop Organization in the Printing Industry: The Chapel." *Human Relations* 13 (February 1960):49–65.

Szekely, Julian. "Radically Innovative Steelmaking Technologies." *Metallurgical Transactions (B)* (September 1980):353–71.

Tamburrano, Giuseppe. *Storia e cronaca del centro sinistra*. Milan: Feltrinelli, 1971.

Taranto, Roberto; Franchini, Mariella; and Maglia, Vittorio. *L'industria italiana della macchina utensile*. Bologna: Il Mulino, 1979.

Tarrow, Sidney G. *Peasant Communism in Southern Italy*. New Haven: Yale University Press, 1967.

Taylor, Frederick Winslow. *The Principles of Scientific Management*. New York: Harper and Brothers, 1915.

Thirsk, Joan. *Economic Policy and Projects: The Development of a Consumer Society in Early Modern England*. Oxford: Oxford University Press, 1978.

Thomas, Konrad. *Die betriebliche Situation des Arbeiters*. Stuttgart: Enke Verlag, 1964.

Thompson, E. P. *The Making of the English Working Class*. London: Gollancz, 1963.

Thompson, E. P. "The Moral Economy of the English Crowd in the Eighteenth Century." *Past and Present*, no. 50 (February 1971), pp. 76–136.

Thompson, E. P. "Time, Work-Discipline and Industrial Capitalism." *Past and Present*, no. 38 (December 1967), pp. 56–97.

Thrupp, Sylvia. *The Merchant Class of Medieval London, 1300–1500*. Chicago: University of Chicago Press, 1948.

Tomasi di Lampedusa, Giuseppe. *Il Gattopardo*. Milan: Feltrinelli, 1958.

Touraine, Alain. "Les ouvriers d'origine agricole." *Sociologie du travail* 1 (July 1960):230–45.

Trempé, Rolande. *Les mineurs de Carmaux, 1848–1914.* Paris: Editions Ouvrières, 1971.

Trentin, Bruno. *Il sindacato dei consigli.* Rome: Editori Riuniti, 1980.

Ugolini, Bruno. "Nessuna sconfitta FIOM e PCI ma seri problemi all'Alfa." *L'Unità,* November 3, 1978, pp. 1, 13.

Unger, Roberto Mangabeira. *Knowledge and Politics.* New York: Free Press, 1975.

Unger, Roberto Mangabeira. *Law and Modern Society.* New York: Free Press, 1976.

Unione Regionale delle Camere di Commercio dell'Emilia-Romagna – CERES. *Il commercio con l'estero dell'Emilia-Romagna: serie storica, 1975–9.* Bologna: Unione Regionale delle Camere di Commercio dell'Emilia-Romagna – CERES, 1981.

Valentine, Charles A. *Culture and Poverty: Critique and Counter-Proposals.* Chicago: University of Chicago Press, 1968.

Veblen, Thorstein. *The Theory of the Leisure Class.* New York: Vanguard Press, 1927.

Vernon, Raymond. *The Dilemma of Mexico's Development.* Cambridge: Harvard University Press, 1963.

Vianello, Fernando. "I meccanismi di recupero del profitto: l'esperienza italiana, 1963–73." In *Crisi e ristrutturazione nell'economia italiana,* edited by Augusto Graziani, pp. 119–44. Turin: Einaudi, 1975.

Vidal, Daniel. "Un cas de faux concept: la notion d'aliénation." *Sociologie du travail* 11 (January 1969):61–82.

Walton, Richard E. "Work Innovations in the United States." *Harvard Business Review,* July 1979, pp. 88–98.

Waterbury, John. *North for the Trade: The Life and Times of a Berber Merchant.* Berkeley and Los Angeles: University of California Press, 1972.

Weber, Max. *Gesammelte Aufsätze zur Religionssoziologie.* 3 vols. Tübingen: J. C. B. Mohr [Paul Siebeck], 1922–3.

Wedderburn, Dorothy, and Crompton, Rosemary. *Workers' Attitudes and Technology.* Cambridge: Cambridge University Press, 1972.

Weiss, Frank Dietmar. *Electrical Engineering in West Germany: Adjusting to Imports from Less Developed Countries.* Kieler Studien 155. Tübingen: J.C.B. Mohr [Paul Siebeck], 1978.

Wells, Louis T., Jr. "The Internationalization of Firms from Developing Countries." In *Multinationals from Small Counties,* edited by Tamir Agmon and Charles P. Kindelberger, pp. 138–43. Cambridge: MIT Press, 1977.

Wells, Louis T., Jr. "International Trade: The Product Cycle Approach." In *The Product Life Cycle and International Trade,* edited by Louis T. Wells, Jr., pp. 3–33. Boston: Division of Research, Graduate School of Business Administration, Harvard University, 1972.

Weltz, Friedrich; Schmidt, Gert; and Sass, Jürgen. *Facharbeiter im Industriebetrieb: eine Untersuchung in metallverarbeitenden Betrieben.* Frankfurt am Main: Athenäum Verlag, 1974.

Whyte, William F., Jr. *Street Corner Society.* Chicago: University of Chicago Press, 1943.

Willis, Paul. *Learning to Labour.* Westmead: Saxon House, 1977.

Woodbury, Robert S. *Studies in the History of Machine Tools.* Cambridge: MIT Press, 1972.

Wright, Eric Olin. "Class Boundaries in Advanced Capitalist Societies." *New Left Review,* no. 98 (July 1976), pp. 3–42.

Wright, Erik Olin. *Class, Crisis, and the State.* London: New Left Review Books, 1978.

Yans-McLaughlin, Virginia. "A Flexible Tradition: Southern Italian Immigrants Confront a New York Experience." In *Industrial America, 1850–1920*, edited by Richard L. Ehrlich, pp. 67–84. Charlottesville: University of Virginia Press, 1977.

Zarca, Bernard. "L'ami du trait." *Actes de la recherche en sciences sociales* 29 (September 1979):27–43.

Zarca, Bernard. "Artisanat et trajectoires sociales." *Actes de la recherche en sciences sociales* 29 (September 1979):3–26.

Zeitlin, Jonathan. "Craft Control and the Division of Labour: Engineers and Compositors in Britian, 1890–1930." *Cambridge Journal of Economics* 3 (September 1979):263–74.

Zeitlin, Jonathan. "Craft Regulation and the Division of Labour: Engineers and Compositors in Britain, 1890–1914." Ph.D. dissertation, University of Warwick, 1981.

Zeitlin, Jonathan. "The Emergence of Shop Steward Organization and Job Control in the British Car Industry." *History Workshop*, no. 10 (Autumn 1980):119–137.

Zelnik, Reginald E. "The Peasant and the Factory." In *The Peasant in Nineteenth-Century Russia*, edited by Wayne S. Vucinich, pp. 158–90. Stanford: Stanford University Press, 1968.

Zweig, Ferdynand. *The Worker in an Affluent Society: Family Life and Industry*. London: Heinemann, 1961.

Index

ABC auto factory, 106, 143
advancement, opportunity for, 57, 58,
    75–6, 88, 92–3
    see also promotion
advertising, 200
Agence National pour le Dévelop-
    pement de la Production
    Automatisée (ADEPA), 65
Alfa Romeo, 161, 164, 256n100, 258n124
alienation, 8–10, 234n23
Allis-Chalmers, 214–15
Altmann, Norbert, 213
ambition, 80, 128, 132, 185
    of craftsmen, 85, 89, 175–6
    of social groups, 231
American Federation of Labor, 253n32
American Liberty League, 141
Andersen, Kristi, 261n164
apprenticeship, 83–4, 85, 125, 229
APT (Automatically Programmed Tools),
    69
Armco, 205–6
army, 191
Arrow, 211
artisanal firms, 40–5, 221
    defined in Italian law, 268n66
    see also cottage industry, high-technol-
        ogy
assembly line, 33–4
    flexibility in, 212–14, 216, 217
    see also Fordism; mass production
Association of Small and Medium Sized
    Industry (Italy), 228–9
authority relationships, 2
    in national culture, 21–2, 24
automation, 2–3, 58, 96–8
    flexible, 211–12, 214–15, 217–18
automobile industry, 103–4, 117, 195,
    203, 237n10

automation in, 212, 217
unionization of (U.S.), 138–40, 141,
    142
see also names of specific firms, e.g., Re-
    nault
autonomy, 187
    of craftsmen, 82, 167, 168, 177, 179
    in ghetto workers' personality, 115
    of migrant workers in Italy, 159–60,
        162
    national, 25–30
    worker, 3, 4, 23–5, 94–6, 214
    of workers with plant-specific skills,
        179, 181
auto-régleurs, 92

Bagnasco, Arnaldo, 251n114
Bahrdt, Hans Paul, 10, 93–4, 96, 179
Baldwin locomotive works, 32
Baltimore, 116
Banfield, Edward, 112
Bardou, Jean-Pierre, 71
bargaining, 63, 111, 170
Barrier, Christine, 184
Barton, Josef J., 119
Berlin, 177
Bernoux, Philippe, 105, 110, 111, 132,
    137, 161
Bethlehem Steel, 207
Beynon, Huw, 142–3
Bildung, 122, 123
Billancourt, 103
Birmingham, England, 40, 41, 42, 43,
    229
Black Panthers, 117
Blauner, Robert, 2–3, 6, 179–80
Bloch, Marc, 129
blue-collar workers, 1–4, 86, 91, 128
    do not form a class, 187–93

293